Moving to Opportunity

Moving to Opportunity

The Story of an American Experiment
to Fight Ghetto Poverty

Xavier de Souza Briggs
Susan J. Popkin
John Goering

OXFORD
UNIVERSITY PRESS

2010

OXFORD
UNIVERSITY PRESS

Oxford University Press, Inc., publishes works that further
Oxford University's objective of excellence
in research, scholarship, and education.

Oxford   New York
Auckland   Cape Town   Dar es Salaam   Hong Kong   Karachi
Kuala Lumpur   Madrid   Melbourne   Mexico City   Nairobi
New Delhi   Shanghai   Taipei   Toronto

With offices in
Argentina   Austria   Brazil   Chile   Czech Republic   France   Greece
Guatemala   Hungary   Italy   Japan   Poland   Portugal   Singapore
South Korea   Switzerland   Thailand   Turkey   Ukraine   Vietnam

Published by Oxford University Press, Inc.
198 Madison Avenue, New York, New York 10016

www.oup.com

Oxford is a registered trademark of Oxford University Press.

Library of Congress Cataloging-in-Publication Data

De Souza Briggs, Xavier N.
Moving to opportunity : the story of an American experiment to fight ghetto poverty /
Xavier de Souza Briggs, Susan J. Popkin, John Goering.
     p.   cm.
Includes bibliographical references and index.
ISBN 978-0-19-539371-2; 978-0-19-539284-5 (pbk.)
1. Housing policy—United States.   2. Urban poor—Government policy—
United States.   I. Popkin, Susan J.   II. Goering, John M.   III. Title.
HD7293.D367 2010
363.5'80973—dc22   2009023187

Printed in the United States of America
on acid-free paper

Preface

This book centers on three questions. First, where does low-income housing assistance belong in the effort to reform economic opportunity policies appropriate to the twenty-first century? This question has assumed a new urgency and new political dimensions in the context of America's most severe economic crisis since the Great Depression and the most sweeping electoral mandate—that won by Barack Obama, the Democratic candidate for president, in November 2008—in more than a generation. The urgency of reform, the prospects of "leveraging" the crisis to create an economy that benefits everyone and not just the affluent, and the tough fiscal choices that confront us at a time of enormous budget deficits—all these factors underscore how important it is to inform the policy debate with good evidence. This is true even, and perhaps especially, when the evidence comes with surprises for those on both the Left and the Right of the body politic.

Second, how can we improve the *quality of life* of poor people—in particular, of poor families who endure the severe challenges of raising children in violent ghetto neighborhoods—even as we also look for ways to help them *escape* poverty? We will show why dramatically improving quality of life, such as by buffering people from violence and the constant fear of victimization, is possible, necessary, and just. But we will also show how different it is from helping people escape income poverty. The failure to see this distinction clearly and judge public policy and private initiative fairly in light of this distinction has led to much disappointment and confusion. Here again, the Left and Right bear responsibility for adding to that confusion and the political impasse it often compounds. If the first question is defined by opportunity, the second reminds us of the importance of security—economic, physical, mental, and other kinds. Security is essential to leading a decent life even if one must live poor or live poor for a time, and ironically, it is easy to miss this by focusing exclusively on "opportunity" in education, work, or other domains.

Third and finally, as the nation responds to the economic crisis that was triggered by a credit crisis in real estate, how should we rebuild the "housing ladder"? How can we take a much more balanced approach, one that does not shortchange affordable *rental* housing for the sake of promoting homeownership first and last? We will show how and why such an approach must include rental housing affordable to those who earn the lowest wages in the economy and who help make our economy function in the nation's most expensive regional markets. It is vital that the policy agenda, now and in the decade ahead, not be limited to crisis management. Real reform and honest answers are required. For example, will we merely change the *way* low-income housing assistance helps millions of the most vulnerable people in our country, or will we address the fact that—leaving the delivery approach aside—such assistance only covers about a quarter of those eligible to receive it?

We cannot offer comprehensive answers to any of these questions, and there are other questions we address along the way. But we believe the lessons of this book to be especially relevant to those three urgent concerns.

We have incurred many debts in the production of this volume, along with the policy briefs, journal articles, and other products of a roughly five-year project to understand an ambitious social experiment. Our greatest debt is to the families who participated in the Moving to Opportunity (MTO) experiment. It is remarkable that parents and children who endure so many daily struggles would allow researchers to repeatedly poke and prod through face-to-face conversation, phone calls, and other channels. The modest financial incentives we offered aside, some of our subjects expressed a heartfelt appreciation for our interest in their lives and views. We are humbled by that and grateful for their trust. We hope we have repaid that trust with a book that will educate the public and the field, leading to better public policy, as well as public and private action. We sincerely believe that MTO is America's experiment. Its lessons matter for all of us, for its success and shortcomings implicate the decisions, large and small, that we each make to shape the country we share.

But as an initiative of the federal government, specifically of the U.S. Department of Housing and Urban Development (HUD), MTO was made possible by those who authorized, funded, and inspired it. HUD Secretaries Jack Kemp and Henry Cisneros are first and foremost among those, and the many members of Congress who supported this social experiment also deserve our thanks. Our friend and colleague, civil rights attorney and activist Alex Polikoff, who successfully argued the landmark *Gautreaux* desegregation lawsuit before the U.S. Supreme Court in 1976, was the one who took the case for an MTO-like demonstration to Washington in the late 1980s. And sociologist James Rosenbaum's results on the court-ordered Gautreaux program in greater Chicago—the forerunner of MTO—were crucial to winning support for the new experiment, as we show in chapter 3. There would have been no results to show, however, if not for the hard-won victories of Chicago's Leadership Council for Metropolitan Opportunity (now closed), which implemented the Gautreaux program over many years.

A social experiment is, in the end, two things joined: a program plus the project of rigorously and thoughtfully evaluating it. For supporting the early efforts to design and fund the longitudinal evaluation of MTO, beginning in 1993, we thank Michael Stegman and Margery Austin Turner, who were appointees at HUD during the first Clinton Administration. We hope that this book and the other publications on MTO's lessons are testimony to the importance of sustaining high-quality research on the nation's complex policy choices and programs. We cannot do better if we do not learn, and while producing evidence does not guarantee learning— as studies of research in the policy process have shown time and time again—solid evidence is certainly a vital ingredient. Sadly, this has not been the view of every administration or policy official.

Our work was made possible through the generous support of HUD, as well as a consortium of private, philanthropic foundations. In HUD's Office of Policy Development and Research, the conscientious support and critical feedback of Todd Richardson and Cheryl Levine were crucial, along with that of Kevin Neary and Bob Gray. As for the foundations, key staff not only championed our work but asked important questions and offered useful leads along the way. In particular, we thank: Ralph Smith and Cindy Guy of the Annie E. Casey Foundation; Amy Bogdon and James Carr of the Fannie Mae Foundation (now closed); Darren Walker of the Rockefeller Foundation; Mark Steinmeyer of the Smith Richardson Foundation; and Bob Granger and Ed Seidman of the William T. Grant Foundation.

We also owe our thanks to a wide array of outstanding social scientists and practitioner experts whose critical advice, encouragement, and other supports helped us enormously. These are very in-demand people—the proverbial best in the business—and we cannot adequately express our thanks for the time they made to help us make progress. We convened a national advisory committee early in the life of our project and periodically sought their advice and feedback on this work (in various forms). The committee included Barry Bluestone, Linda Burton, Thomas Cook, Camille Charles, Ingrid Gould Ellen, Joseph Ferreira, George Galster, Harry Holzer, Christopher Jencks, Philip Kasinitz, Tama Leventhal, Jens Ludwig, Kristin Moore, Katherine Newman, Lynn Olson, Paul Ong, Gary Orfield, Mary Pattillo, Robert Sampson, Barbara Sard, Jeremy Travis, Margery Turner, Sudhir Venkatesh, Thomas Weisner, Terry Williams, and Min Zhou. Beyond that group of formal advisers, key friends of the project include Jeanne Brooks-Gunn, Susan Clampet-Lundquist, Greg Duncan, Stefanie DeLuca, Kathryn Edin, Judie Feins, Frank Furstenberg, Jeff Liebman, Larry Katz, and Jeff Kling. Among them, Greg has been a key adviser since MTO's inception and a particularly generous and insightful colleague.

Over the roughly five-year life of our project, the team included interviewers and data analysts at Harvard, MIT, and the Urban Institute, as well as support staff at the City University of New York, expert methodologists and data storage and security wizards at UCLA's Fieldwork Lab, and doctoral-student ethnographers hired from a half dozen more universities.

We are grateful to many administrative staff at each institution, as well as to the dedicated members of the project.

Our Urban Institute stalwarts included Jeremy Gustafson and Jennifer Comey, who were able project managers and fieldworkers; Elizabeth Cove and Lynette Rawlings, who together conducted nearly a third of the qualitative interviews; Carla Herbig, Laura Harris, Michael Eiseman, Mary Cunningham, and Kadija Ferryman, who were excellent interviewers and data analysts; Barika Williams, who, along with Elizabeth, analyzed the MTO Interim Impacts Evaluation Survey data; Shawnise Thompson and Julie Adams, who helped recruit interviewees and manage the interview data; Thomas Kingsley and Kathy Pettit, who oversaw the analysis of neighborhood indicators and other spatial data; and Margery Turner, who has patiently and steadfastly supported and advised us, especially when a problem arose that called for a fresh, wise outlook.

The team of hard-working and resourceful ethnographers, who juggled many challenges out in the field as well as back in the office, included: Naomi Calvo, Silvia Dominguez, Luis Martos, Maria Rendón, and Gretchen Weismann in greater Boston; Erica Angert, Don Clayborne, Cynthia Duarte, Genelle Gaudinez, Tu Vu, and Ellen Wight in greater Los Angeles; and Carla Barrett, Al Gilkes, Joan Mazelis, and Kim Torres in greater New York City. A subset of these—Cynthia, Gretchen, Maria, and Silvia—stayed on to code and/or analyze our mountain of fieldnotes.

Some of these team members or advisers coauthored papers or policy briefs with us that serve as foundations for chapters of the book: Kingsley and Pettit for the chapter on the unequal geography of opportunity; Leventhal and Weismann for the chapter on moving to security; Ferryman and Rendón for the chapter on finding good schools; Cove, Duarte, and Turner for the chapter on finding work; and Comey and Weismann for the chapter on finding good housing and neighborhoods. We are grateful to them all, for contributions too many and varied to capture here.

At UCLA's Fieldwork Lab, we thank Thomas Weisner and Eli Lieber for generous support, patient troubleshooting, and insightful advice throughout.

A number of colleagues read and commented generously on parts of the book manuscript, in the late stages of drafting and revision, and so deserve our special thanks: Phil Clay, Ingrid Ellen, David Harding, Langley Keyes, Joan Mazelis, James Quane, Barbara Sard, Margery Turner, Larry Vale, and Barry Wellman. We are likewise grateful to the anonymous reviewers commissioned by Oxford University Press for their thoughtful and extremely useful feedback.

David McBride, our editor at Oxford, provided steadfast interest and encouragement. Most important, at least from our vantage point, he shared our vision of making a careful work of research accessible and useful to as broad an audience as possible. He was a pleasure to work with from the start.

Finally, we are grateful to our families for their love, support, and patience—even for some late-night, just-in-time proofreading. These pages and the lessons they contain are what we give back to them and to everyone who hopes for a better world, where "opportunity for all"—the core of the larger experiment that is America—is much more than a dream or a tag line.

December 2009

Contents

Moving to Opportunity

Chapter 1

Places and Lives

BOSTON

"In the hallway, they were always smoking dope," she remembers. "Hookers after 5 P.M., rubbers on the floor. They smoked in the apartments [too].... And I would tell them to go to another hallway. When my son came in, I would search him."

Erika, an African-American single mother, was 55 when we got to know her in 2004. Through an ambitious social experiment called Moving to Opportunity, she and her children moved out of a public housing development—a government-run apartment complex for very low-income families and elderly—in 1996. Erika's former home is in a high-poverty area of Dorchester in inner-city Boston. The "projects," as she still calls them, were dangerous and drug-ridden—a terrible place to try and raise children. "I was too scared to say 'hi-bye.' ... You can't have friends for watching your back." In public housing, she only socialized with her sister, who lived upstairs, and one other neighbor.

In contrast, the family's new neighborhood, in an economically diverse inner suburb south of Boston, was safe and quiet. This is what Erika appreciated most. She talks about the peace of mind as well as the confidence it gives her to live here, on a well-kept side street of single-family and two-family houses with small side yards, in a private apartment, which she rents using a housing voucher provided by the federal government as part of the experiment. This low-poverty area is mostly white.

Here in the Boston suburbs, Erika often leaves her front door unlocked. Apart from the woman downstairs who plays her music loud and gives Erika a migraine, she finds her neighbors generally trustworthy, helpful, and respectful—the police force, too. "When they were selling drugs there [she points to a nearby park], the cops came by on bicycles. And I ain't *never* seen that in the projects. The police are much more responsive [here]."

In Dorchester, she would never let her youngest son, Andre, play outside. "People [were] always saying what they gonna do to you. Different rules, dangerous area...people doing a lot of drugs. Women pulling machetes [big cutting knives] out of their underwear, knife fights over a man. Here, I can talk to the neighbor next door, talk to him for an hour, and the wife don't say anything." She remembers being followed

3

and taunted in public housing, too, and recalls the knife fight that took place right outside her window on the day she moved in. It all made her feel "caged" and hopeless.

Yet it hasn't been easy since Erika and her children moved away from inner-city Boston. For one thing, though they moved out, they didn't manage to escape all of the risks around public housing. Ten months after the move to the suburbs, her eldest son, Antone, who was 18 at the time, was killed on a visit back to Dorchester.

What's more, she hasn't worked for many years due to poor health. She goes to the hospital several times per week, sometimes every day, and takes medication for stomach pain and chronic headaches. The year before we started to visit, she had an asthma attack and was diagnosed with walking pneumonia, then congestive heart failure and the related problem of edema (fluid buildup) in her legs. When walking around became difficult, she became obese, making it harder still to stay active on her weakened legs.

Erika uses an electric scooter now. There's a shopping street and bus stop just a few blocks away. Her doctor is at a respected hospital in Boston. She sticks with that care provider because he's familiar, and she relies on transit to go there—it can take all day, there and back, given her health problems and the transfers she must make—or to visit her mother, who lives in a nursing home in an adjacent suburb.

Then there's "the little one," as she calls Andre. According to Erika, Andre has a sensory disorder, some schizophrenia, bipolar disorder, and attention deficit hyperactivity disorder. Erika attributes this to his birth mother's drug habit. Andre's mother is Erika's niece. He is 11, and for most of the time we visited Erika, Andre lived in a service-intensive residential home back in Dorchester. Several of her children went to residential schools for troubled youth while growing up, including her 26-year-old daughter, Keesha, who is still troubled and lives here with her mother.

Erika and her children are part of a large extended family. Erika is the youngest of 16 children, raised in Tennessee until she was a teenager and her father came north to work on the railroad. She talks to her siblings and grandchildren regularly but only sees them a few times per year now. She doesn't belong to any groups, though there's a church at the end of her block, where she uses the day care and food pantry sometimes. Yet Erika says she doesn't feel isolated. We sit in her tiny but tidy living room as she explains how she ventured beyond her immediate neighborhood, a few years after moving to this suburb, to find the day care centers, after-school programs, the YMCA, library, employment center, and other services.

The local schools have been responsive to Andre's needs, Erika emphasizes, and neighbors have helped him shovel snow in the winter and offered to watch him for her. "A lot of kids know he has bipolar disorder. They gonna be more concerned that he needs to be home if his mother said so." Compared to the inner-city neighborhood the family left behind, she says, "the kids here…are more into 'listen to your mom.'"

Erika struggles with chronic illness, deep loss, and the kinds of barriers to getting ahead that would leave most Americans feeling demoralized and perhaps defeated. But she feels at home and never regrets leaving the dangerous public housing developments of inner-city Boston behind. Her current neighborhood, she stresses, is what a neighborhood should be: "the people that knows you and would stick up for you."

Erika's story is part of a much larger story about ghetto poverty in America—the people and places that were rediscovered, albeit briefly, when Hurricane Katrina put them—and society's failure to address their rights and their hopes—on our TV screens several years ago. We begin with her story, and that of several other families who volunteered to participate in this uniquely American social experiment, before taking a new look, in the next chapter, at ghetto poverty as a national problem.

A total of 170 families, including Erika's, used government-provided rental housing vouchers to relocate from public housing developments in high-crime, high-poverty inner-city ghettos of Boston in the mid-1990s through Moving to Opportunity, or MTO. The program invited residents of public and assisted housing in Boston and four other big cities—Baltimore, Chicago, Los Angeles, and New York—to participate in a randomized experiment. Some families were assigned to the experimental "treatment" group, which received housing relocation counseling, search assistance, and a housing voucher (monthly subsidy) useable only in neighborhoods with less than 10 percent of the population living below the poverty line as of the 1990 census, with the condition that they remain in those neighborhoods for at least one year. A second group, the "comparison group," received the vouchers with no special counseling, assistance, or restrictions on where to "lease up." And a third group, the "controls," received no change in their housing assistance: They retained a unit in public housing, though they were free to move out later, on their own, if they were willing and able to do so.

Policy makers wondered: Would the "treatment" make a difference in otherwise similar lives? In various roles—as the planners, evaluators, and advisers of MTO—we, the authors of this book, have been following the MTO families since the beginning. (As explained below, we were able to examine the greater Boston, Los Angeles, and New York sites in depth, while a second team, using a somewhat different approach, studied the other two sites.) We wanted to understand why the experiment produced such a wide range of outcomes, including several big puzzles we outline later in this chapter.

Some stories of families in the favored experimental group are quite unlike Erika's, for example. There's Danielle, who moved with two young children to an inner suburb north of Boston. As the only black mother in an otherwise all-white apartment complex, she felt harassed and unwelcome. Then a boyfriend caused trouble and got the family evicted. Their next move took them south of Boston, to a suburb where Danielle's daughters, Kia and Shauna, liked the schools and the safe neighborhood.

But when a new daughter was born and Danielle wanted a larger apartment, she moved back to Boston, into what turned out to be a terrible, pest-ridden apartment above a detox center. They had to find another place quickly, which landed Danielle back in Dorchester, not far from the public housing projects she and her daughters had left behind six years before—and close to the relatives that defined most of their social life. The schools were rough in ways Danielle's girls had never experienced. The girls there were "fast" (sexually promiscuous), said Danielle, and constantly fighting. "My girls didn't grow up in these kinds of neighborhoods," she reasoned. "They're not used to this. They [the children at school] bully Shauna sometimes…Kia's gotten beat up." After we had visited for a few months, Danielle decided it was "the worst neighborhood" she had ever lived in. As her girls got into more and more fights in their new school, their grades dropped, and they felt unsafe. Danielle was fed up. She wanted to move again.

LOS ANGELES

Some of the MTO families' stories, such as Eduardo and Monica's in Los Angeles, are even more unlike Erika's.

"I work there, I go to church there. That's too much. I can't do any more at the church!" jokes Monica about a Catholic parish in the neighborhood she left through MTO. But the church is the center of her family's social world, and the ties formed there factor into their success in a variety of ways.

When we first meet them, Monica is 46 and has been married to Eduardo, who is 42, for 18 years. Monica emigrated from Honduras to L.A. in her early twenties, Eduardo from Mexico when he was 17. They both work full-time, Monica as a receptionist at the family's church, which is located in a neighborhood she would rather forget. Eduardo works in an auto repair shop across town.

When the MTO experiment came along, the family was living in a public housing development long known for its entrenched, mostly Mexican-American gangs. In some families, several generations of gang-bangers have been caught up in the cycle of crime and violence.

With their housing voucher, Eduardo and Monica moved with their three sons, Bernardo, Raul, and Eddie Jr., to Hollywood, and after saving for several years, they had enough to buy a small, two-bedroom home in a mostly Hispanic neighborhood of similar "starter" homes in East Los Angeles.

It is almost impossible for us to get these proud first-time homeowners to identify *any* problems with their new neighborhood. They are at pains to distinguish it in every way from public housing and the neighborhood left behind. The distance they have put between themselves and that earlier chapter of their lives in this sprawling, unequal metropolis, seems to be central to their getting-ahead story of themselves. It includes, they make very clear to us, tremendous pride at leaving the government's housing voucher program. Moving out, moving up, getting off assistance, as in: "We're making our own way now."

Looking at us with visible concern on one visit, Monica presses to know why we could possibly want to talk to them, since they're "not MTO anymore." We explain that the program was an experiment, which means that we must carefully follow families for years in order to learn about its impacts and that it's especially important that our view of the MTO experiment include families who do *not* receive assistance to meet their housing costs any more—and who even became homeowners. We need to hear from them, we reassure Monica, in part *because* of how well they've done, not in spite of that.

As in Erika's harrowing account of the inner-city projects she left behind, safety is the biggest difference between the public housing neighborhood where Eduardo and Monica used to live with their children and the neighborhood they live in now. But there is a moral dimension to it, too: Monica feels that getting away from the projects got them away from the wrong kind of people.

The couple has a favorite story, which we heard at least three times over the course of our fieldwork. "I left my car open," says Monica, meaning she left it unlocked one day, "and we left the house for like three days, and nothing happened." Bernardo, age 17, rides the bus home from school in the evening if neither of his parents can pick him up after a basketball game. Monica says she doesn't worry about him walking home from the bus stop nearby.

When pressed some more, she concedes that a park on the edge of their neighborhood is risky: "There are drugs, it's not safe." The regular police patrols there offer proof to Monica, and so the family uses a different park, mostly in the summer, about a mile away. Also, her neighbors have told her that gang activity is prevalent on the perimeter of the neighborhood, near a large through-street. But she believes that gangs won't come around her block because "the neighbors would call the police."

Eduardo and Monica are not members of any associations in the area, and their exchanges with neighbors are much more casual and limited than Erika's are in suburban Boston. Relatives are not a big part of their social world either. Eduardo has a sister nearby, but the two are estranged from each other. His other sister lives in Mexico, while Monica's sister lives in Miami with her mother.

The couple socializes primarily with friends they have made at church. Their children's *padrinos* (godparents) are church friends. So is the person who found them a reliable real estate agent. So is the housing counselor who helped them relocate away from public housing. Their youngest son, Eddie Jr., goes to the primary school run by their church, where Monica works, and the other two boys to a church-affiliated high school not far away. One evening, we accompany them to one of the many fundraisers run by the boys' schools. It's bingo night in East L.A.

With the church as their primary community, this family expects their neighborhood mainly to be a safe and accessible "base of operations." The neighbors seem trustworthy and concerned but aren't close. The family drives outside the immediate neighborhood to work, shop, play, and worship.

Leaving behind one of the most gang-ridden public housing projects in a city infamous for large, well-organized gangs did not put Eduardo and Monica on easy street by any means. Both work hard, for limited wages, in a labor market with the most unequal income levels, across different racial/ethnic groups, of any urban area in America. What's more, as we got to know them and their boys over months of visiting, it became clear that neither parent knew how to advise Bernardo, who was soon to graduate high school, about higher education or career options. Should he go to community college and then try to transfer to a four-year school? Should he focus immediately on a profession? The parents didn't know and so left it to the high school to help their son.

But they were homeowners, their children were safe—or as safe as they could make them in a big American city with persistent danger zones—and, with a boost from the MTO experiment, they had climbed a *long* way from the projects. As a family headed by two steadily employed parents, they were also atypical of families in public housing—and therefore of families in the experiment.

Some 208 families successfully relocated away from inner-city public housing developments in Los Angeles through MTO, some moving northward to the San Fernando Valley, others eastward as far as San Bernardino and Riverside Counties, and others to the south, to Long Beach or nearby suburbs in Orange County.

Not everyone stayed away from high-poverty areas, though. Some, like Patricia, an African-American single mother of three, relocated from Watts in South Los Angeles—the huge district that was called "South Central" until the 1992 riots led to a name change—to a low-poverty neighborhood in the San Fernando Valley. The Valley was a different world. Patricia liked the schools her children had there, the safety, and the fact that more of her neighbors out in the Valley worked. But with no car she felt isolated, and she relied on long bus rides, almost daily, to get back to South L.A. to visit the relatives she was close to and to get everywhere—to stores, services, and church. Eventually, Patricia missed those loved ones too much, so she moved back to Watts, where she attends a nearby church a few times per week.

Her apartment needs many repairs—the latest housing agency inspection identified 14 things—but the landlord hasn't fixed them. And Patricia worries about the gang-ridden schools her three children must attend. Last year, her eldest, 12-year-old Shana, was "jumped" (assaulted) and then suspended. The children at Shana's school have it "organized," says her mother, so that those affiliated with one gang, the Bloods, exit through one gate and those linked to the other gang, the Crips, use the second gate. Her best hope, she told us, was to get her children bused somewhere a bit safer.

Sometimes, Patricia takes the children to her cousin's house on the weekend, and she tells us about the "little stuff" in the neighborhood that shapes their routines:

> We be getting out, spending the night over there, just to get away, cuz lately, there's been a lot of little stuff going on. I don't really like to talk about it, but it be a lot of killing and stuff…it's been some killing over there [points to a neighborhood that is rival gang territory], and people supposed to come back [here] and supposed to shoot up a lot of people, so really we been staying close.

NEW YORK

Lanelle says she doesn't mind living back in the South Bronx, not far from Yankee Stadium. The subway is about eight blocks away, a short walk by New York City standards. She can walk to most of the shops they need. Her younger children are in school nearby, health care is not far—which is important, since Lanelle and her son are managing several chronic illnesses—and the relatives they socialize with live nearby, too.

The apartment is "a little noisy" sometimes, she admits. But given the odyssey it took to land here and become stable, Lanelle is not complaining that her family is no longer in the quiet "suburban" area she moved to in the northeast Bronx when the MTO experiment first came along. She's not complaining even though she liked that area and knew it was much safer than either the public housing development they left behind or this area, where no one in the family will walk home alone at night. At least Marlena, the youngest girl, can walk herself to school and play outside.

Lanelle is African American, age 51. Her daughters are Antoinette (age 21), Jocelyn (19), and Marlena (13). Her grandson Jared (7) also lives with them. Lanelle's only boy, Clark (31), lives alone in another South Bronx neighborhood, suffers with acute sickle cell anemia, and gets by on disability checks. Clark is Jared's father, but it's his grandmother and aunts who care for him mostly.

Lanelle and her children lived in a public housing development in the high-crime Mott Haven section of the South Bronx, for seven years until the MTO "lottery," as she calls it, offered the chance to relocate. Mott Haven was overrun with drug dealing and drug taking, gang shootings, and prostitution—part of the Bronx that was synonymous with urban distress, immortalized in *Fort Apache* and other Hollywood movies.

Leaving public housing with help from the MTO experiment, Lanelle chose an apartment in a low-poverty, mostly residential area in the northeast Bronx, on tree-lined streets. She chose that neighborhood, she remembers, based on a teacher's recommendation of a strong elementary school there. She was also thinking about her older girls' need to use transit to get to their two high schools.

The family lived in the northeast Bronx for three years. There was a mix of ethnic groups, which Lanelle liked, and while there were some drug dealers, "they was more on the hush hush, put away." Things were more expensive there, too, Lanelle remembers. "Everything was so expensive! Clothing, things, you know, I'd find myself going back down to the South Bronx to shop. Food, too, it was more up there. And there wasn't as many free programs for the kids, up there you had to pay for *everything*. Nothing was free." And public transportation wasn't as convenient. Everything seemed farther away. But she was content, everyone in the family felt safe, and she wanted to stay.

Like other families in New York who volunteered to participate in MTO, Lanelle was renting at the time from what the real estate industry considers a "small landlord"—someone who typically rents just one or a handful of units, often living in the same multifamily house as the tenant. Small landlords don't rely on professional maintenance companies much or have the access to capital, when repairs or rehab are needed, that large management companies (corporate landlords) typically do. And these differences can be good or bad, depending on the situation and the landlord.

In Lanelle's case, things took a sudden turn for the worse. When the heat did not work for two weeks one winter, Lanelle got pneumonia. Then she learned that she, Antoinette, and Marlena had all contracted HIV—whether through blood transfusion or some other means, she wouldn't say. Then the housing authority refused to pay the landlord (for failure to make the repairs), and so Lanelle and her children were evicted. Their stay in the "suburban" Bronx was over.

The stock of rental housing affordable to low- and moderate-income families, including the working and nonworking poor, declined sharply in New York City, as it did in Boston and Los Angeles and other "tight" markets, throughout the 1990s and into the new decade. Lanelle and her children had to find another apartment fast—in one of America's most expensive housing markets—where the landlord would be willing to accept the family's government-provided housing voucher. Many landlords won't.

After a brief spell living with her grown son, Lanelle and her girls found a new place with a great landlord, back in the South Bronx but in an area less poor than Mott Haven. But Lanelle's health problems made the fourth-floor walk-up apartment untenable. So after a year there, the family had to move again.

Through her stepfather, Lanelle learned about a good building near Yankee Stadium. And this word-of-mouth referral chain continued: During our fieldwork, several more relatives moved into the building, while others, as we have noted, lived nearby.

When we visited the family in 2004 and 2005, the two eldest girls, Antoinette and Jocelyn, were pregnant. The fathers lived in Louisiana and Texas, respectively, and while Jocelyn had gone to live with the father of her child the first summer, when she attended college "down South," neither young mother was expecting much financial support from these fathers. Both daughters are commuting to local colleges, juggling studies and single parenthood.

Lanelle is frugal. She uses the lowest cost grocery store, relies on the health clinic just three blocks away for her family's care, and regularly heads to the food pantry down the block to get free fruits and vegetables. But the baby shower for Antoinette was a big event. Lanelle hunted special gifts in bargain shops across the city for months ahead of the big day. Then Antoinette gave birth to baby Ava, who became the household's seventh member.

Lanelle was struggling, and a series of unlucky breaks—first in her health and that of her adult son, who needed her hands-on care more and more, then in the city's brutally expensive housing market—had made things much harder. Two of her eldest daughters, one of whom also received regular care to manage HIV, had just become jobless single mothers as young adults. But living near stores, services, schools, and the subway, they had access to the basics. And they had key family supports nearby. Plus, they knew the danger zones in the neighborhood, and crime was down—across the city—since their days in Mott Haven. Lanelle's eldest girls had made it to college.

Lanelle's daughter Marlena shook her head one night, during one of our last visits, as she watched a TV program about young teenage girls getting pregnant in order to "get welfare." Marlena couldn't believe the families of those girls would allow it. Her oldest sister agreed: "How they mothers be letting that go on?"

Lanelle's family is one of 180 families who relocated through MTO in New York. Most of them moved to the northeast Bronx, most rented from small landlords, and like Lanelle, most were not there six to nine years later, when our team started to contact families and make visits. They had moved on or moved back, some toward much poorer, higher crime areas in central Harlem and the South Bronx, where more landlords are known to accept the federal housing vouchers that help very low-income people pay the rent.

DIFFERENT LIVES—OR NOT SO DIFFERENT?

Whether they stayed in safer, less poor areas or not, everyone we have introduced so far lived for some period in a neighborhood environment that was strikingly different from the inner-city public housing communities they had left behind. In earlier surveys and over the course of in-depth, "kitchen-table" conversations with us, they described streets that were safer, less drug or gang activity, buildings that were better maintained, schools that were typically safer and more demanding, and neighbors' expectations that were often different. These are some of the factors that have led the public, and policy makers and researchers as well, to believe for many years that less poor, less risky neighborhood environments can have a significant, positive impact on the well-being of children and families. Help families get out, and they will move up—or so the common wisdom holds.

To help test that idea, another group of families in these three metropolitan areas—Boston, Los Angeles, and New York—were part of the MTO experiment's control group. These are the families who did not win the program's "lottery." Like those who were steered toward low-poverty neighborhoods, these families volunteered for the chance to leave public housing. But unlike the former, families in the control group continued to receive housing assistance, for as long as they remained eligible under standard policy guidelines, in the form of a subsidized apartment in public housing in a high-poverty area. By the time we began to visit families, however, many members of the control group—over 70 percent—had moved on.

Like the lives we introduced above, the control-group families are not a homogeneous group by any means. We introduce a few here, to briefly illustrate what life has been like for those who did not make the high-expectations move through MTO—and how some families manage to be successful regardless of where they live, against incredible odds.

There is Pamela, age 73, who has raised three children of her own—all grown now, with 12 grandchildren and 20 great grandchildren—and who now raises Eamon (age 14) and Clarissa (13), two she adopted as infants. "There's no senior in this citizen," Pamela declares on our very first visit.

Pamela has outlived two husbands, including the abusive first one she had to divorce. And she has lived in the same public housing development in the South Bronx for more than four decades. She knows everyone there, and "they love me," she tells us. Her adopted children—Eamon always has a book in hand, and Clarissa is the social one—seem to be busy every waking moment we spend with them. They are in one of the most competitive charter schools in New York City, thanks to Eamon's high test scores, which won both siblings admission, and Pamela has already had them visit some of the nation's top colleges. Then there are after-school programs, church, and weekend cookouts with extended family in Brooklyn.

Stephanie also lived in public housing for many years. She was born and raised there, like many of her relatives. But she faces very different prospects day-to-day than Pamela does—in a South Los Angeles neighborhood racked by shooting and other gang violence.

For over a year before we met her and her two children, Shari (age 13) and Troy (4), Stephanie had been fighting an eviction order in public housing. The public housing agency claimed to have a photo showing her boyfriend dealing drugs, and "zero tolerance" policies had become more strict, thanks to the epidemic of gang violence in many inner-city neighborhoods in the 1980s and early 1990s. But Stephanie swears that he had never lived with her, that she had never been an accessory to his crimes in any way, and that they don't see each other anymore.

Ultimately, Stephanie gave up her appeal and moved with Troy to her aunt's house in another neighborhood. She left Shari with her grandmother (Stephanie's mother), not far from the public housing projects, so she could stay in her middle school. On that block, most of the neighbors are Stephanie's relatives, so they keep an eye on Shari. Car-less and without special skills, Stephanie has been unable to find work. She and her children rely on welfare.

A long history of exposure to violence marks Shari's family. Her father was killed years ago in the same neighborhood, just a few blocks from the projects. Then a cousin was shot and killed the year before we started to visit her. Then Troy's preschool was caught in a cross fire, so a brick wall had to be built around it.

One afternoon, we sit with Shari and her teen cousins as they contrast the neighborhood where Stephanie is living for the moment—itself a high-poverty, racially segregated area of South L.A.—with the much riskier one near public housing where Shari still goes to school. Cousin Jason chimes in quickly, "It's quiet over there [where Stephanie lives]. You can just sit down and relax. Over here, you got…can't even go to sleep at night. Shooting. One night, when I got in the shower, there was shooting. And when I walk just up to school, there had just been a shooting…and the police was cocking their guns. We saw 'em."

HIGH STAKES AND BIG PUZZLES

Poverty and crime. Safety and security. Sickness and health. Growing up and getting looked after—or not—by parents, relatives, and public institutions. Falling back and "messin' up," too. Living on the bottom in a changing America. Our study is an effort to understand how an ambitious social experiment called Moving to Opportunity took shape and also how it affected the lives of very poor people in greater Boston, Los Angeles, and New York over time.

Much as drugs are tested through trials that randomly assign patients to distinct groups that scientific researchers have defined, the participants in MTO were randomly assigned and then tracked to help public policy makers test the efficacy of a different way of helping poor people meet the high cost of housing—this in markets where even middle-class professionals must scramble, from time to time, to find an affordable place to live in a decent neighborhood. There was more than shelter at stake, since national policy statements declared, beginning in 1949, that every family in America should not only have "a decent home" but also a "suitable living environment."[1] Building on earlier, more limited programs, some of them produced by civil rights lawsuits dating back to the 1960s, MTO set out to test the idea that where you can live in America matters for your well-being and life prospects—and also to test *how* it might matter. This lies at the heart of our effort to systematically examine lives such as those above.

If "bad" neighborhoods are truly bad for children and families, especially the minority poor, can moving to better neighborhoods lead to better lives? Might these families escape poverty, beyond having a better quality of life if they continued to be poor? Federal planners thought so, and in 1994, the U.S. Department of Housing and Urban Development launched Moving to Opportunity (MTO). The $80 million social experiment enrolled nearly 5,000 very low-income, mostly black and Hispanic families, many of them on welfare, who were living in public housing in the inner-city ghettos of Baltimore, Boston, Chicago, Los Angeles, and New York.

But about five years after they had entered the program, many of the families in the favored "experimental" group were living once again in high-poverty neighborhoods. Young women in that group showed big drops in risky behavior and big improvements in mental health, on average, while young male movers did not. The males even showed some signs of increased delinquency if they had lived, at least for a time, in the low-poverty areas. Parents likewise showed major drops in anxiety and depression—two of the crippling symptoms of being chronically poor in high-risk ghettos—but no improvements in employment or income. While skeptics worried that relocating would rob the families of vital social support from loved ones, as well as a sense of community, many movers appeared to be maintaining the same limited social circles—mostly disadvantaged relatives and close friends, with frequent trips to high-poverty areas—despite living in more advantaged neighborhoods.

We wanted to know why.

As we pursued these puzzles, we confronted a host of questions that have absorbed researchers, and sometimes policy makers and the public, too, for decades. For example, in a nation where most people, not a select few, will experience poverty at some point in their lifetime—but most of them only for a short spell—what causes *some* people to experience such chronic and destructive poverty in the nation's most disadvantaged urban neighborhoods? What choices do low-income people make—assuming they have meaningful choices to make—when exposed to a different community context, and why do they make those choices? Why do some kinds of changes improve the *quality* of poor people's lives without helping them *escape* poverty, and how should we invest in both kinds of improvement?

Beyond these questions, the evolution of the experiment itself is a story of great expectations unfolding in challenging times. Among other major trends, the first decade of MTO saw: the biggest and most sustained economic expansion since the Second World War—but with mostly low-wage, limited-benefit jobs for low-skill people; the most significant and controversial welfare reform in a generation; increasing distress in older suburbs; gentrification in "comeback" cities, even in long-distressed inner-city neighborhoods; and also the biggest jumps in rents—sadly, with little media attention when it was poor people facing those skyrocketing rents—that anyone could recall. Housing policy focused overwhelmingly on promoting homeownership, to the neglect of affordable rental housing. As it turned out, this lopsided focus also "greased the gears" for the risky lending and borrowing that produced a foreclosure crisis and then a much wider financial crisis that helped devastate the economy of the United States—and much of the globe as well.

The story we tell of this remarkable experiment is centered on the families who volunteered to participate. But it also includes, as it must, the policy makers, planners, landlords, and administrators who did so much to shape the MTO families' prospects and choices. MTO has been an unusual, and easily misunderstood, but all-too-American experiment to fight ghetto poverty. It holds lessons for the nation about what works, what doesn't, and what could work to overcome one of the most destructive forms of poverty—the "ghetto poverty" that is concentrated in high-risk, distressed neighborhoods in many cities and sometimes in the suburbs, too. But MTO also holds lessons *about* a nation that has, for so long now, let millions of its most disadvantaged live such dangerous, deprived, and isolated lives in the midst of enormous wealth and extraordinary innovation. Likewise, our nation has shown little sustained interest in the "ghetto housing" problems we examine here and yet such concerted political activism around the other social problems—such as chronic and expensive illness, school failure, and violent crime—to which ghetto poverty is closely tied.

ORGANIZATION AND LESSONS OF THE BOOK

In the next chapter, we look closely at America's fleeting "rediscovery" of ghetto poverty and its terrible social costs in the wake of Hurricane Katrina, which left thousands of people, many of them black and poor and without means of escape, stranded in toxic, rising water as millions watched on television. As a tool for helping to rebuild people's lives, Moving to Opportunity was back in the headlines, albeit briefly, thanks to that unplanned event. This is not a book about natural disasters, but Katrina is a window on our central theme: the geography of risk and opportunity and society's obligation to *change* that geography for the ghetto poor. In chapter 2, we examine historical shifts in how "ghetto" is defined in American life, as well as the evolution of efforts to fight ghetto poverty—from the era of urban unrest in the 1960s, the War on Poverty social programs, and the extraordinary series of bipartisan national policy commissions that called segregated and poor ghettos America's greatest social problem through the Reagan era and the harshest years of a political war *against* the poor, as sociologist Herbert Gans has labeled it. In the 1980s, social researchers showed a renewed willingness to examine ghetto poverty, though sharply divergent schools of thought emerged about its causes and what to do about it. From there, the story heads into the era of the crack epidemic and the Clinton Administration's support of the so-called war on crime, welfare reform, MTO, and a large-scale program to tear down many distressed public housing developments in inner-city ghettos and replace them with "mixed-income housing." Like earlier periods, the latest era is studded with controversies about how much "choice" society's institutions actually allow poor people, what those choices really involve, and how poor people make their choices, for better or worse.

Chapter 3 shows how a coalition of academic researchers, policy entrepreneurs, energized government planners, and their supporters in Congress designed a new experiment, with low-income housing assistance as the platform, to fight ghetto poverty. Perhaps not surprisingly, that tale includes the fateful choices that would shape families' experiences more than a decade later, when we went into the field. We highlight major challenges to implementing the grand design—a process that is invariably fraught, say veteran observers of social programs, with unexpected setbacks, unwelcome trade-offs, and more than a few gaps in planners' knowledge.

Chapter 4 examines the "stages" on which the experiment unfolded: America's changing cities and suburbs, its metropolitan housing markets. We focus, in particular, on how poor people have been priced out or regulated out of decent housing and resource-rich communities in economically robust metropolitan regions across the country. We offer a new view of the uneven "geography of opportunity" that MTO was designed to address. The experiment unfolded in five distinct contexts, and the differences and similarities between them help shed light on the outcomes of families in the experiment. We underscore the importance of a massive but quiet crisis: the shortage of affordable rental housing that affects millions of low-income families in the tightest housing markets, where economic inequality is severe but where much of our nation's economic growth is centered.

Chapter 4 highlights the first major lesson of our work: *MTO and the fight against ghetto poverty cannot succeed without a major national commitment to make rental housing affordable in safe, livable neighborhoods.* This is especially critical for the majority of very low-income families who are not subsidized and who face crushing rent burdens that make it all but impossible for them to lead decent lives, let alone get ahead. In spite of the well-founded conventional wisdom in real estate about the value of location, the role of rental housing, and the issue of how location defines housing's value for a healthy and satisfying life, is consistently overlooked in policy commentary on poverty in America, both in journalism and scholarship. As the nation continues to transform—some would say dismantle—the New Deal model of "project-based" public housing in favor of rental assistance for use in the private market, we show why we can no longer ignore the quiet crisis of unaffordable housing. MTO's aims have been significantly undermined by the shortage of available apartments, at modest rents, in what most Americans would recognize as "healthy" neighborhoods. A vital but crumbling rung on the housing ladder, rental housing affordable to low- and moderate-income families, including many at risk of homelessness and the costly social programs the homeless require to get back on their feet, remains overlooked in a society that has been obsessed with homeownership.

We know homeownership to be important and worth supporting for many reasons, and we support efforts to vigorously address the foreclosure crisis, as well as the predatory lending and other financial practices that helped to produce that crisis in recent years. But the classic concept of a rental "ladder" to homeownership, like the so-called ladder to the middle class, cannot function if there are no adequate, affordable rungs at the bottom of the ladder. MTO is the most carefully documented window on how vital those rungs are—and how central they are to any serious effort to address ghetto poverty.

The next few chapters focus on the MTO families' experiences, choices, and outcomes. In the early 1990s when the experiment was launched, some of our ideas about the power of place and the role of neighborhoods in healthy child and family development—not to mention economic advancement, or getting ahead—were based on very optimistic assumptions about higher income neighbors as role models, job brokers, and supporters of strong community institutions. Not everyone expected "escaping the ghetto" to be 100 percent positive, by any means. But most of the "what if's" ranked low-poverty areas better than high-poverty ones in every dimension. And there were other, less explicit assumptions: that young males might reap particularly big gains from moving out (through less peer pressure to join violent gangs), that parents would have an easier time finding and keeping steady jobs outside the inner city, and that those who moved would connect to new, higher status neighbors and gain valuable social resources or "social capital" from those new ties. Was the optimism well-founded?

Chapter 5 looks at the powerful role of "moving to security" as the experiment's most fundamental contribution. Girls, it turns out, have benefited from MTO more than boys thus far, in part because relocating removes young women from the predatory behavior of older boys and young men. This includes gangbangers and others who harassed young girls in the housing projects and pressured them into early sex. For their part, many adolescent males who relocated remain exposed to significant risks—at least some of it in high-poverty neighborhoods they were *not* living in—through their networks of male relatives, an astonishing share of whom are ex-offenders or still engaged in crime.

Meanwhile, MTO parents who relocated show massive reductions in depression and anxiety when compared to members of the control or comparison groups. The constant fear of victimization is tied to crippling anxiety and depression in our country, especially among those exposed to chronic poverty and violence, whether inside or outside the home. Conversely, *freedom* from fear—as Nobel economist Amartya Sen (2001) has called it—is closely linked to feelings of efficacy (being able to shape one's own life through effort) and the ability to strive. Freedom from fear is not a lottery ticket; it does not guarantee a road to the middle class. But as we will show, it is no small thing. Indeed, it is priceless even though a relocation-only social program has not miraculously "boosted" its adult participants out of poverty. As for that kind of mobility, the story of MTO youth—the experiment's next generation—is still unfolding.

Chapter 6 analyzes the social worlds and social capital of families in the experiment, including the many MTO children and families for whom "your neighborhood is not your community." Changing the social relations of participants was not a primary aim of the MTO experiment, and indeed it is the sort of thing that attracts claims of inappropriate "social engineering." But many of the hoped-for positive outcomes anticipated changes in exposure to particular kinds of peers, adult role models, and more successful neighbors who might be sources of useful job information, as well as a positive, motivating influence.

We consider, in particular, the debates about whether poor people who leave poor neighborhoods might lose "community," including ties to relatives and close friends concentrated in ghetto neighborhoods left behind. This concern goes back at least to the 1960s and the backlash against urban redevelopment efforts that dislocated poor people and disrupted their social ties. On one side of the ledger, we find that few MTO families developed new and beneficial ties after relocating; for example, social contacts who might recommend good schools or make job referrals. This was in part because they did not join community institutions and in part because most maintained social worlds dominated by needy relatives, with limited education and job prospects, and by socially similar friends. These social circles represent both benefit and burden to the families we came to know, and this is the other, rarely mentioned side of "the community question."

Sometimes, those kin-centered networks provided vital social support that was, it is true, more difficult to access, post-move, given greater distances to travel. The most extreme examples were in sprawling Los Angeles, for MTO families without a car. But most MTO movers remained embedded in those social worlds, actively socializing and exchanging with loved ones, while other movers *used* relocation to distance and buffer themselves and their children from the demands and risks those social ties posed.

Popular notions of community and scholarly debates over "community lost" have both underplayed the real challenge: forging and managing a range of social ties, some for support and some for advancement, in a range of places. This "managing" cannot assume that relatives and friends are always and everywhere supportive, but they are emotionally significant—and therefore central—in the lives of most poor people. This is the second major lesson of our work, and it is one that challenges both liberal and conservative views of poverty: *that the most vulnerable among the poor are embedded in "communities" of kin that often expose them to extraordinary risk and burden, no matter where they live.*

As mentioned above, many MTO families who got out of high-poverty neighborhoods struggled to stay out of them. Chapter 7 shows why. It focuses on choices families made, over time, in search of good housing in good neighborhoods, and it sets up the linked challenge of finding good schools, the focus of chapter 8. Were the choices driven by information? The shortage of good options? Strong preferences for the familiar over the unfamiliar, however promising the latter might seem to an outside observer? Or by a "culture" people carried with them when they left the ghetto? Policy makers, scholars, and advocates are paying more and more attention to choice schemes that aim to "shock" dysfunctional service-delivery systems and supposedly empower the customer. School vouchers for families in "failing" public school districts were the most visible case in the 1990s, but retirement savings, health care, and other reforms also rely, in various ways, on high-stakes choice schemes. In this light, an honest rethinking of choice in the low-income housing market is sorely overdue.

This leads to the third major lesson of our work: *For poor people who have lived segregated lives in dangerous, high-poverty neighborhoods, conventional choice programs offer little room to maneuver, thanks to the choosers' information poverty, the limited comparisons they are equipped to make, and a logic of choice focused simply on avoiding violence and other risks—not necessarily on garnering "opportunity."* In terms of getting to and being able to stay in better neighborhoods, for example, we show why some MTO families struggled and failed while others succeeded, against the odds. This is a huge issue, since low-income housing policy in America has taken a sharp turn, since the 1970s, toward choice-oriented assistance for use in the private rental market—far more than other wealthy nations, which subsidize a greater share of their populations' housing costs and rely less on the market to meet all housing needs.

Chapter 9 asks how relocating affected employment prospects and employability, both for the single parents who head most MTO households and for their young-adult children—the first "MTO generation" to age into adulthood and the demands of building a career and a life. Policy makers' greatest hopes for MTO included economic advancement: the idea that moving away from "weak" work norms and toward higher status neighbors and suburban job growth would improve job networks, employment, and earnings. Thus far, measurable effects on this dimension have not materialized. While the huge impacts of welfare reform and swings in the business cycle may be hiding "true" effects of the experiment (Orr et al., 2003), we find other factors at work as well. First, MTO relocatees did not necessarily move closer to areas with entry-level job growth. In at least some of these markets, MTO movers gained nothing or even lost ground, at least in spatial terms. Second, movers did not, as underscored above, create valuable new job networks that could provide referrals or endorsements from new neighbors, for example, to help secure work. Instead, movers found work through relatives, prior friends, co-workers, and people they met in training programs. Third, MTO parents struggled to line up a stable match among housing, the workplace, and safe, reliable sources of childcare. That three-legged stool, and not just the "jobs-housing mismatch" that prior research and policy advocacy have emphasized, was the key, and in many cases, each of the legs was shaky.

For all these reasons, as we will show, *neighborhoods* can matter (as locations) even when *neighbors* do not. And where the next generation is concerned, there is more: Relocating clearly enabled some MTO youth to build much more diverse friendships and a broader repertoire of "soft skills," including skills of self-presentation and culturally valued codes of speech, which they perceive to be important for upward mobility. But this came with some pains of acculturating when a young person's previously acquired "ghetto style" (their label, not ours) did not conform to social expectations in a new school and neighborhood. Fitting in is tough for many adolescents, in almost any kind of setting. Moving across major social boundaries in America—divisions of race, class, and culture imprinted on our nation's segregated landscape—only adds to that challenge.

Chapter 10 sums up our findings and discusses their implications in the context of an evolving public debate about what "opportunity for all" now requires in America. Our third major lesson outlines the specific gaps between planners' hopes and expectations and the realities the MTO families confronted. To have a strong and legitimate policy idea is one thing. To deliver on that idea, through effective implementation, is quite another. This sets up a final, bottom-line message: *Housing mobility is a powerful, and indeed essential, tool for fighting ghetto poverty—but one that is extraordinarily vulnerable to the strong-idea-weakly-implemented problem, as well as unfounded assumptions about how persistently poor people can escape the risks of ghettos, regardless of where they are able to live.*

Beyond outlining what it takes to deliver on that potential, which the ambitious MTO experiment did only in part, we underline the importance of improving the quality of life of chronically poor people—in particular by expanding freedom from fear—as well as helping them to escape poverty. We show why simply leaving the ghetto cannot guarantee both kinds of benefit and, nevertheless, why both are important goals for a renewed anti-poverty agenda in America.

In the final section, a methodological appendix, Studying Moving to Opportunity, offers details on our approach in the context of several major research traditions. The appendix also provides key details on the experiment's implementation, diagrams that summarize important conceptual links, and another, final story: how we got to know the families at the heart of this social experiment—that is, how we operated in the field—and how we approached the challenges of using very different types of data to resolve analytic puzzles while also producing practical lessons for policy. We know that such "mixed-method" approaches are tough to implement, but we believe they are indispensable for understanding complex problems and social interventions that make a serious effort to tackle them. We conclude with advice for others who share our goals.

HOW WE DID THE STUDY

As noted above, in the appendix to this volume we detail our study's design and method. For the general reader, we highlight several features and the rationale for them here. We collected most of our data in 2004 and 2005. We took a mixed-method approach, meaning that we collected and analyzed several different kinds of data in an integrated way, to generate richer, more valid answers to complex questions. We used: (a) the MTO interim impacts evaluation survey fielded by an earlier evaluation team (Orr et al. 2003) to help answer key "what" and "how many" questions (for example, how many MTO families who had relocated from high-poverty public housing to low-poverty neighborhoods remained in the latter kind of neighborhood five or more years later?); (b) in-depth qualitative interviewing that was a blend of open-ended and more structured questions—what one might think of as "kitchen-table conversations," with MTO parents and their children, right in their homes; (c) ethnographic field research (a combination of direct observation and interviewing techniques); and (d) quantitative analysis and mapping of census and administrative data, such as on local crime and education patterns.

The latter three types of data were our most important resources for answering "how" and "why" questions about the MTO outcomes. We wanted, in particular, to know why parents, adolescents, and young adults who participated in the experiment made the choices they did, whom they relied on, if anyone, to inform or carry out those choices, and how they (the main subjects) assessed the outcomes of their choices and the challenges "out there," in the world, over time. Many evaluations of major social programs do not shed light on why the participants made the choices they did, but understanding those choices is vital in MTO, for obvious reasons.

To create as representative a view of these issues as possible, for component (b), we interviewed a large random sample of 122 families, but only those that included an adolescent in the household, at three of the five MTO metro sites (Boston, Los Angeles, and New York), while a second research team, whose work we draw on in several chapters to come, focused on Baltimore and Chicago. In each family, we interviewed a parent, adolescent, and, where available, a young-adult child. This sample included those families who were randomly assigned by the program to the experimental group and who successfully made the intended relocation (the *compliers*, in social science shorthand, who received the intended "treatment"), as well as members of the experimental group who were not successful when they enrolled (noncompliers). The sample included the corresponding subgroups from the "comparison group" of families who were allotted a housing voucher but no special assistance or restrictions on where they could lease up. Finally, the in-depth interview sample also included members of the control group, who were randomly assigned to continue receiving assistance in the form of public housing.

We also sampled randomly within that sample, in component (c), to create an ethnographic sample of 39 families who were either in the control group or the experimental-complier subgroup. We visited this subsample repeatedly, an average of 11 times per family. On these visits, our research team, usually a male and female working in a pair, combined several kinds of interviewing—often chatting informally, but with focused objectives, rather than maintaining the sense of a formal interview session—with direct observation of family routines, including home life and errands and socializing outside the house. Researchers have called this approach "family-focused" (Burton 1997), since it emphasizes the context and choices of each family as a unit. This approach does not assume, for example, that the immediate neighborhood of residence or any particular neighborhood was socially salient in each subject family's life, whether family members considered the neighborhood in question to be good or bad, familiar or mostly unknown. We focused first and foremost on each family's daily routines, social relations, and use of neighborhoods (anywhere). We systematically analyzed thousands of pages of fieldnotes, for a total of 430 visits, in this ethnographic component.

As we show formally in the appendix, statistical tests confirm that both qualitative samples are quite representative of the larger population of all MTO families, in terms of background traits, income, employment status, and a range of other social outcomes, including problem behavior by youth.

The fourth element of the study, which we term *scans*, examined the changing contexts in which MTO families are leading their lives, for example the economic and social changes at the neighborhood, city, and metropolitan levels that are reshaping the geography of risk and opportunity over time. The scans analyzed census, market, and administrative data at the neighborhood, city, metropolitan region, and other levels, including racial make-up, crime, concentrations of poverty, rental prices, capital investment, and other factors.

The integration of distinct types of data is crucial for generating richer, more valid results and actionable specifics to guide decision-makers. Mixed-method approaches are also crucial for building better theory, over time, from a base of complex and mixed results. But we caution the reader about the need to appropriately interpret the different types of data. And misconceptions about data drawn from small samples—for example, that it is "anecdotal"—have led to much confusion within and beyond the research community. At the heart of this confusion is a failure to understand two distinct logics of science or, more precisely, logics for making inferences from data, which is the heart of scientific inquiry.

Our ethnographic field data, while drawn from a random sample that generated wide range in the phenomena under study, follows a *case study* logic rather than a *sampling* logic. The case study approach allows us to understand family circumstances as integrated constructs—families as cases that are revealing for the conditions that covary within them—without indicating how *common* those constructs are across the program population as a whole (Ragin 1987; Small 2008). Survey results—which are ubiquitous in a society that loves polls and rankings—often tell us what we can reliably conclude about a large population but with little insight into those underlying rationales or social dynamics at work: little on the how's and why's. Put differently, good survey results, which follow a sampling logic, tell us something basic that we can reliably conclude about a large population—what share of families watched a comedy film in the last month, say, or what share favor a particular policy to strengthen the regulation of handguns?—but with little insight into the social processes or reasoning at work. And this is a major problem if one wants to design and implement better interventions that help people. On the other hand, ethnographic and other qualitative methods provide the depth and texture that illuminate such processes—school and housing choices as the subjects themselves perceive and make them, for example—but typically without precise population estimates. The results are not less "true" simply because we cannot indicate with precision what share of the larger population the cases represent. That is, small-sample (small-N) results are often big (in importance) but this does not settle the issue of how *prevalent* they are. So we use the interview data (from the larger and more representative sample) to indicate prevalence and explore broad patterns, referencing the MTO interim survey results where appropriate, and in presenting our results, we try to indicate the basis for selecting particular, "revelatory cases" for greater depth (Yin 1994). Finally, in some instances (social types in chapter 6, for example), we do not attempt to indicate prevalence, not with point or range estimates that is, while in other instances (housing trajectory types in chapter 7, for example), we are able to link our qualitative data to the survey data and therefore indicate prevalence quite directly.

This is not a typical evaluation of a social experiment. The dominant approach to evaluating experiments—estimating "treatment effects" by comparing statistically valid results for each treatment group—is essential but simply not sufficient for understanding why those results obtain. Nor does that approach adequately explore variation *within* treatment groups—why do people who receive the *same* help fare so differently?—as opposed to between them. We discuss the latter point in several chapters under the label "the myth of the average experience." But the larger point is this: The major aim of our book is rigorous description with important implications for policy and planning. We shed light on powerful and still poorly understood social processes, often by focusing particular chapters on the experiences of those who relocated as MTO's planners hoped and not by directly *comparing* those experiences to other treatment groups. (Enabling very poor people to "move to opportunity" while they remain embedded in dense networks of risky, burdensome relatives is one example of this description; see chapter 6.) Put differently, we have not focused on making strong causal arguments but on revealing what experiences and choices—in particular contexts—are all about. We do, however, offer a range of comparisons as well, since experiments are uniquely structured to allow that.

All personal names in this book are fictive (pseudonyms), and while we use real place names for cities or large districts, we have disguised some small-area names, such as neighborhoods or housing developments, to protect our subject's anonymity. This is our ethical obligation as researchers; it was also a strict rule set by the federal government as a condition for letting us contact the MTO families.

Chapter 2

Ghetto Poverty Before and After Katrina

> Here in America, the land of opportunity, we gave up on the
> poor more than two decades ago.
> —Cynthia Tucker, "Katrina Exposes our Callous Treatment of
> the Poor," *Atlanta-Journal Constitution*, September 6, 2005

AFTER KATRINA: GHETTO POVERTY ON SCREEN

They stood on rooftops, in T-shirts, waving signs that said, "Help us," as helicopters flew overhead with TV cameras rolling. They waded through chest-high water dirtied with raw sewage, dead bodies, and toxic pollutants. They waited, endlessly it seemed, near the stage for some of America's glitziest sporting events—the New Orleans Superdome—for food, water, blankets, medical care, crime protection, and other basics. Some looked for food in flooded and abandoned stores, hospitals, and other facilities. Many had lost everything, not just homes and the possessions inside them but loved ones as well, to one of the deadliest and costliest natural disasters in American history.

And yet, to the astonishment of hundreds of millions worldwide, it was days before basic help arrived for the poor and mostly black New Orleanians, who were the longest stranded and most vulnerable in a deluged city. After Hurricane Katrina made landfall along the Gulf Coast of Alabama, Louisiana, and Mississippi on August 29, 2005, and a day later when flood protection failed and 80 percent of New Orleans was covered by filthy water, the national and international media soon turned a story about breached levees and the unprecedented flooding of a major U.S. city into a very different story. True, the physical event was staggering, even for a city built, as the British newsmagazine the *Economist* bluntly put it, "on low-lying, hurricane-prone swampland surrounded by water on three sides."[1] But the new and less straightforward story was about government incompetence and societal indifference to the thousands of isolated New Orleans residents, many of them from inner-city ghettos, who lacked even the resources to comply with an evacuation order given a day before the mega-storm hit their community.

This new story, then, was about those who had *no way out* and about how, in a land of such wealth, so many people could have ended up in such desperate straits, could have faced terrible and sometimes deadly risks not only because of who they were but because of *where they lived*.

In the media chorus that soon followed the storm, David Brooks, a conservative columnist at the *New York Times*, ventured a broader conclusion about the hurricane and its meaning:

> Katrina was a natural disaster that interrupted a social disaster. It separated tens of thousands of poor people from the run-down, isolated neighborhoods in which they were trapped. It disrupted the patterns that have led one generation to follow another into poverty.[2]

For more than a generation, politicians in an increasingly conservative America had campaigned against the supposedly "undeserving" poor, in word as well as action, as sociologist Herbert Gans observed in his book *The War Against the Poor*. Along the way, argues journalist Cynthia Tucker in the post-Katrina editorial we quote atop this chapter, "We learned that the poor were simply too lazy to improve their prospects and their misery was their own fault." As such, she added, we "not only gave up trying to help the poor, but we also bought the argument that trying to assist them, especially through government programs, would just make matters worse."

Like others in the media, Tucker and Brooks not only attacked the painfully slow and clumsy response by disaster officials to the immediate needs of Hurricane Katrina's victims. The mainstream press also cast a light on the years of neglect and even punitive public policy that helped place so many people in dangerous, high-poverty neighborhoods, isolated from job growth, good schools, basic personal security, decent health care, and—more to the point—from political influence and functioning public institutions.

In the months that followed Hurricane Katrina, the American media and the public briefly rediscovered something—*ghetto poverty*—that had once been the headline theme of national policy debates and presidential commissions. The effects of that poverty, the distress concentrated in poor racial ghettos, had long since been relegated to scholarly debates that tend to be marginal to the nation's political life. Ghetto poverty had become the subject of hip-hop music and fashion and media coverage of the same—the ghetto as a cultural style and multibillion-dollar industry. Finally, ghetto poverty was also the object of a maze of government programs and nonprofit-run interventions that are seldom coordinated effectively with one another or given enough sustained financial and political support, together with high and focused expectations, to make a real difference.

Beyond putting the problems associated with ghetto poverty back on the radar screen, Katrina also led the press to spotlight a little-known set of interventions to help people *escape* ghettos, if not necessarily to escape poverty. Within days of the storm, in fact, top journalists underscored the promise that low-income housing policy, though much maligned since the

Reagan era, could and should help to reduce racial and economic segregation.[3] Hurricane Katrina forced the unprecedented location of hundreds
of thousands of city dwellers, many of them black and poor and from
poor black neighborhoods. In so doing, the storm put the idea of helping
people "move to opportunity," with government housing assistance, into
the headlines.

What most observers missed, however, is the fact that the social conditions Katrina briefly exposed grind on daily, across the country, as more
routine media coverage makes clear. Inner-city public housing, particularly in big cities, is often at the center. In a typical story in April 2008,
for example, the *New York Times* wrote about "hope and hard knocks" in
a Brooklyn public housing development: the seesaw of crime trends, the
economic struggles, the despair and drug addiction, and the remarkable
resilience as well that marked this "federal slum"—one of many enclaves
consigned to ghetto poverty—in one of the world's wealthiest and costliest housing markets.[4]

Ghetto poverty, centered on inner-city public housing, is the most
deadly, chronic, and miserable form of poverty in urban America. It is
an enduring problem that the nation has steadfastly ignored, with few
exceptions, for decades now. By many measures, we ignored it once again
after Katrina. We turn next to one of the exceptions, a source of hope and
also puzzles—the focus of this book.

AN AMERICAN EXPERIMENT

This is a book about the persistence of ghetto poverty and about one very
American experiment to fight it. That experiment—Moving to Opportunity, or "MTO," launched in 1994 and still unfolding—is American for its
celebration of individual choice, for its heavy reliance on market mechanisms to undo social problems the market helped to create, and also for its
deep faith in the power of community to improve human life.

In essence, MTO tests the idea that changing someone's "social
address"—specifically, helping them to relocate from distressed public
housing projects in high-risk, high-poverty urban ghettos to low-poverty
neighborhoods—can change their life for the better. MTO is all about the
geography of risk and opportunity that Hurricane Katrina briefly spot-
lighted—the image of extreme suffering and government abandonment
that played on millions of TV screens.

In this chapter, we look briefly at the appearance and disappearance of
ghetto poverty as a public issue in recent decades—the problem that was
deeply rooted but largely ignored before *and* after Katrina—and at what
the best research has taught us about such poverty. As we will show, our
nation has, for the most part, developed little consensus about what the
policy *goals* (the ends) should be, let alone *how* best to combat the most
destructive kind of disadvantage (the means). And we have a disheartening

tendency, as a society, to repeatedly conclude that nothing works, ignoring evidence to the contrary.

The broad idea we preview in this chapter is that both the power and the limits of the MTO strategy hold urgent lessons for America: about addressing the low-income housing crisis in realistic ways, creating real bridges to social and economic opportunity, and making the most dangerous ghettos livable for young people and their families—even when those families do not move out *and even if they remain poor.*

GHETTOS PAST AND PRESENT

"Ghetto" has not always been synonymous with "poor." For most of history, in fact, the word *ghetto* has referred to districts where particular ethnic groups were required to live, regardless of their income or status, so as to contain their influence and—sometimes—to limit violence against them by other ethnic groups.[5] The word ghetto originated in Renaissance Venice to describe the area where Jews were settled by law, and other groups—German and Turkish traders, for example—were likewise restricted to particular residences in the city. But the label took on horrifying new meaning during the Second World War, in reference to Nazi-controlled ghettos in Warsaw, Krakow, and other cities of Central and Eastern Europe, where Jews were first confined and later shipped to deadly concentration camps.

Likewise, for much of American history, poor neighborhoods and racial ghettos were quite distinct. For example, in the late nineteenth century, when Jacob Riis decried the awful tenement slums of New York City in *How the Other Half Lives* (1890), he was describing a large part of the city, where a low-income, multiethnic population estimated at 1.2 million lived in cramped, unsanitary, and often dangerous buildings and streets. The slums, he argued, were "the evil offspring of public neglect and private greed" (p. 2). But they were also a side effect of rapid growth driven by industrialization. Riis's concern was the brutal economic inequality of manufacturing cities in the Northeast and Midwest, which remained overwhelmingly white, albeit more and more "ethnic"—home to Southern and Eastern European immigrants. Along with other social reformers whose activism helped spur the planning and building codes that made the industrial city more livable, Riis was also concerned about the tendency of the middle class and rich in America, like their counterparts in industrial England, to treat the poor as a morally depraved caste—a group unwilling to better itself (Vale 2000).

Later that decade, W.E.B. Du Bois published *The Philadelphia Negro* (1899), the first great work of American sociology and also a landmark study of race in our country. At the center of Du Bois's account were racially segregated but economically diverse black neighborhoods in that northern city, with preachers, teachers, and paupers, relatively prosperous merchants and low-wage delivery men, living in close quarters thanks to restrictive housing laws and the constant pressure of white discrimination beyond the borders of the ghetto. Three decades later, Louis Wirth (1928) made similar observations about the Jewish ghetto in Chicago.

In sum, until the latter half of the twentieth century, most poor urban neighborhoods—while distressed by many measures and also socially stigmatized—were not racial or ethnic ghettos, and those ghettos—while isolated in multiple dimensions—were not mostly poor.

Making the Modern Ghetto

Three massive changes in the nation's economic and social structure, and one in public policy response, made the contemporary ghetto a very poor *and* very racially segregated place, particularly for black and Hispanic Americans but also for some Asian Americans. First, technological change—the mechanization of agriculture—spurred the Great Migration of rural, southern blacks to cities in the Northeast, Midwest, and far West of the country (Lemann 1991). Wartime and postwar labor shortages, especially in factories, meant that a poor farmhand from Mississippi, say, could make four or five times his farm wage soon after he stepped off the bus in Chicago. All told, about 5 million black Americans left the South between 1940 and 1970 alone—a scale that outranks the migrations of other ethnic groups, such as the Irish, Italians, and Jews, to America during the great wave of European immigration.

The relatively small black populations of cities such as Chicago, Los Angeles, and New York swelled in the mid-twentieth century thanks to this major influx, and many cities rushed to tighten restrictive laws and real estate practices to contain these large numbers of black newcomers (Hirsch 1983; Massey and Denton 1993). Similar economic pressures and restrictions confronted many low-skill Hispanics who migrated to these cities around the same time—Puerto Ricans to Boston, Chicago, New York, and other parts of the Northeast and Midwest, for example, and Mexicans to California and the Southwestern states.

Both the large numbers and comparatively low education and skill levels of these workers figured prominently in the devastating impact of the second major shift: the de-industrialization of the American economy (Bluestone and Harrison 1982; Wilson 1987). Millions of high-wage, unionized jobs—which had defined a secure ladder to the middle class even for those with a high school education or less—not only disappeared fast, in several waves of decline between the 1950s and 1980s. They also disappeared in very distinct geographic concentrations of industrial production that had developed over preceding generations, near large neighborhoods of worker housing that now became areas of concentrated joblessness and sometimes-chronic welfare receipt.

As such, millions of low-skill black and Hispanic migrants and their children, lured to the higher paying jobs in industrial cities and concentrated there in minority ghettos—ghettos of *working* people that included middle-class professionals—now found themselves jobless and dependent on public assistance. Millions of white Americans lost work and/or wages through deindustrialization, too, of course, creating a powerful sense of "downward mobility" that helped split Franklin Delano Roosevelt's New Deal coalition and reshape American politics (Newman 1988; Rieder 1985). White Americans became significantly less likely to support policy measures to enhance the economic security of the most disadvantaged. Millions of whites also abandoned cities for the suburbs, and in the labor market, following an old pattern of "last hired, first fired," minority Americans fared much worse overall in the shift to a postindustrial economy and the millions of low-wage service jobs to which low-skill workers were increasingly relegated (Levy 1987).

But the housing needs of large, jobless, and underemployed minority populations, and public policy response to those needs, also played a decisive role in making the modern ghetto. This was the third major change. The federally funded public housing program, launched as part of the Depression-era New Deal and expanded rapidly in the 1950s and 1960s as part of postwar "urban renewal," increasingly became home to a jobless black and Hispanic population, particularly in the Rust Belt cities of the Northeast and Midwest.

Public housing was created to replace the tenement slums that Riis and other social reformers had indicted a half century earlier. It was to be a low-rent stepping stone to better lives and better housing, not a long-run refuge or isolated barracks. But in many major U.S. cities, public housing was fast becoming the housing of last resort for the minority poor (Vale 1993, 2000; Venkatesh 2000; Von Hoffman 1995). Federal occupancy policies and local tenant advocacy, from the 1960s forward, focused on meeting the shelter needs of the poorest, least resilient families. And racial discrimination concentrated new public housing development in minority neighborhoods, "protecting" white neighborhoods that resisted such development, as well as other forms of subsidized housing (Danielson 1976; Hirsch 1983; Massey and Denton 1993; Schill and Wachter 1995).

The pillars were in place. With important exceptions, such as the fiercely defended enclave of South Boston, where a large concentration of Irish Americans persisted in "the projects," public housing became synonymous with distressed inner-city neighborhoods, the minority poor, and—in the popular view—with a "ghetto culture" disconnected from mainstream American values and habits.[6]

When researcher Lee Rainwater published his findings on the infamous Pruitt-Igoe housing projects in St. Louis, his title—*Behind Ghetto Walls* (1970)—conveyed the isolation, and his subtitle—"life in a federal slum"—implicated public policy.[7] Rainwater presented black families living not only in chronic poverty but in constant fear of crime and exploitation *by their neighbors*. In spite of kin ties within the projects and some bonds of friendship and mutual protection, wariness and distrust

defined life in Pruitt-Igoe, argued Rainwater, as much as broken eleva-
tors, dark and decrepit hallways, and other symptoms of physical distress.
So did the downward spirals that linked prolonged joblessness and experiences of white discrimination with drug addiction, illegal incomes—from
"hustling" stolen goods, illicit drug dealing, or other means—and family
breakdown.

These were the years of civil rights mobilization, profound cultural
change in America, and launch of the federal government's War on Poverty. For the first time, systematic social research such as Rainwater's
entered the political debate over the causes and consequences of persistent poverty, as well as the most promising strategies for addressing it. In
general, researchers emphasized structural barriers to opportunity such as
those we have outlined so far, bad choices by the poor themselves (including "cultural" factors), or both. Researchers who spent time getting to
know poor people and recording their experiences and rationales in their
own words played particularly important roles in this debate and in laying
the foundations we build on a generation later. For example, ethnographers Eliott Liebow (1967), Carol Stack (1974), and Ulf Hannerz (1969)
all provided rich accounts of the "cultural logic" (choice rationales) and
social relations of the urban poor, with a focus on racial minorities.

These and other scholars responded to Oscar Lewis's (1966) controversial thesis that a self-destructive "culture of poverty" doomed many
of the poor to intergenerational disadvantage. Lewis's critics—at least
those who made evidence-based, rather than ideological, responses—
emphasized several factors: the social isolation of the poor from resource-
rich institutions, the resilience of poor people's networks of mutual aid
in spite of that larger isolation, and the chronic unemployment, racial
discrimination, and other barriers that led to coping behavior—such as
"normalizing" hustling or drug dealing—that was outside the mainstream
known to most Americans. The chronically poor, argued these scholars,
largely shared the values of "upstanding," mainstream society but often
found it hard to survive, let alone get ahead, relying solely on the most
socially accepted behavior.

But the window to vigorously debate these issues, having been pried
open by the civil rights movement, progressive exposés of poverty such
as Michael Harrington's *The Other America* (1962), and President Lyndon
Johnson's Great Society program, would not stay open for long. In a controversial 1965 report on the state of the black family, Harvard scholar
and later senator Daniel Patrick Moynihan (1965) argued that the prevalence of single parenthood, in the context of pervasive discrimination
and other barriers, would continue to have devastating effects on young
blacks, reproducing poverty from generation to generation. The backlash
against that report, and more broadly against studying the experience
of poverty, was intense. This helped silence public and scholarly debate,
which, argued the critics, tended to blame the victims for their own poverty. The Left and Right in American politics locked into two seemingly

irreconcilable "frames" for understanding poverty: the former focused on structural barriers and societal responsibility for tackling them, the latter on the need for personal responsibility by the poor (Schön and Rein 1994). And the standoff endured for almost two decades.

When several years of civil unrest culminated in the race riots that rocked dozens of U.S. cities in the summer of 1967, President Johnson's National Advisory Commission on Civil Disorders (Kerner Commission 1968) placed the tangle of economic desperation *and* social breakdown at the core of its diagnosis. The Kerner Commission concluded, "Our nation is moving toward two societies, one black, one white—separate and unequal" (p. 1) and extended the message of expanded opportunity to encompass "all citizens—urban and rural, white and black, Spanish-surname, American Indian, and every minority group." As for responsibility, "white society is deeply implicated in the ghetto," noted the report. "White institutions created it, white institutions maintain it, and white society condones it." But the Commission added:

> The movement apart can be reversed. Choice is still possible....This alternative will require a commitment to national action—compassionate, massive, and sustained, backed by the resource of the most powerful and richest nation on earth.... *There can be no higher priority for national action and no higher claim on the nation's conscience.* (pp. 1–2, emphasis added)

As Goering (2005) observes, the Kerner Commission was the most prominent in a series of White House conferences, commissions, and national policy reports, from the early 60s to the early 80s, to offer essentially the same diagnosis, generally with an unpopular, two-pronged remedy: *substantially "enrich" inner-city ghettos* (to use the Kerner Commission's term) with better investments and services; and *help those who want to leave them to move out*, for example, through special initiatives to expand housing choice.

There was a fourth major factor, which complicated the three we have outlined thus far (race migration and segregation, rapid economic decline in cities, and the unfortunate role of low-income housing policy). The fourth factor centers on the black professionals Du Bois had interviewed in black neighborhoods at the turn of the twentieth century—the higher skill workers whose lives and community institutions, he and later scholars argued, retained prosperity, dignity, and stability in economically diverse black ghettos.

The fourth and most counter-intuitive shift that shaped the contemporary ghetto was the civil rights revolution of the 1950s and 1960s. Once restricted from living in more affluent neighborhoods with better schools and amenities, middle-class blacks and other racial and ethnic minorities could now, at least officially, live anywhere they could afford. Though study after study showed widespread racial discrimination in the nation's housing markets (Turner and Ross 2005; Yinger 1995), meaning that minority homeseekers did not and still do not enjoy the range of housing choices their white counterparts with comparable incomes do, hundreds of thousands of middle-class minorities did manage to leave inner-city ghettos, particularly in the 1960s and 70s (Wilson 1987).[8]

If one migration—that of mostly poor rural workers and families to industrial cities—marked the opening chapter of the transformation, a second migration—the outmigration of the minority middle class from inner-city neighborhoods to other urban as well as suburban areas— marked the final decisive change that shaped the inner-city ghetto. Now they were racially segregated *and* extremely poor, in some cases with intergenerational patterns of joblessness, school dropout, and economic dependency. When sociologist William Julius Wilson recalled our attention to concentrated minority poverty in *The Truly Disadvantaged* (1987), he described ghetto neighborhoods in Chicago, centered on large public housing projects, that were as much as 80 to 90 percent poor, almost entirely black, with some of the nation's highest rates of welfare dependency, substance abuse, and crime.

We return to Wilson's influential account of inner-city life and the problem he identified as *spatially concentrated minority poverty* below. But first a cautionary note: No city had concentrated nearly as much public housing, and thus nearly as many chronically poor families, in racially segregated areas as Chicago had. In fact, based on government-funded audits, many of the nation's million public housing units continued to function reasonably well as low-rise, low-rent housing in modest concentrations.

But in large cities with large concentrations of public housing, including Chicago and the other four cities where Moving to Opportunity would soon be launched—Baltimore, Boston, Los Angeles, and New York— inner-city public housing had, by the early 1990s, become ground zero in a war zone. New threats from highly addictive drugs and the gangs that controlled their distribution, the "war on drugs" and the wave of incarceration that crackdown produced, persistent barriers in a restructuring job economy, and a larger rhetorical "war" in politics and public policy had made things much more extreme than anything Lee Rainwater could have recorded in the "federal slum" he visited in the mid-1960s. Some 43 percent of "family" public housing units were located in neighborhoods of extreme poverty by 1990, and over 200,000 units qualified as "severely distressed" under multiple criteria (Newman and Schnare 1997; Vale 1993).

"BLACK BUCKS" AND WELFARE QUEENS: THE RACIALIZED WAR AGAINST THE POOR

While focusing thus far on the major forces that "made" the modern ghetto, we have hinted at some of the broader trends in American society and politics that set the stage for the MTO experiment, and a new discussion about ghetto poverty, in the 1990s. There was the social policy revolution led by the War on Poverty, the first major expansion of the government-backed safety net since the Depression-era New Deal. The War on Poverty included job training, grants for community organizing and flexible local service delivery by neighborhood institutions ("community action"), early childhood health and education (Head Start), and other new federal initiatives. This array of programs generated new forms of social research and myriad accomplishments but also became a target for political attack. And economic decline along with the welfare rights movement led to a huge increase in the welfare caseloads between the mid-60s and the mid-90s, when that much-maligned cash assistance program was transformed.

Next, there was the deep cultural divide that erupted over opposition to the Vietnam War, plus the loss of a white working-class electoral base in deindustrializing Rust Belt regions, as well as the white Southern vote by the Democratic Party after major civil rights reforms. With the exception of Jimmy Carter, who won the presidency thanks to the blow of Richard Nixon's Watergate scandal, no Democrat was elected to the White House between 1968 and 1992. The Vietnam War also spelled the end of America's powerful, postwar economic expansion and ushered in almost two decades of recurrent recession, inflationary swings, high interest rates, tighter federal budgets and slow-downs or deep cuts in domestic spending—on the social safety net, public infrastructure, and other needs. On the housing front, President Nixon snuffed most of the Kerner-era ambition of the federal government vis-à-vis racial and economic integration of America's cities and suburbs (Bonastia 2006; Goering 2005).

Following the brief interregnum of President Ford and the recession-racked years of President Carter, Ronald Reagan played a central role in the nation's ideological and fiscal turnaround, dramatically slowing the growth of aid to the poor and cutting aid to cities—a basic shift in the relationship between the federal government and localities that hit hardest in the declining industrial regions. Reagan, who defeated Jimmy Carter in a landslide in 1980 as the economy continued to stagnate and America suffered the Iran hostage crisis abroad, sensed and accelerated a major swing to the right in American politics. But more specifically, Reagan mounted an all-out attack on government for supposedly giving poor, unmotivated—and so undeserving—people a free ride (Gans 1995).

As Reagan memorably captured his bottom-line view, "America fought a war on poverty, and poverty won." Here was the politically potent idea that government programs were a large part of the poverty problem that journalist Cynthia Tucker would highlight a quarter century later. A master of the provocative anecdote, however distorted or nonrepresentative it might be, Reagan and other conservative reformers routinely attacked "welfare queens" who cheated the system, collecting government checks under multiple names.

But Reagan also racialized poverty in very politically potent ways. Invoking familiar code language about race at one Florida campaign stop, for example, Reagan expressed frustration that "hardworking people" wait in line at grocery stores while a "strapping black buck" could buy T-bone steaks with food stamps.[9] And Reagan told of a public housing development in East Harlem where low rent garnered a spacious apartment "with a 20-foot balcony, a swimming pool and gymnasium … and the rent begins at $113.20 and that includes utilities"—discounting the actual rent figure by a factor of four and neglecting to mention that the pool and gym were at a community center serving 200,000 low and moderate-income families in a segregated neighborhood (Cannon 2003).

THE NEW DEBATE ABOUT POVERTY

The political mood of the 1980s opened a new window on the issue of persistent poverty and life in ghetto neighborhoods. Following a long silence after the culture wars of the 1960s, in the first Reagan Administration, serious debate began anew. From the Right, scholars and advocates asked whether social policies exacerbated poverty by providing the wrong incentives, or too few incentives, to center family life and economic well-being on work. And from the Left, scholars and advocates emphasized the effects of long-run demographic and social changes, such as the rapid rise in single-parent, single wage-earner families among all racial groups, as well as the changing nature of employment and geographically concentrated urban distress, on the character of poverty.

Major works of this period, including those by journalists who helped shape the public conversation, illustrate the intellectual shifts, as well as shifts in social conditions "on the ground." In *The Underclass* (1982), Ken Auletta, a staff writer for the *New Yorker* magazine, emphasized the urgent need to focus on the "persistently" poor, whom he defined as "unable to climb out of poverty after a generation or two."

With *Beyond Entitlement* (1986) and *The New Politics of Poverty* (1992), political scientist Lawrence Mead helped drive the focus on work requirements that now dominates federal social policy, as did Charles Murray. The latter's *Losing Ground* (1984) offered a scathing critique of welfare—in the form of guaranteed cash payments for the nonworking poor with children—as a disincentive to strive. Murray argued, in particular, that the subsidy programs created by the War on Poverty had lowered the costs and the stigmas associated with being idle and unemployed or bearing children out of wedlock. Murray developed a detailed version of Reagan's causal story: government assistance *causes* poverty, which is why most "antipoverty" programs are doomed to fail.

Though Murray's arguments have not held up well against careful analyses of the relationships among trends in childbearing, unemployment, and social welfare spending and reform (Jencks 1992), a growing body of "point-of-view" (advocacy) research reinforced these highly influential analyses by conservative academics. Decrying a liberal bias in academia as well as the media, for example, conservative think tanks that were committed to slashing welfare spending commissioned more and more advocacy-oriented reports to back up their policy statements, shaping a new generation of Reagan-inspired elected officials, public managers, and jurists as well (O'Connor 2007).

From the Left—or what was now the Left in a more conservative nation—the sociologist William Julius Wilson hypothesized in his influential *The Truly Disadvantaged* (1987) that the major demographic and social changes we outlined above, including the movement of the black middle class and high-wage industrial jobs away from historically black urban communities, had created a new and isolated "urban underclass" defined by *concentrated minority poverty in inner-city neighborhoods*. Citing Chicago public housing as his extreme case, Wilson, in direct response to Murray, added that long-run isolation from regular habits of work, useful job networks, and the sanctions provided by mainstream role models had entrenched a particularly durable form of poverty and social dysfunction, including out-of-wedlock birth, the glorification of gang leaders, and worse:

> If strong norms and sanctions against aberrant behavior, a sense of community, and positive neighborhood identification are the essential features of social organization in urban areas, inner-city neighborhoods today suffer from a severe lack of social organization.…Unlike in previous years, today's ghetto residents represent almost exclusively the most disadvantaged segments of the urban black community. (p. 143)

Wilson's work, which offered a compelling hypothesis, not proof, for his central claims about why poverty persisted so destructively, echoed a concern for what analysts would later term "the geography of opportunity" (Briggs 2005b; Galster and Killen 1995)—and specifically for the unequal housing choice that was part of the Kerner Commission's late-60s prognosis about two Americas, drifting apart. But as a respected black sociologist, Wilson also helped to reopen the conversation about social norms, networks, and family life in ghetto neighborhoods—a debate which had been shut down two decades before, following the backlash against Moynihan's 1965 report on the black family.[10] As we explore below, Wilson's influential concept of concentrated poverty likewise motivated a focus on poverty "deconcentration" policies during the Clinton Administration. That focus propelled MTO, as well as the redevelopment of public housing, which had long been restricted to very low-income people, into "mixed-income" housing.

The new attention to inner-city neighborhoods and their problems included a vigorous discussion, at least among analysts, of the meaning of "underclass" and "ghetto" and how to measure them. In *The Urban Underclass* (Jencks and Petersen 1991), researchers set out the fact and fiction about a perceived "explosion" of underclass poverty. Sociologist Christopher Jencks found, for example, that the welfare rolls and crime rates had in fact leveled off in the 1970s, that high school dropout rates were down and reading and math scores up for schoolchildren, including racial minorities. Birth out of wedlock was up, it was true, but this reflected a broader societal shift that we now know has separated mothering from marriage for all racial groups, at all income levels (Edin and Kefalas 2005). Joblessness and inequality were indeed getting worse, concluded Jencks, but the term "underclass" misleadingly suggested a monolithic category of people for whom *everything* was getting worse—and that group was hard to find in the statistics.

On the other hand, the spatial concentration of minority poverty had indeed worsened considerably since the 1960s, as Wilson argued, and it was virtually unknown among whites, who make up the majority of all poor people in America. Jargowsky and Bane (1991) confirmed a dramatic increase in the prevalence of ghetto poverty during the 1970s, defining a "ghetto" as any metropolitan census tract with a poverty rate of 40 percent or higher. Between 1970 and 1980 alone, they found, the number of people living in such neighborhoods grew by 29.5 percent, from 1.9 to 2.4 million. The black population in ghettos, thus defined, grew by 27 percent and the Hispanic ghetto population by 39 percent over the period.

Yet this growth in concentrated poverty was not universal or uniform across the country. The ten metro areas with the largest concentrations were home to almost half of the ghetto poor, and metro New York and Chicago alone accounted for half of all growth in ghetto poverty. Many small metro areas had seen a decline in concentrated poverty, while sharp growth was concentrated in the Rust Belt cities: the former industrial powerhouses of the Northeast and Midwest. This broad category included cities, such as New York, that were already restructuring dramatically to perform new functions in a global economy, and others, such as Detroit and Baltimore, that were not adapting well at all. (We examine these patterns, which "set the stage" for MTO in its five metro settings, in the fourth chapter of the book.)

Yet not all areas of concentrated minority poverty were home to the underclass behaviors Wilson and others had labeled "aberrant." Demographers Erol Ricketts and Isabel Sawhill showed that about 1 percent of the nation's population, and 5 percent of its poor, lived in neighborhoods that were home to high concentrations of "underclass" social conditions—males out of the labor force, school dropout, unwed parenting, and dependence on public assistance—but some of these areas were not extremely poor by Bane and Jargowsky's criterion. Nearly 4 in 10 underclass neighborhoods were not high- poverty areas, and nearly 72 percent of high-poverty areas were not underclass.[11] So a high rate of neighborhood poverty was not a sure sign of "ghetto" social conditions. And "underclass" was not a synonym for living in the very poorest neighborhoods, as some journalists and scholars had suggested.

Yet researchers, journalists, and citizen activists could widely agree on one thing: Pervasive violent crime was one distinguishing feature of extremely poor, racially segregated "project" neighborhoods, that is, neighborhoods centered on large public housing developments, in big cities. One reason was the expansion of gang-controlled distribution of illicit drugs in the 70s and 80s and the increasingly violent competition for sales territory in urban neighborhoods. Older gang members recruited "shorties"—young teens and even preteens—as lookouts and errand boys, offering cash, guns, status, and more to young people accustomed to severe deprivation. Then there was the scourge of crack. By the late 1980s, the invention of crack cocaine—a cheap, raw, and highly addictive form of the more powerful "freebase" drug—led to an epidemic of addiction and violent, gang-led contests in inner-city neighborhoods.

Journalists offered vivid accounts of life in these extreme environments. Alex Kotlowitz's *There Are No Children Here* (1991) recounted the awful risks and challenges facing two young boys growing up in the Henry Horner Homes, an inner-city Chicago public housing project or, as Kotlowitz labeled it, "the other America." Hallways were unlit and deserted even during the day, so a local politician handed out flashlights during a campaign stop. Residents on welfare received their aid checks at a local currency exchange, because all the mailboxes had been broken into. The lack of social services was so extreme that Mother Theresa of Calcutta, upon visiting Horner in 1982, assigned nuns from her mission to open a soup kitchen and offer an after-school program and other vital services.

Where Pruitt-Igoe in St. Louis had been an early icon of public housing failure in the 1960s—the 33-building project was demolished in 1972 after several failed rehab attempts—the gang-ridden, high-rise public housing projects of Chicago became the new symbols of all that was desperate, violent, and mismanaged in ghetto neighborhoods and the programs that served them—and especially in public housing. Chicago had many infamous high-rise projects in addition to Henry Horner, including Cabrini-Green, Ida B. Wells, and perhaps most infamously, the Robert Taylor Homes—the world's largest low-income housing development, with 28 high-rise buildings clustered on vast superblocks, home to 27,000 very poor blacks at the peak (Venkatesh 2000).

Addressing the larger system of forces that produced such extreme concentrations of poverty, violence, and other distress, sociologists Douglas Massey and Nancy Denton's *American Apartheid* (1993) deepened the account of structural barriers facing the inner-city poor. They showed how racial segregation "produces" concentrated minority poverty (in that poor whites are not similarly channeled into very poor neighborhoods) and perpetuates multiple barriers, formal and informal. This includes isolation from job growth and job networks, for example, but also from political influence and public investment, since middle- and upper-income suburban taxpayers can escape responsibility for the poor who live in cities and since the elected officials who represent more affluent suburbs need not campaign for broader support. Segregation, said Massey and Denton, was the "missing link," glossed over in many discussions of persistent poverty.

It showed, they and other scholars argued, why the term "underclass" should not be used as a synonym for "undeserving poor" (Gans 1990).

Finally, labor economist David Ellwood's *Poor Support* (1988) demonstrated that major structural shifts in employment depressed wages for the unskilled or low-skilled worker, while childcare, child support, health insurance, and other systems had not caught up with the shift from stay-at-home motherhood in families with two working adults to single-parent, single wage-earner family life—or with the low wages and insecurity that characterized most low-skill work in the still-emerging service economy. In this light, the ghetto poor were grappling with these society-wide transformations along with the stigmas and isolation associated with race, class, and spatial segregation. With colleague Mary Jo Bane, Ellwood also helped draw attention to the dynamics of poverty and welfare receipt: Most welfare recipients, they revealed, received welfare only for a short spell, but most welfare expenditures, and the worst stigmas, went to the minority who experienced long spells on welfare and/or cycled back onto welfare soon after managing to leave it (Bane and Ellwood 1986). It was the small group with long spells and frequent "cycling" who were more likely to be racial minorities and who endured the greatest hazards while on welfare. Likewise, while most Americans experience poverty or near-poor incomes at some point in their lives, a much smaller share experienced the very long spells that define chronic poverty.[12] Much poverty persistence in America, they found, reflected the interaction of family formation patterns—divorcing, getting married, losing a spouse or partner's income to sickness or death, and other developments—and economic insecurity in a changing economy.

The rebirth of public and scholarly debate, then, in the 1980s, had sharpened and informed two images of ghetto poverty, at least for those who were paying attention. The first image centered on chronically poor *people*, whose experience of poverty, especially if they were racial minorities in America's big cities, included high odds of exposure to the nation's poorest, most distressed, and most dangerous neighborhoods. This point is central to what motivated MTO: not simply that poor people are clustered geographically in particular ways or for particular reasons but that *the experience of poverty and the prospects for escaping poverty are particularly bad in these places.* But before MTO, researchers did not have any clear view of what "escaping" ghettos might produce for the very poor—or, indeed, whether those who got out would choose to stay out.

The second image of ghetto poverty centered on the *places* and the fact that public policy had offered only piecemeal strategies and market-driven hopes for reinvigorating them after long years of decline.[13]

With a new experiment authorized by Congress and a new president elected—a Democrat known for supporting innovative social policy in his two terms as the governor of a poor Southern state and also for advocating a new, post-Reagan consensus on crime, poverty, and other social problems—1992 would prove a pivotal year. In the final section of this chapter, we look at the controversial shift toward deconcentrating poverty and the political backdrop of Clinton-era reforms. We trace several key reforms into the Bush years and the run-up to the Obama election. The chapter that follows tells the extraordinary story of designing and implementing the MTO experiment in this controversial context.

WHITHER THE GHETTO PROJECTS? THE MOVE TO REDEVELOP AND "DECONCENTRATE"

By the time the 1992 election year arrived, increased media attention to the violence and desperation in many inner-city neighborhoods in the 1980s, together with a conservative swing in politics and a sharp resistance to racial integration policy in America after the early 1970s, had left many government planners and at least some advocates pessimistic about the power of public policy to create significant, positive changes for the ghetto poor and their neighborhoods.

What is more, low-income housing policy was not—then or now—a "top-of-mind" agenda issue in Washington or on the campaign trail. The voting public tends to assume that the market will provide adequate housing to hardworking people, even those on modest incomes. Careful historical research suggests that this tendency goes back centuries in our political culture (Vale 2000), despite the reliance of many of America's early industries, such as textile mills and mining operations, on subsidized worker housing. Furthermore, astute observers have noted a long-standing tendency in America's mainstream culture, particularly over the last century, to disparage *rental* housing in general on moral grounds, and to enshrine homeowners and homeownership as the backbone of good citizenship, community mindedness, stability and prosperity (Vale 2006). In this light, low-income rental housing is the lowest rung on a lowly ladder. It is noteworthy that the few major national policy initiatives to support low-income rental housing over the past half century—most notably the Housing Act of 1949, which addressed major postwar housing shortages—were structured to provide significant benefits for developers, banks, private landlords, and other business interests, as well as those perceived to be "middle class" (Marcuse 1995; Orlebeke 1999).

Yet the image of war-zone public housing and gang-dominated inner-city neighborhoods had become so ubiquitous by the early 1990s that Congress and the Bush Sr. administration agreed to act. The thrust of policy debates, shaped powerfully by William Julius Wilson's concept of concentrated poverty, became "deconcentration." As we detail in the next chapter, this avoided the baggage associated with, and judicial proscriptions against, racial "desegregation." For much of the voting public, desegregation connoted forced busing and government dictating "who should live in my neighborhood."

Long-time observers of public policymaking and public management have observed that "public ideas," such as deconcentration, become powerful in part through their capacity to generate concrete programs of action, not just stir the body politic or reveal new information about a problem (Moore 1990). As a public idea, deconcentration suggested at least two workable strategies for fighting ghetto poverty. The first seeks to demolish highly distressed public housing projects and redevelop them as mixed-income developments, with a share of low-income families living alongside middle-class professionals and other market-rate tenants (who would be attracted to live in inner-city neighborhoods again). The second strategy seeks to enable families living in inner-city public housing developments to move out, using rental housing vouchers (which the federal government created in 1974 as construction of new public housing came to an end). In practice, these strategies worked in tandem, at least in some local housing markets, with administrators "vouchering out" public housing tenants whose developments were undergoing redevelopment—*involuntary* mobility, in effect—and offering volunteers, most importantly in the Moving to Opportunity experiment, a chance to relocate from public housing to a private apartment in a different kind of neighborhood.

The place or project-based thrust of deconcentration in the 1990s took the form of a program—HOPE VI—to transform public housing developments labeled "severely distressed" (Vale 1993). The program, which peaked at $660 million per year in redevelopment grants in the late 1990s, is still unfolding, and it has been subjected to a great deal of praise—including top architectural and government innovation awards—as well as heated criticism and ongoing research.[15] Supporters champion the transformation of public housing's long-standing failures, while critics underscore the human costs of dislocation and—in some cases—indict HOPE VI as the latest ploy to subsidize upscale property development and drive poor people from prized urban land. According to the Center on Budget and Policy Priorities, by 2008, when the Bush Administration excluded new funding for HOPE VI from its budget request, Congress had provided a total of $6.7 billion for the program, which funded the demolition of 155,000 public housing units.[16] A study of 49,000 displaced public housing residents by the U.S. General Accounting Office showed that "displacement" did not tell the whole story: About 50 percent moved to other public housing; about 30 percent moved with vouchers; and the rest were either evicted for lease violations or relocated on their own, that is, without assistance. Some had earned more income and were no longer eligible to receive assistance.

We return to redevelopment in the next chapter (as part of the brief but potent backlash against MTO in suburban Baltimore), in the chapter on MTO families' housing choices (since public housing demolition influenced those choices), and again in our final chapter, where we sum up lessons for policy. But our focus in this book is on the second thrust of poverty deconcentration: MTO and other so-called assisted housing mobility programs that provided rental vouchers for families to lease private apartments, with the federal government paying a portion of the rent up to a designated maximum. The rental voucher program is the nation's largest program for meeting the housing needs of very low-income people, with expenditures of about $16 billion per year to serve nearly 2 million households.[17] Our specific focus is MTO, which took the form of a voucher-based experiment.

THE CURRENT PICTURE AND THE IMPORTANCE OF MTO

By the time prominent journalists showered praise on MTO and similar programs to deconcentrate ghetto poverty, in the wake of Hurricane Katrina in 2005, the experiment had been operating, with little fanfare, for over 11 years. In 2007 and 2008, the nation saw the longest and most expensive presidential campaign in its history, some of which highlighted the staggering growth of economic inequality in America over the past generation, the growing crisis of foreclosures and job loss, the "real" lessons of Katrina—as any given speaker would have us understand them—and a frequent lament that the war in Iraq had diverted hundreds of billions of dollars that we need to protect and improve the "home front."

Under two terms of the Bush Administration, HUD repeatedly proposed major cuts in low-income housing assistance—many of them rejected by Congress, first under Republican and then under Democratic leadership. Most relevant to our story, the Administration showed little enthusiasm for poverty deconcentration, whether through voucher-based relocation or public housing redevelopment, or even for innovative investment in poor neighborhoods. The Administration tried but failed to win Congressional support for the elimination of HOPE VI. And in July 2008, journalist Hannah Rosin, using Memphis as a case, published a highly critical article in the *Atlantic* magazine, with the sensational title "American Murder Mystery." Rosin argued that poverty deconcentration—specifically, demolishing public housing and relocating its residents to new neighborhoods—was a significant contributor to the jump in murder and other violent crimes in formerly peaceful Memphis neighborhoods. Rosin made quick reference to similar crime trends and similar housing reforms in other mid-sized cities. Then MTO made a cameo appearance in the article. Rosin suggested that its effects were modest—more evidence of the "over-selling" of poverty deconcentration—and that what poor people in ghettos needed was support services, not naive reformers' efforts to dislodge them from their communities. Though Rosin's evidence was full of holes, right-wing bloggers had a field day, highlighting the fact that a respected *liberal* magazine, drawing on research evidence, had now exposed the threat of "social engineering" to tackle ghetto poverty.[18] These fears grew as the foreclosure crisis unfolded, weakening housing markets and producing widespread neighborhood decline. If past is prologue, that decline will fuel stereotypes about low-income voucher holders as harbingers, if not drivers, of distress and loss.

Through it all, MTO has continued to unfold, the families going about their lives long after Katrina and other high-profile events left the headlines. Understanding the stories of these families is important for the future of public policy as well as popular debate. Specific plans for dramatically reducing poverty in America are encouraging—in 2007, a progressive think tank outlined an approach to cutting it in half over the next decade, for example[19]—yet it is unlikely that *ghetto* poverty will take center stage in domestic policy in the years ahead. The economic crisis and need for broad-based recovery only make it more likely that political support will favor universal rather than targeted programs.

To be fair, we have underscored that the population represented by MTO does not typify the experience of poverty in America: A relatively small share of people who are ever poor experience chronic poverty and multiple forms of disadvantage in the most dangerous and distressed urban neighborhoods. About 875,000 poor people, 63 percent of them black and 22 percent Hispanic, lived in such neighborhoods as of the 2000 census.[20] But these are children and adults enduring some of the harshest, most extreme burdens and contradictions of a wealthy and increasingly unequal society. If we are lucky, efforts to expand opportunity for *most* Americans— in the most dire economic crisis America has experienced in more than seventy years—will offer special hope for the most disadvantaged among us.

To some readers, it may seem odd that social scientists spent a decade or more, and millions of public and private research dollars, "proving" that high-risk neighborhoods are, in fact, bad for people. But that was not the aim. It was, instead, to examine, through careful tracking and comparison, *what could happen if some people were given a chance to get out.* MTO is a powerful window on that specific idea. But it is also a window on what antipoverty policy should aim to accomplish: Should programs like MTO be considered successful if they dramatically *improve the quality of life of the poor* or only if they help a significant share to *escape poverty* altogether? Is it not enormously important that poor mothers and their children who relocated were not dodging bullets and living in daily fear of victimization and death, in other words, that the program helped sever the invidious link between being poor and living in deadly, depressing surroundings?

In the next chapter, we set the stage for these questions by looking at the great expectations and the muddling through—the impatience, hope, hard work, and political maneuvering—that gave birth to an ambitious social experiment called Moving to Opportunity.

Chapter 3

Great Expectations and Muddling Through

Designing and Launching the Experiment

> The federal government has many programs that are meant to help families. Sometimes they do. Unfortunately, sometimes they fail to help anybody. Sometimes, it seems at first that they are helping, but it turns out that families had plenty of strengths and would have done very well anyhow, and the money that the government spent was wasted.... We want to try a new plan, which has seemed to work very well in certain cities.
> —*HUD Secretary Henry Cisneros, video announcement of Moving to Opportunity to agency staff, March 1994*

WHERE DO SOCIAL EXPERIMENTS COME FROM?

Creating and implementing large-scale experiments that aim to affect people's lives in systematically measurable ways is a tricky business. As careful observers have documented time and again since the 1960s, when the War on Poverty produced a dramatic expansion in social programs, thorny social problems often produce confusion and disagreement over what the root problem *is* and also, not surprisingly, over what kinds of remedies would be effective as well as ethical (Crane 1998; Pressman and Wildavsky 1973; Schön and Rein 1994). Agree on what should (in principle) be done, and there turn out to be gaps in the capacity available to implement the idea well. Frequently, those who are ideally positioned to take on the problem may not be trusted or able to do the job well—the problem persists in spite of them or was made worse, some say, *because* of them—while those trusted to do the job better are not well positioned to take it on (M. Moore 1995). So compromises are made to leave the problem at hand more "tractable," as in: amenable to the imperfect means available for tackling it. Then more compromises are made to assemble the needed implementing capacity, with offers to compensate one agency, train another, and "coordinate" or "consult" with a third or fourth.

Then launching the intervention—in particular, the first contact with real clients as opposed to ideas about clients—leads to a host of surprises. In part, this is because some things cannot be learned except by doing— by trial and error—and in part because, in retrospect, the planners filtered incomplete or conflicting information through half-right assumptions. Then the front-line, client-serving staff reinvent the intervention, in little or not-so-little ways, through how they perform their roles (Lipsky 1980). They juggle daunting constraints and bring to bear their own, informal "practice theories" of what a good program should look like. The implementers respond to incentives, rules, and problems not fully understood by the planners, in the everyday settings—workplaces, streets, homes— where the social experiment actually unfolds.

To make the plot even more interesting, along come the researchers with their own set of needs to standardize and measure things in ways that may have little to do with the priorities of families or implementers in those everyday settings. Then many changes take place, beyond the scope of the intervention, that affect the participants—changes in the job and housing markets, in other arenas of public policy, and beyond. Yet in the end, where there is sustained commitment, carefulness, and a bit of resourcefulness and good fortune, none of these hurdles prevent a worthwhile intervention from happening—or obscure its effects from measurement. And even where the effects are mixed, with both encouraging and disappointing impacts on people's lives, something important can be learned about what works, what does not, and why.

Creating and implementing a social experiment, then, is about great expectations and tons of planning but also a good deal of "muddling through" (Lindblom 1959), with limited information, limited political room to maneuver, and imperfect tools. In this chapter, we briefly outline the story of how the Moving to Opportunity (MTO) experiment was conceived and "authorized"—to use the lawmaker's shorthand—and then designed and implemented. We tell this story first and foremost because it is studded with fateful decisions that shaped the experiences and outcomes of the families who participated in the experiment. That is, the chapter sheds light on the family-level findings at the heart of the book, which define the "bottom line" for any planned intervention. But we also tell this story because it holds lessons for efforts yet to come—efforts to redefine and rebuild an opportunity agenda for America that includes the chronically poor in segregated, high-crime neighborhoods.

In simple form: In act one, the inner-city poor, along with federal policy makers and agency planners, face a distressingly intractable problem, but after years of standoff and running pilot programs on the margins, a seemingly viable "solution" presents itself. In simple terms, it is an idea that has produced results somewhere. In act two, the planners, policy entrepreneurs, and lawmakers outline a new experiment, based on that idea and that limited experience, and codify it—without much detail—in an act of Congress. Then the planners have to figure out how to "pull it off." In act three, they design the research requirements and the local implementers are recruited; the latter introduce their own ideas and challenges; and they begin to enroll and serve the families who volunteer to participate. That fourth act includes a firestorm of opposition at one local site, from "receiving" areas in Baltimore County. Homeowners there were angry, in spite of MTO's very small scale, at what they perceived to be indifferent social engineering that threatened their neighborhoods. The fifth and final act, the long one after families have been placed and research gets underway, is still unfolding.

At each juncture, we underline the dilemmas facing the decision-makers and the choices that would, in the years that followed, prove—variously—enlightened, heroic, or off-base.

THE SEEMINGLY INTRACTABLE PROBLEM: "FEDERAL SLUMS"

As we noted in chapter 2, by the late 1960s, careful observers of high-poverty public housing projects had labeled the projects "federal slums"—the byproduct of sweeping social and economic changes in urban America, the intended and unintended consequences of public policy decisions, and political neglect (Hirsch 1983). Yet conditions were far worse by the late 1980s. In big cities, public housing residents were 90 percent minority (black or Hispanic) and their neighborhoods had a staggering poverty rate of 55 percent, on average (Goering, Kamely, and Richardson 1995; Leif and Goering 1987). Many projects were overrun with gang-controlled drug dealing and the deadly violence it inevitably produced. Chronic poverty and welfare dependency, in families headed by single mothers with children, were the norm. Beyond the terrible distress in the projects themselves, public housing in big U.S. cities typically anchored large, isolated, jobless, and extremely poor racial ghettos, with the nation's highest crime rates (Massey and Denton 1993; Wilson 1987; Wilson 1996). In the most segregated small and medium-sized cities, meanwhile, and in Boston and New York City, local decision-makers often ran dual programs, with some public housing projects unofficially designated ("protected") for whites and others for blacks or Hispanics.

Over this long period of decline, staff at the U.S. Department of Housing and Urban Development, which funds and regulates public housing through hundreds of local agencies, looked on rather helplessly. Most HUD staff were acutely aware of the indifference of the general public and of most policy makers, in Congress and the White House, and skeptical that any workable remedies existed. A host of social programs had failed to turn around distress in inner-city public housing; it functioned for many families as the housing of last resort, and local politics and market forces often seemed to favor ghettoization over any proposal that would integrate public housing, let alone give large numbers of very poor minorities the chance to live in safe and secure communities of opportunity.

One symptom of the deep hole into which HUD had fallen was the growing number of expensive and protracted lawsuits. In a series of class-action cases from Boston, Chicago, Dallas, Kansas City, New York, and elsewhere, legal advocates highlighted the failure of HUD and its local agency partners to treat residents of public housing, especially blacks, in a manner consistent with civil rights laws and constitutional equal opportunity mandates (Goering 1986; Roisman 2007). In 1986, as HUD continued to fight legal attacks for deliberately segregating public housing residents and for housing blacks, in particular, in the lowest quality housing units, a veteran HUD staffer wrote, "It is appalling how little is known, how little has been effective, and how mountainous are the obstacles to change. The costs of segregation are so severe, and the pace of change is so deadly slow, that one can despair of any progress within the next decades" (Goering 1986:3).

Debates inside and outside the agency often focused—frustratingly, from the advocate's perspective—not on bold moves to fight ghetto poverty itself, or to directly alleviate the distress associated with it, but merely on efforts to make high-poverty public housing projects somewhat more racially mixed. Few HUD staff were eager to make demands of local managers and elected officials, and likewise, no local officials asked HUD for help with their segregated housing stocks. In the context of a lawsuit focused on a staunchly segregationist public housing authority in East Texas, for example, one HUD staff member opined that the agency "should just leave those good [white] folks alone."[1] HUD staff spent weeks poring over tenant assignment plans, only to move small numbers of tenants in a hostile context. Soon after two tenant families from the overwhelmingly black Beaumont, Texas, housing authority were moved to all-white Vidor nearby, HUD staff learned that Vidor had become home to an active chapter of the Ku Klux Klan. The racial hostility was immediate, and the two black families quickly moved out. One of the black tenants was soon murdered in an apparent robbery in Beaumont, and the State of Texas later sued the Klan for "intimidating blacks who briefly moved into an all-white public housing project," as the *New York Times* reported.[2]

Meanwhile, HUD's leadership offered neither ideas nor resources to address the problem of federally maintained slums. Indeed, Samuel Pierce, HUD Secretary throughout the Reagan years, seemed to pride himself on slashing the agency's budget to unprecedented levels (Dreier 1995; Orlebeke 1999). The pattern continued under President George Bush Sr. Zero dollars were allocated for desegregation initiatives, and the Administrations consistently voiced their opposition to race-conscious policies or programs of any kind, including a specific HUD mandate to "affirmatively further fair housing" (Roisman 2007; Tegeler 2005).

The impasse would be broken only when a determined, court-ordered local initiative showed that the desegregation of public housing was not only legally necessary but also *achievable* with HUD's own program tools—and, more than that, beneficial to the families who participated.

A SOLUTION MADE IN CHICAGO

Over the course of the 1980s, the nation's then leading organization for promoting housing choice for the inner-city poor—the Leadership Council for Metropolitan Open Communities in Chicago—repeatedly provided HUD with depositions to demonstrate a model. It relocated black families from inner-city Chicago to racially integrated communities throughout the Chicago region without rancor or major administrative problems. The program lined up landlords willing to rent to families who relocated with HUD's then-new *housing vouchers*.[3] Vouchers subsidized a very low-income tenant's own rental payment, beyond a designated affordability threshold (30 percent of household income), up to a rent "ceiling" (determined by periodic surveys of local housing markets), so long as the housing unit was not in substandard condition (passed a basic quality inspection). The Leadership Council's program recruited and counseled tenants, therefore, but it also matched them with willing landlords in racially mixed communities, some of them twenty to thirty miles away from the core of the Chicago ghetto—the city's infamous inner-city public housing projects.

This "assisted housing mobility" program had been developed in the late 1970s, not by legislative or executive initiative but as a court-ordered remedy. It followed a landmark class-action lawsuit, *Gautreaux v. Chicago Housing Authority*, the nation's first successful public housing desegregation lawsuit. Filed in 1966, the *Gautreaux* case went, a decade later, to the U.S. Supreme Court, which upheld a lower court's order to provide "desegregative" housing opportunities to current and former residents of Chicago public housing (Polikoff 2006). Eventually, the program would help some 7,100 black families to relocate using housing vouchers.

But initially, the Leadership Council's claims were viewed by HUD merely as court filings by advocates—and claims that vouchers paired with counseling and landlord recruitment could achieve credible levels of desegregation. There was no credible, independent evidence on either how counseling worked or on the *benefits* of desegregation to the participating families. More importantly, there was no external political support for replicating the Gautreaux program. That would soon change, however, when sociologist James Rosenbaum and collaborators produced survey evidence that the children of Gautreaux families who relocated to major white, middle-class suburbs, and who had lived in those areas for seven to ten years, were more likely to take college-track classes, finish high school, and attend college than counterparts who relocated within Chicago (Kaufman and Rosenbaum 1992; Rubinowitz and Rosenbaum 2000). The earliest results suggested that children whose earliest schooling was in inner-city Chicago struggled to adjust to the higher expectations of suburban schools; many were placed in special education classes, for example, and their grades dropped. But the longer-run view showed impressive gains. Also, the Gautreaux parents who relocated to suburban areas appeared more likely to be employed rather than receiving welfare (Popkin and Rosenbaum 1991; Popkin, Rosenbaum, and Meaden 1993). While the program was not constructed as a social experiment and thus the research had important limitations,[4] a major reason for hope was beginning to appear: Helping inner-city families to leave distressed ghettos could have major benefits, especially for children.

At a small conference in Virginia in 1987, the Leadership Council argued vigorously that its model of assisted housing mobility provided a legally and administratively viable option, as well as a beneficial one, for the seemingly intractable problems associated with inner-city public housing. The will to build on Gautreaux would took shape, however, only when a very determined "policy entrepreneur" nudged HUD to act in spite of its pessimism and its resistance to race-conscious programs.

GOVERNMENT SHOULD ACT

Careful observers of the policymaking process have long noted that desperate social *conditions* may persist for years without becoming *problems* that key elected officials, advocates, and others are willing to invest time, money, reputation, relationships, and other crucial resources to address (Kingdon 1984). Shocking public events, pivotal election outcomes, and other changes may create political "windows of opportunity," but there is still no guarantee of effective action: The problem may remain fuzzy and contested; other issues have more effective advocates; competing "solutions" lead to standoff; or other barriers get in the way. It may take determined policy entrepreneurs to remain optimistic in the face of long resistance, recognize windows of opportunity, marshal the evidence in favor of particular solutions, and connect the players who can become a coalition to support those solutions. Based on careful study of the process by which Congress defined its policy agenda (the issues up for serious discussion) and considered alternatives for acting on that agenda over time, political scientist John Kingdon (1984:129, 130) explained:

> [Policy entrepreneurs] could be in or out of government, in elected or appointed positions, in interest groups or research organizations. But their defining characteristic, much as in the case of a business entrepreneur is their willingness to invest their resources—time, energy, reputation, and sometimes money—in the hope of a future return.... They make calls, have lunch, write memos, and draft proposals...

In decision-making contexts where many ideas and many people are competing for attention—and where many do *not* get a meaningful hearing— successful policy entrepreneurs, argued Kingdon, have "some claim to a hearing" (p. 188), whether because of special expertise, the ability to speak for others, or an authoritative position. In addition, they are known for political connections and negotiating skill. But perhaps most importantly, they are persistent. "Many potentially influential people might have expertise and political skill," Kingdon (1984:189) concluded, "but sheer tenacity pays off."

Confronting the muddle at HUD in the late 1980s, Alex Polikoff, the lead plaintiff's attorney in the *Gautreaux* case, was such a person. His relentlessness on behalf of public housing desegregation went back two decades. He believed passionately in the Leadership Council's mobility program; he knew the value of credible research evidence; and he was willing to compromise to make HUD try something. In 1988, Polikoff formally requested a meeting with HUD staff to discuss the possibility of replicating the Gautreaux approach on a larger scale. But HUD began to draft an official response that put off any such meeting. Inside the agency, the Polikoff proposal had a few allies in HUD's policy development and research unit, but that unit had little funding to invest and limited connections to the program staff that managed the public housing and voucher programs. Their funding and regulatory backing would be crucial to any large-scale housing mobility demonstration. Personal ties among veteran staff members made the difference, as they often do in large bureaucracies. By 1989, HUD's policy and research staff got the director of the voucher program to formally invite Polikoff to Washington to discuss his proposal.

As insiders recall, the meeting at HUD began with Polikoff proposing a single-site replication of Gautreaux in Baltimore, but HUD staff believed there might be room to extend the demonstration further, on the condition that income and not race be used to target "opportunity" areas to which families would relocate. In the absence of a court finding, and given skepticism in the bureaucracy about race as a criterion for targeting, HUD relied on income make-up alone as a metric of neighborhood "opportunity." The legally controversial, race-focused objectives of Gautreaux were replaced with the neighborhood poverty rate threshold.[5]

"De-linking" the program from race, Polikoff acknowledged in a 1991 memo to HUD, "would be accomplished by defining the eligible population as families who are income eligible [for rental vouchers] and who reside in high-poverty neighborhoods.... Eligible receiving areas would be low-poverty neighborhoods." Jack Kemp was now the Secretary of HUD. He had made economic empowerment a major focus of his speeches, and the emerging coalition of staff backing a new housing mobility demonstration won support for it from Kemp's staff by framing the proposal as "providing assisted families the choice of moving from economically depressed areas to areas of high job potential."[6] Yet the planners did not know whether low-poverty areas were in fact areas of "high job potential." Such areas might not be racially integrated either, nor provide the high-performing schools that Chicago's mostly white suburbs had provided to thousands of poor black children who relocated through the Gautreaux program.

Working with Polikoff, HUD staff drafted a short description of a "Moving to Opportunity" demonstration for inclusion in the fiscal year 1991 and 1992 budget proposals to Congress. By this time, Rosenbaum, too, had visited HUD to present the encouraging results of his research on inner-city families who had successfully relocated to suburban Chicago and managed to stay in those communities for seven to ten years. As Polikoff recalls in *Waiting for Gautreaux* (2006:261–262), he built support for the new MTO proposal in the Senate, and—in October 1992, one month before the presidential election—Congress authorized the program, appropriating $70 million in housing voucher funding and an additional $1.5 million for tenant relocation counseling. Congress also directed HUD to employ rigorous standards of evaluation and to report on "the long-term housing, employment, and educational achievements of the families assisted…compared to a comparable population of [voucher] recipients who have not received assistance under the demonstration."[7]

After decades of piecemeal response to distressed and segregated public housing in inner-city America, after the abandonment of serious research on "what works," and after a decade of legal resistance by the nation's housing agency to almost all proposed reforms, Congress had just ordered the largest low-income housing demonstration in decades. MTO offered a specific means to deconcentrate poverty in inner-city ghettos. Under newly elected President Bill Clinton, it would soon become one of the most ambitious social experiments ever attempted.

CHANGING OF THE GUARD: THE CLINTON APPOINTEES AND MTO'S DESIGN

In the spring of 1993, the Senate confirmed Henry Cisneros, the Harvard-educated former mayor of San Antonio, as Clinton's new HUD Secretary. After twelve years under Presidents Reagan and Bush, HUD was decimated and demoralized—its budget slashed, its contracts and staff racked with fraud and mismanagement scandals. Cisneros and the other appointees had to fight not to launch major new policy initiatives but, first and foremost, to save the agency in the face of mounting criticism. The restive mood on Capitol Hill was best captured the following year, when Republicans regained control of the Congress and newly installed House Majority leader Newt Gingrich claimed, "You could abolish HUD tomorrow morning and improve life in most of America."[8]

In spite of these challenges, Cisneros and his team quickly signaled a change of course at HUD. For our story, two moves were particularly crucial: the decision to stop contesting the slew of public housing desegregation lawsuits brought forward in the 1980s and enter into "consent decrees" (voluntary agreements) to settle those disputes; and enthusiastic support for the just-authorized MTO demonstration. To Michael

Stegman, who now directed the policy and research unit at HUD, and Margery Austin Turner, who ran the unit's evaluation portfolio, the Gautreaux model of relocation counseling appeared effective and not unduly expensive, and the benefits suggested by research on Gautreaux were extremely encouraging.

In consultation with academics and policy experts, HUD staff decided on a formal experimental structure in which families in public or assisted housing[9] who volunteered to participate in MTO would be randomly assigned to: the "experimental" group, which would receive Gautreaux-like relocation assistance and a "restricted" housing voucher that could be used to lease up only in a low-poverty neighborhood; a comparison group, which would receive a "regular" voucher with no special assistance or location restrictions; and a control group that would continue to receive assistance in the form of a public housing unit. The agency also decided to fund small grants to researchers who would study MTO families' early experiences and outcomes, proposing innovative ways to understand the program and its impacts rather than reporting on particular outcomes designated by HUD. In the context of an experiment that had such great expectations and faced—more than the planners realized—long odds, the decision to open up the research process proved crucial. In just a few years, the researchers would identify unexpected positive impacts in areas that had never been a part of the Gautreaux discussion—safety, health, and mental health, for example—while highlighting multiple reasons that the most hoped-for benefits, in education and employment, might not materialize as expected.[10]

The emerging MTO demonstration joined other efforts by HUD to tackle problems associated with concentrated poverty and social distress in inner-city neighborhoods: the Bridges to Work demonstration, a "reverse commuting" program to link inner-city job seekers to suburban opportunities with transportation, training, job matching, and other supports; the Jobs-Plus demonstration, which saturated public housing developments with state-of-the-art employment and training services, childcare and other work supports, and rent incentives to encourage public housing residents to find and keep jobs (rather than focus on keeping their rents low by limiting their income from wages); and a large-scale redevelopment of "severely distressed" public housing developments into well-designed, mixed-income developments—the award-winning and sometimes controversial HOPE VI program.

Together, MTO and these other efforts represented an about-face on the problems of ghetto poverty, for which HUD, in the preceding dozen years, had offered only modest physical upgrading through public housing "modernization" grants. And the substantial body of careful research on each of these efforts would produce more knowledge about the social and economic effects of low-income housing policy—a long-neglected, much-maligned domain of public policy—than any work carried out in the preceding thirty or forty years.[11]

FINALIZING THE DESIGN: ASSUMPTIONS, KNOWLEDGE, AND GAPS

Now HUD had to implement MTO. And it had to contend with the fact that for roughly two decades, researchers and planners alike had largely neglected life in inner-city public housing. Would public housing families volunteer for MTO given what planners had designed it to offer? Would mobility counseling and search assistance in fact work to help the families find new homes? Would they be able to relocate to the designated types of neighborhoods? Beyond these questions was the greatest unknown: Given the social dynamics the families were leaving behind, how might relocating actually affect their lives?

In 1970, sociologist Lee Rainwater had reported that because of the fighting, drinking, drug abuse, and stealing around them, residents of the very distressed Pruitt-Igoe housing project in St. Louis felt little attachment to it—were wary and mistrusting of their neighbors—and very much wanted to move out. Likewise, anthropologist Sally Engle Merry's (1981) ethnographic study of crime in and around a public housing development in Boston in the late 1970s illustrated how different ethnic groups—black, white, Hispanic, and Chinese Americans—mostly kept to themselves and coped with an ever-present sense of danger that helped to make the development and its surroundings a "neighborhood of strangers." But since then, only a handful of journalists had done any in-depth investigation, producing, in books such as Alex Kotlowitz's *There Are No Children Here* (1991), incisive and compelling accounts that emphasized danger and hopelessness in and around the projects. These partial accounts focused, as journalism tends to, on the personal stories of a few individuals or families living in a single place. No one had had the need or opportunity to figure out whether and how very disadvantaged families, in a variety of housing developments and cities, would respond to a real chance to get out, especially if that chance meant giving up the long-term security of a public housing lease and if it came with location restrictions or other "strings" attached.

HUD planners would soon learn one lesson, but miss three more, in the final stages of design before MTO launched. First, it became clear very quickly that the primary motivator for MTO participants would be families' strong desire to escape the crime and pervasive sense of insecurity that plagued many inner-city housing projects—not broader hopes for better schools or job opportunities, let alone more integrated living. On an initial visit to the Pico Aliso development in Los Angeles, for example, HUD planners were surprised to find a large gathering of roughly forty women, almost all Hispanic, who had come out to hear about a program that might offer the chance to move away. One mother, speaking through a translator, told HUD staff that her teenage daughter had recently been murdered by her boyfriend, who lived next door. Because the mother was scheduled to testify against him in court, she feared for her life and pleaded to be among those allowed to move out. The staff moved her immediately.

But what those planning the experiment had not realized or allowed for was the fact that many families in the worst public housing projects had become harder to serve since Gautreaux began enrolling families in the 1970s. Beyond having extremely low incomes and little or no work history, many of those living in the most unsafe, distressed projects by the 1990s, many who would be eager to leave, had chronic health and mental-health problems and, in some cases, children or other family members with criminal records or drug abuse problems—an accumulated set of severe stressors. These challenges could affect their ability to relocate. What would a housing counselor helping such families need to do? These serious barriers could also limit the families' ability to *succeed* after relocating—to create functional, satisfying lives in new places. Would such families stay in "better" places long enough to benefit? Finally, such barriers could also affect, in powerful ways, the effects (or noneffects) of staying in the new locations. MTO, after all, was to offer *only* a relocation—with no intensive health or human services or other special supports in the experimental "treatment."[12]

Third, beyond the targeting of eligible families, there was the issue of targeting sending and receiving ("opportunity") neighborhoods. For the former, HUD planners decided to rely on the researchers' convention of categorizing census tracts with a 40 percent or greater poverty rate, as of the latest (1990) census, as "high-poverty" neighborhoods. In fact, MTO families would come from neighborhoods with poverty rates that ranged as high as 80 percent. These were extremely poor areas, far more disadvantaged than the 1960s ghettos. And HUD did not understand them well at all, although its policies and programs were implicated in them. As for the opportunity areas, a threshold of 10 percent or lower poverty rate was chosen as the converse. Further analysis of 1990 census data showed that many low-poverty census tracts were also racially mixed, which led planners to assume that MTO would achieve racial desegregation in addition to poverty deconcentration—and do so quietly, indirectly, without a race-based targeting criterion that might invite political or legal attack. Little additional thought was given, beyond this simple metric, to operationalizing "opportunity." In fact, many other low-poverty neighborhoods were *not* racially mixed; many of those were getting poorer; and many offered neither high-performing schools nor strong job growth nearby.

Nonetheless, HUD planners decided that the MTO experimental group would receive vouchers restricted to use in low-poverty neighborhoods, thus defined, on the condition that the families remain in place at least one year. Beyond that, nothing ensured that the apartments would *remain* affordable and available for leasing or that families would *want* to stay put longer.

Fourth and finally, MTO needed an effective division of labor. Gautreaux had partnered the chronically mismanaged Chicago Housing

Authority with a capable, trustworthy, and highly committed nonprofit organization—the Leadership Council—to provide relocation counseling and match tenants with willing landlords. HUD planners relied on this one successful template in designing MTO: Local public housing agencies would contract with nonprofits to provide the counseling and manage families' search and "lease up" process. The planners had little confidence that public housing bureaucracies could find, train, and appropriately supervise counseling staff that would need to circumvent the traditional, open-ended approach to allocating vouchers. Traditionally, there were no geographic restrictions on the use of vouchers and no special relocation coaching, search assistance, or other support to secure "favored" locations.

But would local public housing agencies be willing and able to work with nonprofits appropriately? Would nonprofits comparable to the Leadership Council even exist in other metropolitan areas to act as reliable implementers? Would they deliver relocation assistance appropriately? HUD assumed so. It did not have systematic data on these questions before finalizing the "notice of funding availability" (NOFA) that made MTO's launch official in August 1993.

IMPLEMENTING: THE HOUSING AGENCIES AND THE "CHAIN" OF COOPERATION

HUD had no real blueprint for a large-scale effort like MTO, and so the temptation was great to rely on a single, tested program model—that of the Gautreaux program in Chicago, which served a somewhat less disadvantaged clientele and operated under different, court-ordered terms. Furthermore, HUD assumed there would be local capacity to implement a program significant enough to constitute an experimental treatment— in plain terms, an intensive-enough "dose" of something good that might generate effects big enough to be detected by evaluators. HUD further assumed, like any organization launching a social experiment, that the program could be implemented faithfully enough to test what planners hoped to test, despite the fact that social experiments, unlike laboratory-based ones, cannot be carried out, and do not evolve over time, under highly controlled or controllable conditions.

HUD's notice of funding availability invited applications from local public housing agencies and their nonprofit "partners."[13] The NOFA outlined the experiment's terms and conditions, announcing $70 million to fund approximately 1,900 new housing vouchers for up to six local public housing agencies that would be chosen, based on explicit rating and ranking criteria, by HUD. In light of the 1992 riots that rocked Los Angeles, that city's public housing agency was told that it would be funded provided that it submitted an approvable MTO application.

HUD's NOFA detailed the nonprofit role in the demonstration and told these organizations to expect about $500,000 apiece in funding, which "may not be sufficient to fund the housing counseling services under this demonstration." The notice called on nonprofit partners to raise matching funds from other sources. As for the counseling to be provided to tenant clients, HUD called for "realistic introductions about the advantages and disadvantages of living in low-poverty census tracts." That was it, and no one at HUD, insiders recall, had a clear sense of what the "disadvantages" might be. The notice also instructed nonprofit agencies to use maps showing the full range of low-poverty neighborhoods, but given the time pressure to place large numbers of voucher holders quickly, that seldom happened. The nonprofits were instructed to screen families by making a "home inspection" of the family's current housing unit, because, said the notice, "a small number of assisted family heads have grown up in dysfunctional families in which they never learned housekeeping skills." Finally, the notice indicated that nonprofit counselors would follow up in the first ninety days post-relocation to check on short-term adjustment and that program participants would be free, after one year, to move on if they so desired. This seemed fair to planners at the time—again, in lieu of research or other guidance on what would create a feasible deconcentration program.

By October 1993, HUD had received a total of sixteen applications in response to the notice. Los Angeles had submitted an approvable application, HUD staff soon determined, and so had just four other local partnerships: Baltimore, Boston, Chicago, and New York. MTO would include five, not six, local sites.

HUD's small research unit contracted with Abt Associates, an experienced evaluation research firm, to help further design and manage the experiment's complex, cross-site operations and training of the local implementers, along with the tracking of an estimated 5,000 families. There was the Gautreaux material to draw on, but HUD and Abt would have to create a full set of operating protocols to ensure that local agencies implemented the program as intended—as one intervention, that is, and not five different ones. And inevitably, there would be surprises, and tensions around those protocols, when local realities did not conform to the planners' hopes or expectations. Plus, the random assignment of tenants to treatment groups had to be bullet-proof, or the demonstration would be worthless as an experiment. HUD was under considerable scrutiny. In 1994, Speaker of the House Newt Gingrich had even put the agency on his hit list for elimination, part of a "Contract with America" that galvanized conservative voters and helped the Republican Party retain control of the Congress for six of President Clinton's eight years in office. HUD could not afford to mismanage a $70 million demonstration or millions in additional funding for the evaluation.

The mechanism for standardizing implementation was an operations manual, plus Abt field staff assigned to each of the five sites. The manual defined eligible families, for example: a family, living in public or assisted housing in a high-poverty census tract, with at least one child under eighteen years old, a solid rental payment history, and acceptable housekeeping. Two of the sites also excluded families with a criminal arrest record.[14]

Abt also directed the random assignment, basing some guidelines—such as ratios for assigning tenants to either of the voucher groups—on the Gautreaux experience. Planners initially assumed, for example, that only about one in five families assigned to a voucher group would successfully lease up; that was the Gautreaux success rate. But MTO sites would soon achieve rates two to three times greater, and so random assignment had to be adjusted to ensure large, statistically comparable populations in each treatment group.

The experiment's operations also mandated "informed consent." Informed consent meant that each family head would have to appreciate what they were getting themselves into over the long haul, since researchers would quite regularly be stopping by for interviews and other data collection. The research component of MTO also required that some level of information should be gathered at the very first stage in a family's enrollment, that is, at a clear baseline point. These measurements were at first required as part of Congressional mandates for biennial reports and later became an integral part of HUD's MTO research program.

HUD and Abt instructed local implementers that their involvement with voucher users would be limited to housing search and relocation counseling, that supplemental services, such as employment or health-focused supports, should be through referral only. This boundary would be put to the test right away, as soon as HUD and Abt gathered staff from the local public housing agencies and nonprofit counseling agencies for a national training. Abt commissioned the Leadership Council from Chicago to brief the trainees on its "proven" approach to counseling, and the planners assumed the local implementers would gratefully accept and act on that advice. The planners were wrong.

On one side, there was the principle of running a standardized demonstration, according to protocol, using the one approach to assisted relocation that had ever been implemented at scale and then studied—the Gautreaux approach. On the other side, there were the staff, primarily with human service expertise, accustomed to dealing with clients and their special needs, their struggles in the housing market, and more—dealing with them in the here and now, in five very different localities, not in a special program implemented years before and only in Chicago. Several of the nonprofits had no interest in implementing what they saw as Gautreaux's bare-bones counseling approach. They recognized, as HUD planners had not, the need for intensive supports that many public housing families would need, and they argued for a much more comprehensive case management approach to help ensure families' success. The Los Angeles site's nonprofit partner added that it would have to provide intensive job counseling in order to meet HUD's stated goal that counseling should "build the capacity of enrolled families to become independent and survive on their own."

Beyond not calling for such supports, neither Congress nor HUD had budgeted for them, and HUD's notice of funding availability had obviously generated expectations, among the local implementers, that were broader, and more expensive, than the Gautreaux model. There were other challenges. The New York site's nonprofit partner had failed to raise the needed matching funds and thus requested a special HUD grant to fund the gap or the leeway to implement a stripped-down version of MTO in which they would simply contract with rental brokers to find reasonably priced apartments. HUD had to deny the request and soon provided them a special allocation to run a "bare-bones" program.

HUD planners did concede that the local nonprofits could customize their approach to counseling and search assistance, in order to ensure the highest possible lease-up rates, as long as the approach fit within program budgets and the demonstration's research requirements, and as along as it was designed to "empower" families to become independent after relocating. Program recruitment and enrollment began in the summer of 1994.

While all five sites steadily "leased up" clients in the experiment's two voucher-holding treatment groups, success rates varied widely. This was, in part, a function of the differences among the housing markets, which we analyze in the next chapter. Some rental housing markets are tighter than others, and this affects whether, where, and how quickly voucher holders can find suitable apartments and sign leases with private landlords. But the variation in local performance also reflected the uneven management capacities of the public housing agencies and their nonprofit partners, as well as the degree of effective coordination between the two parties.

There are over 3,000 local public housing agencies in America. They are creatures of state law but funded by the federal government, beginning with the Housing Acts of 1937 and 1949. These agencies serve some of the nation's most severely disadvantaged families and poorest elderly, primarily in urban areas (Quercia and Galster 1997). Some agencies are consistently well managed, in spite of underfunding and in spite of stigmas—those associated social welfare administration in general and housing the very poor in particular. This includes very large housing authorities, such as New York, which manages 180,000 units in 2,700 buildings—a resident population the size of the city of Atlanta—and smaller ones, such as Minneapolis, which consistently rate highly in federal performance reviews. In recent years, deep funding cuts under George W. Bush's two terms threatened the capacity of even these capable agencies to run viable programs. Over the decades, the worst performing public housing agencies have fallen into periods of such operational and fiscal failure that they are taken over, via temporary receivership, by HUD.

Indeed, in the fall of 1996, HUD ended the Chicago Housing Authority's (CHA) implementation role in MTO and put in its place the private contractor that managed Chicago's very large voucher program. Among the many reasons for terminating the CHA's role was that landlords and tenants each complained—often loudly and bitterly—that the Authority was consistently late in sending rent payments to landlords. Clients also complained that the Authority was late or negligent in carrying out required housing quality inspections for the apartments they had found. These issues—distrust of the housing authority by both landlords and tenants—had to be addressed immediately by the new contractor. But the CHA's failures produced significant delays, and the Leadership Council, the nonprofit partner for MTO, performed poorly as well. Enrollments in MTO took almost an additional year, as families waited and waited for the two agencies helping them—the new contractor and the nonprofit MTO counseling agency—to work together effectively. Partly as a result of these problems, the lease-up rate for families in the treatment group in Chicago was only 34 percent in the end, compared, for example, to a rate of 61 percent in Los Angeles.

It was not just the public housing agencies, then, but the nonprofit partners that presented a mix of strengths and weaknesses. While nonprofits have a long record of involvement in providing social services, coaching prospective homeowners, and developing and managing low-income rental housing in the United States, few had any experience counseling public housing tenants on a move to "opportunity." Nor did they have experience coordinating with the public housing agencies, which signaled some resentment that HUD had required them to contract out for any portion of a housing voucher demonstration. Add to that the fact that two of the nonprofits that came forward to be part of the MTO program were fair-housing *advocacy* organizations with a history of suing local landlords and public housing agencies—the very players whose cooperation was essential in MTO. In Chicago and Los Angeles, these two nonprofits were ineffective and had to be replaced.[15] In Boston and Baltimore, the housing agencies had a significant incentive to cooperate for MTO lease-up: They had to accommodate an aggressive schedule of public housing demolition as part of the HOPE VI redevelopment program.

Like human service providers throughout the country, the nonprofit partners in MTO struggled with large workloads, staff turnover, and limited funding and other resources (Lipsky 1980; Feins, McInnis, and Popkin 1997). Ironically, the Leadership Council, which helped to inspire MTO through its success at the Gautreaux housing mobility program, floundered most with MTO's much harder-to-serve client population. Its success rate was abysmal, as we noted above, and it gave up its contract to counsel MTO families in Chicago.[16] Baltimore, Boston, and New York worked with the same nonprofit partner throughout MTO placement. New York's counseling agency did, in the end, rely heavily on real estate brokers to find landlords willing to rent to voucher holders in low-poverty neighborhoods. Their placements, not surprisingly perhaps, were heavily concentrated in a single corner of that vast metropolitan housing market: racially transitional neighborhoods in the Northeast Bronx. We take up this theme—the trends reshaping the "geography of opportunity" around the families, as the experiment unfolded—in the next chapter, as well as chapter 6.

The final MTO lease-ups occurred in Los Angeles in the spring of 1998, almost five years after the experiment enrolled its first clients. As a HUD-funded assessment of MTO counseling and relocation success confirmed, the five local implementation partnerships used a variety of approaches (Feins, McInnis, and Popkin 1997), but they allocated all the funded vouchers and, in several instances, added more vouchers, from their own "regular" voucher allocations, enlarging the number of households in the demonstration by more than a quarter. Costs per family counseled averaged $1,200, with a low of $590 in New York (where the nonprofit relied solely on HUD funding) and a high of $1,600 in Baltimore, where the nonprofit raised nearly half the funding on its own and employed very comprehensive counseling and early supports to help families succeed (U.S. HUD 1999). Having operated in five tough housing markets, including three of the nation's tightest and most consistently expensive—Boston, Los Angeles, and New York, our three study sites—MTO's lease-up success rates were generally below the national average for HUD's rental voucher program, with a cross-site average of 47 percent for the experimental group. Yet they were much higher than the Gautreaux program's rate of 20 percent.

In only one site did the MTO program face a far more daunting challenge than the ones we have thus far described: overt, well-organized political opposition by "receiving" communities. In the next section, we examine the firestorm that met HUD planners in Baltimore County. This episode is instructive about how the wider public often views the stakes in programs to help the minority poor move out of the inner city—not the question of whether "better" neighborhoods are good for families leaving ghettos but whether those families are "good" for the neighborhoods that receive them.

COMMUNITY OPPOSITION IN THE BALTIMORE SUBURBS

In the spring of 1994, before MTO began to enroll clients at any site, a government employee who lived in the eastern section of Baltimore County asked to come to HUD to make a copy of the MTO application that had been submitted by the Housing Authority of Baltimore City. His anxieties were clear: He said he feared for the quality of his own neighborhood and was concerned, more specifically, that his young daughters might date a black person from one of the MTO families. He was also bothered by the fact that the MTO demonstration appeared to be a "secret." It seemed that no one in the county had been informed about the demonstration. His visit to HUD was an effort to learn whether Baltimore County had been targeted as the new home for people from the city's public housing ghettos.

As a large body of research would predict, these fears about MTO reflected a preexisting perception of decline and unwelcome demographic change.[17] Like many older, inner-ring suburbs across the country, parts of

Baltimore County, particularly the towns of Essex and Dundalk in the east, had, by the early 1990s, begun to experience their own troubles with job loss, poverty, and crime. Topping this list was the decline in the number of industrial jobs, as steel and aviation plants moved elsewhere. Many of the residents of the eastern section of the county were working-class families, whose members had worked in the steel and shipping factories along the county's waterfront (S. Newman 1995). But these once-prosperous blue-collar areas had now begun to deteriorate. Unemployment in Essex, for example, was double the rate for the rest of the county in 1990. More-over, the minority population in the county had increased, albeit from a relatively small base, by 60 percent in the 1980s, while the increase in the Essex area was over 90 percent in that one decade (Lucas 1997). Despite the growing need for affordable housing, the county had resisted apply-ing for federal funds that carried requirements for building low-income housing. County officials rejected building public housing but welcomed privately owned, subsidized rental housing developments, and large num-bers of these developments had been placed in the declining areas of the county (Galster, Tatian, and Smith 1999; Lucas 1997; McDougall 1993).

After the official HUD announcement of the MTO agreement with the Housing Authority of Baltimore City in March 1994, a small number of county residents joined a new group, the Eastern Political Association (EPA), which decided to openly oppose MTO. EPA's stance was heavily influenced by media coverage that linked the impending demolition of some of Baltimore's worst public housing, through the HOPE VI redevel-opment program, with the arrival of MTO and the wider sense of decline and vulnerability in eastern Baltimore County communities.

EPA sponsored a number of community meetings with the purpose of distributing information against MTO. Central to this effort was their belief that the small numbers of MTO families—who would be widely dispersed across a large housing market—were not the only public hous-ing residents headed their way. "Many residents see MTO as the first step in a government plan to tear down the city's housing projects and move the residents to eastern Baltimore County," reported the *Baltimore Sun*.[18] Residents saw the claim that MTO would only fund vouchers for 145 families as a "smoke screen" concealing government plans to move in all 18,000 families in public housing. An anti-MTO poster in the town of Essex, naming some of the city's infamous inner-city housing projects, warned:

> HEAR US SHOUT. People living in drug and crime-infested Lafayette homes and Murphy homes could be moving to Essex. The Moving to Opportunity program could affect our neighborhoods, our schools, and the number of families receiving County social services. But this is not a racial issue. It is a matter of safety and quality education for Essex residents.

"Despite the small scale of the Baltimore MTO program," writes econo-mist George Galster and colleagues (1999:881), "it became a lightning rod for opponents of dispersed housing subsidy programs." For the increasingly vocal opponents, who soon turned a local Fourth of July parade into a de facto rally against MTO, the program symbolized forced integration and social engineering. To make matters worse, some County residents became convinced, thanks to the organized opposition, that "their economically depressed neighborhoods have been targeted to become new ghettos by well-paid, uncaring federal bureaucrats who live in wealthy suburbs far away."[19] One of the leaders of this movement, Jerry Hersl, explained his feelings to a reporter: "People here moved from Baltimore city, and they worked for that move. Now somebody could move in down the street, not have a job, get a 100-percent rent subsidy, and send their kids to the same school I'm sending my kids to. And that's not fair."[20]

HUD planners and Baltimore City housing officials attempted to address the rumors and angry opposition by participating in a public meeting held at a local high school on June 21, 1994. The planners brought maps to show that large portions of the eastern section of the county actually had poverty levels too high to qualify for MTO. However, after only a few minutes of presentation, HUD research director Margery Turner was interrupted by hecklers and peppered with questions from the audience of roughly 200. The meeting then "turned into a noisy, racially tinged free-for-all," as the press reported.[21] Some of the audience shouted out, "If they come here, we will riot and burn their houses down." Another said, "I don't want those low-income nobodies from Murphy Homes in my neighborhood." Nothing the government officials could say helped stem the anger and fears so palpable in that school auditorium.

After that, despite numerous statements by federal and some local officials, county political leaders convinced local residents that unwanted neighborhood change was soon going to be forced upon them. It was an election year, and almost every candidate for federal, state, or local office in the Baltimore County area expressed opposition to MTO. A candidate for the Maryland House of Delegates, for example, told a Baltimore County newspaper, "MTO is a Democratic project, and Republicans believe it is a total waste of taxpayers' money." A Democrat in the state house, Lou DePazzo, was quoted as saying that, while he didn't "have anything against the poor," many people in public housing were "undisciplined, unskilled, take dope, and have to be taught how not to steal." Another candidate stated, "I pledge to lead community efforts against any infringement of nuisance laws, health standards, or housing standards that may have been brought about by MTO. I also pledge to provide leadership in lobbying landlords in our community not to participate in MTO." The Republican candidate for governor, State Delegate Ellen Sauerbrey, stated that she too opposed the program as "social engineering" and added that "once you start messing around with people's property values, you're asking for trouble."

United States Senator Barbara Mikulski of Maryland had long been a staunch supporter of federal housing programs, and she was a key supporter of the HOPE VI program to redevelop distressed public housing. But MTO's local opponents quickly got to Kevin Kelly, Mikulski's lead staffer on housing issues, to argue that their suburbs were already struggling from the loss of local employment and that there simply were no jobs or real opportunities there for MTO families. No one at HUD, Kelly felt, was dealing with the problem, and MTO implementation had been botched in Baltimore. He pressured the HUD secretary to kill the program.

In a compromise measure, HUD agreed not to launch the *second* stage of MTO with funding that had already been appropriated. On September 3, 1994, a joint-conference committee on appropriations ended the provision that would have financed the second year of funding for MTO.[22] Senator Mikulski commented at the time that, "The program has been bungled by the city administration and by the group that was supposed to administer it.... There has not been enough consultation with the community out there. That has exacerbated discontent to the point that it would be only a hollow opportunity for the poor people in the program."[23] HUD kept MTO alive, but the agency had suffered a major, and very ugly, setback in its efforts to promote regional housing mobility, for example through expanded public housing desegregation across the nation.

As a reporter observed, "No one wants the poor around, particularly the black poor.... In the grim shadows of the post–civil rights era, the black poor have become our modern lepers. It's easy to understand those people in Dundalk and Essex: There is a lot of crime committed by poor blacks."[24] But the reporter also singled out the local politician for his role: "Instead of reasons (he) plucks fears. He brings stereotyping back into season. And his timing couldn't be more calculating." By March 1995, the *New York Times* had published MTO's obituary under the headline "Housing Voucher Test in Maryland is Scuttled by a Political Firestorm."[25]

MTO AND PUBLIC HOUSING REDEVELOPMENT AFTER THE FIRESTORM

Hostilities in Baltimore County cooled by late 1994, with virtually no public meetings or protests following the November election. Congress had responded quickly to the opposition and appeared to "cancel MTO." But the experiment did not end. It proceeded apace, without the planned, second-year expansion.[26] This progress included the greater Baltimore site: The intended number of families were counseled and moved. The largest, most systematic effort in American history to understand the effects of neighborhood context on the lives of low-income children and families has proceeded ever since, mostly out of the limelight. The keen interest in MTO after Hurricane Katrina is, as we described in the last chapter, the major exception.

In retrospect, the communities where opposition to MTO organized were right to be worried about government plans, which is not to say they are to be excused for the race or class bigotry that flared. The city did plan to demolish all of its public housing, and that demolition soon occurred, with large-scale relocations that did reach eastern parts of the county. HUD planners were naïve not to prepare for, and address, that larger prospect, which dwarfed MTO and fueled the view that the federal planners were heartless and out of touch. More generally, HUD was unprepared for NIMBYism as it launched the experiment. And even if the fears about MTO per se were based only on perception—there is very little evidence, after years of careful research, that assisted households drive down neighborhood property values, for example[27]—this naïveté is unfortunate. There is a long and virulent history of territorial opposition to low-income housing, and the belief that it leads inevitably to ghettoization, across the country.

None of the other MTO sites experienced any comparable opposition from community activists or elected officials. By way of epilogue: In the decade since MTO enrolled its last families, there have been no new federal proposals to initiate an MTO-like program, though civil rights lawsuits have spurred innovative desegregation initiatives in Dallas, Baltimore, and other localities (Briggs 2003; Popkin et al., 2003; Roisman 2007). And following the policy turnabout on "federal slums" that the Clinton years represented—under HUD Secretaries Henry Cisneros and Andrew Cuomo and their staffs—the administration of George W. Bush (2001–2008) reverted to the strategy of Presidents Reagan and Bush Sr. As severe housing needs grew among low-income renters nationwide (see chapter 4), the public housing and rental voucher budgets were slashed;[28] opportunity-focused housing mobility—as an aim of the voucher program—was ignored; desegregation complaints were contested; and the agency's response to Hurricane Katrina was widely attacked. In the ultimate blow to the agency and its leadership under President George W. Bush, a succession of corruption scandals led, in March 2008, to the resignation of HUD Secretary Alphonso Jackson.[29]

SUMMARY AND IMPLICATIONS

In act one of this story, a remarkable, court-ordered initiative to fight ghetto poverty and racial segregation in greater Chicago offered federal planners and policy makers what appeared to be a viable solution to an intractable problem. Academic research provided encouraging evidence that the approach was beneficial for the inner-city families who participated, not just administratively feasible or legally advisable. A persistent and skillful policy entrepreneur used that emergent body of research evidence, and hard-won experience about how to implement a housing opportunity initiative for the inner-city poor, to advance the idea of a national demonstration for "assisted housing mobility." That demo proposal became Moving to Opportunity.

That entrepreneur and his allies inside the bureaucracy successfully pushed HUD to act. Two HUD secretaries, one a Republican and the other a Democrat, accepted his advice and agreed to allocate substantial funding for both the program and a rigorous research effort. Winning this support was no small feat after decades of floundering, neglect, and, during the Reagan and Bush Sr. years, direct opposition to all racial desegregation efforts as well as most attempts to make innovative new investments in low-income housing. But basic compromises were made, in the outline of a new social experiment, that limited its reach in important ways: defining the fuzzy concept of an "opportunity" neighborhood, for example, as a census tract with a low poverty rate rather something more direct, such as an area with high-performing schools, job growth, or other traits.

In act two, a new and very supportive group of political appointees at HUD—President Clinton's team—embraced the MTO proposal as part of a larger portfolio of efforts to fight spatially concentrated "ghetto poverty." MTO was constructed then as a formal experiment, with rules for eligible "sending" neighborhoods (points of origin), eligible families on housing assistance, and eligible receiving areas (relocation destinations), among other key features of the program.

In act three, lacking a roadmap for a multisite program of this kind, and with limited information on how the families to be served might respond, HUD planners relied strongly on the one model available—Gautreaux— and it turned out to be a quite limited guide. For one thing, the families MTO would soon enroll were far more disadvantaged than the average Gautreaux family and far more so than federal planners had imagined. For another, "partnering" local public housing agencies with nonprofit counseling agencies was easier said than done. Local capacity to implement the experiment left much to be desired, and what is more, local implementers had their own ideas about what it would take to help the MTO families succeed. Some compromises were made between the formal experiment's need for consistency with strict protocols and the service providers' push to customize delivery according to client needs. As families began to relocate, it became clear that many low-poverty areas did not meet wider "opportunity" criteria. Some of the nonprofits, and one of the public housing agencies, were dismissed for nonperformance, and replacements were assigned. Virulent community opposition in Baltimore killed the second round of funding for the experiment and led to inaccurate headlines that it had been "scuttled." But the experiment chugged on, completing its intended placements after four long years (1994–1998).

Because the success of voucher-based assisted housing mobility programs, like that of the housing voucher program generally, hinges on a chain of cooperative action by landlords, tenants, housing agencies, and sometimes organized interest groups, Briggs and Turner (2006:59) conclude, "This element of the nation's opportunity agenda is particularly vulnerable to the strong-idea-weakly-implemented problem." Understanding crucial design decisions and implementation challenges, as well as the context in which they emerged, is important for that reason alone: Ideas deserve a "best shot" when they are to be tested with large public investments, and understanding how good a shot they have received is essential to interpreting the results of any test.

In the end, nearly 5,000 families participated, and about half of the experimental group successfully relocated to eligible neighborhoods, and the strict methodological requirements for a social experiment—including carefully managed random assignment, baseline surveys, and long-term tracking of participants—were effectively managed. The integrity of this MTO "research platform" has endured, and it provides the basis for our in-depth inquiry.

In the next chapter, we look at the uneven "playing fields" on which the experiences and choices of each MTO family unfolded—the five dynamic metropolitan areas that shaped the experiment's outcomes. The subsequent chapters look in depth at those outcomes, in the texture of families' lives and, as much as possible, in their own words.

Chapter 4

The Unequal Geography of Opportunity

Consider a simple thought experiment. There is a metropolitan area with many kinds of neighborhoods to choose from. Like the squares on a checkerboard, each neighborhood has clear boundaries that distinguish it from adjacent areas, and the major features of each neighborhood—the income and racial mix, safety, the quality of local schools and services available, access to jobs outside the area, and other traits—remain constant over time. At the center of the checkerboard is a city, and around that core are suburbs. Each family who volunteers for the Moving to Opportunity experiment is randomly assigned to relocate within this checkerboard. Each family stays in its new neighborhood for at least twenty years. From a research standpoint, the ideal version of the experiment enrolls only childless families who give birth after relocating—children who are raised, that is, from the cradle to early adulthood, in a single neighborhood that does not change over the course of the experiment. Researchers compare outcomes for these children over time.

The actual Moving to Opportunity experiment evolved in the real world, of course, and not under such controlled laboratory conditions. The squares in the checkerboard were not static, unchanging contexts for child and family development—anything but, as we show in this chapter. And the checkerboards themselves—the five local housing markets where MTO was launched—were themselves evolving as people migrated in and out, the regional economy restructured, the physical fabric got reshaped by public and private investment, shifts in tax and spending policies affected household budgets and options across the income spectrum, and schools and other institutions changed in dramatic ways—sometimes in remarkably short periods of time. Also, the high cost of housing, sickness and other life shocks, and the constraints associated with relying on government housing vouchers pushed many MTO families around on the checkerboard, leaving them with little room to maneuver.

MTO was created, as we showed in the last chapter, to test the power of place, and specifically the potential effect of relocating from one place to another, on the lives of extremely low-income families with children who were living in public housing in the early 1990s—some of the very poorest and most disadvantaged families in urban America. But places change, and families move on, as many families in the MTO experimental group did after the initial relocations triggered by the program (its rules let the families move after at least one year residing in place). The major forces defining places (contexts) and changing them over time were *structural* forces, that is, beyond the control of the MTO families, which is why we focus first on these forces. They often compelled the families, including those in the experimental group, to swim upstream.

FOUR MAJOR PATTERNS

What did these metaphorical checkerboards look like when MTO began, and how were they changing as families lived their lives and—in most cases—moved about? We briefly explore four major structural patterns.

First, and notwithstanding the economic crisis that had engulfed the nation by 2008, MTO was launched in five economically healthy metropolitan areas. This is the first key reference point for understanding the contexts that MTO families were navigating as the experiment unfolded. Although poverty rates in the inner-city public housing neighborhoods where MTO families were living in the early 1990s were extremely high, these metro areas were—and still are—part of a distinctive category: expensive metropolitan areas where much of the nation's economic growth is concentrated. MTO was not implemented in any declining regions—America still has many—that offer a lower cost of living as well as limited economic growth (or "negative growth").

Second, as a corollary, the poor are increasingly priced out of these regions and particularly the gentrifying downtowns and residential neighborhoods that have made a comeback over the past decade—with significant new investment and major increases in housing prices. These are highly unequal regions, where incomes have essentially been flat, for those on the bottom of the job market, for decades while the real cost of housing and other essentials for a decent life have increased sharply. While homeownership has commanded center stage in our culture as well as our policy debates, and while the mortgage meltdown generated the biggest shocks in the economy, the brutal gap between incomes and cost of living, for both the working and nonworking poor, has been most acute in the arena of rental housing. New supply has not kept up with growth in demand, yet rental housing, particularly entry-level rental housing affordable to low- and moderate-income families, remains the "neglected child" of U.S. housing policy, as long-term observers have put it (Downs 2007). Preservation has been especially overlooked: The nation loses more low-rent units each year, through demolition and other "erosion" of the stock, than it adds through all new affordable rental programs combined (Joint Center 2006a).

As we preview below and examine more closely in chapter 6, MTO families confronted tightening housing markets that grew more costly and challenging, especially for renters on the bottom, as the experiment unfolded. At the same time, federal program reforms made it easier for landlords to opt out of the voucher program and rent to higher income tenants.

Beyond the program, however, one byproduct of the broader rental housing crisis is *the wrong kind of housing mobility*: Unable to secure a safe and affordable home, low-income renters in America move much more often than others in the housing market, undermining stable connections to schools, health care providers, and other formal and informal sources of support—the very systems that MTO hoped low-income families would benefit from in "better" neighborhoods. The epidemic of foreclosures nationwide has had multiple spillover effects: forcing many renters out of their homes when landlords lost their properties, reducing rents in some markets, and adding many new renters (the former owners) to the pool of renters competing for units. (It is not yet clear how these changes have affected MTO families, since the crisis followed our fieldwork in the 2004–2005 period.)

Third, in addition to being highly unequal, the MTO regions, like most regions in America, continued to be highly segregated, by both race and income. And ghettoization—the social and economic isolation of the least favored neighborhoods—has persisted over the course of the experiment, even where the boundaries of the ghetto shifted somewhat. The extreme poverty concentration that helped motivate the launch of MTO—the number of neighborhoods with poverty rates of 40 percent or more—declined in most regions of the country in the 1990s, particularly in the formerly industrial Rust Belt. Major forms of racial segregation likewise declined somewhat in the nation's most segregated regions, including the MTO regions, over that decade. Yet local housing markets still offered highly unequal choices to families of different races and income levels, and this has powerful implications for access to job growth, safe and healthy environments, high-performing schools, and other opportunities. Conversely, in terms of exposure to *risk*, major disparities in exposure to violence, environmental hazards, poor schools, and other problems—disparities by income and even more so by race—are rooted in disparate housing options.

The shape of this disparity, in the literal sense of its geography, trended in a very specific way as MTO unfolded: Many urban neighborhoods became attractive to middle- and upper-income households and so "upgraded" again, while other urban neighborhoods, along with many neighborhoods in older suburbs, saw sharp increases in poverty and social distress. In programmatic terms, the "successful" movers in the MTO experimental group—those who managed to move from high- to low-poverty areas—tended to relocate to such transitional neighborhoods. They were successful only to a limited extent, as we explore in the chapters ahead.

The unequal geography of opportunity is a major challenge for our nation, which has—for more than a generation now—been getting more ethnically diverse and more economically unequal at the same time. This unequal geography helped ensure that MTO did not produce racial integration, as the court-ordered Gautreaux program had, simply by targeting low-poverty neighborhoods. It also put many MTO families in neighborhoods that had low poverty rates at the start of the experiment but were getting poorer over time—areas declining in ways that tend to offer more risks and fewer resources to newcomer parents and their children.

Fourth, in its current form, low-income housing assistance in America tends to reflect and reinforce, not improve, the unequal geography of opportunity. It does little to reduce segregation or mitigate its costly effects.[1] On one hand, this is the very reason that MTO was conceived, as we showed in the last chapter: to address, after years of neglect and half measures, the "federal slums" mired in the most destructive kind of poverty and isolation. But far more than planners of the experiment realized, the public housing and rental vouchers on which the experiment hinged provided families little room to maneuver—in the housing market, that is—in the face of the major structural forces outlined above. This fact, and not just the neglect of affordable rental housing generally, necessarily frames the discussion of how an ambitious social experiment *built on low-income housing subsidies* affected the families it intended to benefit.

SOME REGIONS ARE ECONOMICALLY VIBRANT—AND EXPENSIVE

The United States has 331 metro areas, and together they are home to eight in ten persons who live in our country. A large body of work has described the trends in metropolitan America, including population and job growth and contraction in recent decades[2], while a related and more complex literature has debated the causes and consequences of those changes. For our purposes, two patterns are critical. First, a host of factors—including migration patterns, the restructuring of industries in a global economy, policy decisions, climate, and other major forces—have favored some metro areas in America over others, meaning that some regions are vibrant while others, in the same nation, remain stagnant or in decline. Second, among the favored, perhaps two dozen U.S. metro regions are driving much of the nation's economic growth—and feature the highest costs of living. This presents back-breaking challenges for the poor, including the millions of working poor who help keep these regional economies afloat by working the least desirable, lowest paying jobs.

The five MTO metro areas—metropolitan Baltimore, Boston, Chicago, Los Angeles, and New York—are in that economically vibrant but expensive group. This remains true in spite of the economic crisis. While there are important differences among the five to be sure, these regions are winners, in relative terms, in a process of demographic and economic restructuring that has left large swaths of the country with flat or declining metro populations, and little or no economic growth, for decades or longer. Many of the latter are former industrial powerhouses, such as Flint, Michigan, and Gary, Indiana, that have not replaced the manufacturing jobs they lost. By contrast, the MTO regions are established economic magnets that have, to varying degrees, repositioned themselves successfully to compete on new terms, largely around high-wage export sectors, such as regional and international finance, trade, high technology, tourism, health care, and higher education—anchor industries that generate government, retail, construction, and other jobs in the local economy.[3]

The largest—metro Chicago, Los Angeles, and New York—are some of the most diversified regional economies in the world. The smaller MTO metros—Baltimore and Boston—are, in the former case, anchored by large government and information technology bases in Washington, DC, and Northern Virginia and, in the latter case, propelled by information and communications technology, biotech, world-renowned health care, and—tied to all of these knowledge-intensive sectors—the largest concentration of colleges and research universities in the world. As we outline below, there is extreme inequality within these regions, however. The continued decline of the city of Baltimore—its hollowing out amidst job loss, the drug trade, and gang-fueled violence—was the extreme case as MTO unfolded in that otherwise competitive region.

In some of the MTO regions, central cities and their suburbs have been growing—or bouncing back from earlier decline—together. Between 1990 and 2005, for example, the population of New York City grew 10.3 percent, reversing earlier decline, and Los Angeles grew 10.3 percent, while Chicago grew a modest 2.1 percent.[4] But the core of the Baltimore region continued to hollow out. Though the region expanded, the city's population continued the decline triggered by major industrial job loss in prior decades; the city lost about 100,000 people, or nearly 14 percent of its population, between 1990 and 2005. It is the one exception to the rule of high-cost cities in MTO. Boston's population dropped 2.6 percent, 15,000 people, over that period, as the job market rebounded and real estate boomed; many families left for lower cost communities.

Immigration is an important part of the urban population trend. Metro Chicago, Los Angeles, and New York are the initial destinations (gateways) for more than half of all immigrants to the United States, with central-city neighborhoods receiving a large share of this migrant wave—and the enormous economic activity it generates. Immigration contributed a third of all population growth in America in the 1990s. All of the nation's 100 largest cities would have shrunk in the 1990s if not for immigrant newcomers.

But economic magnetism has a down side, given the dramatic growth in income inequality in America since the 1960s. Because of strong demand, the MTO regions are among the nation's most expensive to live in and were getting more so as MTO unfolded. The Consumer Price Index rose 33 percent in metro Boston between 1997 and 2006, for example, compared to the national increase of 26 percent, and energy prices in the region increased the most (93 percent) over that period.[5] While inflation flattened as the economy went into recession in 2008, the long-run structural gap holds: Wages on the bottom of metro Boston's labor market, along with that of the other MTO metro areas—roughly comparable to wages in less prosperous regions of the country, in spite of the higher cost of living—have simply not kept up with the cost of living. Expensive housing, including rent and utilities, represents the biggest share of that cost and of that gap.

THE POOR ARE PRICED OUT, MOST OF ALL IN RENTAL HOUSING

Large and economically healthy metro regions show some of the worst economic inequality in an increasingly unequal nation, and one symptom of this is the "pricing out" of the poor.

To put the broader trend in perspective, between 1973 and 2000, the top 1 percent of taxpayers saw their incomes rise by 93 percent, and the top 5 percent group by 45 percent, while incomes of the poorest Americans declined, in real (inflation-adjusted) terms. In 2005 alone, the annual incomes of the top 1 percent rose more than 14 percent, to an average of $1.1 million. In the 1990s, though the economic boom lifted incomes for those on the bottom for the first time in decades, income inequality continued to increase, simply because gains were so much greater for those on the top of the income distribution. As sociologist Douglas Massey (2007:36, 40) observes:

> By the end of the twentieth century, all of the declines in inequality achieved during the New and Fair Deals [of the 1930s and 1950s] had been wiped out, and the United States had unambiguously returned to levels of inequality not seen since the laissez-faire era of the 1920s.

In 2005, the *New York Times* reported that the top fifth of earners in Manhattan made 52 times what the lowest fifth made in the prior year—about $366,000, on average, versus $7,000.[6] This income inequality takes on a distinctly racial character in many American cities, including the MTO sites. Los Angeles, for example, has the worst income inequality by race of any large city in the country—the product of very high incomes for the best-paid occupations, which are overwhelmingly white, and a massive, low-wage, largely nonunionized labor force that is overwhelmingly non-white (Bobo, Oliver, Johnson, and Valenzuela 2000; Milkman 2006).

While high health care costs—and, more recently, surging food and energy prices—tend to garner more headlines, housing is the biggest living expense for most families. The fact that poor people are increasingly priced out of economically healthy metropolitan areas is particularly severe in the arena of rental housing. The trend has worsened since MTO was launched, and this is enormously significant, since the experiment—and the larger rental voucher program, America's dominant approach to meeting the housing needs of low-income families—rests on the assumption that decent, affordable apartments are *available* in the private market. We focus briefly on the key national patterns, then the conditions in the MTO housing markets. But chapter 6 revisits this theme from the street-level perspective: the lived experiences of the MTO families who struggled to find decent apartments in decent neighborhoods as markets grew tighter around them.

Scholarly research and government reports have highlighted a severe lack of affordable rental housing, particularly for those with very low incomes, for more than two decades.[7] A major contributor is the loss of low-rent units from the nation's housing stock. Some 1.2 million low-rent units—units costing $400 or less per month, including utilities—were lost between 1993 and 2003, for example (Joint Center for Housing Studies 2006b). Meanwhile, the number of households experiencing "worst-case housing needs," has increased sharply, surging by 16 percent, or some 817,000 households, between 2003 and 2005 alone (U.S. HUD 2007).[8] Families with children saw the largest increase—475,000 households—and a large share of those family households (41 percent) faced worst-case housing needs in spite of being employed full time. A total of nearly 6 million households had worst-case housing needs in 2005,[9] 91 percent of them based on severe rent burden, and two-thirds of all extremely low-income renter households in America (those living at 30 percent of the area median income level or below) had worst-case needs.[10] This was up from about 3.6 million households in 1978, when HUD first reported the data (Quigley and Raphael 2004). But affordability problems affect a much broader swath of renters: in 2005, nearly half (45.7 percent) of all renters were spending more than 30 percent of their income—the federal threshold of affordability—on housing costs.

It is easy to forget, in the face of such statistics, that affordability is about the gap between income and housing costs, between what the labor market pays (for the majority of low-income people, who are employed) and what the housing market supplies at a given price. So the "housing" problem has long included a very big earned income problem: Too few jobs in our economy pay wages sufficient to rent or buy decent housing in good locations. In her best-selling *Nickel and Dimed* (2001), for example, journalist Barbara Ehrenreich, who tried to get by on minimum-wage jobs in three different regions of the country, vividly captured the near-impossibility of juggling dead-end jobs and high-cost, often unfit housing.

On average, a parent working full-time had to earn $17.32 per hour in 2007, or about three times the federal minimum wage, in order to afford a "modest" two-bedroom home or apartment, by federal standards (Pelletiere, Wardrip, and Crowley 2008).[11] That minimum "housing wage" was much higher in many of the nation's strongest metropolitan economies, including the MTO markets on which our study focused: more than $26 per hour in metro Boston, $25 in metro Los Angeles, and $25.35 in metro New York. Rates were somewhat lower for the other two MTO sites: $19.48 per hour in metro Baltimore and $18.15 in metro Chicago. But all of these asking rents are far more than the federal minimum wage—and will remain so even after planned increases in that minimum.

According to leading housing economists, the gap between real, inflation-adjusted incomes and real housing costs, adjusted for changes in the size of the average American housing unit, has grown substantially since the 1960s—but only for low-income households (Quigley and Raphael 2004). Figure 4.1 shows how disproportionately severe housing-cost burdens fall on lower income groups in America—but also how the burden spikes upward for the *lowest* income quintile in particular, wherein households pay a staggering 78 percent of their pre-tax income, on average, to meet the costs of housing (and see Belsky and Drew 2007).

A substantial driver of the long-run, upward pressure on housing prices is the breakdown, in many housing markets, in what economists call *supply response*: the response of supply to demand that should bring a market into equilibrium, for example, where population or income growth is driving up demand for housing (Glaeser, Gyourko, and Saks 2006; Quigley and Raphael 2004; Schill 2005). In the 1950s alone, Los Angeles expanded its housing stock by nearly 60 percent and New York City by 20 percent. Yet since 1960, new construction, as measured by permit requests, has fallen off sharply in many large metropolitan areas,

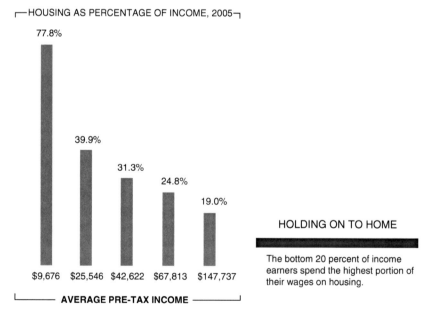

Figure 4.1 Housing Cost Burden by Income Quintile, 2005

Source: Bureau of Labor Statistics

especially in high-value markets (Glaeser, Gyourko, and Saks 2005). Land values in these increasingly built up and restrictive local jurisdictions—both cities and their suburbs—plus high growth in construction costs in some markets have made the cost of building new housing rise much faster than median incomes.[12] In 2005, 203,000 multifamily rental units were added, while 195,000 units were lost through demolition or conversion to condos—for a net growth of just 8,000 units in the entire country. Only 12 percent of the newly built rental units in America had asking rents of $650 or less (Joint Center for Housing Studies 2006).

Growth restrictions reflect deeply entrenched political preferences as well as race and class stereotypes, not just the unintended consequences of regulations that are meant, say, to safeguard the environment or otherwise improve the quality of local development (Danielson 1976; Pendall 2007; Pendall et al. 2005).[13] Local political resistance to new construction of moderately priced, multifamily rental housing—as opposed to luxury condominium units—is particularly widespread. The mere mention of building "apartments" is enough to send many a suburban zoning hearing into frenzy (Fischel 2001; Pendall 2007).

Tied to the upward pressure on rents is what we referred to above as the wrong kind of housing mobility. While residential mobility has declined for most demographic groups in America in recent decades, it has increased for low-skill, low-income households. They are much more likely than higher skill counterparts to be renters, who move four to five times as often as owners, and to make *involuntary* moves, for example, because of job loss, death, divorce, eviction, fire, unaffordable mortgage or rent, or nonrenewal of lease, such as when a property is sold (Fischer 2002; Schacter 2001). Involuntary moves and the long-run loss of housing affordable to the lowest income households may help explain why children move much more often in the United States than in other wealthy nations (Long 1992). This gap reminds us that some forms of residential mobility, especially frequent moving in search of a secure and affordable setting, can be a big negative for families.[14]

Drawing on fieldwork among low-income African Americans, recent research and family interventions have emphasized the importance of securing "the homeplace"—comprising "individual and family processes that are anchored in a defined physical place and that elicit feelings of empowerment, rootedness, ownership, safety, and renewal" (Burton et al. 2004:397)—and the difficulty that many of the nation's most vulnerable families face in securing such a homeplace. Frequent moves converge with other risks to create a cumulative set of stressors affecting poorer children and adults (Quane et al., 2008).

How did the MTO markets reflect these national trends in housing affordability? Four of the five MTO sites had tight housing markets before the demonstration began, and they remained significantly tighter than the national average over the course of the demonstration (figure 4.2). In 1990, only Chicago's vacancy rate essentially matched the national rate, with Baltimore and Boston close behind. Los Angeles and New York were, even at that recessionary point, at or below the 4–6 percent vacancy rates estimated for the typical rental market's "natural" vacancy rate, that is, equilibrium corresponding to no downward or upward pressure on real rents (Gabriel and Nothaft 1988, 2001). By the end of the decade, as rental markets grew tighter in many metros nationwide, vacancy rates plummeted in all five MTO metros and most of all in those places that began the decade as tighter markets. Greater Boston, L.A., and New York—our study sites—became extremely tight, with vacancies in the 3–4 percent range, and in the L.A. case, the trend toward an ever-greater scarcity of vacant rentals persisted into the new decade, right through the early 2000s recession.

Research has shown that it is much more difficult to lease apartments using federal rental vouchers in such tight markets (Finkel and Buron 2001) and also that while most households are able to use vouchers to find an affordable apartment, the national success rate declined from 81 percent to 69 percent over the past two decades (Katz and Turner 2007). Not only were there fewer available apartments, relative to demand, in very tight markets, but landlords appeared less willing to accept subsidized tenants—confident that they could find reliable, *un*subsidized tenants and avoid the hassles of dealing with government-required housing unit inspections, payment processing, and eviction procedures.

As figure 4.3 shows, trends in HUD-designated fair market rents (FMRs), based on local market surveys, mirror the vacancy rate trends.

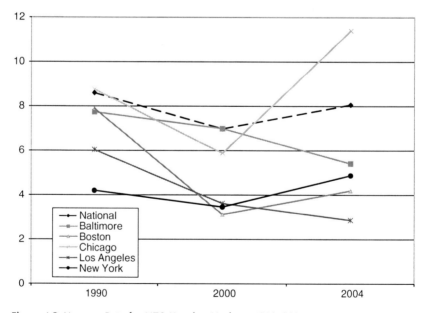

Figure 4.2 Vacancy Rate for MTO Housing Markets, 1990–2004

Our three study sites began and remained the most expensive of the five MTO metropolitan housing markets, clustered in the $1100 to $1300 per month range by 2006. Los Angeles saw gross rents jump 13 percent between 2000 and 2004 alone, compared to the national increase of 6 percent, while Boston and New York saw sharp increases (9 percent) as well.

As housing costs rose, HUD made things tougher on families receiving low-income housing assistance. For example, payment ceilings and other features of the rental voucher program that were designed to respond to tight markets were frozen in place or cut back in order to reduce federal spending. Earlier reforms made it easier for landlords to opt out of the voucher program as prices jumped in the market. Very tight rental markets are simply not friendly to the rental voucher program, much less a demonstration aiming to give voucher users a secure foothold in safer, more resource-rich neighborhoods. And MTO did not include mechanisms to shift these incentives.[15]

By 2004, when we first visited MTO families, the rental markets in Los Angeles and New York were imposing very widespread hardships. Based on county-level data from the American Community Survey, more than half of *all* Los Angeles and New York City renters (54 percent and 51 percent respectively), and nearly half in Baltimore, Boston, and Chicago (48 percent), paid more than 30 percent of their income for housing, compared to the national rate of 44 percent of renters (who paid more than 30 percent). Each of the five MTO markets saw an 8 percent jump in that hardship rate between 2000 and 2004 alone—twice the national increase.

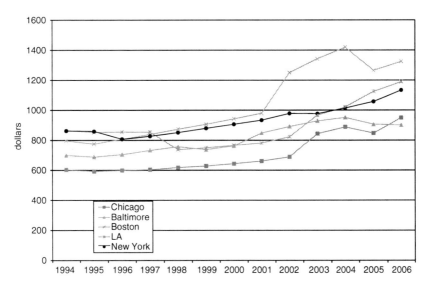

Figure 4.3 Fair Market Rents (FMRs) for MTO Housing Markets, 1994–2006

Source: U.S. Department of Housing and Urban Development, "FMR HUD History 1983–Present," two-bedroom data. Note: Geographies are FMR areas.

Average asking rents are much higher in the central cities than these metro-wide figures suggest, and they continued to climb through the onset of the foreclosure crisis and the slowdown in home sales: Industry researchers reported an average asking rent for Boston that increased more than 4 percent to $1,650 in the first quarter of 2007, compared with a year earlier. In New York City, average monthly asking rents increased 7 percent over the same period, to a staggering $2,605, as the already low vacancy rate of 2.8 percent dropped to 2.5 percent.

In sum, while three of the five MTO markets—metro Boston, Los Angeles, and New York—are notably tighter and more expensive than the other two, the broad pattern is one that prices lower income people out of the very cities and suburbs that offer economic growth. The net result of growing demand in the face of near-static supply is higher rents. These rents are out of reach for millions of Americans, including millions of low-wage workers drawn to the nation's economic engines—its vibrant metropolitan economies. In turn, higher rents in dynamic markets spell more involuntary mobility among the poor and near poor—the lack of a secure and stable place to call home—as well. In effect, MTO aimed to learn about the effects of living in "better" neighborhoods just as those places were priced further out of the reach of low-income families.

HOUSING MARKETS REMAIN HIGHLY SEGREGATED BY INCOME AND RACE

Beyond being costly and highly unequal, in terms of incomes and housing burden, America's cities and suburbs remain highly segregated by income and race—far more so than those of any other wealthy nation. This profoundly affects the housing options available to all families but especially to low-income and minority families, such as those who volunteered for MTO. When they entered the experiment, MTO families were obliged to strive against the forces that persistently segregate our housing markets. This is true for all three treatment groups in the demonstration, but its effects are most evident for the experimental group—the relocation group randomly assigned to make "moves to opportunity"—as we show in chapter 6.

Using census data from 1950 to 2000, sociologists Douglas Massey and Mary Fischer (2003) find that income segregation increased within metropolitan areas—that is, at the level of neighborhoods and local jurisdictions—over the past half century.[16] On the other hand, within any *given* metropolitan area, people of different incomes were less likely to share the same neighborhoods in the year 2000 than in 1970 or 1950. The trend is not limited to one racial group; for example, using the top and bottom fifths of the income distribution to describe "rich" and "poor" (respectively), the segregation of the rich from the poor increased

34 percent among whites and 27 percent among blacks between 1970 and 2000. There is an expanded class divide within each racial group, then, as well as a greater tendency in general for people with different financial resources, social contacts, political habits, and housing options to live apart within local housing and job markets.

Yet with the exception of the West, extreme poverty concentration in metropolitan areas—the ghetto poverty phenomenon we introduced in chapter 2, which is rarely experienced by the white poor—declined sharply across the country in the 1990s. The number of persons living in neighborhoods that were 40 percent or more poor declined from 4.8 to 3.5 million over the period (Jargowsky 2003). The number of extremely poor census tracts also declined sharply, most of all in Rust Belt areas of the Northeast and Midwest, while the number of moderately poor (20–40 percent poor) tracts expanded significantly (Kingsley and Pettit 2003).[17] This was in part because the number of poor families dropped (via income gains) and in part because of residential mobility patterns: higher income households moving in to gentrify urban neighborhoods, for example, and lower income households moving out. There is some evidence of reconcentration since,[18] and the nation's economic crisis could affect these patterns in a variety of ways.

As table 4.1 shows, blacks and Hispanics in four of the five MTO metro areas saw big drops in the share concentrated in extremely poor neighborhoods; metro Los Angeles was the striking exception.[19] The MTO metro areas also differ sharply in the number of extremely poor or poor tracts "available" as housing options (data not shown). In metro Boston, for example, by 2000, 90 percent of *all* households lived in neighborhoods with a poverty rate under 20 percent, while only about two-thirds of all households did so in metro New York (63 percent) and Los Angeles (67 percent). The city of Boston had just 12 extremely poor neighborhoods, while New York City had 248 and Los Angeles 103.

Table 4.1. Change in Extreme Concentration of Poverty by Race in MTO Metropolitan Areas, 1990–2000

Metropolitan Statistical Area	Blacks			Hispanics		
	1990 Share	2000 Share	% Change	1990 Share	2000 Share	% Change
Baltimore	34.7	21.5	−38	9.7	3.5	−63.9
Boston	12.5	6.2	−50.4	10.7	8.1	−24.3
Chicago	45.3	26.4	−41.7	12.4	4.7	−62.1
Los Angeles	17.2	21.3	23.8	9.1	16.9	85.7
New York	40.1	32.5	−18.9	40.9	32.2	−21.3

Source: Jargowsky (2003), table 3. Shares are percentages of the racial group who live in census tracts with poverty rates of 40 percent or more.

Poverty shifted somewhat, away from resurgent, in-demand urban neighborhoods and toward older suburbs, particularly in the nation's 100 largest metropolitan areas. There, between 1980 and 2000, the number of suburban census tracts with poverty rates of 30 percent or higher grew 89 percent, and the number of poor residents more than doubled, according to the census. As political scientist Peter Dreier observed in the *Nation* magazine in 2004, "Stereotypes about the 'inner-city poor' and the 'suburban middle class' no longer reflect how we live."[20] One MTO mother who had moved to an inner suburb of Boston described the trend to us more bluntly: "I left the ghetto, but the ghetto followed me."

In another reflection of the spatial pecking order, cities and suburbs lost a large number of middle-income neighborhoods over the past generation, further dividing local housing markets into low-income versus high-income areas. While middle-income neighborhoods constituted 58 percent of all metropolitan neighborhoods in 1970, they had declined to 41 percent of the total by 2000; in the central cities of the 12 largest metro areas, the drop was much sharper: from 45 to 23 percent (Galster, Cutsinger, and Booza 2006).[21] Lower income families also became more likely to live in lower income areas over this period: where 55 percent had lived in middle-income neighborhoods in 1970, only 37 percent did so in 2000.

Middle-income areas that might have served as affordable entry points for relocating MTO families declined sharply in the highly unequal markets we studied: from 42 to 30 percent in New York City over the period, for example. Among the 100 largest metro areas, only Los Angeles (28.3 percent) ranked lower than New York (29.6 percent) in the share of neighborhood representing a middle-income option. Boston ranked somewhat higher, with 44.5 percent.

The unequal housing market pattern also reflects persistently high racial segregation. This segregation is only partially explained by income differences among races, that is, by racial differences in ability to pay for particular kinds of housing in particular places (Schill and Wachter 1995). Beyond reflecting a distinct class divide, then, housing markets remain distinctly "color coded," as sociologist Camille Charles (2005), who studies racial attitudes and the neighborhood make-up preferences of different racial groups, puts it.

Beyond the preferences of minority households for a social and psychological "comfort zone" created by having people of one's own racial or ethnic background as neighbors, racial segregation reflects active discrimination in the real estate market and—often—the avoidance by whites of neighborhoods with even a modest minority presence. Illegal discrimination includes real estate professionals steering minority homebuyers to different neighborhoods than white homebuyers, landlords misleading minority callers to think that advertised rental units are no longer available for rent, providing differential leasing or financing terms, and other practices (Turner and Ross 2005; Yinger 1995). Meanwhile, white avoidance of more racially integrated areas (when whites are on the market for a new home) has a far greater impact than so-called white flight from neighborhoods undergoing racial change (Ellen 2000). White avoidance—when not steered by a real estate agent—is perfectly legal, though it undermines the quest for a more integrated society and makes it less likely that low-income minority homeseekers in particular, such as those in MTO, will be able to find communities that are racially integrated and remain so.

The latest decennial census provided a very mixed picture of segregation levels and trends in the United States at the turn of a new century. On one hand, rates of the most commonly used metric of segregation (unevenness of population distribution across census tracts) in the most hypersegregated metro areas—rates of black segregation from whites, most of all in older cities of the Northeast and Midwest—continued to fall in the 1990s (though not in New York). This continued a three decade-long trend and, in national terms, represented a drop in black/nonblack segregation to its lowest point since 1920 (Glaeser and Vigdor 2001). In general, neighborhoods that integrated black and white households became much more numerous, as well as more stable, in the 1980s as compared to the 1970s (Ellen 2000, 2007). Over three-fourths (76.3 percent) of tracts integrated by 1980 remained so by 1990, while 16.6 percent of those tracts became majority black and 7 percent predominantly white. Many integrated neighborhoods continued to be mixed in the 1990s. The continued decline of black/white segregation during the 1990s appears to have come primarily from the partial integration of neighborhoods that were once exclusively white, not significant rates of white in-moving into minority neighborhoods (Rawlings, Harris, and Turner 2004).

At the same time, black/white segregation rates remain distressingly high in absolute terms, particularly in Rust Belt cities of the Northeast and Midwest. This includes four of the five MTO markets: metro Baltimore, Boston, Chicago, and New York. These are some of the nation's most racially segregated markets. For its part, metro Los Angeles saw an increase in Hispanic/white segregation.

In terms of exposure, the average white in U.S. cities and suburbs lives in a neighborhood that is overwhelmingly white—about 84 percent—and thus offers little exposure to other racial/ethnic groups. Nationally, the average black family earning over $60,000 per year lives in a neighborhood with a higher poverty rate and lower educational attainment than the average white family earning less than $30,000 (Logan 2001). Furthermore, blacks remain more segregated from whites than do Asians or Hispanics.[22] Not only is the median rate of segregation higher for blacks nationwide, but the black/white rates range upward to extremes that Hispanics and Asians do not experience in any metro area (table 4.2).[23]

Yet even middle-income immigrants are relatively isolated from white neighborhoods—a pattern that is even more evident for blacks. Furthermore, some of the fastest growth in immigrant and black suburbanization

Table 4.2. Segregation by Race, 1990–2000 Index of dissimilarity (D), 330 U.S. Metropolitan Areas

	White-Black	White-Hispanic	White-Asian
Maximum index	84.7	75.4	58.8
Median index	52.3	38.2	35.2
Minimum index	20.2	11.6	14.5
Change in median index, 1990–2000	−6.2	−4.6	−11.8

Source: Authors' calculations using Lewis Mumford Center (University at Albany) census datafile.

Note: Dissimilarity (D) measures unevenness in two population distributions (whites versus blacks, say), on a 100-point scale. The index indicates the percentage of either group that would need to move in order to make the racial composition of each neighborhood (census tract) match that of the metro area as a whole. Higher scores thus reflect greater unevenness (higher segregation). On measures of segregation, see Massey, White, and Phua (1996).

is occurring in "at-risk" suburbs that feature school failure, weak fiscal capacity, and other problems long associated with vulnerable cities (Orfield 2002)—and now a heavy concentration of foreclosures as well. One reason is that neighborhoods with concentrations of minority homeowners were targeted heavily by "predatory" subprime lenders (Apgar and Calder 2005). When MTO families reached the suburbs at all, it was almost always to these vulnerable suburbs, as we explore in chapter 6, not to the upper tier of communities (and school districts) within each metro region.

The costs of segregation, for MTO families and for millions more nationwide, are multidimensional, reflecting lower access by racial and ethnic minorities to high-performing schools, the job growth that has centered on suburban America for several decades now, and safe and healthy communities. Health researchers have shown a particularly strong interest, in recent years, in the "social determinants" of health—such as being able to live in a safe and environmentally healthy neighborhood—after a half-century focus, in the field, on behavioral determinants of health, such as good diet and exercise, and on improved treatment once illnesses have been diagnosed. High-risk, segregated neighborhoods can affect health in a variety of ways, from higher rates of pollution and other environmental health hazards to greater violence, poorer access to care, the long-run effects of stressful living conditions—what experts have termed "weathering" (Ellen, Mijanovich, and Dillman 2001)—and other factors (Acevedo-Garcia 2003; Krieger 1994).

Over the course of MTO's first decade, then, the low-income families in the program, including the experimental group for whom expectations were highest, found themselves struggling in high-cost, segregated markets—some of the nation's most expensive, in fact, and most segregated by race and income. What is more, they were doing so with limited help from the low-income housing assistance that was supposed to *expand* the geography of opportunity open to them.

LOW-INCOME HOUSING ASSISTANCE OFTEN COMPOUNDS THE PROBLEM

Since America's landmark Housing Act of 1949, and in policy statements made regularly ever since, the goal of U.S. housing policy has been to provide "a decent home" as well as a "suitable living environment" to every family in the country (Newman and Schnare 1997). In chapter 2, we showed how and why many inner-city public housing projects had, by the 1960s, come to fail on the latter dimension—and how, by the 1980s, the failures had become catastrophic, especially in big cities, making the projects deadly war zones in a gang-dominated drug trade.

Nationally, the federal government's largest program for addressing low-income housing needs—the rental housing voucher program formerly known as Section 8—does much better, on average, than public housing at subsidizing housing costs for very low-income families outside of ghetto-poor neighborhoods and even outside of central cities. The voucher program also does better than most of the other supply-side housing programs, which have focused increasingly, since the 1970s, on private and nonprofit management of small to medium-sized apartment buildings.[24] The typical development financed by these important programs, which often do not serve the lowest income renters,[25] is in a moderately poor, moderately segregated urban neighborhood. Yet only a relatively small share of voucher users, particularly if they are racial minorities, live in low poverty or racially integrated areas. And in general, the best available data on trajectories over time indicates that assisted households—a category that combines vouchers with public housing and other supply-side programs—tend to move from poor or extremely poor areas to other poor areas, and only rarely to more advantaged areas.[26]

In terms of reducing *housing cost burden*—the main reason vouchers were created a generation ago—the program is among the most successful social policies in America, according to assessments by federal budget authorities and others.[27] Yet it falls short of most hopes in terms of neighborhood quality. Like other forms of low-income housing assistance, vouchers have often exacerbated, not mitigated, segregation in housing. In chapter 7, we show why. There, we address a major puzzle that has dogged the MTO experiment so far: If many families who initially "escaped" high-poverty neighborhoods, thanks to the program, have struggled to stay out of them, was it mainly because of choices they made—for example, wanting to live closer to loved ones, even if it meant returning to much poorer, more dangerous neighborhoods—because of forces beyond their control, or a bit of both?

SUMMARY AND IMPLICATIONS

Although leaving behind some of the most distressed and dangerous neighborhoods in America represented a "move to security" for MTO families who relocated with a housing voucher—the boon that is the focus of the next chapter—these families were forced to swim upstream against the factors that reproduce extreme economic inequality, and also a very segregated geography of opportunity, in America. First, with the important exception of declining Baltimore, MTO operated in economically healthy but very high cost metropolitan markets. Our three study sites—Boston, Los Angeles, and New York—illustrate this at the extreme. The poor are increasingly priced out of these places, and the safety net is weak. As the latest recession has underscored, economic insecurity—a much broader condition than poverty—has been extending up the income ladder, forcing many middle-class families to face a measure of what the poor have endured for so long.

Second, while other issues receive more attention from the public, the media, and the policy establishment, the fact that poor people are priced out of these economically vibrant regions is nowhere more evident than in the rental housing arena. This is a particularly acute, and largely unaddressed, feature of the broader, dual-economy pattern. As the nation continues to undo the New Deal formula of large-scale subsidized rental housing developments, we face a crisis that will loom, whether recognized or not, over any discussion of a reinvigorated "opportunity agenda" in America: The gap between incomes on the bottom and the supply of housing at affordable rents has grown dramatically, in real, inflation-adjusted terms, since the 1960s. The shortfall is massive in many housing markets. Even the most progressive proposals for raising the minimum wage and supplementing it with tax credits or other transfers now fall short of asking rents in the metro regions where most of the country's economic growth is taking place.

Third, though the extreme poverty concentration that helped motivate MTO declined dramatically in the 1990s, economic and racial segregation—the twin foundations of ghetto poverty—persisted through the decade and into the 2000s, over the experiment's first decade. This confronted MTO movers with a far more restricted and starkly divided set of housing choices than planners had hoped.

Fourth and finally, low-income housing assistance has tended to exacerbate, not mitigate, this unequal geography of housing opportunity. Politicized siting decisions at the local level have concentrated most subsidized housing developments—even many of the newest and most attractive ones managed by private and nonprofit agencies—in moderately poor, relatively segregated urban neighborhoods, excluding them from more affluent areas of cities as well as exclusionary suburbs. But even vouchers, which, on paper, should maximize housing choice in the much larger market of private rental housing, typically channel the very low-income families who use vouchers to relatively poor and segregated areas. Gautreaux is among the few well-documented exceptions, and in hindsight, its success may have given MTO planners too much faith in the power of a voucher subsidy supplemented by some relocation counseling.

Perhaps it should not surprise us, then, that many MTO families who escaped dangerous, high-poverty areas—the great *initial* achievement of the experiment—struggled to stay out of such areas as MTO unfolded. In the next few chapters, we examine, respectively, the glass-is-half-full and glass-is-half-empty aspects of that pattern, tackling the how and why puzzles that motivated our work with MTO families.

Chapter 5

Moving to Security

TWO WORLDS

Denise and her children have lived in a quiet, low-poverty neighborhood near the Los Angeles airport since the late 1990s, when she used her Moving to Opportunity (MTO) voucher to move out of one of L.A.'s most notorious public housing projects. Denise grew up in public housing and, before MTO was announced, had become increasingly concerned about the negative effects that living in such a crime-ridden environment was having on her children. She is very happy with her current neighborhood. She sees it as safe and secure—an excellent place to raise her two sons, Wesley, 16, who is a junior in high school, and Shawn, 21. She explains:

> You don't walk down the street and see people gambling on the corner or people drinking on the corner, you know, stuff like that...Everybody pretty much works and take care of business. I mean that is what they [my kids] see.... There is nothing to steer them, you know, towards anything other than good as far as I can see around here.

Contrast Denise's positive picture of her neighborhood with the fortunes of Beverly and her daughter Tonya, who were living in public housing when we met them in 2004. Beverly also received an MTO experimental voucher and moved to a low-poverty neighborhood. She chose one in the San Fernando Valley but soon found life out there too isolating and moved back to Watts, in South L.A. The family ended up losing their voucher, briefly became homeless, moved back into public housing, and in short order, ended up back in the development where they had started. Tonya, who was only 16 when we met her in 2004, was pregnant. Beverly's younger son was in boot camp for armed robbery, and her older son was a gang member legally barred from living with the family because of his arrest record. The picture Tonya painted of life in her development, especially for girls, was starkly brutal:

> Foul. Just like in any other projects....They'll call [women] B's [bitches], ho's, tramps, sluts, stuff like that. They don't care. They don't have no respect for females at all. They beat up females over here and all that, throw them out of windows. Oh, my God. These projects is crazy. They throw their girlfriends out of windows and everything else, pull out guns on them and stuff. They don't really too much care for females over here.

In this chapter, we explore what leaving such troubled communities and moving to security has meant for lucky MTO families. We focus first on the overall benefits and then on the puzzling finding that this dramatic life change seems to have affected adolescent girls and boys in very different ways. As we discussed in chapter 1, MTO families moved from some of the nation's worst inner-city public housing projects—developments such as the one Tonya describes, where drugs are rampant and violence is commonplace. The developments in Chicago and Los Angeles were especially notorious, dominated by those cities' powerful gangs—the Gangster Disciples, Latin Kings, Bloods and Crips—but the situation in the other MTO cities was little better. The problems in many large, inner-city public housing developments were long-standing. Rainwater (1970) and his colleagues found a community overwhelmed with crime and disorder in St. Louis' Pruitt-Igoe in the 1960s. Likewise, Gautreaux participants in Chicago, who moved out of public housing in the late 1970s and early 1980s, were still traumatized by the violence years later, and many talked to researchers about improved safety as the most important benefit of leaving (Rubinowitz and Rosenbaum 2000). In a seminal study of children growing up in war zones, Garbarino and colleagues (1991) considered the trauma and psychological damage for children growing up in Chicago's public housing high rises to be on par with that experienced by children who lived through civil wars in other countries.

The consequences of living with chronic fear of crime are serious, leading to extreme stress and sometimes to social isolation for residents (Perkins and Taylor 1996). Because of the extreme physical concentration of problems, the effects of living in highly distressed public housing are particularly severe and have serious consequences for mental health (Roman et al. 2009). Beyond the projects, moreover, research indicates that living in dangerous, high-poverty neighborhoods is especially harmful for children and adolescents, putting them at risk for poor physical and mental health, early and risky sexual behavior, and involvement in delinquent and criminal activities.[1] In particular, exposure to violence can have profound—and lingering—effects on children's mental health and development (Kilpatrick et al. 2003).

But the risks in these war zone environments are somewhat different for boys than girls. Boys growing up in these communities are at greater risk for delinquency than girls and face pressure to be tough; girls face pressure for early sexual initiation and the risk of sexual violence, as well as the possibility of pregnancy. All children are at risk for dropping out of school and having trouble in finding work. Severely distressed public housing developments, such as those the MTO families came from, are among the worst environments for children—and adults—in the nation. Their residents are likely to suffer some of the worst consequences of concentrated poverty and racial segregation. Adding to the misery, because of years of poor management and neglect, these developments were often plagued with maintenance problems—broken plumbing and heating, infestations of vermin—and were littered with trash and debris and covered with gang graffiti.

Many public housing developments in America are not nearly so distressed, of course, but tens of thousands of families, including those who volunteered for MTO, struggled to raise their children in these horrific conditions, often because they had no alternative. The crime, poor maintenance and security, and changes to rent policy had driven many working families out of these developments, leaving the poorest and most vulnerable families behind. The damage to the residents who endured—and sometimes contributed to—the misery was profound. Many were addicted to drugs, abused or neglected by drug-addicted parents, killed or injured in the drug wars, arrested or incarcerated, or simply traumatized by the stress of coping with the constant violence and disorder in distressed projects (Popkin et al., 2000). As we previewed in chapter 2, the design of these developments made them ideal territory for gangs and their drug dealing. When combined with ineffective policing, criminals were easily able to dominate these communities. And in many cities, including the five MTO sites, the crack epidemic of the late 1980s and early 1990s swept through public housing developments like a storm.

By 1992, a National Commission on Severely Distressed Public Housing had declared that hundreds of inner-city public housing developments were "severely distressed" and that the nation needed a bold, new approach to address the multiple challenges of crumbling buildings, devastated neighborhoods, and vulnerable residents (National Commission 1992). The $6 billion HOPE VI program grew out of the Commission's recommendations, providing funding to replace many of these developments with new, mixed-income housing intended to both revitalize neighborhoods and provide new opportunities for residents (Popkin et al., 2004). Ironically, given the design of the MTO experiment and its intent to compare the experiences of voucher holders and public housing residents over time, many of the developments that MTO families came from were eventually targeted for HOPE VI. Some participants who did not relocate initially (through the program), either because they failed to "lease up" with their MTO voucher or because they were assigned to the control group, ended up moving later, because their development was being torn down. At the interim evaluation point, some four to seven years after enrolling in MTO, about 70 percent of the control group had moved out of public housing.

LOOKING FOR A WAY OUT

In the mid-1990s, HOPE VI was just getting underway, and MTO offered families a chance to escape distressed projects. Over 5,300 of them volunteered for it. Not surprisingly, given the overwhelming crime plaguing their communities, when participants enrolled in the program, the most common reason they cited for signing up was to get their families away from drugs and gangs (Orr et al., 2003). As we showed in chapter 3, the planners who designed MTO hoped that helping public housing families move to lower poverty, more resource-rich neighborhoods would spur the kinds of employment and educational outcomes that Gautreaux families experienced. Early on, the planners thought that parents might choose MTO primarily because they sought those better opportunities, especially better schools for their children. Instead, many MTO parents were focused on safety first, last, and always, viewing getting away from the pervasive violence and disorder as the most important thing they could do for themselves and their children.

Despite the terrible conditions in public housing, it was not clear that MTO families would really be better off as a result of moving to "better" neighborhoods. In fact, some researchers and advocates suggested that relocating would disrupt important social support networks and leave residents struggling in unfamiliar communities without a safety net. Many of these families had lived in public housing for decades. Some had lived there all their lives. Bad as they were, these developments were their homes, and these residents—even those who looked forward to the opportunity—faced great uncertainty as they contemplated a move to parts unknown.

But the interim evaluation of MTO clearly showed that like Denise, most successful movers in the experimental group believed that they were far better off and had attained their top goal: getting away from drugs and gangs (Orr et al., 2003). The movers were much more likely to report feeling safe in their neighborhoods at night (85 percent) than were families in the control group (55 percent). Likewise, the movers were significantly less likely to report problems with drug trafficking and gangs than those who remained in high-poverty neighborhoods. (Similarly, studies of families relocated through the HOPE VI program show that improved safety is the most important benefit of leaving distressed public housing, cf. Popkin and Cove 2007, Popkin et al., 2009.) Our analysis of neighborhood crime data from three of the MTO sites for which the right data are available—Boston, Chicago, and Los Angeles—shows that residents' perceptions of greater security reflect very real differences between different neighborhoods in recorded crime rates. Experimental-group movers in these three sites started out in neighborhoods where the rate of violent crime averaged 39.8 per 1,000, while the neighborhoods they moved to initially averaged just 11.2 per 1,000. Even after five years, these families were living in neighborhoods that were substantially safer, with violent crime rates about half what experienced in the projects (Kingsley and Pettit 2008).

THE MEANING OF SECURITY

Escaping the constant fear and anxiety of living in the projects had profound and unexpected benefits for MTO families—at least, for the mothers and daughters. Erika, a mother in the Boston experimental group who moved, echoed the sentiments of many movers when she said that the "rules are just different" in lower poverty neighborhoods. She moved with her grandnephew, Andre, from a public housing development in Dorchester, a high-poverty neighborhood in the city, to Quincy, a working-class suburban community:

> "I'm always telling the little ones I don't like kids doing drugs, smoking, and drinking. Get into it, and that's gonna be your life. Some kids like it, some don't. They respect you. At Dorchester, you go home at 4 P.M. in the evening, and somebody is going to try and do something to you." She said, "Quincy's different than Dorchester. It's a different ball game, with people and respect." [Fieldnote]

Like Denise and Erika, many mothers spoke of feeling profound relief when they moved out of public housing, and believed they had succeeded in saving their children from serious dangers and bad influences. Stacey and her four sons (ages 11 to 20) have moved three times since receiving their MTO voucher. Their first move was to a suburban area in the San Fernando Valley, where they all felt safe and liked the schools and neighborhood. But, they soon faced a challenge that confronted many MTO families who relocated to low-poverty areas through the program: Their landlord raised the rent substantially, and they ended up moving again, the second time to Long Beach, where Stacey's oldest son got into trouble and dropped out of school. Although things are not perfect in their current neighborhood, a moderately poor area in Los Angeles, and there are sporadic problems with drugs and gangs, Stacey views this as much safer than the public housing development they came from. Her family still attends church in their old neighborhood, near the projects, and she is able to contrast her sons' experience to those of their peers who stayed behind in public housing:

> Well, I'm so grateful to be moved out of there.... I told you my church is over there. Last week was Vacation Bible School.... I got a chance to teach the 15- to 18-year-olds. And I got a chance to see the young men, and I watched my sons. My sons are totally different...from those young boys. The [other] boys are hyper acting, they're all over the place. They're not mannerable, they're not respectable, they're rude, even the girls. And my sons are more laid back.

Four out of five of the women we interviewed cited safety as the primary reason for choosing their current apartment, even if they had moved several times since they left public housing. Feeling safe not only meant less worry about their children, it meant *freedom* from the constant fear and anxiety that had colored their lives in public housing. Like Stacey, Anique and her daughter, Clara, made several suburban moves after they left public housing in the mid 1990s. They were living in San Bernardino County, to the east of Los Angeles, when we got to know them in 2004. Anique told us she did not realize how much the violence had affected her until she no longer had to live with it every day:

> So far, since I've been here, I've never heard no gunshots, no none of that. That was a big thing that I, I don't know, I didn't realize it, but once you've grown up in a neighborhood and that's something you heard on a daily basis, you don't know that that's not how it's supposed to be. So then when I actually moved out, and I wasn't hearing nothing, I was like, I couldn't sleep, because it was too quiet. And I didn't know that that was affecting me that way. I did not know that. And it's really weird, but I didn't. And then, after I did, I knew that that's not something I wanted my daughter to get adjusted to.

The major gains in safety and feelings of security have had a profound impact on the mental health of women in MTO. According to the interim evaluation, psychological distress and depression were reduced by 3.5 percentage points, or over one-fifth, relative to the control group (Orr et al., 2003). To put this in perspective, such a reduction is comparable to that achieved by some of the most successful drug treatments for depression and related disorders. There is no question that for adult women, *moving to security* alleviated one of the most serious sources of stress in their lives and brought about profound improvements in their feelings of well-being.

But what about their children?

A GENDER PUZZLE

The interim evaluation of MTO offered more puzzles than answers about the effects of the program on adolescents. Researchers focused on that age group not only because adolescence is a crucial developmental stage, fraught with possibility and risk, but also because young people who were adolescents, ages 15 to 19, at the time of the evaluation survey in 2002, had moved between the ages of 8 and 15. They were young enough that the move and adjustment to new neighborhoods—in some cases, more than one since the initial relocation—were still relatively recent. But they were old enough to participate in surveys and to have significant behavioral records, which, in some cases, included school disciplinary problems and even criminal records.

Despite early-impact findings that suggested potential big benefits for adolescent boys and minimal gains for girls, the interim evaluation found that girls were significantly better off—in mental health and avoidance of risky behavior—thanks to relocating while boys were struggling (Kling, Ludwig, and Katz 2005; Orr et al., 2003). The researchers combed a slew of measures. Yet there were no improvements in mental health for boys, and there seemed to be negative effects on delinquency and crime. Boys in the experimental group were more likely to have been arrested, and among those arrested at least once, the frequency of arrests for property crimes was higher. Also, the self-reported problem behavior for boys in the experimental group was higher. Researchers acknowledged that "the increase in arrests might reflect more stringent policing in new locations, rather than (or in addition to) more criminal behavior" (Orr et al., 2003:xi), and they later acknowledged that self-reports are subject to the norms of the comparison group. That is, experimental-group boys might be more likely to rate their own behavior as problematic if other boys—in their lower poverty schools and neighborhoods—show relatively few problem behaviors; for boys in high-poverty areas, such acting out could seem to be the norm (Clampet-Lundquist et al., 2006; Kling, Ludwig, and Katz 2005). But these points suggest only that we should not exaggerate the evidence of negative effects on boys. The striking difference between boys and girls—only the latter clearly benefited, based on the wide range of measures employed by evaluators—remains to be explained.

For the rest of this chapter, we explore the question of how MTO affected adolescents, focusing on the gender puzzle. Given the best-available evidence on child development, there was no obvious reason why youth of both genders would not benefit from escaping dangerous and violent neighborhoods. Our analysis, based on our qualitative interviews and ethnographic fieldwork, suggests two distinct hypotheses: first, that girls have benefited by getting away from gender-specific dangers, specifically sexual harassment and pressure; and second, that boys have had more difficulty forming new social networks when they move, and instead have tended to maintain risky connections to the old neighborhood or other high-poverty neighborhoods, thanks largely to relatives that live in those areas. Below, we also draw on the work of researchers who have examined the MTO adolescent puzzle in Baltimore and Chicago, using somewhat different methods. Their work suggests that differences between girls and boys in social habits (where and how they spend free time), reception in the new neighborhoods (a more hostile reception for young males), and connections to role models (weaker ones for males) may also be contributing to the gender differences observed so far.

Early-Impact Gains, Interim Surprises

Shortly after the MTO experiment began, HUD funded a set of single-site, early-impact studies, with the aim of informing long-term research on MTO (Goering and Feins 2003). Researchers in both the Boston and the New York sites examined MTO's impact on children and adolescents' mental health roughly two and a half years post-move. The Boston study, focusing on children ages 6 to 15, found that experimental-group boys displayed fewer of six behavior problems, such as disobeying parents or trouble sitting still, than control-group boys; it found no program effects for girls (Katz, Kling, and Liebman 2001). Likewise, the New York study, focusing on children ages 8 to 18, found that experimental-group boys self-reported fewer behavior problems than control-group boys; again, there were no program

effects for girls (Leventhal and Brooks-Gunn 2003). Finally, researchers at the Baltimore MTO site, using juvenile arrest records, found a
significant favorable program impact on adolescent boys' arrests for
violent crime (Ludwig, Duncan, and Hirschfield 2001). These early,
single-site findings led observers of MTO to expect that the cross-site,
larger scale interim evaluation would show powerful effects on boys,
perhaps reducing the risk of delinquency and criminal arrests, but no
significant effects on outcomes for girls.

As we previewed above, just the opposite happened. Like their mothers, experimental–group girls reported significantly less psychological distress and anxiety than girls in the control group. Moreover, they were less
likely to report marijuana use or smoking than control-group girls. The
Section 8 comparison-group girls showed reduced risk of arrest. Meanwhile, adolescent boys in the experimental group reported *more* behavior
problems: were more likely to smoke, more likely to be arrested for property crimes and—perhaps most surprisingly—were no less likely to be
arrested for violent crimes than their counterparts in the control group.
These findings have been highly controversial, leading some to pronounce
MTO a failure—or even a threat to receiving neighborhoods.[2]

Prior research had suggested that that low-poverty neighborhoods
might improve the life chances of adolescents through several distinct
mechanisms: because of higher levels of neighborhood *social organization*—for example, neighbors monitoring behavior and enforcing rules—
that reduce the threats of violence and disorder (Browning, Leventhal,
and Brooks-Gunn 2005; Sampson, Morenoff, and Raudenbush 2005);
stronger *institutional resources*, such as higher quality schools, youth
programs, and health services (Jencks and Mayer 1990; Leventhal and
Brooks-Gunn 2000); more positive *peer-group influences* (Brody et al.,
2001; Elliott et al., 2006); and more effective *parenting*, thanks to parents' living in safer, less stressful neighborhoods and enjoying better
mental health or parents' becoming employed (McLoyd 1998; Simons
et al., 1996).

But while families in the experimental group who moved successfully did end up in dramatically safer neighborhoods, and while MTO
mothers' mental health did improve, MTO did not seem to affect
other factors that might improve adolescent outcomes, such as parenting practices or parental employment. And, as we will show in
chapter 8, MTO movers in the experimental group generally stayed in
the same central-city school district, meaning that the *average* MTO
adolescent in the experimental group was not in a substantially better school than the one left behind. Furthermore, many MTO families
maintained strong ties to high-poverty areas rather than developing
new social worlds in new neighborhoods. Thus, beyond the improvement in neighborhood safety, there is no obvious explanation for the
puzzling adolescent outcomes—either the improvements for girls or
the apparent setbacks for boys.

THE FEMALE FEAR

Having ruled out the most likely explanations for the gender differences in MTO's effects on the mental health and risky behavior of young people, we need to probe more deeply for alternatives. Our interviews with MTO families suggest that a factor that may explain at least some of the difference in outcomes is that safety has a different meaning for girls than it does for boys. Specifically, it appears that low-poverty neighborhoods are protective for girls in a way that they are not for boys. By moving to lower poverty neighborhoods, MTO girls dramatically reduced their level of the "female fear," Gordon and Riger's (1989) term, based on a comprehensive study of women and violence, for the fear of sexual harassment, coercion, and rape—and the ways in which this fear impedes women's lives. While Gordon and Riger argue that all women experience this fear to some degree, women in poor, minority communities are affected most.

As Tonya's description of life in her public housing development indicates, girls growing up in high poverty face specific risks because of their gender—the demoralizing effects of omnipresent and constant harassment; pervasive domestic violence; and a high risk of sexual assault. In addition to the fear of actual victimization, girls in these communities also experience pressure to become sexually active at increasingly younger ages. Early sexual initiation brings its own hazards: pregnancy, the risk of sexually transmitted disease, and dropping out of school to care for children (Alan Guttmacher Institute 1994; Albert, Brown, and Flanigan 2003; Cooksey, Rindfuss, and Guilkey 1996; Tubman, Windle, and Windle 1996; Johnson 2009).[3] Another, less serious consequence is very different parental expectations and attitudes toward male and female adolescents. Boys generally have more autonomy and, as we discuss below, often have more freedom to move around independently. In contrast, parents are more likely to try to restrict girls' activity and keep them close to home in order to protect them from perceived risks (Quane 2008).

Girls in many types of communities—not just very poor, high-crime ones—experience at least some verbal and physical harassment from men. But in the socially isolated world of distressed public housing, the pressures for sexual activity are much greater, the threats more blatant, and the risk of victimization much more immediate. Women who grew up in these dangerous environments often report having had to run a gauntlet of men and boys each time they left their homes and having had to cope with the fact that domestic violence and other violence against women is an everyday occurrence (Alvi et al., 2001; Popkin et al., 2000; J. Raphael 2001; Renzetti 2001). One study of girls in high-risk neighborhoods found that more than a third reported some form of victimization—including being physically threatened or hurt by someone trying to have sex with them—during any given year, with most girls reporting repeated victimization (Menard and Huizinga 2001).[4]

A number of in-depth qualitative studies have highlighted the sexually exploitive attitudes that adolescent males in distressed neighborhoods often hold toward their female peers. Certainly, not all men and boys in these communities behave this way, but enough of them do to create a sense of menace for women and girls. For example, Silverman and his colleagues, in their study of dating violence among low-income young men found that their respondents expected to have multiple partners; sought status through claims of sexual activity; and perceived girls who claimed to have been raped as liars (Silverman et al. 2006; Raj et al., 2007). Elijah Anderson's (1999) ethnographic work revealed how male peer groups in a poor urban neighborhood emphasized sexual conquest and bravado, and also how gang activity promoted the sexual exploitation of adolescent girls. Other research has found that in dangerous neighborhoods, girls frequently barter sex for protection from gang violence (Vera et al., 1996). In his field study among drug dealers in New York, Bourgois (1995) vividly described the ways in which the young men involved in this world used sexual violence to demonstrate their toughness, routinely using gang rape as a means of initiating new members into their group.

Even when violence is not involved, research suggests that sexually exploitive attitudes are prevalent in dating relations in very poor and segregated neighborhoods, with male youth more likely than female youth to view dating partners as possessions or objects of sexual gratification and to condone infidelity (Harper et al., 2004). Again, it is not that all men and boys hold these attitudes, but they are pervasive enough to create an acceptance of these views as "normal" (Harding 2006). Edin and Kefalas's (2005) study of how poor women make choices about childbirth and marriage provides a window into how these widespread attitudes affect young women, likewise documenting the pressures for early sexual activity from male partners and the limited choices poor women face—choices that often lead them to stay in relationships with abusive, risky, and unfaithful partners.

Girls Feeling Safe, Escaping Risks, Comparing Neighborhoods

Girls growing up in high-poverty neighborhoods must daily confront both norms that emphasize macho sexual values, female objectification, and early—and potentially risky—sexual activity, and a high risk of partner violence. It is not surprising, then, that moving out of these environments, and out of the war zone of distressed inner-city housing projects in particular, could have a profound impact on their sense of well-being and efficacy (the feeling that one has control over one's life). For MTO girls, moving out of public housing meant less harassment, less pressure for sexual activity, and a reduced risk of victimization.[5] And, in fact, our interviews indicate that girls whose families successfully moved to lower poverty communities experienced both a substantial reduction in their level of the "female fear" and a sense of freedom from pressures for sexual activity. Compared with their counterparts still living in high-poverty neighborhoods, experimental-group movers *who were still living in low-poverty neighborhoods when we visited them* reported less fear, less harassment from men and boys, and less pressure to engage in sexual behavior. The difference in pressure to engage in sex is especially significant for very young girls, who in high-poverty neighborhoods begin experiencing harassment and pressure during early adolescence, for example at age 12 or 13. It is striking, furthermore, that these girls and their mothers often talked about what has happened to their friends who still live in public housing and how they feel they have avoided that fate. Boys also spoke of the corrosive attitudes toward women and girls that they saw as widespread in their communities, describing the objectification of women and girls, expectations for men to be "players" and have multiple partners, and the casual acceptance of name-calling and harassment.

The difference in concerns about pressure and harassment, between mothers and girls in high- versus low-poverty neighborhoods, held regardless of whether the family had left their original public housing development and spent some time in a low-poverty neighborhood and then moved back to a higher poverty neighborhood or never left at all. Nearly all the experimental-group girls still living in low-poverty areas, as well as their mothers, described feeling confident that they are safe from those types of risks, while most living in high-poverty neighborhoods described living with pervasive harassment. Specifically, 18 female adolescents and young adults in the experimental-complier group (the compliers are those who successfully relocated, upon enrollment, to a low-poverty neighborhood) said they experienced no harassment, compared with 3 who said they did. In contrast, 18 experimental noncompliers (who did not manage to relocate after enrolling) and 10 control-group girls described harassment, fear, and the like, compared with 9 controls who did not report these experiences. There were less distinct patterns across experimental groups for the boys, partly because harassment was not as salient an issue for them. But those that did describe harassment were generally those still living in high-poverty communities.

Cassandra is a 15-year-old girl in the experimental group. Her family has lived in the same low-poverty suburban neighborhood, outside of Boston, since they moved there from public housing in 1994. She told us that she felt safe from harassment in her neighborhood, because it was simply unacceptable. "How do the guys treat women around here?" we asked. "They know not to touch them," she replied. Likewise, Matthew, the 20-year old son of Stacey, who spoke about the differences between her sons and the boys she taught at her church in her old public housing community, said that in his current, low-poverty neighborhood, "you have to be a gentleman."

Terri, a 16-year-old girl in the experimental group, who was living in a low-poverty, suburban neighborhood in San Bernardino County east of L.A., could not even imagine that men in her neighborhood might treat women badly. Likewise, her mother Robin spoke poignantly about how moving from a public housing development in Watts to a suburban community had affected her daughters' lives:

> I'm glad we are out here, far as that part, I'm glad we are living out here, cuz there is more intimidation and everything down there [in Watts, where we lived before].... Those boys down there are bad, say all kind of stuff.... I'm like, 'Man, look at these kids.' It's a faster pace. [Fieldnote]

Parents often used that word—*fast*, as in: too young to be acting that way—to capture what researchers, likewise, report as "accelerated" development, acquiring adult behaviors, and often risky ones, much too early.

Some girls talked about friends they left behind who already have children. Antoinette is a young woman in her early twenties, in the New York experimental group, whose family has lived in several low- and moderate-poverty neighborhoods in the Bronx (areas that were 5 or 10 or 15 percent poor) since they left public housing. She described what she thought would have happened to her if she had stayed in the projects:

> Because a lot of kids in my [old] neighborhood, like the girls, wound up not finishing junior high or just starting high school, like one of my best friends. I mean, we were in every single class since we started school together. We even went to the same high school. And then, like ninth grade, she had a kid and that was it.

Leah is a parent in the New York experimental group. She now lives in a low-poverty neighborhood in the North Bronx. Her relief at having gotten her 14-year-old daughter out of what she saw as a very dangerous situation in public housing was clear:

> Oh, them girls at [our former housing project] is wild, so I know they'll be different. Her [my daughter's] best friend is calm. She is not into boys. Those girls at [the project] is into boys at 12 year old.... Into boys, having sex, kissing, all that stuff. No, that's why I'm glad I moved out of [the project].... Can't let her grow up in these projects.

As Leah's comment indicates, an issue of particular concern for many of the mothers and girls was the pressure for early sexual initiation—in her case, girls being "fast" and interested in sex too early. Another issue was especially what they viewed as older men and boys preying on very young, impressionable girls who could be lured with drugs or money. Brianna, a mother from the experimental group in Los Angeles who successfully relocated, talked about how hard it would be to raise her daughter if she had stayed in the projects. When asked what her rules for her daughter would be if she still lived in public housing, she brought up her fears about men preferring young adolescent girls.

> BRIANNA: I have thought about that before, if I was living there still, how would it be. I think the type of person I am, I would have control of it, but I wouldn't be able to trust it, because of the guys...that try to hit on younger girls. So I wouldn't trust it.

INTERVIEWER: Do you think that happens more over there than it does
here?

B: Yeah, it does. I'm not going to lie to you. It does.

I: How does it happen over there, or how did you see it happen?

B: That's what they're like. They don't like the women my age. They go for
the 12-year-olds, the 11-year-olds, and give them drugs, and that's not
good.

…I have seen a lot of young girls like that…I refuse for my daughter to be
like that. [Fieldnote]

Then we asked Brianna if she thought there were those same kinds of
pressures on girls in her current, lower poverty neighborhood. She said
no, that it was different:

I pay attention, and it's different. The girls, they're different around here.
I always say that. It's different. It really is. You know, if I would compare
them to out here, out here they better…. You don't see them walking and
hanging out and drinking and something that…a teenager don't supposed
to do with a grown man. [Fieldnote]

THE GIRLS WHO ARE LEFT BEHIND

Related research, on families who relocated out of public housing as part
of the HOPE VI program, has found that moving benefits children who
leave, while girls who stay behind are at great risk for behavior problems
and delinquency (Gallagher and Bajaj 2007). Nearly all of the girls—and
mothers raising girls—who were living in high-poverty neighborhoods
when we interviewed them talked about their fears. Patricia, a member
of the experimental group in Los Angeles, intially moved her family to
a low-poverty neighborhood in the San Fernando Valley. However, she
felt isolated, and after three years, moved her family back to the same
neighborhood that they came from—literally across the street from their
former public housing development. Although she was happy to be back
near family and friends, she worried about the effect on her 12-year-old
daughter. And she was especially concerned about the pressures for early
sexual initiation:

When she at home, I make her stay to herself, she have friends that come
over from school. But, I don't let her socialize with too many people, because
the girls, they fast, they got boyfriends, they having sex, and I don't want my
daughter having sex. She only 12 years old, you know! And some girls get
jealous because, you know, I don't know, it's just crazy. [Fieldnote]

Patricia's daughter, Shauna, was also aware of the risk. We asked about her
friend, Tracey, whom Shauna had described:

I (fieldworker) asked, "Do you think she is sleeping around with guys?" She
said, "She is." I asked, "Are the guys older than her?" She said, "They are too
old for her, like 20, and she only 13. She in the seventh grade. She go with

boys like 15, 18."... I asked, "Do you think she does other things like drink
or smoke, like marijuana, or anything?" She said, "Marijuana. Her momma
sell it." [Fieldnote]

These widespread concerns about harassment and early sexual activity
reflect the reality that girls who live in distressed public housing often
pay a steep price—one that that can clearly affect their mental health and
their life chances. The potential risks include pregnancy, contracting sexually transmitted diseases—especially HIV—and experiencing domestic
abuse, sexual coercion, and sexual violence. Sexual violence and coerced
sex are common experiences for girls living in high-poverty neighborhoods. Even if they are not the victims, they usually know others who
are. Nearly all of the girls—and mothers raising girls—who were still living in high-poverty neighborhoods talked about how badly men in their
neighborhood treat women. Charmaine, a Hispanic 14-year old girl from
Los Angeles, was an experimental-group mover whose family initially
relocated to the suburbs. But they were evicted and ended up back in
a high-poverty neighborhood of L.A. She said that guys in her current
neighborhood treated women "terrible":

> They come at them wrong ways. They'll talk about their bootie or they'll
> just come to them straight, "Do you want to have sex?," or they talking
> about they use a girl. Yeah, they'll use a girl and they said, they call it "pimp
> a girl out."... Just get between her legs and just go on like nothing.

Boys living in high-poverty neighborhoods provided similar descriptions.
Juan was a 14-year old whose family, like Charmaine's, had briefly lived
in the San Fernando Valley before high rents forced them back to a poorer
part of Los Angeles. By the time we interviewed him, he was struggling
in school and was involved in a gang. When asked how guys treat girls in
his community, he said, "They pretty much treat them like animals....
They be calling them bitches and all that.... They just say bitches, whores,
that's it."

Javon, a 14-year old boy from the control group in Los Angeles who
still lived in public housing, observed, "People, they treat women...like
they was just objects, as if they owned them or whatnot. There are the
women who are independent enough not to take that and all...you can
either mistreat a woman or the woman is going to mistreat you."

Some MTO girls have experienced serious consequences as a result of
the pervasive sexual pressures and violence. Carla and her teenage children
moved back to public housing in New York after living for years in a lower
poverty neighborhood. Carla described the many bad things that had happened to her daughter since moving back—getting involved in risky sexual
activity, catching herpes, being exposed to violence. Because of all these
problems, she urgently wanted to move again to a safer neighborhood.
"I really want to get out of this neighborhood," she said, "because Maribel
[her 16-year old daughter] gets involved in things she shouldn't." Carla
then told us about a drug dealer ex-boyfriend who gave Maribel herpes.

A small number of older girls described being in abusive relationships or being coerced by their boyfriends to have unprotected sex. Tonya, the pregnant teen we introduced early in this chapter, told us that she was "kind of asleep" when her boyfriend first started having sex with her. Like Charmaine, Juliana is a 15-year old Hispanic girl in the Los Angeles experimental group whose family ended up moving back to a high-poverty neighborhood after living for a while in a low-poverty area, in this case because her family gave up their voucher in order to buy a house. Juliana got involved with an older man, became pregnant, and dropped out of school to care for her child. She and her mother both talked about how her boyfriend had physically abused her and how they had to force him to move out of their apartment. She also talked about the appeal of older men—that they have more money and resources and can "offer more" to a girl. But Juliana now feels she was taken advantage of and has suffered real harm as a result:

> I just think that at some point...girls stop trying to look for loving, whatever in an older guy, but then older guys take advantages, too.... They can offer you more, but they can also do more harm....To me, it would have been nicer to experience someone my own age...someone that he experienced something his first time and I did it too. I don't know. Something's different, because my experience wasn't very nice. And I regret it.

Even worse, a few girls spoke of being raped or molested by older men—in one case, by a mother's boyfriend—and the consequences that that experience has had for their lives. Lilian is an adolescent in the New York experimental group whose family moved out of public housing to a low-poverty neighborhood in the Northeast Bronx, then to a higher poverty area after their landlord told them he wanted the apartment for a relative. Lilian told us about being raped at the age of eight and the ongoing fears that continue to constrain her life:

> When I was younger, I got raped. When I was about 8, 8 years old.... And that was by my mom's boyfriend. She didn't know about it, and my sister and me were raped at the same time. But we never knew [about each other's rape] until I was like 13.... She [my mother] didn't know at all. Until my mom asked me, I was 13, are you a virgin, and then I told her, 'Ma, I got raped.' So she was like, 'Why didn't you tell me?' And when we told the cops, they couldn't do nothing about it, 'cause we waited so long to tell.... It took me a while to get over it. Now I can't be in a room with an older guy alone.

While many mothers and daughters feel intense anxiety about the risks, those who have suffered domestic abuse or sexual violence are especially traumatized. Those who have managed to move to—and stay in—low-poverty neighborhoods are acutely aware of having escaped from a dangerous environment. Those who have had to move back and those who never left speak of the extreme risks and the constant need to be alert, aware, and protective.

Adolescent girls respond to the threat of harassment and violence in a variety of ways. Some, like Antoinette in the Bronx, try to show they are tough by the way they walk, talk, or dress.

> I got a way. When I walk down the street, I look real evil.... I don't even smile like nothing, nothing. And if you did say something to me, it's like...Why you talking to me? Something like that... I don't respond to people. I have never responded to anyone. I think one time I responded to somebody, and that's because the guy touched me.... Because...somebody could be crazy. You could be crazy, I could be crazy.... You know, that's disrespectful.... I don't think you should touch people to say 'hi.' If you say 'hi,' and I don't say nothing back, that mean I don't want to be bothered. But don't touch me, because it makes me nervous, and you don't know what's going to happen after that.

Others avoid risky places where they know they might face danger, including staying to themselves and staying inside the house. And some, like 13-year old Georgiana, an experimental-group mover living in suburban Boston, rely on siblings or friends to walk them to and from school and home.

> "I just avoid it. Other girls aren't as tough as me. They go along with it and talk back to them and let them flirt," she said. While some girls engage boys, according to Georgiana, she also said that often "girls will walk with their brothers" as well. Georgiana shared that she often walks with her brother to avoid boys. I (fieldworker) asked her if she feels safe with him, and she said that she does. "He may be short and skinny, but he could put up a good fight!" she said proudly. [Fieldnote]

Similarly, a few boys, who acknowledged that some guys in their neighborhood harassed girls, spoke about protecting their sisters.

Mothers adopt a range of strategies to protect their daughters from the sexual pressures, from allowing their daughters to have a boyfriend "so they won't do it behind my back" to closely monitoring their daughter's friends and activities. About half of the girls across all experimental groups mentioned that their mothers had rules for them about dating or curfews; only two boys mentioned any restrictions on their dating behavior. Like many other mothers in our study, Patricia, the mother who had moved her family back from the Valley to an apartment across the street from her original public housing development, said she was strict with her daughter about where she can go when she leaves the house. When asked where 12-year old Shauna could go, Patricia said:

> Just to my Momma house and my house. Only here and my Mom's.... She do go to the candy house [the corner store]. When she do go, somebody always go with her, I don't let her go by herself. I always tell Frederico [her brother] to go with her, cuz boys...they be, at least my son, he a boy, but I ain't gonna say he know, but he know when people ain't supposed to talk to his sister, grown mens, he know.

Some parents who relocated through MTO, such as Robin in Los Angeles, talked about the contrast between their children and their friends' children still living in the projects:

> My kids are slow [not "fast," not sexually active at an early age]. So when my kids go down there [to their old neighborhood] now, and they [the other kids] look at them, like, "You guys are different."… They tell 'em that they are different or whatever, "You guys changed since you lived out there." They talk about them. That's why I say, it's kind of good that we are living out here. I know me, even if I was living in L.A., it'd be hard for me, because the kids that they hang around, or the environment that they are around, it would be hard, for them as kids too…[Fieldnote]

The comments of those, such as Robin, who feel they have succeeded in getting away from pervasive risks indicate a profound sense of relief. The mothers feel their daughters are safe and the girls feel free to move around without the need to be always on alert. The consistency of these patterns supports the argument that reduced levels of the "female fear" and the freedom from pressures for early sexual initiation help explain the substantial improvements in girls' mental health and well-being.

RISKY TIES

While boys evidently did not face the same threats in the projects as girls, moving could have enabled them to escape from equally powerful ones, for example, pressure to become involved in gangs and drug dealing, as well as the threat of violence and victimization of a different kind. MTO boys did not experience the same gains in mental health or reductions in risky behavior as girls. Further, and of great concern, MTO experimental-group boys were no less likely to be arrested for violent crime than their counterparts in the control group and were actually more likely to be arrested for property crime.

The answers to this part of the gender puzzle are less clear and our data do not provide a full explanation, but our evidence, and that from other researchers, suggests that several factors were at work. Other research has found that low-income parents have very different expectations and rules for their daughters and sons; girls have more household responsibilities and, as the stories from these MTO families indicate, are often kept close to home. Boys are not as restricted, and generally have less supervision and more autonomy.[6] Most significantly, our interviews indicate that parents gave boys substantially more freedom than girls to move around the metro area. Some were able to maintain their connections to risky social networks—including relatives and friends—in the old neighborhood or in similar, high-poverty neighborhoods. Perhaps because they had these connections, and perhaps because youth in the communities they moved into viewed them as threats, MTO boys also seem to have had more difficulty than girls in forming new social connections in low-poverty neighborhoods. Finally, we must consider the possibility that police in lower poverty communities monitored young, low-income minority youth more heavily than those in higher poverty areas—although young men from both types of neighborhoods complained about police harassment.

As we outlined above, there is considerable evidence that living in high-poverty neighborhoods increases the risk that adolescents will engage in risky and delinquent behavior. In general, boys have been more likely than girls to take these risks—to drink and use illegal drugs and become involved in criminal activities, such as vandalism, drug dealing, auto theft, and violent crime. Policy makers and scholars have become increasingly concerned about the problem of "disconnected" youth in inner cities—young men who are not participating in schooling or the labor market and who are at high risk for becoming involved in criminal activities (Holzer 2006).

As many researchers have underlined, neighborhood traits interact with parenting practices and peer influences in complex ways to shape adolescent behavior and outcomes (Elliott et al. 2006; Furstenberg et al. 1999). Generally, our data indicate that because of their concerns about sexual pressures and risks, MTO harassment, pressures, and assaults, mothers tend to monitor their daughters closely, while allowing their sons more freedom to move around independently. As Theresa, a mother who had moved with a regular Section 8 voucher (in the comparison group) put it, she was more protective of her daughter than her son because, "she's a girl and she has a body like a woman." Although the interim evaluation survey did not uncover differences in parenting among the mothers we interviewed in depth in our study, there was a greater expectation that boys would explore and might act up. We repeatedly heard indulgent attitudes along the lines of "boys will be boys." With their freedom to move around, male youth often spent time going back to their old neighborhoods—and often because their parent or a relative took them. But they also encountered risks in their current neighborhoods—other youth who regarded them as threats, as well as opportunities to get involved in trouble.

Both boys in the experimental group who moved to low-poverty neighborhoods and boys in the comparison and control groups who did not were clearly struggling. Regardless of where they lived, they were facing pressures to fight, deal drugs, and join gangs. Avoiding these threats required extraordinary effort on the part of both the boys and their parents, and it often meant that the youth spent much of their time indoors, isolated from potentially bad influences. Boys living in all types of neighborhoods spoke of not being able to rely on their family and friends and of having fathers who were in jail, abusive, or simply out of the picture. And, these minority youth consistently complained that police (in all neighborhoods) regarded them as trouble, assuming they were up to no good even when they were simply standing on the sidewalk.

While research on poor families and neighborhoods—as we explore in the next chapter—often portrays kin networks as resilient and supportive, our fieldwork shows that many ties to relatives have been, at best, a mixed blessing for MTO youth, especially boys. Using our data, Weismann (2008) finds that virtually every young male in the in-depth ethnographic sample (39 families) and most of those in the larger interview sample reported knowing someone who was or had been in jail. In many cases, it was their father who was in jail or had a criminal record. Weismann finds that close social ties drew male adolescents from the experimental group back to risky neighborhoods, often because they were bored and seeking excitement they could not find in their new, lower poverty community. Associating with friends and family was potentially risky because much of the adolescents' extended family was involved in risky and often criminal behavior.

Similarly, Clampet-Lundquist and colleagues (2006), in their qualitative interview study of families in the Baltimore and Chicago MTO sites, find evidence that the experimental-group boys were less successful than girls at forming positive peer networks in their new neighborhoods. In particular, girls were more able to make friends at their schools, who seemed to facilitate their acclimating to low-poverty neighborhoods. In contrast, boys failed to form new networks, often encountering hostility and even violence from local boys, who regarded them as threats. As a result, they also found that boys maintained closer ties to networks grounded in the projects left behind or other risky neighborhoods.

Our interviews confirm that mover girls in the experimental group were more likely to view their friends as being positive influences, while boys were more than twice as likely to say they were bad influences. However, boys were no more likely than girls to report engaging in risky behavior.[7] Illustrating the risks, Fernando, an 18-year-old boy from the experimental group, who had moved with his mother to an apartment complex in a quiet suburb outside Boston, described a peer and kin network heavily engaged in criminal behavior. Like many MTO youth whose families had moved to low-poverty communities, Fernando had few friends in his current neighborhood, and he told the interviewer he had smoked marijuana, smoked cigarettes, drank beer, and had been arrested for drug possession. He also told the interviewer that "half of my family is in jail" and that his cousin had been arrested for stealing cars.

Lionel, another boy in the experimental group; his mother Blair; and his older sister Jasmine were living in a moderately poor neighborhood outside of Boston when we interviewed them in 2004. They had to move from their first apartment in a predominantly white, suburban neighborhood because the building burned down and they could not find another apartment, in the same area, that they could afford. Although his family had been in the current neighborhood for several years, Lionel opted to attend a high school near his old public housing development. He was struggling with anger and told the interviewer he had tried drugs, smoked, and drank. He had been in a number of fights and was injured when he was jumped at school. Even worse, a close friend of his had been killed.

Youth still living in public housing struggled with the same pressures, often magnified by the broader crime and disorder around them. Javon, the 14-year-old boy in the Los Angeles control group whom we quoted earlier on relationships between men and women. He was living in public housing with his mother Jeanine. He spoke of the extraordinary efforts it took to avoid getting pulled into his family's risky network. He said his father was "a gangster," and his mother would not allow him to spend time with his father. She told us that she had cut ties to her relatives with "a big knife." She had also cut ties with her daughter's father, who was in prison, and to Javon's uncle, who was arrested during a drug raid. Javon said that he tries to "really stay distant away" from people that are "like gangbangers." His mother is very protective, and he says he avoids trouble because of "what she'll do to me." He and his mother both told us, in one-on-one interviews, that they were very close to one another and that they talked regularly about how to resist the pressures in his neighborhood.

Cora and her 17-year-old son Craig were also in the control group and still also living in public housing in Los Angeles when we interviewed them in 2004. They had been in their development for six years. Craig's comments highlight the challenges that many of these young men faced in trying to escape the influence of risky networks. He did not view anyone in his family, including his mother, as a positive influence. Craig told us that he hoped to join the military and said he stayed inside or went to the library to avoid the gangs and drug dealers. He had spent time in a "probation school" because he was caught with a knife at his regular school. He described a host of the negative influences in his life, including his abusive father and his mother's boyfriends, who he said abused her, too. And he told the interviewer:

> My biggest worry is that I don't get to join the military, and I stay here for the rest of my life.... My other worry is that when I leave here, I don't want to keep in touch with anybody here. I'm not going to give them my phone number or anything, I'm just going to move away.... I don't want to be bothered with them...the relatives, most of my relatives.

SHARED STRUGGLES

Even youth in the experimental group who were living in low-poverty neighborhoods had not escaped the pressures, or were concerned about the pressures, to become involved in gangs and illegal activity. About two-thirds of the adolescents we interviewed—male and female—mentioned pressure to fight or join gangs. And boys living in low-poverty neighborhoods were just as likely to cite these pressures as those still living in high-poverty public housing projects. Weismann also shows in her analysis that youth often perceived risk in neighborhoods where their parents did not. For example, April, a Haitian immigrant, had lived with her family in the same apartment in suburban Boston since she received her MTO voucher.

She views her neighborhood as completely safe for herself and her children. Yet her daughter, Georgiana, is one of the girls we described earlier talking about needing protection from her brother to feel safe from harassment in her neighborhood. Georgiana and her brother showed us where there were drug dealers and needles on the ground, near the family's apartment complex.

Certainly, not all the boys we interviewed were involved in delinquent or criminal behavior or were as unhappy and alienated as Craig, Lionel, and Fernando. But it was clear that avoiding trouble meant taking extreme measures—strictly limiting access to risky networks, including friends and relatives, and deliberately seeking out positive influences. A few boys had fathers or stepfathers in their households or nearby who served as role models. They enforced rules, checked on grades, and encouraged the young males to do well in school.

Far more common was a mother who went out of her way to ensure that her son was monitored and protected—a pattern documented by research on "successful" parenting in high-risk neighborhoods (Furstenberg 1993; Jarrett 1999). For example, Stacey, whom we introduced earlier describing the differences between her sons and those she taught in bible school back at her church in her old neighborhood, made extraordinary efforts to protect her four sons. She limited her sons' contact with their father, who had a criminal record. She enrolled her younger sons in a private, Christian school. She arranged mentors for them through her church. And she encouraged her sons to form relationships with positive role models, such as their coaches. Likewise, Marsha, a mother in the experimental group in New York, described tight restrictions on her 13-year-old son, Reese. Marsha was unusual for an MTO participant. She was a well-educated teacher, and her stint in public housing—where the family became eligible to participate in MTO—was the result of temporarily falling on hard times because of an abusive spouse. Marsha encouraged Reese to hang out only with friends from church and school. She did not let him have any contact with boys in their Harlem neighborhood.

POLICE MONITORING

It is difficult to determine from our data what role policing in different types of communities may have played in the arrest rates for MTO experimental-group boys, particularly for property crime. One hypothesis is that police in lower poverty communities viewed these minority youth as a threat and monitored them more closely. Another possibility is that lower poverty communities provided more opportunity for property crime—more and better cars to steal and the like. However, our data offer no clear answers about the role of police or opportunity in creating the problematic outcomes for MTO experimental-group boys. The argument about police monitoring would seem stronger if these youth had moved to predominantly white communities where they would be more visible; but as we discussed in chapter 4, they mostly moved to lower poverty minority communities where they may or may not have stood out relative to other youth. And our interviews indicate that regardless of where they lived or what experimental group they had been assigned to, these minority youth reported feeling harassed by the police, and a few boys from every group described being involved in drug dealing, joy riding, and vandalism.

While Denise, the experimental-group mover from Los Angeles whom we described at the beginning of this chapter, was pleased with her safer neighborhood, her older son, Shawn, complained that he got "harassed by the police for standing outside." He said that police bothered him and his friends about half the time they were outside, often demanding that they empty their pockets. He said, "They just mess with the young looking [dudes] that dress weird to their eyes." Likewise, Lionel, the experimental-group mover living in a working-class Boston suburb said that the police frequently "hassled" him:

> One night when I was walking to my house, and they stopped me. I was walking over this way and I cut through the yard. I went around because it's like a lawn and you can cut through. So you won't have to walk all the way around the corner, and the detectives were rolling up the street. They seen me. I looked at them and I stopped and then I kept on walking. They backed up and came down my street. Stopped right here in front of my house. They do that all the time.

But boys living in higher poverty communities—both those who had failed to move and those in the control group—had the same types of complaints about police harassing them and stopping them. For example, Roberto, whose family lived in public housing in Boston, said that the police were "suspicious for no reason" and stopped him because he was waiting outside for a friend to pick him up.

SUMMARY AND IMPLICATIONS

For mothers and girls, at least, relocating through MTO meant moving to security. It brought freedom from fear—for mothers, the fear that their girls would become "fast," or be harassed and preyed on, especially by older men and boys, and for girls, the fear of being pressured for sex, harassed, or victimized. Mothers are less stressed and anxious. Girls have seen improvements in mental health, too, as well as risky behavior. As Anique put it at the beginning of this chapter, some MTO parents did not realize how much the constant fear was affecting their lives until they moved to a place where they felt truly safe. On this front, MTO has been enormously successful, with the main caveat being that many families struggled to stay out of high-risk neighborhoods after initially escaping them. This insecure foothold in more secure places is the focus of chapter 7. The comments of the girls and their mothers make clear the distress many felt about returning to an environment where daughters were once more subject to the pervasive harassment and pressure for sex. Clearly, any benefits these families have gained by living in safer communities can be quickly lost once they return to distressed neighborhoods.

Moreover, the picture is a sad one for adolescent boys in MTO, regardless of where they live. Unlike the girls, they cannot point to positive gains from moving to low- (or lower) poverty neighborhoods. The experience of safety, we have argued, was different. Girls experienced a profound drop in sexual pressures, predation, and related types of risk, while boys—who did not face this particular threat in the projects—did not. Boys appear to have faced more hostility from local teens—in low-poverty neighborhoods, that is. They had more trouble making new friends in new settings. Furthermore, most of these boys had more freedom than their female counterparts to seek out risk, usually because poorer areas, where relatives lived and hung out, were more fun, but sometimes because the boys' own parents emphasized sticking close to relatives, centering the family's social life on these kin, as we show in the next chapter. Avoiding the risks was also tremendously stressful and required boys to accept being as isolated and overprotected as their sisters, which sometimes produced anger and withdrawal. Low-poverty neighborhoods did not necessarily present more institutional resources, and when they did, parents and their children did not necessarily learn about or use them. MTO was a relocation-only intervention. It did not provide support services that could have benefited these young people, the boys in particular.

While the experience may be very different for boys who moved as very young children—or who were born in low-poverty neighborhoods, after their parents moved through the experiment—the outcomes for these boys illustrate the danger of simple assumptions about what makes a neighborhood "better" for a young person, especially a young minority male who is growing up poor.

Chapter 6

When Your Neighborhood Is Not
Your Community

Ain't nothing like family…and sometimes, you can't even get
along with them.

Tessa, MTO Boston

DIFFERENT STROKES

For families in the Moving to Opportunity experiment, like families generally, a change of neighborhood does not necessarily entail a change of
"community"—in the sense that the people and routines at the center of
one's life may not change much at all. For example, when Crystal, a member of the MTO experimental group, moved from the South Bronx to a
low-poverty area in the Northeast Bronx and then to a nearby suburb, she
took a large nuclear family with her. There were her two daughters, Nina
(age 4) and Tammy (18). There was Michael, her adolescent son, plus
her infant granddaughter, Tammy's daughter. There was her husband, too,
though his drug addiction soon led Crystal to kick him out of the apartment. The new neighborhood was safe, and Crystal felt that the schools
were giving Michael a better education than had schools in the Bronx.
Yet her ties to high-poverty neighborhoods in the Bronx and Manhattan
remained strong. The main reason was extended family.

Crystal's mother, whom she visits weekly or more often, lives with
Diane, one of Crystal's sisters, in Manhattan. Then there is her grandmother Essie, whom Crystal feels close to and whom she "takes things
to," plus her other sister, Shanelle, who lived in Crystal's new apartment
for a while—hoping to enter the shelter system so she would get moved
up on the waiting list to receive a housing voucher of her own—and her
brother Terry. Crystal has two nieces and one nephew, plus her cousins,
aunts, and uncles. She's also in close touch with her stepbrother Milo
and his wife Rhonda, whom she turns to for advice and encouragement,
plus friends from church and childhood, most of whom live in the South
Bronx. Though Crystal and her father, who lives outside the New York
region, don't see each other often, they talk frequently by phone. He calls
her because Crystal doesn't have long distance service.

As for the others, Crystal visits them regularly in their neighborhoods. They eat and talk, sometimes go to church together. They "fellowship," she says. They also help each other out, usually with babysitting, giving rides to the doctor or other services, giving and taking small loans in emergencies. Beyond these personal ties to the area she moved away from, Crystal works as a teacher's assistant in a school there, not far from the public housing development she used to live in. It's a 30-minute drive from her apartment, and she often does her shopping there in the South Bronx, on the way home from work. Her youngest daughter, Nina, goes to day care there while Crystal is at work.

Crystal's eldest daughter, Tammy, splits her time between Crystal's place and the South Bronx, where her boyfriend, the father of her infant daughter, lives. All of Tammy's friendships are in the old neighborhood in the Bronx. As with other young people in our study who lived in low-poverty areas, at least for a time thanks to MTO, most of Tammy's exposure to risky behavior—heavy drinking, drug use, drug dealing, fighting, and other problems—reflected kin ties that drew Tammy back to high-poverty, high-crime areas. Her nuclear family had relocated away from the ghetto, but not left its social influence behind. The main reason was her relatives and her mother's choice to keep her nuclear family strongly connected to the lives of relatives who were concentrated in one or more high-poverty neighborhoods.

It's not that Crystal dislikes her new neighbors. Three of the families in her apartment building are "Spanish" (Hispanic) and one is Chinese, she says. Crystal thinks they're nice, and she thinks she could ask to borrow a screwdriver, say, or some bread if she needed to. But their interactions are casual, "hi-bye," like many neighborly interactions in America.

Though Crystal's ties to the neighborhood left behind are particularly strong and multistranded—kin, work, church, friends from church and childhood—the structure of her social world was common among the MTO families we got to know. The neighborhood of residence might, when things worked out, be a safe base of operations and a place to find somewhat better schools (see chapter 8), but it was not the *community* where the family's most important relationships were located. There was a neighborhood left behind, or some other neighborhood where relatives lived and where our subjects went regularly—not necessarily, and in fact not usually, the former public housing development itself—that played a central role in daily life, providing companionship and vital practical supports, such as childcare and money, but sometimes posing overwhelming obligations as well.

Almost always, it was kin—relying on them, feeling obliged to them, organizing social life around them—who were the magnets drawing MTO families to those other neighborhoods. We took to calling them "second neighborhoods" because they were neighborhoods of some influence, and even places where MTO children or other members of the household sometimes stayed for a while, though not the family's primary neighborhood of residence. Some families had more than one such place.

A less common pattern was the *transplant*—the family with weak social ties, if any, to the place left behind, some of whom worked to minimize contacts, to distance themselves, from that place and people who lived there, and some of whom maintained steady ties with relatives or friends who had also left behind ghetto-poor neighborhoods—that is, MTO movers who maintained ties to people who had also moved away.

In the first category is April, a Haitian immigrant who relocated with her husband, Jean, and two children, Georgiana and Tevin, from inner-city Boston to an inner suburb north of the city. Though most of her husband's friends live in the area they left behind, in neighborhoods of Dorchester or Mattapan, April avoids those neighborhoods as much as possible and encourages her children to do the same.

The suburb April lives in now has a "ghetto part," she acknowledges. It is an older suburb that, like similar areas in the Boston region and other metro areas, has become poorer and more racially diverse over the past decade (see chapter 4). But it's nothing, in April's mind, like the ghetto they left behind—with trash everywhere, as she recalls, teenagers selling drugs on the corner, children cursing, men coming on to her ("Hey baby, are you married?" she mimics), and the constant threat of violence. Though her children walked us around their neighborhood, pointing out spots where teenagers smoke weed or drink, April sees none of the ghetto behavior she was so eager to leave behind. There's even a security guard and a sign-in at the entrance to her apartment complex, which she likes.

April's children have no memories of inner-city Boston, where they were born. When we asked them to map their neighborhood for us, to point out people and places that were important to them, it was clear, in fact, that Tevin had no knowledge of the family's history in inner-city Boston. His older sister teased him playfully about it. But when she visits her father's relatives in Dorchester, she notices that young people there dress differently and carry themselves differently—act tougher, talk louder. We asked how she (Georgiana) was different. "I'm not ghetto or gangster," she said. Her mother doesn't like to visit Dorchester at all. Many of her husband's friends don't work, says April, and they live in the ghetto.

April doesn't know her neighbors in the apartment complex, and in general, she told us, she avoids making friends, whether in the neighborhood or anyplace else. Having friends would be nice, but they tend to bring problems, as she first learned as a young woman in Haiti. The hard part about friends, she says, is "finding a good one." April's church, one of the largest Haitian-American congregations in the Boston region, is in the suburb where she and her family live, and she and her two children are there all day every Saturday, for services and choir practice, while husband Jean visits his friends and relatives. When her husband cannot be home and she needs someone to keep an eye on the children, she turns to a few "old church ladies" to stay in the apartment.

April has little time to socialize anyway, she says, and many working parents in MTO echoed this sentiment. She works in a nursing home a short drive from her apartment, usually from 3 to 11 P.M.. She values the steady work and the fact that she can earn more in the Boston region than in Florida, where she and Jean met and where they worked before their children were born. April values her job even though she has been the target of racial slurs. Some of the elderly patients ridicule her dark skin. "Get your dirty hands off me," they say. One called her "nigger," and another called her a "black monkey," she remembers. The Italians are the worst, she says. This kind of treatment was *not* a part of the ghetto she left behind, where most of the residents were dark-skinned. But she takes it all in stride. If one of her patients insults her, she explains to us, she'll reply, "That's ok, you're almost done. You're heading out."

Their housing situation is not ideal. Her two teenagers are squeezed into a single bedroom, for one thing. April would love a bigger apartment, she told us, but she won't leave the quiet and safe suburb, with better schools, that she found through MTO—not for anything (see chapter 7).

Other MTO parents were transplants after relocating, though not like April. Some are the caregivers—the responsible, reliable, and often exhausted hubs—in networks of struggling kin. In Los Angeles, Roxanne's neighborhood is the center of her social world, and her days are long. Though all but one of her own nine children have grown up and moved out, she has custody of four grandchildren: two toddlers from a homeless daughter, and two teenagers from her drug-addicted daughter, who still lives in public housing. Roxanne struggles with diabetes, arthritis, and frequent shortness of breath. Her exhaustion was visible on many of our visits. Yet she was the matriarch of a large and dependent extended family. The barbecues were at her place, when we visited on the weekends, and the courts turned to her whenever her children could not take proper care of their children.

We got to know the family just after a move to Long Beach from a nearby suburb, and within a few months, Roxanne and her family had recentered their routines on the new place, learning its shopping and services and befriending a few neighbors. Some of them were "ghetto," Roxanne told us, in that they liked their music loud and let children hang out at all hours. But several were parents and she felt she could count on them to keep an eye on her children, too, and help out in an emergency.

Other MTO parents moved *in order* to put distance between themselves and their constantly needy relatives, some of whom were in and out of jail, drug addicted or alcoholic, and irresponsible with money—or prone to expecting too much and giving little back. These families did not want to center their social worlds where their kin lived. In Los Angeles, for example, Jeanine relocated with her housing voucher several times, and after the latest move, when we got to know her, she withheld her address from most of her relatives. "My little brother doesn't even know," she said, "Six of my aunties and five uncles don't know where I stay. They don't even have the phone number. They live close by, but they don't know I'm here."

Jeanine has six siblings, but she cannot count on them for help, and more than that, she felt, they have abused her trust and goodwill in the past. Her parents were crack addicts who became homeless and died in their fifties, leaving Jeanine to raise her younger sisters and brothers on her own. Now, she is one of the few members of her extended family with a steady job and a decent credit rating, so she has helped several family members by buying things, on credit, in her name. Her uncle's house is in her name, for instance, because she applied for the mortgage. And this arrangement worked fine, she says, because he paid on time and helped her out in little ways, too. But Jeanine also helped her brother buy a car and motorcycle by signing on the loans. Then he went to jail, and it turned out that he was not paying the loans, so Jeanine was strapped with the expensive monthly payments. To make matters worse, the car got impounded, and she had to come up with $2,500 to retrieve it. "Why am I making $1,500 every two to three weeks and I'm still broke?" she asked us rhetorically, with exasperation. "And I can't even get food stamps or anything."

Finally, for a small share of MTO families, the neighborhood was merely a secure place of residence, and no neighborhood served as a community, in part because no one place was the epicenter of kin ties or other strong ties. Some of these families were isolated socially, but others simply found an *institutional* community. For Monica and Eduardo, for example, two immigrant parents who relocated through MTO in Los Angeles and then managed to get off housing assistance and buy a small starter home of their own, the church is the social world. Monica works as a receptionist at the church. Their children attend its school—on a scholarship Monica learned about from a co-worker. The couple met the MTO counselor who helped them relocate, and later the real estate agent who helped them buy their home, at the church. They attend church regularly and volunteer for its special events (one of our visits led us, with the family, to bingo night). Monica's mother and sister live in Miami. Eduardo has a sister in Los Angeles, but the two are estranged. His other relatives are out of town or back home in Mexico. Their friends were made at church, and the closest are *copadres* (godparents) to their children. Otherwise, they avoid close relationships, including neighborly ties.

When is a neighborhood not a community, we wondered, especially for those who relocate hoping for a better life? Those who planned the MTO experiment believed it could reduce the "social isolation" that was, argued leading scholars, a core feature of life in segregated, high-poverty ghetto neighborhoods (see chapters 2 and 3). A move to more resource-rich "communities" should encourage poor parents to get ahead and provide them with the services and other formal supports, plus the informal connections and the motivation—in the example of successful, rather than welfare-dependent or drug-addicted, neighbors—to make that getting ahead possible. Yet by the interim evaluation mark some four to seven years after families enrolled in MTO, few of the parents who moved to low-poverty neighborhoods reported having ties to more educated, higher income people living nearby, and many reported regular contact with the ghetto-poor neighborhoods they had supposedly left behind.

To help explain why, and to explore the assumptions about social connection that lay behind MTO and the push to "deconcentrate" poverty, we begin with basic questions that have long stirred the American public even as they bedevil our public policy debates: What is a "community"? Where do people find community, and what does it mean, in today's world, to have one? More to the point, where do poor people find or not find community as they juggle deaths and other losses, moves, births, new jobs, and other changes in their lives?

SOCIETY, COMMUNITY, FAMILY, NETWORK

Americans evince a never-ending fascination with the *idea* of community along with considerable ambivalence toward the real thing. The thread runs from the first European settlers, who arrived in religious groups to found "moral communities," to the Native Americans they encountered and soon displaced. It runs from the slaves who created parallel community institutions—for example, the black church—in part to preserve their cultural traditions and in part because they were denied access to white-dominated society, to the vibrant neighborhoods—the Little Italies, Chinatowns, and other ethnic enclaves—established, in booming industrial cities, by immigrants from southern and eastern Europe, China, and elsewhere. Throughout this history, America's public conversation, and much of its social research as well, has associated "the good society," and even the ideal of citizenship, with belonging to some kind of community (Bellah 1985).

Moreover, some of the earliest systematic social research in America, in sociology most prominently, focused on "the community question"— specifically, whether those migrating from stable farming communities to rapidly changing industrial cities would form "true" communities. Might they, instead, become isolated and detached from fellow city dwellers, leading to lawlessness and alienation? Urbanization, scholars and activists worried, might lead to the loss of community altogether (Tönnies [1887] 1955). Yet sociologists in the influential Chicago School soon defined immigrant enclaves and other neighborhoods as the basic "ecological" zones that differentiated cities and provided boundaries among communities defined by class status and ethnic identities (Park et al., 1925; Park 1952; Wirth 1938). Bonds of ethnicity, class, and kinship even made some city dwellers behave as "urban villagers" in their neighborhoods, researchers concluded (Gans 1962).

By the latter half of the twentieth century, however, observers argued that in a changing "mass society," with its high rates of mobility, widely dispersed interactions, exposure to mass media, and increasingly far-flung communication channels, community was less and less attached to the residential neighborhood (Janowitz 1952; Kasarda and Janowitz 1974). Perhaps it had been "liberated" from place—even if realtors and developers continued to market places to live *as* "communities." Some scholars proposed de-emphasizing the neighborhood-based conception ("spatial community") relative to one of "personal community," defined as a network of meaningful social ties—"strong" ties that are useful and/or emotionally important (Wellman 1979; 1988). Many neighborhoods, at least when measured by important social ties, were not communities at all, it turned out. The network alternative to spatial conceptions of community, and the image of personalized community in a "network society," has had a broad appeal since the rapid emergence of the internet and other information and communication technologies (Wellman 2001). The "liberated" network alternative now contends with influential findings, most famously by Robert Putnam (2000), on the consequences of a long-run decline in face-to-face community engagement by Americans since the late 1960s, including engagement in neighborhood activism.

But the search for a best definition of community, however illuminating, and the debate over trends in various measures of community involvement, miss several important things relevant to our story, the story of an experiment to fight ghetto poverty. First, community can mean different things, *each* of them meaningful, to different people—and even different things, to the same people, at different times. Sometimes, it is a broad reference to peoplehood, to shared traditions and common experiences within a larger national history or a specific region, as in "the Jewish community in America" or "the black community in Los Angeles." It may refer to occupational, political, or other bonds that provide a sense of identity, place, value, and commonality, as in "the teaching community." It can certainly center on kinship or other strong ties, as it does for many MTO families, even if those ties mostly lie outside one's immediate neighborhood, even if they are sometimes burdensome and frustrating.

But second, and conversely, neighborhoods can still "supply" uniquely valuable functions of community, for example, a felt connection and trust among neighbors, which provide the foundation for acting in concert to accomplish shared goals, such as keeping the streets safe or keeping young people on track (Sampson 1999). Ties among neighbors, where they *are* organized, need not be emotionally close in order to be effective and useful. To use a simple example, a loved one who lives many miles away may provide comfort, money, and other aid when needed, but that person is not in a position to keep an eye on your home when you're away. Your next-door neighbor might do that and perhaps even intervene, with other adults in the neighborhood, to keep local children, especially those unsupervised by their parents, "playing by the rules." Urban analysts have come to call this form of community, once again centered on the residential neighborhood, *collective efficacy*. Typically, it appears to be greater in residentially stable, not transient, neighborhoods, and in relatively homogeneous, not ethnically or socioeconomically diverse, ones (Sampson, Raudenbush, and Felton 1997).[1]

But what might a move from a high-poverty, segregated neighborhood to a low-poverty one do to someone's sense of, or access to, "community"? One response to this question, and one critique of poverty-deconcentration proposals since the Kerner Commission report that followed the urban riots of the 1960s, is a version of what sociologists call the Community Lost thesis: The poor might lose access to their most valuable source of social support and companionship—or "fellowship," as Crystal called it—if it came from relatives and other loved ones who lived nearby (Downs 1973; Greenbaum 2006; Venkatesh 2000; Wellman and Wortley 1990). This concern reflects a larger concern about policy decisions that dislocate people—even though MTO was a voluntary program—and threaten to disrupt their most important social ties (Fullilove 2004).

But is this a well-founded concern in the case of MTO? It is true that the social networks of the poor and working class tend to be more "localized" and kin-centered than those of middle- and upper-income people (Briggs 1998; Fischer 1982). The image of Community Liberated from space, with social networks made up of far-flung friends and acquaintances, largely reflects a focus, by many researchers, on the middle-class experience of social life. That is, we should note, the more common experience in a large and wealthy nation. But it is not the only one and not the most relevant one, of course, for poor people, especially if they are racial and ethnic minorities. There is strong evidence that the personal ties of African Americans, in particular, tend to be very kin-centered and more local than those of whites, and there is some evidence of the same pattern among Hispanics (Fischer 1982; Menjívar 1995; Oliver 1988).

Behind these network patterns is a more fundamental point about whom Americans think of as "family." The dominant conception, and the typical reference point in public policy debates, is the *nuclear* family living in a single household. It reflects the social relations of the white Anglo-Saxon Protestant middle- and upper-income group, which has defined America's mainstream culture over generations. This was the model in Senator Daniel Patrick Moynihan's infamous *Report on the Negro Family*, which contributed to such polarization of the poverty debate after its publication in 1965. Moynihan's concern was that fewer and fewer African-American nuclear families fit that "healthy" mold (see chapter 2). But as researchers have documented since at least the 1970s, other groups—not just people of color but many "white ethnics" as well—lead social lives centered on the *extended* family. Relatives are not just "related," they are family—to be kept close, relied on, supported (Jarrett and Burton 1999). This difference in conception and in day-to-day experience and commitments, is especially important in the lives of the minority poor, such as the families who predominate in MTO.

In one of the most influential studies ever conducted of African-American families in poverty, anthropologist Carol Stack showed, in our *All Our Kin* (1974), how parents and their children survived in networks of exchange and mutual protection. These were not aberrations, wrote Stack, but resilient arrangements created to cope with extreme and chronic deprivation in an exclusionary society. Responding to Moynihan and to claims about a dysfunctional "culture of poverty" among the persistently poor, Stack concluded:

> Distinctively negative features attributed to poor families, that they are fatherless, matrifocal [female-headed], unstable, and disorganized, are not general characteristics of black families living substantially below economic subsistence in America. The black urban family, embedded in cooperative domestic exchange, proves to be an organized, tenacious, active, lifelong network. (124)

But Stack also noted that obligations to kin could be draining, preventing parents from accumulating savings and otherwise getting ahead, because there was always some needy member of the extended family who wanted help and who, according to the norms of the network, should receive that help. There is significant evidence that poor people's networks are not only more localized and limited in range (make-up) but more strained, on average, than those of middle- and upper-income people (Fischer 1982; Kadushin and Jones 1992). This is true not only for chronically poor African Americans but also for certain immigrant groups, who may get stuck for long periods, along with their kin, in weak labor markets with little income or other resources to give back to the network and little in the network to draw on (Menjívar 1995).

Stack went so far as to argue that "survival demands the sacrifice of upward mobility and geographic movement [including housing mobility], and discourages marriage" (124–125). In contrast to an influential scholarly essay on the value of having far-flung acquaintanceships—"the strength of weak ties" (Granovetter 1973)—we will refer to the sobering down side of Stack's classic findings as *the weakness of strong ties*.[2] Strong ties may provide support, but they typically come with enormous obligations as well—this is the very idea of reciprocity and mutual reliance—and sometimes perpetuate the exposure of children and youth to risky social influences, too, such as cousins involved in gangs or uncles engaged in crime.

Later research, while qualifying some of Stack's claims, has corroborated the general finding that failures to save, move away, pursue "opportunities" that involve distance and risk, and other patterns, while perhaps puzzling to the uninformed outsider, make sense in the context of strong kin networks focused on the survival of all members, not the mobility of a select few (Burton and Jarrett 1991; Hainer 1991; Jarrett and Burton 1999). Members of the kin network, argue Stack and Burton (1993), are bound and directed, in their behavior toward one another, by "kinscripts." Likewise, researchers have shown that these patterns apply to Hispanics and other groups, when kin attachments and kin reliance are strong, and not just African Americans, and that maintaining *survival networks* does compete sometimes with efforts to create *mobility networks*, that is, networks for getting ahead (Briggs 1998; Dominguez and Watkins 2003; Menjívar 1995).

This evidence suggests that staying close by, rather than moving away, is central to the community lives of many poor families—and also that this is a mixed blessing. It is notable, for example, that MTO parents, in the experimental group who had more kin ties, were less likely to relocate. But the scholarly evidence also suggests that studies of how relocating affects the loss or gain of "community" should be careful to distinguish the kinds of social resources that provide support for coping or survival (getting by) from those that help parents or their children to get ahead. Moving could trade away some of one resource for more of the other type—helping those who left behind public housing in segregated ghettos to meet people with different backgrounds, for example, and different kinds of information or value as role models—or it might affect neither very much (Briggs 1997; 1998).

On the optimistic end of this assessment, even weak ties, such as acquaintanceships with neighbors who are better informed about educational opportunity or other topics, might make the networks of poor movers more useful in their range and function (meaning: the variety of uses the networks might serve).[3] Again, a neighborly tie need not be "strong" (emotionally) to be useful somehow. Research on Gautreaux reported that low-income African-American mothers who managed to stay in middle-income, mostly white suburban areas did form helpful ties with their neighbors, who helped them navigate school bureaucracies and sometimes offered rides, or kept an eye on children, in an emergency; they were more likely than counterparts who moved within the city of Chicago to report interracial friendships and just as likely to regard their neighbors as friendly (Rubinowitz and Rosenbaum 2000). This is a version of what sociologists call the Community Found thesis: Given time, people who move to new neighborhoods will create or "find" community in those new places. This outlook emphasizes the ties people choose, such as to friends and acquaintances, not the ones they are born into.

The Community Lost perspective is skeptical that moving would help the poor create useful new connections, especially the kind needed to help them get ahead. Early observers of the Clinton-era efforts to deconcentrate poverty through housing policy acknowledged that race and class barriers to neighboring, as well as the lower participation rates of low-income, less educated adults in neighborhood institutions (Fernandez and David 1992), made the formation of such "social capital" less likely, also that policy debates should not assume that poor people's "communities" were the poor neighborhoods they lived in (Briggs 1997).[4] Trusted kin and close friends aside, much research showed the behavior of poor people in poor neighborhoods *toward nonkin neighbors* to be wary and distrusting, shaped by fears of victimization, moral boundaries that people set between themselves and "the wrong kind of people" or culturally different people, and the desire to keep needy, desperate neighbors—or people the respondents perceived to be so, at any rate—out of one's "business" (Hannerz 1969; Merry 1981; Rainwater 1970). The networks of poor relocatees might already be more "liberated" from geography, or at least the immediate residential neighborhood, than the Community Lost critics held.

What is more, MTO children, particularly if enrolled in local schools, might have many more opportunities to connect with new neighbors than their parents would. That is, the younger generation might benefit most from the positive peer influences and collective efficacy, as well as the beneficial social networks, thought to be available to young people in healthier neighborhood contexts (Ellen and Turner 2003; Jencks and Mayer 1990; Leventhal and Brooks-Gunn 2000; Sampson, Morenoff, and Gannon-Rowley 2002).

Prior to our work on MTO, then, contending conceptions of community in contemporary America—Community Lost, Community Found, and Community Liberated, in particular—pointed to a range of possibilities for very low-income families relocating away from ghetto-poor neighborhoods to less poor places. The debate suggested we pay at least as much attention to personal communities (networks) as to spatial ones (neighborhoods) and also that we find out *which* neighborhoods were most important to MTO families, not presume their residential neighborhood to lie at the center of their lives—beyond the basic function of providing shelter at a given address, that is. Furthermore, the distinction between social resources for getting by and those for getting ahead suggested we should examine both sides of the coin. Plus, life stage demanded our attention: Young people relocating through MTO might have very different experiences of community than their parents. Finally, though it received much less attention than the critics' loss-of-community, loss-of-support worry, the concept of collective efficacy suggested that even if relocatees did not actively neighbor in their new neighborhoods—*even if they did not like their neighbors very much, in fact*—their families might benefit from the built-up social cohesion in neighborhoods more able to enforce norms of good behavior.[5]

In the early pages of this chapter, we offered a preview of how things have turned out for MTO families. We expand on that next, emphasizing what did change through moving and, even more, what did not.

FINDING COMMUNITY

The social worlds of most MTO families, whether or not they moved out of high-poverty, high-crime neighborhoods through the experiment—and, for those who moved out, whether or not they managed to stay out, too—are centered on relatives and a few close friends. For those families who persisted in low-poverty areas after relocating, few of the most important ties lie within the neighborhood of residence, where MTO adults, at least, typically perceived neighbors as busy and "keeping to themselves." In some cases, though not often, racial tension was also a deterrent to neighboring, whether tension was between African Americans or Hispanic in-movers and their white neighbors or between minority groups—in transitional areas of metro L.A., in particular.

Plus, MTO families have moved around quite a bit, often struggling to stay out of high-poverty neighborhoods because of high rents or landlords' unwillingness to accept government housing vouchers (see next chapter), and after each relocation, there was no easy way to form ties to new neighbors. Few MTO parents have joined community institutions, for example. Instead, the most important social ties tend to lie in second neighborhoods, as we previewed early in this chapter, and only some of those were the public housing neighborhoods left behind. Those important social ties tended to displace new ones, such as ties to neighbors—even if they might have been useful. Crystal's family is an example of this pattern. In general, few MTO movers have made friends in their new neighborhoods, and this pattern is typical of families moving about in urban and suburban America. In this sense, many of the destination neighborhoods, no matter how appealing, were not "communities" for MTO parents. This was only somewhat less true for MTO children and youth who relocated.

Yet there is little evidence to support the Community Lost thesis—that a move away from familiar surroundings, loved ones, and in some cases a church or other institution, would rob families of vital social supports. The main reason is that in the most common pattern, the social worlds of these families, centered on relatives, remained intact, with socializing and other routines typically focused on the neighborhoods those relatives live in. These were the ties MTO parents and their children were born into, the ones they felt most obliged to and, often, the most dependent on. Is this Community Liberated then? No, at least not in the sense of having far-flung, diverse networks. The important social relations of many MTO families are not so much disconnected from neighborhoods in general as detached from the immediate neighborhood of residence—and anchored elsewhere, where loved ones live. In some extreme cases, MTO families' adult relatives and their children cannot survive independently and so rely on the MTO household, whatever the neighborhood, to provide shelter and care, as well as socializing. It becomes what researchers have termed a "base household" for the extended family (Martin and Martin 1978). Roxanne's place exemplifies this. Roxanne transplanted her social world to center on her current neighborhood, though not in the neighbor-seeking, social-capital-building way that some MTO planners and advocates had hoped for.

Where this kin-centered world was not the outcome, we found, it was generally because MTO parents wanted to buffer themselves and their children from the neediness and the risks their relatives imposed. Jeanine is a case in point. She withheld her latest address from a number of relatives in order to keep them and their constant demands at bay. Such distancing took different forms for different parents, but it was always motivated by a desire to protect the immediate family unit from what MTO parents perceived to be excessive risk and burden. This distancing is at odds with the classic depiction of low-income kin networks as reciprocal and focused on every member's getting by (survival), at the expense of getting ahead (mobility). Some MTO parents felt they had to cut ties, even to kin they cared about, because their survival and mobility, as well as that of their children, depended on it. In some cases, such as Jeanine's, the issue was excessive obligation and financial risk. In other cases, other risks, such as exposing one's children to "the wrong example," was a major worry for MTO parents, many of whom had siblings or cousins or uncles—it was almost always male relatives—with criminal habits or records as well as drug addiction problems.

On the other hand, the evidence supports only a limited version of Community Found. Few MTO families have joined community institutions in low-poverty areas or formed significant relationships there—the kind that provide aid, for example. Their ties to neighbors, like the ties most adults report in most neighborhoods in this country, tend to be cordial but casual on one end of the spectrum—what Crystal called "hi-bye"—and wary and distant on the other end. The differences among neighborhoods probably explain some of this—the high-poverty neighborhoods, while generally more dangerous, also tended to be more social—but MTO adults' own preferences and perceptions—the desire to keep to themselves regardless of where they live, for example—have also played a powerful role. April is a case in point. Since she thinks it is hard to find the kinds of friends worth having, and because she is focused on work and childrearing, she keeps to herself in her low-poverty suburban neighborhood, as she did in her prior neighborhood. Other MTO parents, such as Erika in chapter 1, have been more outgoing. Having lived for years in the same inner suburb of Boston, and in the same neighborhood in fact, Erika got to know many of her neighbors, and—as a basic but important indicator of supportiveness—she felt she could count on them to help her keep an eye on her emotionally troubled son, who attends a nearby school, like other children in the neighborhood.

Based on the survey evidence, even if they kept to themselves, the families in the experimental group who moved to low-poverty areas were more likely than counterparts in high-poverty areas to believe that their neighbors, even if they were strangers, would intervene to curb bad behavior. MTO parents, particularly since they were often motivated to leave ghetto neighborhoods because of perceived risk to their children (see last chapter), valued this capacity for *informal social control*, as social scientists describe it, even if it came without neighborly socializing, let alone emotional closeness. Such control is a reflection of collective efficacy as we defined it earlier.

So what explains these patterns?

The Myth of an "Average" Experience

Early-impact surveys of MTO participants, conducted within two years of enrollment in the program, found that holding motivation, family size, and other factors equal, families in the experimental group were more likely to relocate successfully (becoming "compliers") if they had fewer social connections to the old neighborhood (Shroder 2003). A special survey of compliers in Chicago also showed that both experiment-group and Section 8 comparison-group adults reported that their main sources of advice, loans, and companions for socializing were neither in their current neighborhood of residence nor in the "old" neighborhood but "someplace else" (Rosenbaum, Harris, and Denton 2003). The interim evaluation survey, which included a few general measures of social connection four to seven years after families enrolled in the program, provided additional clues about these patterns. It found no effects of the experiment on the size of participants' friendship circles or the likelihood that they were attending church, when members of the experimental group were compared to members of the control group or Section 8 comparison group (Orr et al., 2003).

But average measures in those highly structured (questionnaire-based) survey studies, like averages in most such studies, hide much of the story: There are more and less *common* patterns in the experiment, to be sure, but not "average" ones. Different types of families had qualitatively different experiences of community, in part because of the choices they made and in part because of the character of their kin networks, the context for neighboring around them, or other factors largely outside their control. These differences have important implications for the supports and obligations, the benefits and the risks, that MTO parents and their children experienced in their lives and, more to the point, for the effects or noneffects of moving and of living in particular kinds of neighborhoods.

Table 6.1 summarizes the major types we uncovered, focused on the experimental compliers—those who relocated, at least for a time, to a low-poverty neighborhood. We constructed the typology around these families because planners' expectations, after all, were highest for this group: They received the experimental treatment. Our ethnographic fieldwork, which allowed us to examine social relations, daily routines, and patterns of engagement in one or more neighborhoods, in depth, was limited to experimental compliers, including those who managed to stay in low-poverty areas and those who had moved back to very poor ones, as well as control-group members. So we use those data, supplemented by the interview data on the same families, not to make causal claims about

Table 6.1. Experimental Compliers: Types, by Neighborhood Engagment and Social Relations

Type	Description	Context (circumstance and choice factors)
1. Kin-centered nonlocal social world, mainly *outside* neighborhood of residence	Social worlds anchored in a second neighborhood, though not necessarily the one left behind.	Socializing and/or exchanges of support are focused on the key neighborhood(s) where relatives, such as MTO household head's parents or siblings, live.
2. Kin-centered transplant, social world anchored mainly in neighborhood of residence	Social worlds anchored where subject family lives, though engagement with nonkin neighbors limited.	Family moved to a neighborhood where relatives live, or vice-versa (MTO household provides stable base for extended family).
3. Kin-avoidant, friend-centered	Avoids close ties and steady contact with some or all kin. Social world may not be anchored to any neighborhood.	Uses physical or emotional distancing strategies to buffer self and children from excessive kin obligation and/or risk. History of abusive, estranged, and/or exploitative kin relations. Friends made in school, at work, during childhood in public housing, or through church or social programs, not current neighborhood of residence.
4. Broader social world	Some kin ties, large friendship circle, plus useful "associates" or acquaintances. Limited neighborhood engagement.	Tend to be more educated, better employed MTO parents. More likely to participate in associations; neighborly ties pursued where useful.
5. Social isolate	Avoids personal ties generally.	Chronic illness or demanding work and childrearing routines, together with wariness about close personal relationships, discourages connection. Kin physically and/or emotionally distant.

Source: Three-City Study interview and ethnographic field data.

the treatment but rather to carefully describe the patterns about which most prior research has only conjectured. In simpler terms, we are focused here on understanding in depth *what movers' experiences have been*, not detecting *effects of the program* per se (or the experiences of control-group members who were never offered relocation help, conditional on moving to low-poverty areas).[6]

The first two types in table 6-1 were the most common, the latter three exceptional. Crystal's family is an example of the first type, and typical of this type, she saw little need to form closer ties to her neighbors even though she viewed them in a generally positive light. Her active ties were to kin, and those ties were anchored, had long been anchored, elsewhere. Multiple moves since entering the MTO program had not changed that. This pattern was also clear among control-group families and experimental-group families living, unlike Crystal, in high-poverty neighborhoods: Social life centered on kin and perhaps a few trusted friends. The difference is in how *other* neighbors (those who were not kin) were viewed: In high-poverty areas, MTO families saw many of their neighbors not as busy or keeping to themselves but as gossipy, prone to fighting, and likely to cause trouble if one brought them close. A number of MTO mothers described interacting with these neighbors strategically. While they were not be trusted as friends, they should not be angered or alienated either, and occasionally, they kept an eye out in helpful ways. But there was virtually no basis for neighbors to exert significant social influence or provide significant aid.

As we explore in detail in the next chapter, for a small share of experimental compliers, connections to kin and other strong ties were an important reason for moving back to high-poverty neighborhoods. Take the example of Patricia, a single mother in the Los Angeles experimental group. When we began to visit her, she was living, once again, in a high-poverty, high-crime neighborhood of South L.A., albeit not the public housing neighborhood she and her children had left behind when they enrolled in MTO and moved to a low-poverty neighborhood in the San Fernando Valley. Patricia loved the Valley neighborhood and found her neighbors there "very nice," as she recalls. "They were the neighbors that loved my kids and took them places." She also found a "church home" she liked in the Valley. Yet all her loved ones were in South L.A., and because they did not have a car, she and her children had to take a bus, several hours each way, to visit them several times each week. The need to be with her mother grew when her brother was killed in their old neighborhood. He and Patricia were close, and it was the sixth homicide the extended family had suffered. The loss sent Patricia's mother into a great depression. Patricia and her children also had to catch a bus to the church she liked in the Valley. Patricia had other reasons to stay connected to inner-city Los Angeles. She did not have a regular job, so she made her apartment an informal hair salon and kept in touch with friends from the public housing projects. They were her steady clientele. "They know that I need the money and stuff, so they come and help me out," she says.

As we explore in chapter 9, other MTO parents, including those with steady jobs and childcare needs, even moved in with relatives, at least for a time, when they could not align the location of their job with an affordable apartment and reliable source of childcare (which usually entailed getting their children to and from a relative's home each workday).

Roxanne illustrates the second type in table 6.1. As the matriarch of the family, she provided the shelter and care, not only for her own youngest child but for several of her older children's children as well. Like Crystal, Roxanne had generally positive views of neighbors but little time or inclination to form ties with them. Likewise, April had transplanted her life to her low-poverty neighborhood in a Boston suburb, but work, church, and childrearing filled her time. She was happy to have her children focus on their peers in the new neighborhood, unlike her husband, who socialized regularly with relatives and friends back in inner-city Boston. Plus, April was wary of friendships in general. Here again, neighbors are relegated to the background as sources of either aid or influence.

Jeanine, whom we also introduced in the opening pages of this chapter, exemplifies type three in the table. In her case, parents were out of the picture. They had both suffered drug addiction and died young. Jeanine's siblings, whom she largely raised herself, had become unreliable, even exploitative from her vantage point, by the time she and her children enrolled in MTO. She had become as choosy about her extended family ties as many people are about friends; some were worth it and deserving, others not. She had moved on and let go.

A similar family history shaped the social world of Pamela, age 73, who continued to live in public housing in a high-poverty area in the South Bronx when we began to visit her. As a young girl, she had been sexually abused by men in her mother's life, as well as frequently left alone, for days on end, by her mother. "I was the oldest," she told us, "and so I ended up taking over, going out, stealing food, stealing clothes, washing clothes." Pamela was now estranged from most of her siblings and their children, keeping just two siblings close—including her youngest sister, whom she had raised as her own child. She relied on none of them for regular support.

MTO parents who did this distancing, which ranged from seeing relatives less often to cutting them out entirely or only allowing children to visit them when the parent came along, tended to be wary of close social ties in general. Here again, there was little to make any new neighborhood a community, as distinct from a base of operations for the family's daily routines.

Few MTO adults are in the fourth category: parents whose social worlds reflect neither the avoidance of kin nor centering one's life on kin but rather a much broader engagement with friends and weaker ties, such as acquaintances. These are adults with social ties that are both diverse in make-up and expansive in geography: the networks "liberated" from place that, sure enough, reflect a middle-class education, institutional access, and outlook. Jessica, for example, lives in Harlem with her two sons and teaches science at an elementary school in the area. Though Harlem has gentrified considerably over the past decade, with a large number of professionals moving into once-distressed blocks, it is still much poorer than the low-poverty area Jessica moved to when she left public housing through MTO. But the current neighborhood is conveniently located to shopping and special programs, which Jessica taps for her younger son, James, in particular. Jessica told us she had few people she counted as friends but many reliable "associates" she could turn to for social support and useful information. She met most of them on the current job or earlier jobs, some through a church she attends each week, not through neighboring. While we were in the field, Jessica was working to earn a graduate degree online, and she had plans to move to Florida and buy a home there.

Other parents in MTO, while not as connected as Jessica, described a single individual in their lives—a helpful pastor, for example, or a childhood friend who was a teacher—as a treasure trove of information and advice. We revisit this theme, and the opposite problem of information poverty, which was widespread among MTO families, in the chapter on finding good schools.

At the other extreme from the Crystals and Jessicas in our study—women with large support networks, albeit of very different kinds—is the fifth and final type, the social isolates. These are highly disadvantaged MTO mothers with virtually no support from either relatives or friends. Some are immigrants whose relatives live in other states in the U.S. mainland or elsewhere, such as in Puerto Rico, Mexico, or the Dominican Republic. For example, Luisa, who used her MTO voucher to move to a southern suburb of Boston, has a sister in the city, but she cannot easily rely on her to get rides in an emergency. Her other relatives are scattered across several other states, and Luisa does not make friends easily or find her immediate environment a supportive one. She moved into her apartment complex only after the MTO program's lawyers alleged housing discrimination by the property management company. Luisa senses racial tension in the building still—a reflection of the increased presence of people of color in the suburb—and she keeps to herself.

The boundaries among these types are not bold and bright in most cases but rather blurred. Many parents in our study faced some of the challenges that Luisa did, for example, though without the extreme isolation as the outcome. And many faced the burdens that come with strong ties, especially to relatives, and not just the supportiveness that discussions of the importance of "community" tend to emphasize. Before we turn to those burdens, we look briefly at the realities of getting and providing aid, since the Community Lost perspective highlighted the risk that relocating through MTO would lead to a loss of access to vital aid. That rarely happened.

Getting and Giving Help

The 39 mothers, most of whom were single mothers, in our ethnographic sample relied on very small support networks: an average of two relatives and one friend provided rides to places, babysitting, and small cash loans or gifts, or more nonroutine aid, such as help moving, finding a job, or fixing a car.[7] Typically, these relatives and friends were also poor or working-class people with limited resources to offer. Sometimes, they were needy, too. Not surprisingly, married mothers in the sample had less need for help from outside the household.

The character of the relationship, accessibility of the aid giver, and the nature of the need generally dictated whom MTO parents turned to for aid, whereas life experience and family structure shaped overall access to aid. This was true regardless of treatment group or neighborhood type.

For example, Gloria in Los Angeles relied only on her father, because he was willing and able to help—"If I need something, he don't ask no questions, he's just like, 'Here you go,'" she told us—and also because she felt estranged from her mother, who had been abusive during her childhood. For Nancy and her husband José, also in Los Angeles, proximity is a huge boon. Her brother bought a duplex, which allowed Nancy and her family to leave public housing. Her mother lives with her brother next door, so the two households can babysit each other's children, and Nancy can get rides from her brother when she needs them.

The oldest MTO parents had grown children they could rely on, usually one or two who were particularly reliable, whether or not they lived in the same neighborhood. Tessa in Boston, age 72, has lived in the same inner-city neighborhood for almost 50 years. She tends to rely on her daughter Cheryl, even though Cheryl lives in Rhode Island, for rides to the doctor or to get groceries. But sometimes, Tessa relies on her older daughter, Terry, too.

When kin lived too far away or were emotionally distant or to be avoided, MTO parents typically turned to a single close friend or two or, less often, a neighbor. For example, Elena in Boston relied reluctantly on a neighbor, one of the two friends she identified in her life, for occasional babysitting. Though she stayed in close touch with her relatives, they all lived in the Dominican Republic, where Elena was born and raised, and she was wary of trusting new people.

Mara, also in Boston, relied on a friend and ex-roommate, Juan. In the first low-poverty suburban area she moved to with her MTO housing voucher, she told us, "There were no buses, no trains, and when my car used to break down, Juan was there…He never says 'no' when I ask him to do anything." Her relatives, on the other hand, were in Puerto Rico as well as Boston, most importantly her four sisters living in public housing. But while Mara's daughter Alma, age 23, had a brain-damaged son who needed constant attention, her sisters offered little help, she said, only gossip about her and judgment:

> Family didn't ever give me any credit…only negatives. Do you remember how they were giving me so much shit when my grandson was in the hospital and they were questioning whether I was giving him good care? We don't have to give any explanations…and then when we were in Puerto Rico, they kept asking me how come I had not brought my grandson.… They were trying to make me feel bad because we didn't bring him. Were they nuts? Didn't they know how difficult it was to care for him?

But beyond being unsympathetic or in other ways unsupportive, some kin ties were burdensome or posed special risks. We examine these down sides of maintaining close ties next.

The Weakness of Strong Ties: Burden and Risk

As we discussed earlier in this chapter, the 1960s-era debates about chronic poverty, and the claims about family dysfunction in particular, led some researchers to focus on the resilience of kin networks among poor people. Carol Stack, for example, emphasized the tenacity, resourcefulness, and strong norms of reciprocal obligation that enabled African-American extended families, linked by blood and affection, to survive extreme and chronic deprivation and exclusion. But she also showed how the constant demands of needy relatives also thwarted upward mobility, as well as housing mobility—moving up or moving out, that is—for any one nuclear family in the network. Sociologists have found the same for immigrants embedded in chronically overburdened networks.[8] We take this finding further by examining not only the burdensome nature of many strong ties that MTO families took with them (did not lose) when they relocated but also the risks some of these ties posed in the form of negative influence on children.

About half the adults in our ethnographic sample of 39 families identified at least one burdensome tie, with an average of two to three. Burdensome ties were usually relatives with chronic illness and corresponding care needs, those who taxed MTO families financially by constantly asking for help the family could not afford, or those who exploited trust and defrauded their own kin: a cousin who stole something or a brother-in-law who "ripped me off." Jeanine's experiences with her siblings, who exploited her good credit rating and her willingness to help them, illustrate these burdens. Some burdensome relatives were those who asked for babysitting, a place to stay, or other informal support much too often or for too long, at least from our subjects' vantage points. A smaller share were children, such as Roxanne's, who were not in shape to care for their own children. The sense of obligation to many of these people, in spite of the burden they represented, led to mixed emotions, including frustration and guilt.

The strains were particularly severe for MTO mothers who were themselves quite ill or otherwise burdened day to day. At the interim evaluation point, nearly one-quarter of MTO adults were receiving SSI, a benefit primarily granted to individuals who are unable to work because of chronic health problems. Shenice, for example, is a mother in the Boston experimental group. She lives in a quiet, low-poverty neighborhood in the southwest part of the city. She was diagnosed with lupus after moving through MTO, and her condition had deteriorated significantly in the several years before we began to visit in 2004. By then, her illness was affecting what she was able to do on a daily basis, and her doctors had given her just a few years to live. On some of our visits, she was barely able to walk, talk, or even breathe. She often complained of severe pain and spent some days in bed because of it. At other times, her lupus caused Shenice to experience a loss of appetite, diarrhea, fatigue, or migraines. Her daughter Bianca sometimes went with her on errands, so that Bianca could steer the car or otherwise help her mother.

In spite of these severe physical challenges, and the emotional strains they created, Shenice was determined to support her mother, a cancer survivor who received regular dialysis, and her sister, who suffered from diabetes and was going blind. Shenice felt obligated to visit her family daily, in particular to make sure her mother took her medication and made it to all her medical appointments. Plus, Shenice was expected to drive her sister to work each night because her sister was unable to see at night to catch the bus—including the cold winter nights, without a working car heater. In general, the extended family relied heavily on Shenice. At the beginning of our fieldwork, her brother was moving out of Shenice's apartment after having lived there with his girlfriend for free. Bianca and the girlfriend had had an argument, which led Shenice to ask, apprehensively, that her brother move out. Bianca felt that the girlfriend did little to help out around the house, in spite of Shenice's poor health.

Over the months we visited the family, Shenice began to feel worn out, and her daughter became fed up with relatives' demands. "I tried to help my brother out," Shenice said one day, "because he's my brother, my family, and because that is how my parents raised us." But she soon added, "Given my condition, they shouldn't be so dependent on me." Even the errands she ran for them had become too much. "It's become very difficult for me to go to the store. My bones hurt a lot. I can't," she explained. She felt that her sister and mother, in particular, were in denial: "They don't want to accept how sick I am."

Bianca was often late for school, or missed school days altogether, due to the heavy demands of her relatives, and she grew frustrated at what she perceived to be their lack of consideration. "I don't like it when they [family members] call sometimes, especially when my mom is not feeling well. They tell me it's an emergency, and I know it's not an emergency." Shenice told us that one time, when family members told Bianca it was an emergency, they were in fact calling to find out when she could pick things up for them at the grocery store.

Beyond burden, most families in our in-depth ethnographic study had relatives whose risky behavior posed risks—relatives with alcohol or drug abuse problems, abusiveness at home, criminal records and time in jail, and/or a history of fighting or other violence. Overwhelmingly, these were male relatives: ex-husbands, boyfriends and ex-boyfriends, brothers, uncles, cousins. About half the adolescents in our study had fathers with one or more of these traits. One-fifth of the sample had male relatives who had been shot or killed. Marisol, in Boston, told us about the drugs that had been "all around" in her life. She called off the drug addicted:

"My brother, my dad, her dad [pointing to her daughter]. It's been all around me." She had moved from home to home, staying with relatives, as she tried to stay away from her abusive ex-boyfriend, her daughter's father. In one fight, he tried to strangle her. In another, he pulled a knife. Marisol's mother had suffered similar abuse. "My dad beat her so bad [once]," she recalled. "She was hospitalized for like over three weeks, almost a month. They didn't let us see her at first, because her face was so messed up."

When MTO parents distanced themselves from relatives, friends, or other strong ties, it was often to protect their children. As we showed in the last chapter, attachment to kin back in high-poverty neighborhoods exposed many MTO youth to risky behavior, often by relatives themselves—cousins in gangs, fathers or stepfathers or uncles who stole or got in fights—even after the (nuclear) family's relocation to a safer neighborhood. As Gretchen Weismann concluded, using our data, MTO parents were less conscious of the risks posed by these relatives than those posed by risky neighbors or former neighbors to whom they were not related.

But some parents cut ties to kin, as we have shown, and sometimes, it was a marked change of behavior that "crossed the line" in terms of what MTO parents would accept. Mothers avoided sisters, cousins, or others who began to drink or take drugs and date the "wrong kind" of men, and more importantly, they made sure their children stopped visiting those relatives, too. Some parents also looked outside the family to find role models, especially for their male children. A few were lucky enough to find a strong and attentive coach, teacher, or guidance counselor, for example.

Beyond excessive burden and risk, there is a third, less intuitive "weakness" of strong ties: Centering one's life on them tends to crowd out other kinds of ties, including weaker ties that can be enormously helpful—as Jessica, with her large circle of associates, knows well. It is true, as Tessa observes in the epigram atop this chapter, that there is nothing quite like family (as in kin). She is also right, our own experiences and our data tell us, that sometimes, you cannot get along "even" with them. But as important as so many kin ties are to the day-to-day survival of MTO families, in most cases, those ties are not enough—not enough, as we will show, to help families find the best possible neighborhoods to live in, the best schools for their children, the best job or training opportunities open to them. Some families had relatives with helpful information, advocacy skill, perhaps even favors they could call in. But most families did not enjoy that kind of access through kin, and some could not count on their kin even if the latter were well positioned to help. The experiment did not specifically enable or encourage MTO parents to build more diverse and effective networks, whether inside or outside the neighborhood.[9]

Before recapping the major findings of the chapter, we consider a final question: Since young movers have institutions—schools, in particular—and developmental needs that are different from those of their parents, did MTO youth find community in new neighborhoods, old ones, or someplace else?

YOUNG PEOPLE'S SOCIAL WORLDS

To our initial surprise, even the young people who relocated to low-poverty neighborhoods through MTO often named relatives among their best friends. While some made friends at school or found playmates in the neighborhood, the social worlds of MTO's next generation, like that of their parents, often revolved around kin in second neighborhoods, not the nuclear family's neighborhood of residence. Habit was one reason, but for young people for whom adult-type obligations to kin have yet to take hold, the other reason was parents' distrust of nonkin. As we showed above, MTO parents differed in their relationship to kin, but in the common pattern, the kin-centered type, the kin network *seemed* a protective circle, an antidote to the risk that children might hang out with the wrong friends at school or in the neighborhood. Young cousins of a similar age were thus often on the friend list, and some MTO youth hung out with older relatives, including those involved in gangs, fighting, theft, and other trouble. Adolescents in the experimental group described a number of relatives, in fact, including young cousins, who first exposed them to drinking, smoking weed, gun toting, car theft, and other risky behavior. Perhaps because of kinscripts, MTO youth were less able to isolate themselves from these risky peers (to whom they were related) than other peers they deemed to be a bad influence.

In the control group, young people named friends made at school in addition to relatives, and the pool of peers at their schools often included young people involved in gangs, drinking or drug taking, or other risky behavior. The risky behavior we learned about was more serious, the risky peers more available, more likely to drop by the home. The main point is that exposure to such peers did not change—for those who relocated—nearly as much as MTO planners had hoped, and the main reason was MTO participants' attachment to kin who were still living in high-poverty neighborhoods and whose children attended some of the poorest, most segregated, and most gang-ridden and dangerous schools in these regions. Adolescents identified some of their relatives as distinctly negative influences, including those that got them into gangs or into smoking weed, as well as those who set bad examples for their children, dropped out of school, or became homeless.

On the positive side, adolescents in the experimental group, more often females than males, invariably identified relatives among their role models—when they could think of role models at all. Regardless of treatment group, successful aunts, uncles, and cousins—or their own parents—who stayed in school, found steady work, and formed healthy relationships are the people these youth look up to. Faith, age 13, sees her aunt Diana, her mother Juana's younger sister, for example, as a role model:

> [Diana] was able to make it through school and work, and she's really done what she wanted to do, and now she has a really good life.... She went to high school, then to college. She got a nice house and a nice car and a nice boyfriend. I want all of that. She's always happy. She's different from the others [in the family]. She put her mind to it. I think I could be like that.

But about half the adolescents could not think of anyone they considered a role model or mentor, which we let them define broadly as someone to look up to or seek guidance from. Relocating per se had no clear effect on this. When we pressed Carmela in Boston, Marisol's daughter, for someone in her life whom she thought of as a model or guide, she could think of no one. "Only TV and stuff like that," she said "It's depressing." Michael in Los Angeles named Tupac Shakur, the popular rapper who was killed in 1996, because he was successful without forgetting his roots "in the neighborhood." "Do you look up to anyone you *know?*" we asked. "No," he said. "I don't have mentors." José, in New York, chuckled when we asked him about sources of advice on getting into college specifically. And then he replied, "I ain't got no support. Nobody tells me about that. They don't tell me anything." This kind of isolation, which we revisit in the chapter on finding good schools, affected young people in the experimental group as well as their control-group counterparts.

Kia in Boston, whose mother emphasized self-reliance and material success whenever we visited, was emphatic that particular adults might offer an example of *how* successful one could be, but looking to others for guidance was not something she needed or wanted: "Me. I'm my role model," she told us flatly. "Is there anyone you look up to?" we pressed. "I depend on myself. I take care of myself," she said firmly. Her mother, Danielle, and her grandmother had taught her this. Kia then shouted to her sister, Shauna, in the next room. "Shauna! Who's your role model?" she asked. "Me!" came the reply.

SUMMARY AND IMPLICATIONS

One reason that social experiments defy straightforward interpretation is that, at least on some key dimensions, there is no "average" participant experience. Finding community, as we have shown, is a many-splendored thing. Different families made different choices, but several major patterns stand out. First, new neighborhoods provided much greater security to many families, and MTO parents and their children typically viewed low-poverty areas as better monitored—in keeping with the view that neighborhoods can "supply" community in the form of collective efficacy even if particular residents are not actively engaged in neighboring, joining local institutions, or otherwise contributing to the stock of social capital.

In this limited way, the Community Found perspective finds support in the experiences of very low-income families who moved to low-poverty areas. As we show in the next chapter, however, MTO families in the experimental group struggled to stay out of high-poverty neighborhoods over time, and their ongoing housing mobility discouraged deeper integration into the social life of their neighborhoods.

Following on that point, second, for most MTO families, like many other families in America, the new neighborhood was not a community in the sense of being a social world for interaction and mutual support. A network of kin played that role, and obligations to kin loomed large in the lives of most families, in keeping with prior research on how the chronically poor—both disadvantaged, native-born African Americans and disadvantaged immigrants or descendants of immigrants—cope with deprivation. Only rarely did families show evidence of losing access, through relocation, to loved ones and the support they provided—as the Community Lost school of thought worried. To the contrary, in the most common pattern, some second neighborhoods where a key relative(s) lived, and not the neighborhood of residence, provided the context for socializing, getting and giving help, and other interactions. Less commonly, MTO families transplanted their social world to a new neighborhood, either because their home was the extended family's base, a church or other institution acted as the central social site, or because they—the MTO parent—chose to cut ties with burdensome or risky relatives. This distancing, we have emphasized, is at odds with the common depiction of extended-family ties as mutually supportive and comforting. MTO parents have also been abused, ripped off, enticed to abuse drugs or alcohol, and threatened by their relatives—especially male ones—and sometimes, a change of address was part of a larger strategy to insulate themselves and their children from such emotional and physical violence, taxing financial demands, negative social influences, and other problems. We are not able to claim that MTO made this easier on a program-wide basis, but clearly relocating helped some families cut burdensome ties.

Beyond the burdens and risks, kin-reliant, kin-centered living displaced opportunities to form broader ties, leaving the networks of many MTO adults insular and limited in the aid they might provide. These three traits—excessive burden, sometimes overwhelming risk, and insularity—define what we have called the weakness of strong ties.

Regardless of these choices and circumstances, however—we cannot choose the kin networks into which we are born, after all—the outcome is that MTO families almost never "converted" a new location into significant new social resources. This thwarted hopes that relocation away from ghetto neighborhoods would generate better access to information about good housing, schools, jobs, and other opportunities. In other words, moving rarely led to the loss of social capital in the support or survival dimension, but nor did it generate new social capital of the kind useful for getting ahead, at least for MTO adults. While some movers experienced harassment or racial tension, most thought their neighbors friendly enough—but not to be approached. Ironically, most MTO parents found neighbors in low-poverty areas to be generally less social than the neighbors left behind and *at the same time* less troublesome. Some parents, we should underline, avoided interactions of any kind and seldom formed friendships. They were wary of relationships anywhere, in any type of neighborhood, and this outlook was rooted in painful family histories, exploitative friendships in the past, or the messages imprinted by parents, not the experience of relocation.

Third, kin-centered community also shaped daily routines and important social relationships for MTO youth to a significant extent. Though some made good friends in new neighborhoods and schools, the good friends they described to us were often relatives, for example cousins— or uncles, aunts, nieces, and nephews of a similar age. Parents were the mediators of this contact, as we have noted above. Children and even adolescents depended on them to return to the second neighborhoods, though not necessarily the "old" neighborhood of public housing residence. And while this provided some support, it also made young people's networks more insular and sometimes more laden with risk. Some MTO adolescents whose families had successfully relocated to low-poverty areas described relatives who exposed them to drug dealing, car theft, gun toting, smoking weed, drinking, early sexual behavior, and other risks. Yes, many young people in the more disadvantaged areas were "fast" in those dimensions, but the point is that many MTO youth who relocated to low-poverty areas remained exposed to such fast behavior—"street" behavior—because they were so embedded in kin networks that their parents chose to keep front and center.

Yet neighborhoods, as we will show, can matter even when neighbors do not. How did MTO families fare on the most basic aim of the experiment: to move to and stay in better neighborhoods? We turn to this, and the punishing demands of tight housing markets, next.

Chapter 7

Struggling to Stay Out of High-Poverty Neighborhoods

Finding Good Housing

> It is often remarked how difficult it is to get a family to move out
> of the slum, no matter how advantageous the move may seem
> from the material point of view, and how much more difficult it
> is to keep them from moving back into the slum.
>
> Harvey Zorbaugh, *The Gold Coast and the Slum* (1929)

CHASING THE DREAM

After they enrolled in the MTO program, Tameka and her children relocated to a low-poverty neighborhood in the Los Angeles suburbs. She
was very pleased with this neighborhood, she told us, but when her
landlord stopped accepting housing vouchers because the red-hot market gave him the chance to rent to much higher income tenants, she was
forced to find a new apartment. This drove her back to the city, though
she had looked hard for a decent, affordable place in the suburbs. With
a great deal of effort, she found a vacant house that she liked in L.A.
She remembers:

> Well…it's really a tricky thing when you're moving, because…especially
> when you're a working, single parent…. I know I have a certain amount of
> time to be out this apartment, to be relocated. So I went to this place where
> people find a place for you. You pay them this fee, and they look for like
> apartments and houses for you, for people that work and stuff. And you pay
> 'em a fee, like $150 or something…. And…they give you like a listing every
> week. And every time they give you a listing of maybe, I'd say roughly 100
> places, maybe 80 of the places is already rented, been rented out already
>
> …But it took me about 45 days and, um, at work, even on my break,
> I was in newspapers and doing anything I had to do to find a place. Actually,
> I found this house…in *La Opinion* [an Hispanic newspaper], and I had my
> co-worker to like read it for me…. And they had a open house and I came,
> and I was like, "Oh, I know a lot of people gonna be for this. Don't think
> like that, don't think negative." And when I came for the open house, I was
> the only person here.

The landlord was willing to accept Tameka's housing voucher, but to make things work, she had to help him prepare the unit to pass the government's required housing quality inspection. "I looked at a lot of places in [an inner suburb to the south of Los Angeles]…a lot of places that were vacant and available, they did not accept Section 8 [housing vouchers]," she says. "So you run into that… and if you're not determined and a focused person, you will really give up."

Tameka's story is like that of many low-income, working parents who must navigate high-cost housing markets in America. As we detailed in chapter 4, much of the nation's economic growth is concentrated in these high-cost regions, yet the supply of affordable rental housing has become more and more inadequate over the past decade, and many landlords refuse to accept tenants with government housing vouchers—the roughly 1 in 4 eligible, very low-income families who are lucky enough to obtain those vouchers at all.

What is more, the geography of opportunity, including access to good schools, safe and healthy neighborhoods, affordable housing, and job opportunity, is highly unequal, reflecting persistent segregation. As journalist Jason Deparle wrote—amid Congressional cutbacks in low-income housing assistance more than a decade ago—"Housing problems are far more central to the lives of the poor than a number of issues—immunizations, school lunches—that have made recent headlines. The cost of shelter breaks the budgets of low-income Americans, crowds them into violent ghettos, far from good jobs and schools—or both."[1]

Central cities and older suburban public school districts educate most of the nation's poor and minority children, for example, with the highest rates of dropout and school violence and other failures, while higher income, mostly college-bound children study in private schools or more exclusive suburban public school districts.

These patterns made the goal of securing good housing in a community with good schools—two foundations of the American Dream for most families—elusive for Tameka and her children, as well as many other families in the MTO experiment. That fact, in turn, made the fortunes of MTO families over time very different from those of the successful movers, in the late 1970s and early 1980s, in Chicago's Gautreaux housing program, which provided both the inspiration and the template for MTO.

In chapter 5, we focused on the initial relocation to safer neighborhoods and the impacts of those moves on families' sense of security and well-being. Yet according to an interim evaluation of MTO conducted four to seven years after families enrolled in the program, many families who had successfully relocated to low-poverty neighborhoods were living back in high-poverty ones (though not necessarily the ones they had left behind). These disappointing location outcomes have led some observers to wonder whether deconcentrating poverty is more a reformer's ideal than a priority for the families served by the nation's low-income housing programs and to question both the feasibility and the wisdom of intervening in the complexities of housing choice for low-income people (see, e.g., Clark 2005). Some wondered whether the experiment had simply failed to address the fact that the minority poor prefer and need familiar urban neighborhoods, with loved ones, churches, and other supports close at hand.

We will show that MTO's housing outcomes raise another serious question. It is a question about the potential of any MTO-type effort: How would it deliver on the promise of positive "neighborhood effects" if it could not ensure a stable, secure, affordable foothold in better neighborhoods? Housing stability is a precondition, frequently overlooked in policy debates, for more engagement by low-income families in schools and community life, especially in less poor, less racially isolated, and also less familiar places. Without stability, there is no "community"—and there are fewer positive effects of place.

In America, educational access and outcomes are closely tied to housing opportunities. MTO was inspired by the apparent successes of the Gautreaux housing desegregation program in metro Chicago, as we detailed in chapter 3—in particular, by the striking educational gains made by children who relocated from inner-city neighborhoods to racially integrated, middle-income suburbs and managed to stay in those areas for 7 to 10 years. Yet MTO showed no measurable impacts on school outcomes, and only modest differences in school quality, for the experimental group at the interim mark. Educational failure is one of the costliest and most visible problems associated with ghetto poverty, yet thus far, MTO has not made a dent for the average child who participated.

Why? In this chapter, we address the first puzzle—about struggling to stay out of high-poverty neighborhoods after escaping them—and in the next chapter the second, about children not securing significantly better educational opportunities *even if* their families managed to stay in the experiment's low-poverty "opportunity" neighborhoods. The two puzzles are closely linked, since, for most American families, housing choices *are* school choices: About 7 in 10 children who attend a public school—as almost all MTO children do—are assigned to their school based on the neighborhood they live in (Briggs 2005a).

The lessons of MTO help inform the contentious, ongoing debates over the potential of choice to transform the "public service market" of education and the complex public-private system of low-income housing, which has received much less attention in research on choice-oriented public policy. We begin with a brief look at advocates' great expectations about choice—and the much harsher realities of choice for the disadvantaged in America.

CHOICE AND CONSTRAINT

Like other parents in MTO, Tameka, whom we introduced above, had "run into" quite a few barriers, as she said, but the specific choices she made mattered, too. Both the choices and the structural constraints have shaped the experiment's outcomes, yet to date, researchers have had a very difficult time explaining *how*. And this is a problem in a country deeply enamored of choice as a mechanism for improving lives, both in consumer markets and public policy.

In public education, for example—with the move toward charter schools and school voucher experiments that claim to "empower" disadvantaged children and their parents (Ladd 2002; Peterson and Campbell 2001)—and in health care, social security and retirement savings, housing assistance and other domains, the past two decades have seen a proliferation of choice-oriented reforms, especially voucher-based subsidies, counseling, and "organizational report cards" (Gormley and Weimer 1999; Greener 2008; Hipp and Warner 2008). Proponents claim that *under the right conditions*, these mechanisms promise greater competition, efficiency, transparency, and quality in "public service markets," where most analysts have focused, and also in housing, a complex private market shaped by government policy in a host of important ways.

Yet there are major challenges on both the supply and demand sides of this promise. On the demand side, for example, a growing body of evidence from careful experiments indicates, as psychologist Barry Schwartz explains, that "while the upper and middle classes define freedom as choice, working-class Americans emphasize freedom from instability."[2] Less educated and more economically insecure Americans, particularly if they are not in a position to make better informed choices on their own, associate choosing with demands that pose risk and threaten their well-being. This leads to less comparison shopping and a less-informed search for alternatives.

Moreover, some choices—among retirement savings plans, "exotic" subprime mortgages or other credit instruments, and, for many families, the right schools and neighborhoods—are particularly complex to make. Choosing well demands not easily acquired types of information and subtle judgments about that information—not just being able to find out the educational credentials *and* classroom management ability of a school's teachers, for example, but understanding just why those two very different things, the latter of which is harder to measure and report, might matter for your child's learning in math, science, or other subjects.

The choices "supplied" are also at issue here, particularly if providers have incentives to lower quality to keep costs down, as appears to be the case for both housing and training when government vouchers are used (Briggs and Turner 2006; Hipp and Warner 2008). Some of the most influential new research and commentary, grounded in the field of behavioral economics, is aimed squarely at improving choices without constraining people to do what social engineers think best. For example, in their book *Nudge: Improving Decisions about Health, Wealth, and Happiness* (2008), Richard Thaler and Cass Sunstein argue for shifting "choice architecture"—the presentation of choices and of "defaults"—in ways that, according to the evidence, are likely to improve outcomes without limiting freedom to choose. (A widely cited example is enrolling employees in retirement savings plans automatically, but allowing them to opt out, rather than offering them the chance to opt in. In demonstrations, the opt-in default produces dramatically higher enrollment rates.) But for now, their work and most other work in the field remain focused on the problem of *choosing well within a relatively good set of choices.*

The fact that many in our country do not, as a practical matter, have very good options to choose *from*, even if they are given housing or school vouchers or other forms of assistance, suggests an even wider gulf between optimistic, middle-class conceptions of choice as empowering and the realities of choice for the most disadvantaged. We return to this point in the book's concluding chapter. In an age of piecemeal public supports and numerous choice reforms, it is especially important to understand why and how the most disadvantaged people served by social programs make the choices they do *and* how those programs and the market have, in fact, "supplied" and structured the choices as well as the capacity to choose. Being formally and legally "free" to choose is not very meaningful at all, or very laudable, if one cannot, as a practical matter, exercise that freedom with the limited resources one controls.

LESSONS: A PREVIEW

By combining market analysis with accounts from the many MTO families we visited, we confirmed, on the housing front, that these families faced major barriers in tightening markets. Yet two very different housing trajectories emerged, with some families reverting to high-poverty areas within a few years of the initial relocation and others managing to stay in low-poverty neighborhoods, even if they changed apartments.

First, we found that some families in the experimental group who successfully leased up were less lucky, in their initial relocation, than other families. In plain terms, the unlucky ones secured lousy housing units in better neighborhoods. And some of them were soon willing to trade away location—in particular, greater safety and the chance to buffer their children from "ghetto" behavior—to get larger, better housing units in less secure, higher poverty neighborhoods. Other families, faced with the same choice, were simply not willing to make that trade. They would do anything, they told us, to stay out of the ghetto—or anywhere that reminded them of the ghetto. Differences in the kinds of *trade-offs* families are willing to make, and why they are forced to make them, have been obscured in much earlier research on housing, which merely asked respondents to list the things that are important to them when they choose neighborhoods.

Second, different MTO markets offered different ranges (distributions) of neighborhood opportunity, as we previewed in chapter 4. In two of our sites, for example—Los Angeles and New York—there were hundreds of overwhelmingly minority-occupied, high-poverty neighborhoods (where affordable rentals and landlords willing to accept housing vouchers tend to concentrate). In Boston, there were only a dozen or so. Our analyses of where all housing-voucher holders were living in these markets, compared to the MTO families in all three treatment groups, underscore this finding about the impact of differences between metro regions, as opposed to differences between neighborhoods or between families.

Third, sharp rent increases, disputes with landlords, and landlord decisions to sell the housing unit, plus many family-level shocks—sickness, job loss, divorce, and other changes—produced many involuntary moves. Each one forced MTO families to find decent housing in decent neighborhoods against long odds. Like a roll of dice that have been loaded to undermine the dice-thrower, each move put families in these tough markets at risk of sliding back into the riskiest neighborhoods, regardless of their preferences. Yet housing instability of this kind—frequent and often involuntary moves, which undermine hopes of connecting the disadvantaged to new opportunities in better neighborhoods—is rarely mentioned in current debates on housing need and low-income housing policy in America.

Fourth, and contrary to what some have assumed about poor families who are relocated from inner-city neighborhoods, access to social networks or services "left behind" in poorer neighborhoods seldom drove moving decisions. A small share of MTO movers did feel very isolated in new, low-poverty areas and focused, in moving again, on finding housing closer to loved ones and/or "church homes," which typically meant a move back to inner-city neighborhoods. But for most, those factors shaped daily routines and assessments of neighborhoods—that is, decisions about *where* to move, since access to valued people and institutions counted—but not the decision *to* move. We will show why this distinction is so important for the families and for future policy.

Fifth and finally, while the public and scholarly debates over MTO have focused almost exclusively on the program's up-front effort to counsel families and restrict the neighborhood choices of those in the experimental group, numerous subsequent moves were brokered by rental agents—not by the program's design but of necessity, as Tameka explains in the first part of this chapter. Those agents provided shortcuts to landlords with affordable units open to voucher holders—shortcuts that these busy, low-income single parents prized—but helped steer them to particular housing units. This factor, too, shaped the location outcomes of MTO as the experiment unfolded, over and above family's preferences in the abstract. But brokering has not been factored into the debates over choice by low-income renters. We tend to think of real estate brokers only in the context of homebuying, usually by middle- and upper-income households.

In the next section, we briefly describe the divergent housing fortunes of MTO families as of the interim mark and then examine the factors that explain those fortunes.

DIVERGENT PATHS

Lanelle, a mother in MTO's New York experimental group, loved living in a low-poverty area in the Northeast Bronx. She chose her neighborhood based on a teacher's recommendation of a strong elementary school there for her two girls. It was quiet, too, and felt like the suburbs. But when the heat in their apartment did not work for two weeks one winter, Lanelle got sick. Then the housing authority refused to pay the landlord, citing failure to keep the housing unit in compliance with government's housing quality standards for the rental voucher program. So Lanelle and her children were evicted. After a brief spell living with her grown son, they found a new place, with a great landlord, in a moderately poor neighborhood that still seemed much safer than the public housing the family had left behind. But Lanelle's health problems made the fourth-floor walk-up apartment untenable. Through her stepfather, Lanelle learned about a good building near Yankee Stadium in the South Bronx, and so she and her children moved there. During our fieldwork, several of Lanelle's relatives moved into the building as well. The area is much poorer than the Northeast Bronx, and no one in Lanelle's household will walk alone there at night. But services, shopping, schools, friends and family, and the subway are all nearby. Marlena, Lanelle's youngest daughter, can walk herself to school and play outside.

Lanelle's family illustrates one of the two housing trajectories that emerged in MTO's first decade: what we call the "move-back" pattern. Families on that trajectory did not necessarily return to the neighborhood left behind, but were living once again, when we got to know them, in a high-poverty area. What do the patterns above suggest about why some families were move-backs while others, in the second pattern, persisted in low-poverty areas, even if they had to move on from the apartment or neighborhood to which they had initially relocated through MTO?

Consider the start of the experiment and the early location outcomes: Of the 1,820 families who were randomly assigned to the MTO *experimental group*, which received relocation counseling and assistance and a voucher useable only in a neighborhood with a poverty rate of 10 percent or less, just under half (48 percent or 860) found a suitable apartment and moved successfully (leased up) in the time allotted—a 20 percent improvement over the success rate for the Gautreaux program. Those who leased up successfully, completing the initial relocation per the program's design, are MTO's *compliers*, in that they received the initial treatment intended. The half who did not do so, though they were offered the same programmatic "opportunity," are the *noncompliers*. Recall that all other families who volunteered for MTO were randomly assigned to a *control group* (1,440 families), which continued to receive project-based housing assistance (unless they later chose to move out), and a Section 8 voucher *comparison group* (1,350 families), which received the standard voucher, with no special support or use restrictions.

The experimental-group families most likely to relocate successfully at program enrollment had fewer children, access to a car, more confidence about finding an apartment, greater dissatisfaction with their origin neighborhood, and no church ties to the origin neighborhood. A looser rental market and more intensive counseling services were also significant predictors of success (Shroder 2003).

As we explored in chapter 5, the program's early impacts included dramatic improvements in neighborhood poverty rates, by design, and also participants' reported safety and a sense of security but not rates of racial integration. By the time of the interim impacts evaluation that surveyed families four to seven years after they enrolled in the MTO program, several key aspects of housing status that are closely tied to choice of neighborhoods—such as whether the family rented or owned their housing unit, whether they continued to receive government housing assistance (of any form), and how often they had moved by the interim mark—were not significantly different across treatment groups in the experiment (table 7.1a). This was true whether we consider everyone assigned to the experimental group (the "intent-to-treat," or ITT, column in the table, which includes both compliers and non-compliers) or just those who successfully relocated to a low-poverty area at the initial point (the "treatment-on-treated," or TOT column).[3] On the other hand, the experimental group and Section 8 comparison group reported significantly higher housing quality (i.es., unit quality) than their control-group counterparts. This was especially true of those who did the initial relocation to low-poverty neighborhoods. On average, then, relocating meant "trading up" both in terms of neighborhood and in terms of housing unit. And relocating to low-poverty areas with some help produced bigger improvements, on average, in both than did relying on an unrestricted housing voucher (with no special assistance) to find a place to rent.

In addition, most MTO households, in all three treatment groups, continued to receive some form of housing assistance; about 90 percent were still renters, and the low-income renters who dominate the MTO patterns showed the comparatively high rates of residential mobility that characterize poor renters nationwide.

By the time of the interim evaluation, in fact, ongoing housing mobility—not the initial, planned relocation but subsequent ones, which were not in the plan at all—was reshaping outcomes for all of the treatment groups in significant ways. First, two-thirds (67 percent) of the experimental complier group had moved at least once more, that is, beyond the initial relocation, by the interim mark, and that group was only half as likely (18 vs. 38 percent) as compliers who stayed put to *still* be living in a neighborhood less than 10 percent poor (data not shown, see Orr et al. 2003). The most common reasons for compliers' moving on were involuntary, including: problems with the lease (22 percent), which may include failed unit inspections, rent

Table 7.1a. MTO Interim Impacts: Descriptives and Impacts on Housing Outcomes

Descriptives (adult survey)	Control	Experimental	Section 8
Current tenure: Share who rent	89.3%	90.4%	91.5%
Length of time in current housing unit			
Under 1 year	15.3%	17.9%	16.1%
1–2 years	21.0%	20.4%	20.0%
5–10 years	26.7%	26.9%	27.8%
Number of moves since random assignment			
None	34.0%	28.6%	31.1%
1–3	61.1%	66.9%	62.5%
4 or more	4.9%	4.6%	6.4%

Impacts (multiple sources)	Control mean	Experimental vs. Control Impacts		Section 8 vs. Control Impacts	
		ITT	TOT	ITT	TOT
Current total monthly housing cost (n=3562)	$412	$25 higher	$53 higher	$6 higher	$10 higher
Current total housing cost burden (n=3113)	31.2%	1.6% higher	3.5% higher	1.1% higher	1.8% higher
Housing insecurity					
Rent or mortgage payment problems (n=3502)	29.3%	4.2% lower	9.0% lower	0.046 lower	0.077 lower
Utility payment problems (n=3509)	27.0%	10.5% higher*	22.3 higher*	0.072 higher*	0.120 higher*
Homeless, doubled up or evicted (n=3521)	8.0%	1.4% higher	3.0% higher	1.9% higher	3.2% higher
Reported facing discrimination or bias in search (n=3520)	3.0%	3.7% higher*	8.0% higher*	6.4% higher*	10.7% higher*
Housing assistance (admin n=4248)					
Currently receiving assistance	65.7%	3.2% higher	6.7% higher	10.0% higher*	16.2% higher*
Currently living in public housing	43.5%	18.4% lower*	38.8% lower*	22.6% lower*	36.6% lower*
Housing unit quality					
Share reporting problem with vermin (n=3524)	52.8%	4.7% lower*	10.0% lower*	0.7% lower	1.2% lower
Share reporting problem with heating/plumbing (n=3514)	39.3%	3.8% lower	8.2% lower	0.6% lower	1.0% lower
Share rating current housing as excellent (n=3525)	52.0%	9.9% higher*	21.0% higher*	7.1% higher*	11.9% higher*

Source: Orr et al. (2003: p.61, 64, 66, C-16, D-1).

Note: ITT = intent-to-treat (includes compliers and noncompliers), TOT=treatment-on-treated (compliers only). Control means and impact estimates are regression-adjusted with robust standard errors (not shown). *Housing insecurity payment* measures index late payment or threat of eviction or foreclosure during past 12 months. Number of observations reflect survey n's except where administrative data (admin) indicated.
* p<.05.

Table 7.1b. MTO Interim Impacts on Neighborhood Outcomes, as of Interim Impacts Evaluation, 2002

	Control mean	Experimental vs. Control Impacts		Section 8 vs. Control Impacts	
		ITT	TOT	ITT	TOT
Neighborhood traits					
Poverty rate (n=3675)	38.5%	7.8% lower*	16.7% lower*	6.2% lower*	10.2% lower*
Percent minority (n=3670)	87.6%	4.5% lower*	9.6% lower*	1.3% lower	2.2% lower
Share of adults employed (n=3669)	81.0%	3.5% higher*	7.5% higher*	3.2% higher*	5.2% higher*
Share of persons with incomes twice the poverty level (n=3670)					
Share of owner-occupied housing units (n=3670)	23.0%	9.5% higher*	20.1% higher*	6.2% higher*	10.1% higher*
Proportion of months since random assignment living in areas with indicated poverty rates (n=4248)					
Below 10%	3.9%	12.8% higher*	27.0% higher*	2.0% higher*	3.2% higher*
At least 10% but less than 20%	8.5%	12.3% higher*	25.9% higher*	8.4% higher*	13.6% higher*
40% or above	58.3%	22.4% lower*	47.2% lower*	21.6% lower*	35.1% lower*
Household assessments (adult survey)					
Share reporting feeling safe at night (n=3482)	54.9%	14.2% higher*	30.3% higher*	9.3% higher*	15.6% higher*
Share any household member a crime victim, last six months (n=3499)	20.9%	4.0% lower*	8.5% lower*	5.3% lower*	8.9% lower*
Share reporting litter/trash/graffiti/abandoned buildings (n=3502)	70.4%	11.1% lower*	23.6% lower*	7.6% lower*	12.7% lower*
Share reporting public drinking/groups of people hanging out (n=3489)	69.5%	17.0% lower*	36.0% lower*	9.9% lower*	16.6% lower*
Share very satisfied or satisfied with current neighborhood (n=3524)	47.5%	13.8% higher*	29.3% higher*	10.8% higher*	18.0% higher*

Source: Orr et al. (2003: p.42).

Note: On treatment group labels, see note for table 1a. Neighborhood traits are as of Census 2000 but for locations surveyed in 2001–2002.
*p<.05.

increases and decisions to sell the unit or for other reasons not renew the voucher holder's lease; and conflicts with the landlord (20 percent). But almost as many families (18 percent) reported wanting a bigger or better apartment.

MTO had helped families *get* to particular kinds of neighborhoods, not *stay* in them or move to *similar* neighborhoods over time. Still, a strong desire to stay in similar neighborhoods was evident by the interim mark, when two-thirds of those who had moved since initial relocation reported searching for housing in the same neighborhoods.[4]

Second, many of the low-poverty areas that served as initial destinations for the experimental group have changed over time, through no choice of the participants. Census data show that while most were more or less stable, almost half (45 percent) were becoming poorer in the 1990s (Orr et al., 2003), even as many inner-city neighborhoods were becoming less poor.

Third, about 70 percent of the control group had also moved by the interim mark—most to other poor neighborhoods but with a reduction in average neighborhood poverty rate from 51 percent to 34 percent (when compared to control-group members who did not move). One reason for these moves was public housing demolition and revitalization programs, which received a major boost from the new federal HOPE VI program, and supportive mayors and other local advocates, just as MTO was starting up. But the key point is that many members of the MTO control group became movers, too, with about one quarter living in neighborhoods below 20 percent poverty by the interim point, rather than members of a fixed-in-place comparison category.

Despite some convergence, then, in neighborhood conditions among the three MTO treatment groups over time, at that interim point in 2002, which preceded our fieldwork by two years, families in the MTO experimental group were about 13 percent more likely than the control group, and experimental compliers 27 percent more likely, to be living in very low-poverty areas; the experimental group had also lived in such areas for much longer periods of time, and families in that group continued to rate their neighborhoods much safer, more secure, and less disorderly, on average, than members of the other treatment groups (table 7.1b).

Many families in the MTO experimental group have had an exceptional experience vis-à-vis the dominant pattern for low-income housing assistance nationwide, yet the struggle to stay out of high-poverty areas after escaping them was very evident just four to seven years after the families enrolled in MTO—in Lanelle's case and many others. Neighborhood change—the fact that many families moved to transitional areas that were getting poorer over time—was clearly part of the story, and that factor was beyond the families' control. But how did that factor and others combine to produce the divergent trajectories we discovered?

UNDERSTANDING CHOICE IN THE HOUSING MARKET

As we showed in chapter 3, there was no true road map or precedent for MTO. Even the court-ordered Gautreaux program proved a limited guide, because many families in the MTO population were much more disadvantaged than their Gautreaux counterparts had been, HUD used different criteria to identify "opportunity" neighborhoods in MTO, and the local housing agencies and nonprofit partners did not place families in the same way. But more to the point, HUD planners did not design mechanisms to ensure that families could stay out of high-poverty areas— assuming they so chose—once they got out of them. The planners did not realize that they had to.

Researchers have identified several factors that might explain the struggle to stay out of high-poverty areas and the divergent housing trajectories over time. These forces operate on the demand and supply sides of the housing market, and they concern two distinct decisions that drive location outcomes: the decision *to* move and decisions about *where* to move.

Most research on the decision *to* move has focused on the large majority of housing consumers, who are not "assisted" by the government subsidies targeted to low-income households.[5] This research emphasizes the importance of life cycle factors, including age and family status, for example, heading off to college, having a child, taking in a relative, experiencing a divorce or separation, or having one's children move out of the house.[6] These factors trigger moves by affecting satisfaction with one's housing unit and/or neighborhood. In any population, in other words, including MTO, we should expect moves triggered by this range of factors.

But "satisfaction" connotes a certain freedom to choose when and why to move, and for millions of people, such latitude is rare. To use the census bureau label, *involuntary* factors, such as job loss, death, divorce, eviction, fire, an unaffordable mortgage or rent, or nonrenewal of lease—for example, due to property sale or a dispute with the landlord—also trigger moves. They do so more often for low-income households, such as those in MTO, than higher income ones. Also, renters move four to five times as often as homeowners, and most lower income households, including almost all MTO families, rent their housing (Fischer 2002).

But residential satisfaction and mobility rate studies do little to explain *where families move to*, whether at points in time or in trajectories of moves over time. Economists analyzing "locational choice" emphasize that households try to optimize a multiattribute bundle of housing traits, which includes safety, access, and other traits of locations (Galster 2003). The economist's perspective emphasizes choice, as well as the complexity of the bundle: Movers must size up a variety of traits, some difficult to gauge, and also weigh trade-offs among the things they want. But other research highlights, among other factors, the importance of racial attitudes, discrimination, and patterns of neighborhood change over time.

These factors suggest the limited selection and control that many "choosers" have in the marketplace.

First, most households prefer some racial or cultural "comfort zone" (Charles 2005). Yet there is frequently a mismatch between such neighborhood make-up preferences and the neighborhoods actually available, and this helps reproduce segregation (Bruch and Mare 2006; Pancs and Vriend 2004; Schelling 1971). Minority households, for example, consistently express a desire to live in more racially integrated areas but find a limited supply of available, affordable neighborhoods that fits their preferred range; some also rely on referral networks—networks dominated by friends and relatives of their own ethnic group—that lack information on such places (Charles 2005). For their part, whites in America report a growing tolerance of, if not always an appetite for, greater neighborhood integration but tend to define their comfort zone in ways that lead them to avoid areas with a substantial presence of minorities, especially blacks (Charles 2005; Ellen 2000).

Second, while racial discrimination in rental and ownership housing markets has declined overall in recent decades, it continues to affect minority as well as white housing choices, adding an informal "tax" (for example, higher lease-up or other fees) to the costs of moving and/or steering households in different racial groups toward different neighborhoods in ways that help reproduce segregation (Turner and Ross 2005; Yinger 1995).[7] The chooser has no control over these forms of *disparate treatment* (in the language of civil rights law) by sellers, landlords, lenders, or brokers (real estate agents) in the marketplace. And there is evidence that discrimination begins over the phone, through "linguistic discrimination" in which those who advertise housing for sale or rent infer the caller's ethnic or class identity from speech patterns; discrimination against speakers of the Black English dialect is particularly evident (Massey and Lund 2001).

Third, racial minorities and the poor are more likely than whites or middle- and upper-income households to move to neighborhoods that are transitioning downward over time. One reason is the relative affordability of such neighborhoods, but steering by realtors and the self-reinforcing cycle of minority presence attracting more minorities—while dissuading prospective white in-movers—appear to contribute as well (Ellen 2000; Quillian 1999; Schelling 1971). As we will show, MTO families relocated not just to a category of neighborhoods (those with low poverty rates) but to specific kinds of *zones* within larger metropolitan housing markets: mostly to vulnerable, increasingly distressed areas shaped by the larger processes of metropolitan change we surveyed in chapter 4.

Thus far, we have focused on evidence about the majority of housing consumers in America, who are "unassisted." What additional factors shape the moving decisions and housing location outcomes of assisted households—those low or very low-income households who are eligible for and lucky enough to receive oversubscribed government subsidies?

As for *preferences*, prior research has largely been confined to identifying priorities: Safety and proximity to relatives and friends rank particularly high for assisted households, and there is some evidence that these are threshold concerns—more important, on average, for clients than good schools or proximity to job locations (Basolo and Nguyen 2006; Johnson 2005; Varady and Walker 2007). Voucher holders—who are very low-income family, senior, and disabled households—also tend to identify proximity to public transportation as a priority; housing counselors who work with voucher holders likewise tell researchers that "accessibility" or "getting around" are top concerns for their clients, especially those who live in relatively transit-rich central cities and are asked to consider moving farther out (Varady and Walker 2000, 2003).

Research has also emphasized important demand-side *barriers* of two main types. First, there are the debilitating mental and physical health problems found disproportionately in the housing-assisted population—including the so-called hard to house.[8] Looking for new housing and orchestrating a move with children in tow is a particularly daunting prospect for very low-income parents suffering from chronic depression or anxiety or from severe asthma, arthritis, or other physical problems. Second, even for the more able-bodied and mentally healthy, there is the problem of limited time, money, transportation, information, and other resources important for comparison shopping and other aspects of effective housing search (Basolo and Nguyen 2006; Pashup et al., 2005).

Beyond preferences and demand-side barriers, researchers consistently identify a range of *supply*-side barriers as well. First, there is reported discrimination based on race, family status (for example, the presence of children), or source of income, that is, the use of the voucher itself. In most states, landlords are not required to accept government housing vouchers, and requirements elsewhere are loosely enforced. There is some evidence that source-of-income discrimination is even more prevalent than racial discrimination, at least in some local housing markets (Varady and Walker 2003, 2007).

Next, as we detailed in chapter 4, there is the scarcity of affordable, adequately maintained, and otherwise voucher-appropriate housing units in many communities (McClure 2006; Pendall 2000). This scarcity reflects the dwindling supply of decent rental housing affordable to those at the lowest incomes, including the working poor. The tendency of many low-poverty jurisdictions to exclude such housing is at issue here as well. That is, the scarcity problem reflects the geographic *concentration* of accessible supply, not just the limited *volume* of that supply (Briggs 2005b).

Finally, market conditions also shape outcomes: As of 2001, the latest year for which national data are available, housing voucher recipients in very tight markets were about 20 percent less likely than those in loose ones (61 percent vs. 80 percent) to lease up anywhere (Finkel and Buron 2001). Market tightness, as we will show, was especially important for

MTO families who wanted to stay in low-poverty areas but had to move repeatedly.[9]

According to a 2003 HUD report that examined the nation's 50 largest housing markets, the spatial clustering of vouchers is far greater than the dispersion of housing units at affordable rents would predict: 25 percent of black recipients and 28 percent of Hispanic recipients live in high-poverty neighborhoods, compared to only 8 percent of white recipients, and yet the voucher program utilizes only about 6 percent of all units with rents below the HUD-designated fair market rents (Devine et al., 2003). That study could not determine the units actually available to interested voucher users, of course: If landlords are unwilling to rent to them, for example, rent levels do not matter much.

Minority voucher holders typically live in, and move among, moderate- to high- poverty neighborhoods (Feins and Patterson 2005; Newman and Harkness 2000; Newman and Schnare 1997). Some of these neighborhoods are in distinct corridors or "hot spots" where affordable rental housing tends to be more abundant and minority concentration high (Hartung and Henig 1997; McClure 2001; Wang and Varady 2005). At least some of these areas are poorer neighborhoods or racial ghettos— where housing demand is weaker and landlords more likely to accept government-subsidized tenants—that are vulnerable to decline (Galster, Tatian, and Smith 1999; Wang and Varady 2005).

Moreover, the evidence that positive effects of special supports—that is, "assisted" mobility—on location outcomes *persist* over the long run is thus far limited to long-run data on the Gautreaux program. Those data indicate sustained racial and economic integration over more than a decade (DeLuca and Rosenbaum 2003). It is simply not clear why Gautreaux sustained this relative success.

The picture that emerges is that of a housing consumer poor in time, information, transportation, health, and other essentials for finding and relocating to decent housing, not just someone who lacks enough money for rent and utilities. Then there is the dual housing market that puts low-income renters at great disadvantage and voucher holders at even greater ones. The end result is the need to face an extreme version of the trade-offs that face all families in the housing market—between the cost of housing, the quality of the housing unit, and the other things that define the value of housing, including conditions *in* the neighborhood and access *from* the neighborhood to things that are valued, such as jobs, school, loved ones, churches, and other institutions.

Yet with the exception of the Gautreaux housing desegregation program and a local survey study or two,[10] research on efforts to help voucher users live in less poor areas has focused on initial relocation outcomes: what kinds of neighborhoods voucher holders move from and to in a single relocation the researchers have observed. There is no research on the important question of how supply and demand–side factors interact *over time* to shape location outcomes for the families in the government's largest low-income housing program: rental vouchers. That interaction is best understood, as we show below, when housing choices are viewed in the context of dynamic housing markets, the structure of neighborhood opportunity over time, and families' larger life strategies and challenges, in other words, more holistically than prior research has been able to do.

EXPLAINING FAMILIES' OUTCOMES IN MTO

The Relocation Zones

The first reason that MTO families who escaped high-poverty neighborhoods struggled to stay out of them is that the geography of affluence and poverty shifted as the experiment unfolded, and the families were concentrated in declining (transitional) areas where landlords were willing to accept government housing vouchers. Yet the distribution of housing opportunity was quite different from site to site (market to market), with MTO families in metro Los Angeles and New York facing tougher neighborhood prospects than counterparts in metro Boston.

Many discussions about the impacts of MTO stop at comparing mean neighborhood poverty rates over time, ignoring the character of the areas to which families relocated—*zones*, considered in the context of a broader, dynamic housing market. The Gautreaux program placed many families in advantaged zones: middle-class, mostly white suburban communities 15–20 miles from their mostly black origin neighborhoods in Chicago. By contrast, in all five MTO metros, the first relocation made by experimental compliers was typically to much less advantaged zones—specifically to a low-poverty, majority-minority neighborhood in the outer ring of the central city (about two-thirds of all compliers) or in an economically diverse inner suburb proximate to the central city (about one-third), within a few miles of, or in some cases adjacent to, the ghetto-poor origin neighborhoods—not to more distant, affluent, or racially integrated communities.

The initial MTO housing locations reflected the way the voucher program structures housing options, not just families' neighborhood preferences. Again, the contrast with the Gautreaux program is instructive: In Gautreaux, housing counselors acted as placement agents, lining up units, in a relatively loose market, that were offered on a take-it-or-leave-it basis to those on the waiting list. In MTO, where clients would choose their units, supply-side constraints quickly led to a variety of local compromises: Early assessment suggested that while all five sites tried to expand the pool of participating landlords, limited staff capacity and limited payoff curtailed such efforts (Feins, McInnis, and Popkin 1997). Counselors found their preexisting landlord lists, with units concentrated in particular communities, most "productive" as sources of vacancies. Also, vacancies for certain types of rental housing were not advertised and thus were difficult to learn about through mailers and other conventional outreach by the program implementers. Finally, rental brokers provided shortcuts to landlords who were willing to accept vouchers, at least at some sites. Boston program staff estimated, for example, that 20 to 25 percent of their placements were secured through brokers.

Like Lanelle's family, which we introduced above, New York City compliers were concentrated initially in small rental properties in the Northeast Bronx—where the nonprofit placement agent's landlord contacts were concentrated and where vacancies were numerous—while a handful moved to Staten Island, having relocated primarily from public housing in Central Harlem and the South Bronx. This program-induced mobility tracked a larger movement of people of color, including middle-income black and Hispanic homebuyers, to the city's outer core and inner suburbs, which became both poorer and more nonwhite. Harlem and a large zone in Brooklyn, the historic centers of black settlement, gentrified and became home to more whites, while the South Bronx became evermore Hispanic thanks largely to immigration (Furman Center 2005). But deep pockets of poverty remained in those three areas, where many of the city's most affordable rentals are concentrated. Meanwhile, the market squeezed renters: According to HUD, inflation-adjusted gross rents jumped 23 percent in New York City from 1990 to 2005. The combination of these trends created a strong draw back to poorer neighborhoods for families in the experimental group who were compelled to move again, sometimes—as in Lanelle's case—within a few short years of the initial relocation.

Boston MTO families relocated from the inner-city neighborhoods of Dorchester, Roxbury, and South Boston mainly to small rental properties in the city's economically diverse outer core neighborhoods or to transitional inner suburbs to the north and south of the city, such as Brockton, Quincy, Revere, and Randolph. Those suburbs became poorer and more racially diverse in the 1990s as the job-rich western suburbs along the Route 128 high tech corridor, where school districts are strongest, remained overwhelmingly white and middle to upper income (McArdle 2003). As of the 2000 Census, three-quarters of metro Boston's poor lived in the suburbs.

The initial relocations by families in the Boston experimental group tracked a larger race and class divide in the region's mobility patterns. Guy Stuart (2000) found, for example, that half of the home purchases made by black and Hispanic homebuyers outside the central city between 1993 and 1998 were made in just 7 of the metro region's 126 municipalities. Those 7 were relatively affordable towns, where poverty and fiscal distress grew in the 1990s and where school district performance is much poorer than the affluent suburbs. Meanwhile, many central-city neighborhoods gentrified dramatically as crime dropped, real estate boomed, and middle- and upper-income households moved in. Gross rents jumped 15 percent in real terms between 1990 and 2005, according to HUD, and some neighborhoods saw much bigger increases.

In Boston and New York, MTO experimental compliers left behind high poverty and high crime but transit-rich areas that were close to the central business district for areas with dispersed services and job locations, where having a car is crucial. In sprawling Los Angeles, their counterparts left inner-city neighborhoods in South and East L.A. for transitional southern suburbs nearby (e.g., Compton and Lynwood), as well as communities in the sprawling San Fernando Valley (about 15 to 30 miles from origin, to the north), Long Beach to the southwest, and rapidly expanding and increasingly diverse eastern suburbs and satellite cities 40 to 60 miles away, mainly in adjacent Riverside and San Bernardino Counties to the east—the once-agricultural "Inland Empire" where many low- and moderate-income Angelenos have moved in response to the city's desperate shortage of affordable housing. Transit options in most of these destination communities were poor, which became a major problem for the MTO families that lacked reliable access to a car.

Opportunities for racial integration declined in metro L.A. over the course of the experiment. Far more so than Boston or New York, metro Los Angeles saw a large outmigration of non-Hispanic whites, together with rapid immigration from Asia and Latin America, throughout the 1990s and into the new decade (Frey 2006). The region also saw growth in extreme poverty concentration, counter to the national trend of decline in such concentration (Jargowsky 2003). Closer to the streets, those aggregate changes were reflected in dramatic patterns of ethnic change and competition (Zhou and Myers 2006). For example, many long-black neighborhoods in South L.A. became mixed areas of poor black and Hispanic, or even majority-Hispanic and Spanish-language-dominant settlement.

Though some trends, such as sharp increases in real rents and the suburbanization of poverty, affected all of the MTO metros, several notable differences remained among them in the typical neighborhoods experienced by participants in the demonstration by the interim mark and by all other households in the metro area, as table 7.2 shows. The locations of MTO families over time reflect these different distributions of housing opportunity in each housing market. For example, the share of experimental-group compliers living in neighborhoods with poverty rates below 20 percent ranged from a high of 71 percent in metro Boston to just 45 percent in metro Los Angeles. Even members of the control group in Boston were three times more likely to be living in such neighborhoods than were their counterparts in Los Angeles and four times more likely than counterparts in New York. While these outcome differences may owe in part to site differences in program effects—for example, the effects of different approaches to counseling or assistance early on—these location outcome differences in 2002 track the sharp differences in mean exposure to poverty for all households in those metro areas. That is, there are fewer housing opportunities in low-poverty areas *overall* in metro Los Angeles and New York than in metro Boston or the other MTO metros.

Table 7.2. MTO Neighborhood Locations, 2002, by Treatment Group and Site (Metro Area)

	All sites	Baltimore	Boston	Chicago	Los Angeles	New York
Percent in tracts with poverty rate <20%						
Experimental Group (all)	35	39	44	31	31	26
Experimental compliers	59	57	71	64	45	57
Section 8 Comparison compliers	26	29	33	21	22	12
Control Group	17	26	23	19	7	5
All metro households (2000)	78	86	90	85	67	63
Percent in tracts with share minority <60%						
Experimental Group (all)	18	21	42	7	12	8
Experimental compliers	27	29	61	13	18	12
Section 8 Comparison compliers	16	19	38	5	5	7
Control Group	13	13	34	3	4	6
All metro households (2000)	69	80	93	74	44	53

Source: Geocoded Interim Impacts Evaluation data, plus Three-City Study interview and ethnographic field data.

Note: Control group N=1133; See other row N's in table 7.3.

A parallel pattern emerges for racial mixing: Boston is the standout in terms of MTO location outcomes at the interim point (with more families in comparatively mixed neighborhoods). The striking gap between the two metros with the lowest rates (L.A., New York) tracks the big gap in racial exposure for all households when those two markets are compared to the other three MTO sites. In metro Boston, 93 percent of *all* households live in neighborhoods with moderate or lower minority concentration, while fewer than half of all households do so in metro New York and Los Angeles.

In additional analyses not shown in the table, the trends reshaping these housing markets—shifting patterns of racial and economic segregation, a spike in subprime lending targeting poor and minority neighborhoods, sharp declines in city crime rates, the shift to majority-minority make-up in the central city in some cases (Boston) and the metro in others (L.A., New York), and more—indicate how dramatically the geography of housing opportunity was changing around the MTO families over time. But again, that geography—particularly with respect to the number of racially mixed, low-poverty neighborhood options—remained very different in each of the three MTO metro areas on which our study focused. Movers in each market faced very different prospects, in part because the choices available varied so dramatically.

It is against these changing backdrops, and the options they provided over time, that MTO families have shown two quite different trajectories, as we described earlier. We turn next to how families made their choices and how they experienced the markets changing around them.

Family Fortunes: A Closer Look

Roxanne, a member of the MTO experimental group in L.A., lost her apartment when the landlord decided to sell. Yet she quickly found another affordable one, in a low- poverty neighborhood in a nearby suburb—and so stayed far away from the inner-city public housing community she and her children were living in when she volunteered to participate in MTO. In the same housing market, though, Patricia was dissatisfied with her relocation to the San Fernando Valley, not because of the character of the neighborhood but because she lacked access. Her family and "church home" were too far away; the family had no car; and loved ones did not come to the Valley to visit them. So Patricia opted to move her children to a high-poverty, racially segregated area in South L.A.—an area much like the public housing neighborhood they had left behind at the start of MTO.

Likewise, in metro Boston, Sabrina and her children centered their lives on the suburban area to which they had relocated, in spite of the fact that most of her relatives continued to live in much poorer, inner-city neighborhoods. But different priorities and a series of unlucky moves landed another MTO family, Danielle and her daughters, back in inner-city Boston and schools rife with fighting and academic failures, after years in a much lower poverty inner suburb—where her girls liked the schools.

How common were these distinct trajectories, and how did different families end up on one versus the other? Using the survey data from the large and highly representative interim impacts evaluation, we examined the neighborhood poverty rates for MTO families in all three treatment groups at three points in time: initial relocation, the year 2000, and again at the interim evaluation point in 2002. MTO families have been mobile—but not necessarily more so than low-income renters as a whole. On average, experimental and Section 8 families moved the same number of times (2.6 moves), while control-group families moved somewhat less often on average (2.1 moves; Orr et al., 2003:C-16). We did additional analyses of the families who initially relocated to areas that retained very low poverty rates (less than 10 percent poor) through the 1990s. This allowed us to focus on those MTO compliers who were positioned, through their initial relocation, to receive the treatment planners intended (prolonged exposure to a neighborhood that retained a very low poverty rate).[11]

We discovered two main trajectories and a third, uncommon one, with the shares and context for each shown in table 7.3. Type 1 households managed to stay in very low- to low-poverty neighborhoods (less than 20 percent poor) at all three observation points, whether they moved or

Table 7.3. Experimental Compliers: Trajectory Types and Shares, by Circumstance and Choice factors

Type	Share	Description	Typical Residential Mobility Rate	Context (circumstance and choice factors)
1	40%	Remained in very low to low-poverty neighborhoods.	None to low (0–2 subsequent moves)	Strong preference for low-poverty areas evident. Either retained original rental unit or managed to find an additional rental(s) in similar areas. Daily routines more centered on neighborhood of residence; kin attachments to inner city limited/bounded. High-average neighborhood satisfaction.
2	56%	Reverted to moderate-to high-poverty areas and remained in such areas.	Low to high (2+ subsequent moves)	Variable neighborhood preferences. Stronger kin attachments and/or obligations in inner-city neighborhoods. Involuntary moves common (apartment sold, unit poor, landlord conflict, etc.), but some moves motivated by preference for better unit, access to loved ones, etc. Lower average neighborhood satisfaction.
3	4%	Reverted to moderate-to high-poverty areas and then again to low-poverty area.	High (3+ subsequent moves)	Variable patterns: life shocks, changes in employment status, and family obligations shifted housing demands. Preference for low-poverty areas evident, but opportunities insecure.
N	193			

Source: See table 7.2.

Note: Very-low-poverty neighborhoods are less than 10 percent poor, low-poverty neighborhoods 10–20 percent poor, and moderate-to high-poverty neighborhoods over 20 percent poor as of Census 2000. Shares are percentages of the compliers whose initial relocations were to areas that remained less than 10 percent poor between the 1990 and 2000 censuses.

did not move again after initial relocation. Type 2 households, the move-backs, were already in a moderate- to high-poverty tract by 2000 and remained in one (though not necessarily the same one) when observed again in 2002 (or in 2004–2005 when we visited them). Type 3 house-holds "bounced" from the initial, very low-poverty neighborhood to a moderate- to high-poverty neighborhood by the second observation and then back to a very low-poverty tract by 2002.

The bifurcated pattern is striking: Most households either stayed in a very low- to low-poverty tract (40 percent of the subgroup of compliers we described above) or moved on within a few years to a moderate- to high-poverty tract and then *remained* in that type of tract (56 percent). Only a small fraction (4 percent) followed the Type 3 trajectory, returning to a very low-poverty location after some time in a much poorer one.

As we noted above, some MTO housing markets offered better odds than others. Type 1 represents a slight majority (56 percent) in Boston, compared to just 34 percent for New York and 24 percent for L.A. Con-versely, Type 2 is a large majority in New York (66 percent) and even more so L.A. (74 percent), compared to just over one-third (36 percent) for Boston. Type 3 is a very small share at each site. Treating the shares above as odds, relocating initially to a tract with a stable, very low-poverty rate gave MTO households at our three study sites a roughly 50–50 chance, on average, of being in a very low- to low-poverty tract at the interim point—but much lower odds in New York and L.A.

Not only were the Type 1 families in our ethnographic sample luckier, on average, in the marketplace, but they also tended to express particularly strong preferences for "better" areas—defined as safer and more economi-cally diverse than the inner city—and more limited kin attachments and obligations that tied them to inner-city neighborhoods. It is not surprising, in that context, that their social lives had moved with them—even, in some cases, over multiple moves across a wide geography. In simple terms, these families were comparatively fortunate, satisfied, independent (less kin reliant), and well adapted.

For example, Roxanne, who lost her apartment in one L.A. suburb when her landlord opted to sell the property, found out about another "good" neighborhood through a friend. While the new neighborhood was roughly 15 miles away, Roxanne and her family once again centered their lives on the new place. Ditto Sabrina in suburban Boston, who com-plained about ghetto neighbors moving in from the inner city but focused her children on the safety, recreational programs, and shopping in her suburban neighborhood, not the inner-city neighborhoods where most of her relatives continued to live.

In contrast, Type 2 families, such as Lanelle's in New York City, were generally drawn back to living in the inner city through an involuntary move—usually because of rent increases or problems with the landlord—but sometimes through social obligation and preference. Sick or otherwise needy kin loomed large for the most constrained families, whose social lives revolved around relatives and close friends back in the inner city even when the (subject) family resided in a low-poverty area elsewhere in the metro. Though our sample sizes are small, parents in this group also appear less likely to have access to cars. This was especially serious for the L.A. move-back cases who relied on welfare or had unstable jobs. But it applied to a transit-reliant family living in a poor section of Staten Island, too, whose support network of relatives was concentrated in the South Bronx.

Some Type 2 cases endured not one but a series of bad breaks in the rental market. Lanelle's family in New York, whose trajectory of relocations we detailed above, is one such case. She loved living in a low-poverty area in the Northeast Bronx, but a combination of problems with the unit and landlord, plus health problems and a kin network that connected her to an affordable apartment, put her family back in the South Bronx, in a high-poverty neighborhood near Yankee Stadium, by the time we got to know the family.

Type 3, the rarest trajectory type, showed variable patterns along these same dimensions. The few cases in our ethnographic sample (of 29 experimental-complier families) that fit this type struggled to align life goals—which included a better neighborhood for the children—with insecure or inadequate housing and employment opportunities as well as hard-to-reach social support, such as vital childcare provided by a parent or sibling living at a distance.

For example, Anique is the single mother of Clara, age 11. The family has moved five times since the initial relocation. They initially relocated from the housing projects in South Los Angeles to an apartment in the nearby southern suburb of Gardena. But Anique soon moved back to South L.A. because she wanted more space and because she worried about Clara living too close to a swimming pool. The new home was larger, but the neighborhood turned out to be too dangerous in the evening. So Anique and Clara soon moved again to a home in Compton, also an inner suburb to the south. Anique's failed attempt to buy this house caused her to lose her housing voucher. But she landed a job in Riverside County, more than 70 miles to the east, where an aunt and uncle lived and were willing to provide childcare. So Anique and her daughter moved there. But before long, their relatives left California, and lacking alternative sources of safe, affordable childcare, Anique moved with her daughter to Long Beach to live with Anique's mother and sister. Then Anique was laid off from her job, needed financial help, and so stayed with her mother. Then she got a new job in Riverside County, so her commute was nearly 80 miles each way, and she left the house at 4 A.M. each day. By the time of our final fieldwork visits, Anique had scraped together enough money to rent a small one-bedroom apartment across the street from her job.

Anique's case is revealing, though this trajectory represents a small share of MTO families: She is an extremely persistent single mother whose job, housing, and social support locations remained unstable for a long period of time, challenging her to align the three and keep them aligned. We revisit this problem, as a barrier to employment, in chapter 9.

In light of the constraints, what explains the different priorities of different families? Did MTO, in fact, reflect the so-called reformer's ideal more than the real needs of the families it aimed to serve? We look next at the true nature of preferences and trade-offs for a range of MTO families.

What Counted Most

Recall that MTO families made two kinds of decisions that shaped their neighborhood (location) outcomes over time: *whether* to move and *where* to move. The more often a family had to move, or chose to do so for its own reasons, the more important the search process, preferences, and barriers to choice—in the marketplace—became.

As we noted earlier, moving is always, in some sense, a roll of the dice for a family. Will the housing unit, as well as the location, work out as we hope? Will both meet our needs over time, as things change in our lives and the neighborhood changes? But for the very low-income families in our study of MTO, in three of the nation's costliest and tightest rental markets, the odds were especially daunting.

Whether to Move

MTO families, including those in the experimental group who had escaped high-poverty neighborhoods, moved on (over time) for a variety of voluntary and involuntary reasons, the most important of which were: *dissatisfaction* with their housing unit, landlords, or neighborhoods; *leasing problems*, such as a unit being sold, rented above the voucher program price ceiling, or removed from the voucher program; or *life changes*, such as birth, death, job getting and job loss, divorce, or domestic dispute. These factors drove second and later moves and continued to be the major reasons for moving years after the interim evaluation.[12]

But we find that only rarely did being closer to loved ones act as a reason for moving for experimental compliers; more importantly, it factored into the assessment of neighborhood options (where to move) and helped shape important daily routines—around the accessibility of child-care provided by a relative, for example, or where socializing took place. This is important, since debates over MTO and similar approaches to addressing ghetto poverty often lead to claims that very poor, minority families find, after some time living outside ghetto neighborhoods, that they need to be with the loved ones left behind. There is more to the story, as we show here.

Families in the Section 8 comparison group who reported moving on were particularly likely to cite dissatisfaction with their neighborhood—a lack of safety and sometimes noise or more generally "the wrong environment for my children"—as a main reason for moving. This is consistent with the comparison group's greater exposure to high-poverty areas and with their much lower reported neighborhood satisfaction in the interim evaluation of the experiment.

For the experimental-complier families—those who leased up in low-poverty areas as the program intended—substandard physical conditions were a major culprit. Either the family chose to move because they were not satisfied with landlord maintenance and repair, or the unit failed to meet inspection standards set by the housing voucher program—as in Lanelle's case in the Northeast Bronx. Some families reported health problems related to toxic home environments, such as carbon monoxide poisoning and mold, and we observed serious problems firsthand in some units: kitchens overrun with cockroaches as we sat to conduct interviews, heat that barely functioned in the cold winter, and more.

But there was dissatisfaction with landlords as well: Some families found the lack of privacy too restrictive (e.g., where the landlord lived in the same building), especially when it prevented family and friends from visiting. And some parents could not handle landlords' expectations about keeping their children quiet. We did not and could not interview landlords, so we have only the tenant's side of these stories.

As for the third treatment group in the experiment, control-group families who had moved from public housing projects by the interim mark—and they represented 70 percent of that group—either highlighted "pull" factors (such as receiving a voucher outside the MTO demonstration), the decision to leave subsidized housing altogether, the desire to get better units and/or neighborhoods, or push factors beyond their control: most important, being "vouchered out" through HOPE VI or other redevelopment programs that required resettlement.[13] Here, too, belying the statistics, there was no "average" experience. One family in Los Angeles was so desperate to get out of high-crime public housing that the mother borrowed from relatives and gave up her housing assistance altogether. Others found involuntary resettlement extremely difficult even if they came to value some things about new housing in a different neighborhood.

Where to Move

Beyond the main reasons for moving (anywhere), our work sheds light on why MTO households made the specific housing unit and neighborhood choices they did, showing how needs changed (for example, as the household grew) and also how a willingness to make trade-offs among desired outcomes—for example the willingness to stay or not stay in a lower quality housing unit *in order* to stay in a safer neighborhood—varied widely among families.

Prior research on MTO has emphasized neighborhood safety—in particular, the chance to get away from the drug dealing and violence in high-risk neighborhoods—as the primary motivator for participating families' initial relocation. Years afterward, parents in all three treatment groups continued to emphasize this *avoidance* factor—as distinct from the attractions of a resource-rich neighborhood—sharing "horror stories" of the neighborhoods left behind. But distancing children from what subjects perceived as undesirable "ghetto" behavior was a factor as well, some parents recalled.

Distinctive behaviors invariably lead to perceived social boundaries within neighborhoods—not just across them—and often to sharp judgments as well, as ethnographic studies of "street" versus "decent" or "upstanding" cultures at play in urban neighborhoods have found for more than a generation (E. Anderson 1991; Hannerz 1969; Pattillo 2007; Small 2004). In terms of understanding why families in MTO made the choices they did, what is important is that these perceptions remained distinct and strongly negative, even years after families entered the program, constituting a second avoidance factor. For example, some experimental-complier parents in our ethnographic sample recalled loud and frequent partying, hanging out on the street corner as a sign of idleness, gang banging (participating in gang-organized drug dealing, violence, and socializing), being confrontational and quick to fight, young girls acting "fast" (too sexual for their age), and people dressing or carrying themselves in ways our subjects thought inappropriate and low class—"ghetto style," as they put it.

April, a mother in the Boston experimental-complier group who is originally from Haiti, has lived in the same neighborhood since her first relocation. It is in a mixed-income suburb north of Boston in which, says April, people "are nice, go to work, dress nice." On one of our visits, she contrasted her "suburb" neighborhood (her label) with the "ghetto place" the family moved away from, and she emphasized how much more important these location qualities were to her than the features of a housing unit:

> You know, over there [in the old neighborhood], people are "Blah! Blah!" Loud! The music is high, there's ghetto people. You even hear eight-year-old kids F-talking!... You know those kids are trouble.... I don't care if people give me $5,000 and I get a big apartment, with three bedrooms or more in [my old neighborhood]. I never want to live in the ghetto.

These judgments carried over to experimental compliers who noticed the in-migration of poorer families in their low-poverty areas—the "ghetto followed me" dynamic we mentioned earlier. Sabrina, an experimental complier in Boston, explained her intent to move again, though she and her children were well integrated into the routines and institutions of their neighborhood:

> Sabrina said, "I'm looking for another apartment, better suited for my needs, something more, on a better street. Not so close to the people around here." *I (the fieldworker) asked who she didn't want to be around and she replied,* "The ghetto people in the building down the street. The whole building is low-income and everyone is coming from Dorchester [in inner-city Boston]. They bring with them their Dorchester behavior, and I don't like that."

But making these negative judgments about some neighbors did not stop less wary MTO parents from relying on such neighbors for support. For example, Roxanne, an experimental complier in Los Angeles, thinks her neighbors are mostly "ghetto" because they like loud music and "let people hang out." But she also thinks she could turn to any of them for help in an emergency, in part, she reasons, because they are parents in their thirties and forties, and they care about children. Other experimental- complier parents expressed the same sentiment, distinguishing their immediate neighbors' watchfulness and helpfulness from the issue of the wider neighborhood's character, which they hoped would not turn all poor and nonwhite.

Avoidance aside, and regardless of treatment group, there were common attractions to particular kinds of neighborhoods and neighbors: living near people who are working and/or "middle class," as well as "respectful" or "peaceful," and—while the emphasis on privacy versus social engagement varied—wanting to live in places where "everybody minds their own business," which are "a nice family environment." Some MTO parents specifically emphasized homeownership, neighbors' investment in place, and maturity. As one parent in New York told us, "There's nice places in the Bronx. It's the people. Got to find people who care about the community. I should do my research and find a place with less kids [and more] older people."

How did social supports and obligations—the role of loved ones and close friends living in other neighborhoods—matter? Our data point to a range of types: parents who *prioritize* proximity to loved ones or cherished institutions, such as a church; those who *factor in* such proximity but do not make it a priority when deciding where to live; and those who use vouchers to *distance* themselves from relatives because they perceive those relatives to be risky and burdensome. Crosscutting this variation in priorities was variation in the geography of families' ties: Members of the control group often reported extended family networks in and around their public housing developments, whereas compliers in both treatment groups tended to report strong ties residing at greater distance (outside their neighborhoods). This is consistent with the finding, in research on MTO's early outcomes, that experimental-group members with fewer social ties to the old neighborhood were more likely to successfully lease up in low-poverty areas (Shroder 2003).

As we showed in chapter 6, most MTO families organized their social worlds around relatives and a few close friends rather than new social contacts garnered in workplaces or—even more rarely—in new neighborhoods. But some chose new housing locations that kept relatives particularly close at hand. For example, Larissa, a Section 8 complier in New York, originally had trouble finding an adequate apartment with her voucher. She was relieved to find one near her mother:

> It is down the block from my mother, because I try to stay next to my mother, because I have two brothers, but they don't help her. I do, so I try

to stay. And it was convenient. She helps me. We all help each other. So it was good. I took it. I was like, "Okay, it is two bedrooms and better than what I had before."

That priority led a small share of experimental compliers (<10 percent of our interview sample) to move back to inner-city neighborhoods, though not necessarily the ones left behind at first relocation, in order to be close to loved ones and sometimes the church. Almost all of these cases were in Los Angeles, where compliers moved much farther on average and where public transportation is famously inadequate. In the shorthand of social network analysis, the attractions of a move back were both *instrumental* (strengthen social support, whether giving or receiving or both) and *expressive* (more socializing with loved ones).

Overwhelmingly, for example, compliers in our ethnographic sample reported that socializing with loved ones meant driving or taking transit back into the inner city; their close ties rarely visited them in their new neighborhoods. Patricia, the experimental complier in Los Angeles who had no car access and felt particularly isolated, explains why she moved from a low-poverty neighborhood in the San Fernando Valley back to South L.A. (though she also called the Valley safer and "nicer"):

> The reason why I moved by here, because I wanted to come closer to my family down here because I was the only one in the Valley, and everybody stayed over here [my relatives], or over there [my children and myself], and nobody would come visit me or my kids because they was like, "You stay too far, you stay too far," you know. And I was like…" But still, can't you all come get us?"… We used to be down here like every weekend catching the Metro all the way from the Valley, all the way here. I found a church home down here in L.A., and I liked it and I wanted to be closer to my church home. So I moved down here with my mother and my sister and my family and stuff. I liked it out there [in the Valley], but I wanted to move closer to my loved ones…. My kids, they was like, "Mama, don't nobody come visit us."

Other families adapted much more successfully to low-poverty neighborhoods, whether because they had more resources under their own roofs initially, transportation made access to loved ones living elsewhere much easier than Patricia found it, a job worked out, or for other reasons.

Finally, as we also explored in the last chapter, some MTO families used the MTO relocation to distance themselves from the neediness or perceived negative influence of relatives, including those with a criminal past, no housing, no steady work, a drug addiction problem, or all of these. Wary social relations, including self-isolation from the strains of kinship and other strong ties, have been a theme of qualitative work on ghetto poverty, including public housing environments, at least Lee Rainwater's *Behind Ghetto Walls* (1970) and Carol Stack's *All Our Kin* (1974). But the debates over public housing transformation in recent years have generally de-emphasized this feature of social life among the chronically poor, highlighting the opposite patterns of cohesiveness and positive, mutual reliance (e.g., Greenbaum 2006; Venkatesh 2000).

The distancing strategy appeared in all three treatment groups, including control-group cases such as Jeanine, who left public housing in Los Angeles after an escalation of gun violence. When we visited her, she and her children were still in a risky neighborhood, with prostitution taking place right outside their front door. But Jeanine said she felt much safer there and added:

> "I don't want my family to know where I stay. I have three aunties and two other uncles who don't know I'm here." *Fieldworker: What would happen if they knew?* "They would come visit, and they would become a problem, wanting to borrow, coming to stay. I got a cousin who has been in jail over 13 years, looking for a place to stay. I was like, 'Oh no you're not. You been in jail. I wouldn't be comfortable in the same house with you.' My kids say, 'Why you keep me away from my family?' I'm like, 'Protecting you from the bullshit!'"

HUD planners expected that MTO families would value and make use of better schools, after-school programs, and other resources in low-poverty areas. Yet very few families we talked to in the experimental group identified such resources or amenities as main reasons to live in particular neighborhoods. Some movers—notably the families in our ethnographic sample who had remained in low-poverty areas for more than five years—did most of their shopping and some of their socializing in those "new" neighborhoods, while other families in that group preferred to attend church and to shop in another neighborhood. Many commented on the greater convenience and affordability of shopping in poorer areas, where more stores priced their goods for low-income shoppers.

Trade-Offs and Priorities

Complier families faced more complex choices after the initial relocation, including unwelcome trade-offs between the things they valued: a decent housing unit and a decent neighborhood. Above, April makes clear that she would not trade "the right place" (as she defines it) for a much better housing unit—or for all the proverbial gold in Fort Knox. But most parents in our ethnographic sample of experimental compliers maintained close ties with kin or a small circle of close friends in high-poverty neighborhoods left behind and/or emphasized unit features more than April did. These parents weighed the location-unit trade-off very differently, especially if they were not as lucky as April had been to find a decent unit.

In moving on, some had more bad luck in the housing market, landing in a poorly maintained unit and needing to move on quickly again or ending up on a street that was more dangerous than it seemed during the search. Some faced changing housing needs, too, as the make-up of their households changed, with sick or homeless relatives moving in or a newborn requiring an additional bedroom.

For example, Danielle and her two daughters, Shauna and Kia, left public housing in inner-city Boston for Danvers, an overwhelmingly white suburb about 25 miles north of the city. That first neighborhood was not comfortable for the family. Danielle remembers the neighbors in her apartment complex as unfriendly. "They would never say 'hi' to me," she says. She thought them racially prejudiced as well. "They was scared of me.... When I would take out my girls to play, they would take their kids inside. How am I going to be hurting them with my two kids?" Before long, Danielle and her daughters were evicted from this first apartment due to a fight between her then-boyfriend and her ex-boyfriend. Given what she perceived to be an unwelcoming climate there, however, Danielle told us she "wasn't about to stay there" anyhow. So the family moved to Brockton, a southern suburb of Boston that is about one-fifth black. Danielle and her daughters liked Brockton and lived there for five years.

But by the time we began to visit them in 2004, they had just made another rushed move. Danielle had given birth to her third child and wanted an additional bedroom. She made clear, throughout our months of visiting, that providing materially for her girls, beyond the basics, was very important to her. But the first three-bedroom apartment she found was above a detox center. Her landlord neglected the place, which was physically decrepit and overrun with rats. Only after threatening to call the local media was Danielle able to break her contract and get out, but the abrupt move meant that she had to take whatever three-bedroom apartment she could find quickly. This last move landed the family back in inner-city Boston and its schools, in a neighborhood close to Danielle's relatives in public housing. That was a big plus, she thought at first, but she soon described it as "the worst neighborhood" she had ever lived in. Her daughters missed the Brockton schools immediately. The girls in Shauna and Kia's new schools were "fast," said Danielle, and constantly fighting, not like in Brockton. "You see, my girls didn't grow up in these kinds of neighborhoods. They're not used to this. They bully Shauna sometimes.... Kia's gotten beat up."

Trading away a better neighborhood and/or school to get a bigger or better place, then, was not about preferences in the abstract but problem-solving under tight constraints. In addition, our fieldwork highlighted how the gaps between adult and child priorities—especially if the children are adolescents craving independence and creating a social life for the first time—sharpen under relocation to much lower poverty areas. Neighborhoods that are "peaceful" to parents are often "boring" for teenagers, especially males, offering the latter little to do (according to them) and, in some cases, the need to adapt to a different class culture, with its unwritten rules about appropriate speech, dress, and conduct. We revisit these cross-cultural encounters, and the strains of acculturating in new schools and neighborhoods after moving, as part of the employment puzzle in chapter 9.

The pressures are particularly great for adolescents, given their need to fit in with their peers and develop a meaningful, dignified identity. Adolescents with strong kin ties to inner-city neighborhoods were more likely to visit those neighborhoods often, we found, to maintain peer relationships there (often with cousins), and seek out some of the very risks their parents feared, as we showed in the last chapter.

Housing Search in Tighter Markets

Beyond preferences and trade-offs, our data indicate how opportunities and constraints—most reflecting the structure of the voucher program and its weaknesses in expensive housing markets, some reflecting the challenges of low-income single parenting—contributed to housing choices over time by shaping families' information sets, their approaches to housing search, and other key factors.[14]

First, while complier families relied on a mix of search strategies for the initial relocation—about one-third relied on program counselors, and the rest were evenly divided among public housing agency lists, private agents, and newspapers—the majority who moved on again had to rely on their own devices, including rental agents they paid directly, classified ads, and word of mouth (referral networks) to find adequate housing units and landlords willing to accept the housing voucher. One reason, as affordable housing became scarcer, is that the lists of landlords and rental vacancies that were provided by public housing agencies were routinely out-of-date and therefore useless.

The qualifier for this point is that MTO's relocation counseling clearly got some families to consider areas they had never heard of and were not (until then) exploring—areas where we found them five or more years later. For those families fortunate enough to find housing units and locations that worked and to avoid (or manage) the chance events that trigger many involuntary moves for very low-income households, counseling effects on location outcomes endured for years. This underscores the pivotal role of housing stability *after* families have relocated. Again, this is not something MTO's planners had planned for. It is difficult to ensure, moreover, in a program limited to voucher subsidies.

Second, when additional moves proved necessary or desirable for whatever reason, landlords' refusal to accept housing vouchers, especially in "better" neighborhoods, and the number of units that did not meet the government's housing quality standards, constrained the housing search in significant ways. For these reasons, and because of the time and other constraints on wider search, voucher users did focus on what they perceived to be their best prospects, which generally meant units in poorer and more dangerous neighborhoods—a pattern hypothesized by earlier MTO evaluators (Orr et al., 2003:31). In fact, MTO parents expressed surprise and relief when areas *they perceived to be much better* offered them a viable housing option, but this called for incredible persistence. Tameka's successful housing search, recounted in her words in the early pages of this chapter, is a case in point.

These were not static markets, as we showed with vacancy and rent trends in chapter 4. Martina, a Latina Section 8 complier in Los Angeles, explains:

> It's been very difficult to find an apartment with Section 8.... [It took] (a)bout three years to find the one in Larga. You do find them, but not in good areas. I have children and I do it for them, not for myself. There are less expensive areas, but you don't wake up alive, or they rob or kill you. You can find them, but very far away from here. This area is expensive. In Larga, we paid $800, and the man is currently renting it for $1,500. That is why he asked us to move out, so he could raise the rent. [I lived there] five years. He wanted to raise the rent. Section 8 does not allow that. If $800 was being paid, he was not going to be allowed. That is why he told us to leave. It was hard to find an apartment. [Mine is] very expensive.... I'm going to see what I can do to pay for my rent because Section 8 will give me $500. I will pay the rest. This apartment costs $1,100.

In New York, Tina used her MTO voucher to relocate from the South Bronx to Staten Island. She didn't know anyone there and worried about being isolated from her brothers and sisters. But after seven years in public housing, she was desperate to get out (she remembers moving into public housing, with an infant, only because her brother's drug problem made it impossible for her to continue to live with him and with her mother). Plus, the "realty lady" recommended Staten Island as "quiet and nice." And she loved her first neighborhood there, but she had to move on, after a few years, because the landlord decided to sell the home. So then she looked at seven apartments quickly, all on Staten Island, but none were approved by the voucher program. She took her current place on the Island—a run-down, moldy apartment she doesn't like in a neighborhood that's much more dangerous than the one she liked so much—because she was running out of time and had to use the voucher somewhere. (It wasn't clear why *this* one had passed the housing inspection.) It's still safer than much of the Bronx, she reasons, and the schools are better.

Amber, a Section 8 complier in Boston, likewise describes the change in apartment hunting in the Boston area and why relying on a broker was important as the market tightened and she tried to find a new place in "nicer" neighborhoods:

> Looking for a new apartment, just doing the newspaper, don't help. So I end up going to a real estate [agent]. The real estate agent had to help me find a apartment. I found this apartment, which I had to pay them a fee. And the rent was going up to like $1,600, $1,800. So it was very hard calling [by] myself. And when I went to Section 8 [the unit of the local public housing agency that manages the voucher program], I tried to do the same list thing. That wasn't working out. They either wanted me to move way far...meaning at least 45 [minutes] to an hour away from my family. I didn't want to do that. So my best [bet] was to go to a real estate, and that's what kind of

helped me to get this apartment in Hyde Park [a low-poverty neighborhood in the outer ring of Boston]. I didn't want to go to Mattapan [a high-poverty, racially segregated inner-city neighborhood in Boston]. I didn't want to go to Roxbury [also inner city]. I wanted to stay, live in Hyde Park or West Roxbury [another low-poverty area in the city's outer ring], which I think both the neighborhoods are a little bit nicer. The schools are a little better.

Real estate agents made the search for an adequate, voucher-accepting unit more efficient, in part by narrowing the range of locations considered vis-à-vis an open-ended exploration of the housing market. But from another vantage point, with time, information, and other search resources at a premium, agents probably expanded the location alternatives for some families who would have otherwise settled on the easiest-to-search neighborhoods, those in the weakest rental submarkets—the poorest, highest risk areas.

SUMMARY AND IMPLICATIONS

Some MTO families who moved as part of the experimental group got out and stayed out of high-poverty neighborhoods, while others were living, once again, in such areas, within a few years of entering the program. Shifting patterns of poverty and distress in these segregated local housing markets—which analysts summarize with the rather clinical label "neighborhood change"—explain why the average neighborhood poverty rates were converging across the three treatment groups over time. But those patterns, which were beyond the control of the experiment's participants, do not explain the divergent fortunes: why some families persisted in much safer, lower poverty areas while others—*in the same MTO treatment group*—did not.

As we have shown, this puzzle in fact has two parts: Why did some families move more often than others, and why did they choose the neighborhoods they did if and when they moved? On the first part, involuntary factors, including illness and divorce and other family events, triggered many moves, as did problems with the housing unit or landlord (or both) and rent increases, landlord refusal to continue renting to a government voucher holder, landlord decisions to sell the unit, and other signs of a hot housing market. Only rarely did families choose to move because the neighborhood was the problem, and only some of those cases reflected the need to live closer to loved ones and familiar institutions, such as Patricia's "church home" in inner-city Los Angeles. Yes, some families who moved out later moved back and valued the access they regained to loved ones; this was especially true, in our small ethnographic sample, for families without reliable access to a car. But it is also the case that those ties proved burdensome and draining sometimes and that some parents moved in part to distance themselves from perennially needy relatives or relatives who posed special risks, such as addicts and ex-offenders that

MTO parents perceived to be bad influences on their children. Likewise, some parents had to deal with dissatisfied, adolescent children who found safer neighborhoods boring. There is limited evidence, then, to support the notion that MTO and initiatives like it merely represent a reformer's ideal about what the poorest families want in a neighborhood or how well they can adapt.

On the second part of the puzzle, when they did move, MTO families in metro Boston, Los Angeles, and New York confronted an increasingly tough market over the experiment's first decade. The supply of good choices—acceptable units in desired neighborhoods—shrunk substantially. In chapter 4, we surveyed the market trends that included skyrocketing rents and dipping vacancy rates. In this chapter, we recounted the struggle—as families experienced it, on the "demand side" of the market—to find affordable units, in reasonably safe neighborhoods, where the landlord was willing to accept the housing voucher. In some cases, rental agents, whose ongoing involvement had never been contemplated by MTO's planners, assisted these moves, helping to steer families toward promising landlords and neighborhoods—and thus affecting the location outcomes.

But we also found that families who moved on showed a range of priorities. Some would do anything to avoid unsafe neighborhoods and what they described as ghetto social behavior. They did not want to be around it or, more importantly, to have their children anywhere near it. Some of these families were willing to deal with a decrepit apartment in order to stay in neighborhoods they perceived to be much better for their family. Other parents in MTO were not willing to make the same trade-off, particularly if they judged the norms of behavior, in neighborhoods left behind, less harshly.

Very low-income families on housing assistance take what they can get, making the most of proximity to loved ones (given the need to obtain vital social support from them, provide it, or both), managing in substandard or crowded units for the sake of their children, and otherwise settling. The larger issue is why families served by the nation's largest low-income housing program should be forced to make that devil's choice in some housing markets, given a series of national policy declarations, going back half a century, about ensuring a "decent" home *and* a "suitable" living environment (neighborhood) for all. But in terms of the struggle to stay out of high-poverty neighborhoods, MTO families' priorities did matter, by steering families in the face of limited choices.

The differences among otherwise similar housing markets figured into those limits. Metro Boston, Los Angeles, and New York are among the nation's costliest markets, and for years now, affordable supply has not kept pace with demand. But important demographic differences remain. The Boston market, for example, offered many more options in low-poverty, racially mixed areas—in that such areas make up a much larger share of all neighborhoods there as compared to L.A. or New York.

As a window on choice by disadvantaged people within a choice-oriented social program—the rental housing voucher program—MTO belies optimistic conceptions about empowering the consumer. A combination of limited resources for making choices, a limited range of choices actually available to those who hold government subsidies, the difficulties of getting information about those choices, and other factors combined to limit the effectiveness of the voucher—the key mechanism on which the success of this experiment hinged.

For some families, getting a housing voucher is "like [winning] an Oscar" (as one told us), inspectors and landlords cooperate in textbook fashion, and the unit remains affordably priced for years. For others, the dearth of minimally acceptable units, the insecure opportunity to live in a safer neighborhood when one does gain a foothold, and each arduous new search are all reminders of what it means to rent housing on the bottom of the income ladder in extremely costly and tight markets—and with a government housing subsidy that is often stigmatized and rejected in "better" neighborhoods, even when the advertised rent is within reach.

In the next chapter, we look at how housing outcomes over time, together with other aspects of choice and constraint, shaped the educational opportunities that MTO created or failed to create.

Chapter 8

Finding Good Schools

For some parents, choosing schools is less an opportunity than an occasion for disappointing one's child—at least in the short run.

April, for example, is a Haitian immigrant in Moving to Opportunity's Boston experimental group. She, her husband Jean, and their three children relocated from a public housing development in Dorchester to a suburb north of the city. They had been living there for more than 10 years when we got to know them. April, whom we introduced in the previous chapter, said she would love to get a better apartment but not if it meant moving back to the "ghetto" neighborhoods of Boston, where they used to live, where most of her husband's friends and relatives still live.

We asked how she had chosen the middle school for her children. "My kids told me," she said. Yet her two oldest children, Georgiana (age 13) and Tevin (12), disagreed about which school to attend. Tevin wanted to be with friends at the nearest neighborhood school, but Georgiana wanted to attend a school slightly farther away because it had more honors classes, better teachers, and was "less ghetto," as she put it. Like many inner suburbs, April's community became poorer and more racially mixed over the past decade, creating real strains, including some perceptions that—bluntly put—the ghetto was moving in.

When we asked if she knew anything about either of the schools her children preferred, April replied, "Not really." So in the end, April learned a bit about each school and settled the disagreement with a safety-first emphasis. Georgiana explained, "My mom said, 'No! Nobody is going to [Tevin's preferred school] because there are too many gangs and too many fights.'"

Over the past two decades, advocates for expanded choice in public education—a movement that includes school voucher experiments, less controversial charter and magnet schools, opportunity scholarships for study in private schools, and other mechanisms—have argued that "the best way to improve education is to put parents in charge."[1] But as we outlined at the start of chapter 7, the choices actually available to disadvantaged families, as well as the ways they make their choices, often belie hopes that are grounded in middle- and upper-income Americans' experiences of choice and opportunity. Those experiences typically feature a wide array of good (or better) choices, the information and other resources needed to make useful comparisons among them, and a determination to win long-term benefits from choices made today—that is, the conception of education, housing, career, and other choices as high-potential investments in one's self or one's children. The poor and working class, on the other hand, are more likely to experience big choices as risky and burdensome—the chance to get it wrong.

The sharp contrast between the idealized, higher status model of choice apparent in many policy debates and choice-in-practice for the poor and disadvantaged applies to the school experiences of many families who participated in the MTO experiment. This is in spite of the hopes that MTO would replicate the Gautreaux program's success, that of the low-income black children from inner-city Chicago who got to and stayed in high-performing, middle-class suburban schools thanks to a court-ordered housing mobility strategy (see chapter 3). Researchers found that those children were more likely than counterparts who remained in Chicago public schools to finish high school and attend college (Kaufman and Rosenbaum 1992; Rubinowitz and Rosenbaum 2000). Across the five MTO sites, in the interim survey, a majority of parents in all three MTO treatment groups, and 55 percent in the case of the experimental group, cited safety concerns in the old neighborhood ("getting away from drugs, gangs") as their most important reason for wanting to move, as we highlighted in chapter 5. But 16 percent cited "better schools for my children" as the top reason. Yet MTO showed no significant impacts on school outcomes, and only modest differences in school quality, for the experimental group after four to seven years. The hope that MTO would help families get ahead—especially in the domains of education and economic opportunity—have not materialized thus far.

A major difference between Gautreaux and MTO, then, was in the access to higher performing schools: 88 percent of children in the Gautreaux suburban sample attended schools with standardized test scores at the national average or above (J. Rosenbaum 1995), but less than 10 percent of the MTO experimental-group children, and only 14 percent of compliers (those who successfully relocated to low-poverty neighborhoods after enrolling in the program), attended schools ranked at or above their state average in terms of mean test score (Orr et al., 2003). As of the interim evaluation mark, MTO did not have statistically significant effects on educational effort (e.g., as measured by study behavior), achievement (measured by test scores), or attainment (grade or school completion), that is, when the experimental group was compared to the comparison and control groups at the interim evaluation point. So we focused our attention on school quality—a fundamental indicator of access to educational opportunity—and the question of why the experiment failed to change that opportunity dramatically for families who relocated.

Not only did MTO families' struggles in the housing market, the subject of the last chapter, weaken their access, over time, to better school options in low or relatively low-poverty neighborhoods, but parents and their children also had a variety of priorities, not just academic excellence, and limited resources to draw on. *And relocating did not change these things.*

PRIORITIES AND RESOURCES

Most MTO families in the experimental group did not move—in their initial relocation or later ones—to communities with substantially better schools, and for reasons we explored in chapter 7, some of those who did get to somewhat better school assignment zones moved on within a few years. Where parents had meaningful choices among different schools (from a given housing address), their choices were typically driven by poor information. The social networks of most MTO families, even those who relocated to low-poverty areas and stayed in them over time, remained insular, as we detailed in chapter 6. These networks centered on relatives and a few friends who had similar social backgrounds—and the same limited information about educational opportunity or how to judge schools. In part for this reason, most MTO parents, whether they moved to low-poverty neighborhoods or not, remained information poor—about schools, careers, and more.

Moreover, the logic driving choices was a limiting factor for some families who had meaningful school choices to make. Many MTO parents were schooled in very poor, segregated inner-city schools, and so were most of their relatives and friends. When choosing new schools in new neighborhoods for their children, the choice rationales of some parents centered overwhelmingly on avoiding ghetto-type school insecurity and disorder—making sure that schools were orderly and relatively free of gang violence, for example—and not garnering academic opportunity. In plain terms, the "cultural logic" of choice centered on avoiding terrible risks rather than seeking out terrific opportunities for their children. Like information poverty, this logic persisted in part because of the insular social networks many MTO families maintained.

These factors contributed to keeping MTO children, including many in the experimental group who successfully relocated to lower poverty neighborhoods, in relatively low-performing schools even when more academically promising choices appear to have been available. In this section, we briefly explain and illustrate each of those factors before turning, in the subsequent sections, to the lessons of prior research on these issues and to the MTO experience in greater depth.

First, in sizing up schools, just like sizing up neighborhoods, many MTO families put safety first, as April did, and sometimes last. Contrary to the notion of choice as making the most of an investment, a way to garner academic opportunity, many MTO families, who had long been exposed, like their loved ones, to some of the nation's most violent urban neighborhoods and most disorderly schools, focused on avoiding risk, not seeking out academic opportunities they did not understand or had never experienced. Denise, for example, is a black single mother in the Los Angeles experimental group. She talked to us about the differences between the "ghetto" school in her public housing neighborhood and the school her children attend now, in a low-poverty neighborhood outside L.A.:

> Q: But you said part of the reason you moved was to get into better
>   schools.... How do you think it compares to the other schools...like
>   in [the neighborhood where you used to live in public housing before
>   MTO]?
> A: Oh, you can forget about in [the old neighborhood]. Those schools
>   were, I don't know, just living in the ghetto basically.
> Q: So tell me about his current school.
> A: It's a great school.... They don't play around with anything. They have a
>   lot of rules and stuff and that's what I like about it.... They keep an eye
>   on them. Really, they don't play. There's school security.... They just
>   don't tolerate a lot of things. So that is what I like about it.

For families in the MTO experimental group who got out of high-poverty, inner-city neighborhoods but did not *stay* out of such neighborhoods, the contrast in schools could be striking. But this was no guarantee that parents were informed or resourceful enough to make the best available choices for their children. To the contrary, many remained information poor, and MTO was not designed to address that.

Kia, age 11, is the daughter of Danielle, a black parent in MTO's Boston experimental group whom we introduced in the previous chapter. The family moved to an inner suburb of Boston, where they were evicted after less than a year, then on to another suburb where they lived for about six years, and then back to a poor, mostly nonwhite inner-city neighborhood. In the process, Kia and her sister Shauna, who is a year older, lost ground in terms of school quality. Kia's new Boston school, unlike the one she had attended in the family's suburban neighborhood since entering the public school system, was rife with classroom disorder and fighting in the hallways and lunchroom. Kia complained of "teachers who don't teach," classes where "I sit there and do nothing." It was not like her suburban school at all, she explained, giving illustrations of higher expectations and tougher rule enforcement in that suburban school. Kia then explained to us how her mother made the latest school choice, once the family moved back to inner-city Boston:

> Q: How did you decide which school to go to?
> A: I didn't decide. It was my cousin Allana, and my mom just said, "She'll
>   see if that school is good." If it's not good, she'll look into a different
>   school.

The only advantage that Allana provided to Danielle was that she had slightly older children who had attended Boston schools. Yet Allana, a resident of the housing projects where the family once lived, was unable to provide them with genuinely useful information. Also, she applied the same limited outlook that Danielle brought to the choice among schools. In effect, Danielle's "intelligence network" was insular and limited, made up primarily of relatives and a few close friends whose backgrounds and life fortunes were much like her own.

Toward the end of our ethnographic fieldwork, Danielle had shifted her outlook on the new school from "wait and see" to real alarm. But like other parents in MTO, Danielle was ill prepared to make use of additional information about good schools even when she obtained it. For example, she had also heard about METCO (Metropolitan Council for Educational Opportunity), a voluntary desegregation program that buses academically promising children from inner-city neighborhoods to some of the highest performing school districts in suburban Boston.[2] Danielle considered placing her daughter Kia in the program. Yet in a conversation about schools, Danielle clearly indicated to our ethnographer that she did not understand how this special program worked, thinking METCO was a particular school:

> "I wanted to sign them up for the METCO school," said Danielle. I [the fieldworker] asked her where she heard about METCO, and she said that she "just heard it was a good school."... Danielle explained, somewhat confused, "But I have to wait because Kia has to take a test or something, and they give that test only some time, some grade."

On another visit, Danielle's younger daughter Shauna said to our ethnographer, "I want to go to [Boston] Latin Academy," a high-performing and selective exam school within the district. When we probed, Shauna added that she knew Latin to be "a really good school." Her mother, who was listening, had not heard of the school, nor did she question Shauna about it. Later, we learned that Danielle was unaware that Shauna's school had after-school programs—until Shauna mentioned it to our ethnographer in Danielle's presence.

Sadly, the main features of Danielle's experience and that of her daughters appeared again and again among families in the experimental group who successfully relocated to low poverty: the moving on toward poorer areas over time; the focus on basic safety concerns—a precondition for learning, to be sure—but not broader academic opportunity; the information poverty of the family's social networks; and the parent's own weak educational background—a limited resource for assessing, and interacting with, the schools.

But as we have stressed throughout the book, there was no "average" MTO family or experience. More informed and resourceful MTO parents were able to make very different schooling choices, even if they remained in, or returned to, poor inner-city neighborhoods.[3]

For example, Pamela, a 73-year-old black mother in the New York control group, successfully enrolled her children, Tricia (age 13) and Eamon (14), in one of the most competitive college preparatory schools in the city, a charter school in the Bronx, where she has lived in the same public housing development for 45 years. Pamela calls herself "the matron of the building," telling us, on our first visit, "there is no senior in this citizen!"

Pamela adopted Tricia and Eamon when she was 63, after raising three children of her own. Tricia and Eamon participate in after-school programs and special classes at school, and the family is active in a church outside the neighborhood. Though the children were only in middle school when we first met them, Pamela was encouraging them to think about which colleges to attend. Eamon has even flown to Boston to visit Harvard and MIT, and Tricia, at the time our fieldwork ended, was set to visit colleges in California. Pamela, who went back to school to become a nurse after dropping out as a teenager, obtained a computer for Tricia and Eamon to use for school work, and she visits their school to check on their progress. Pamela was more than resourceful. This "retired" 73-year-old was never at rest. Over the course of our visits, she was running several small enterprises, including a mentoring program and a food charity for the poor, out of her apartment.

Jessica, a Caribbean immigrant in the New York experimental group, moved back to Harlem, finding an apartment in a gentrifying neighborhood, after using her MTO voucher to move out of state, for several years, with her son James (age 12). Jessica is an elementary school science teacher with a college degree. She no longer receives a rental voucher or any other form of housing assistance. She is a member of a group for professional black women and told us she had a variety of "associates," not close friends, mostly from prior jobs, whom she could call on for information. Jessica very carefully researched her son's school choices when they moved back to Harlem. She monitors his homework and academic progress constantly. She also keeps track of enrichment opportunities in and around their neighborhood, where James is part of an after-school program. Jessica is much more educated than Danielle, April, or most MTO parents. The fact that she was living in public housing when the MTO solicited volunteers reflects a cash-poor spell in her life as a single mother, not chronic and extreme disadvantage.

So was it the resources or resourcefulness of the family, not the relocation opportunity, that mattered most? Prior research has had much to suggest about this, not because of MTO specifically, but because many of the hopes about transforming public education, particularly for the most disadvantaged students and their families, hinge on improving the choices that families make about where their children go to school. Likewise, research has examined the effects of high-risk neighborhoods on schooling, and these effects helped motivate the federal government to launch MTO.

HOPES AND EVIDENCE

When MTO was designed, planners inspired by preliminary results on the Gautreaux program hoped the new experiment would give children access to more resource-rich and high-performing schools, with better instruction and supports, as well as positive peer groups made up of young people who were more confident than their inner-city counterparts that education would pay off for them. These positive pathways might lead to healthier aspirations, better attendance, more study time, or other educational effort and, in turn, to higher attainment (school completion) and achievement (review in Orr et al., 2003). On the other hand, moving to new neighborhoods and schools could have negative consequences for those who move. For example, low-income children might respond negatively to competition with more advantaged peers (Jencks and Mayer 1990; J. Rosenbaum 1995), or teachers might single out the newcomers for sanctions, for example, as part of racial or other disparities in the practice of school discipline (Carter 2005; Skiba et al., 2001). Also, moving itself, even to a more resource-rich environment, tends to be disruptive for children's education and social development, and multiple moves can be even more damaging (Pribesh and Downey 1999; review in Sanbonmatsu et al., 2006).

But it was evidence on Gautreaux that most directly informed expectations for MTO, as we detailed in chapter 3. In general, Gautreaux parents who moved to the suburbs reported more concerned teachers who had more resources to help their students, as well as peers who worked harder, were less disruptive, and were more likely to expect to go on to college than the peers left behind in Chicago's inner-city schools. After nearly a decade had passed, follow-up research found that many of these suburban movers struggled for a time with higher standards and unfamiliar cultural expectations in their new schools. The mover children's grades also dropped in the short to medium term—in part because standards were so much higher than they had been in the inner-city Chicago public schools. Yet when compared to a second group of movers who stayed in Chicago (and whose children stayed in its public schools), the suburban mover children were more likely to have completed high school and gone on to college (Kaufman and Rosenbaum 1992; Rubinowitz and Rosenbaum 2000).

Planners wondered: Could MTO replicate this success? Or might the experiment's random assignment of families to treatment groups, and its much more complete tracking of families from enrollment forward, show that Gautreaux's educational success applied only to a select group of low-income families who escaped the inner city?

MTO'S EDUCATION EFFECTS

At first, the evidence on MTO was very encouraging. Early-impact studies conducted at the Baltimore and Boston MTO sites, which focused on outcomes one to three years after random assignment, indicated significant improvements in school quality at both sites (Katz, Kling, and Liebman 2003; Ladd and Ludwig 2003). Baltimore findings further indicated positive impacts on reading and math scores (Ludwig, Duncan, and Ladd 2003).

But survey researchers flagged constraints on housing and school choice as factors to watch as MTO evolved, and additional in-depth interviews at multiple sites indicated that some MTO children were not attending neighborhood schools after relocation, whether because of special needs, safety concerns, or concerns about grades dropping (Popkin, Harris, and Cunningham 2001). These early studies provide limited insight, however, into how and why MTO families made the school choices they did.

At the experiment's interim mark, some four to seven years after random assignment, the evidence was far more disappointing: Children in the MTO experimental group were doing no better academically, across all sites, than children in the other treatment groups, at least as measured by standardized test scores (table 8.1).[4] This finding held even when subgroups of children, such as those who moved at a younger age, were analyzed. Modest "treatment effects" were observed only in Baltimore and Chicago—and there only on reading scores.

Moreover, it was clear that experimental-group children were attending schools with only small advantages relative to controls in: performance (as measured by their school's percentile rank on state exams); poverty rate; exposure to white classmates; or exposure to students with limited English proficiency—a commonly employed set of "contextual disadvantage" measures (table 8.1). They were also somewhat less likely to be attending magnet schools.

School-level integration with white peers, like neighborhood-level integration with white neighbors, has long been used to index access to school opportunity (Clotfelter 2004), and both dimensions point to limited gains by the MTO experimental group—or even by the complier half. Further analyses of these survey data indicated that the young children who showed early-impact benefits in Baltimore did not sustain those gains, that there were no measurable treatment effects on school climate or resources as reported by MTO children themselves, and that *substantial access to high-performing schools is the major opportunity that MTO has failed to produce, let alone sustain* (Sanbonmatsu et al. 2006).[5]

The failure to produce such access is due, in part, to the fact that 80 percent of the MTO experimental group, and 70 percent of the subset who successfully relocated, stayed in the same school district, and, in part, because of how MTO families used the school choices they had. As for the first factor, inequalities in educational opportunity are mainly about between-district rather than within-district differences, and this is much more the case now than a generation ago, thanks to the abandonment of central-city school districts by many middle- and upper-income families, especially whites (Clotfelter 2004). As we noted above, a large majority of Gautreaux's suburban movers were enrolled in relatively high-performing schools when researchers studied educational outcomes in the program, and MTO children whose families relocated outside the central-city school district were more likely (20 percent versus 8 percent) to be in schools with mean test scores at or above the state average

Table 8.1. MTO Interim Impacts on School Characteristics and Educational Achievement

	Control mean	Experimental vs. Control Impacts	
		ITT	TOT
School characteristics			
Percent free lunch (n=3562)			
Current school	65.7	6.6 lower*	13.0 lower*
Average school	72.1	6.7 lower*	13.3 lower*
Percent white (n=4875)			
Current school	10.6	4.0 higher*	8.9 higher*
Average school	8.6	4.7 higher*	10.1 higher*
Percent Limited English Proficient (n=4019)			
Current school	16.8	2.7 lower*	5.8 lower*
Average school	18.1	3.0 lower*	6.3 lower*
Magnet school (n=3945)			
Current school	24.9	5.1 lower*	11.3 lower*
Average school	18.2	3.5 lower*	7.7 lower*
Achievement outcomes			
Woodcock-Johnson broad reading score (n=5169)	497.31	0.92 higher	2.04 higher
W-J broad math score (n=5187)	501.23	0.22 higher	0.49 higher

Source: Orr et al. (2003:110,117).

Note: ITT = intent-to-treat (includes compliers who successfully relocated to low-poverty neighborhoods at enrollment and noncompliers who did not), TOT=treatment-on-treated (compliers only, divided by the site lease-up rate). Control means and impact estimates are regression-adjusted with robust standard.

* p<.05 (Statistically significant at the 95 percent confidence level)

(Orr et al., 2003). Tracking the differences in housing trajectories that we explored in chapter 7, this exposure to suburban schools, researchers found, varied substantially across MTO sites. At the interim evaluation mark, experimental-group children were more likely to be outside their origin district in greater Boston (32.9 percent) and Los Angeles (37.8 percent) than Baltimore (23.6 percent), Chicago (18.3 percent), or New York (13.8 percent).

There is also evidence that school- and district-level changes over the course of the experiment narrowed the gaps among schools in the three treatment groups; that is, the evidence is that school contexts shifted, not just that children transferred across those contexts in ways that produced only modest changes in educational opportunity for the favored experimental group (Orr et al., 2003). First, as we noted in chapter 4, poverty grew much more rapidly in the suburbs than in central cities over the experiment's first decade. Second, because of aggressive school reform in some cities, and because most of the control group moved at some point, control-group children were also in schools with higher average test scores and were more likely to be in magnet schools—which indicate expanded choice—than they were at baseline.

The key question about school choice in MTO, then, is this: How did families *who had meaningful school choices* make those choices? What were their priorities and challenges in making those choices?

THE CONTEXT OF SCHOOL CHOICE: HOW MUCH AND HOW?

Nationally, about three-quarters of children in public schools still attend "assigned" schools (Briggs 2005a), and 71 percent of MTO children did so continuously from baseline to the interim point.[6] That is, school enrollment is generally determined by neighborhood or other attendance zones, making parents "nonchoosers" in the shorthand of educational research. The family's housing and neighborhood choice *is* its school choice, at least in terms of public education opportunities. But the share of children attending neighborhood schools has dropped over the past decade as magnet school programs, charter schools, and school voucher initiatives expand choice nationwide; also, wider choice has been the rule for years in some MTO communities, such as Boston and New York, either at the elementary or secondary level or both. Finally, a small share of MTO children had attended private school for some period of time by the interim mark. At that point, 10 percent of program children at the New York site had attended either a magnet, charter, or private school chosen by the family, as had 12 percent in greater Boston and a whopping 54 percent in greater Los Angeles. Consistent with the five-site proportion of choosers, just under one-third (31 percent) of the adolescents we interviewed had attended a nonassigned school by the interim mark.[7]

As a rule, education researchers have not addressed housing choice extensively, except to note that housing choices and prices within metropolitan housing markets are sensitive to school quality indicators, including major differences in average test scores across districts—a pattern driven by where middle- and upper-income households choose to live and school their children (Briggs 2005; Clotfelter 2004). This gap in research is especially glaring in the case of low-income minority families who tend to have the worst school outcomes and the poorest housing choices. Still, analyses of school choice have expanded and diversified rapidly in recent years, as school vouchers, charter schools, and other innovations grow in scale, variety, and visibility. The commonly held view in the field is that parents choose schools according to the three "p's": how well the school performs; how pleasant or welcoming it is (climate); and how proximate or close to home it is (Bell 2005). But considering the wide range of priorities and specific approaches expressed by parents, especially across social-class differences, researchers have proposed three models of school choice: resources, cultures, and choice sets.

The *resource* model compares parents by socioeconomic status, race/ethnicity, and other traits according to the resources they can or do bring to bear in the choice process. Key resources include time, transportation, and relevant information—for the same reasons these things matter for housing choice, as we showed in the previous chapter. This model grew out of the effort to understand 1960s era school reforms and their successes and failures (Jencks 1970; Wells 1993). The choice model emphasizes low-income parents' lack of access to reliable information for making better school choices, from barriers to obtaining and using the information made available by institutional sources such as school staff to social networks of relatives and friends that are similarly situated and therefore ill equipped to provide effective advice (Bell 2005). Recent experiments suggest real gains from systematic efforts to make information on school performance, for example, more transparent and available to less educated parents (Hastings and Weinstein 2007).

Another research-based model argues that, resources aside, parents bring different *cultures* of decision-making—repertoires of school experience and beliefs about the role of schooling in their children's lives—to bear on choices (Bulman 2004). Even middle- class parents, for example, appear to differ widely on the degree to which the school environment should emphasize ethical values as opposed to narrower academic notions of achievement or the degree to which schools should help less academically inclined children to obtain practical vocational skills versus prepare for college. A key unresolved question in this research is whether and how school-choice cultures and practices *shift* with changes in context, such as relocation to less disadvantaged neighborhoods.[8]

Third and finally, Bell (2005) presents evidence on why differences in *choice sets* ("the actual markets within which parents choose") matter as much as, or more than, choice process or priorities that vary by parents' class status, ethnicity, or other traits. As she notes, "The vast majority (up to 97 percent) of parents with children in failing schools choose to leave their children in those schools even when it is their legal right [under the No Child Left Behind Act of 2001] to do otherwise" (1). Drawing on in-depth qualitative interviews with "choosers," Bell finds that parents quickly narrow their searches to limited sets, based on nominations by trusted contacts and also "customary attendance patterns" (where parents themselves or people they know have enrolled). These criteria lead to big differences in the sets of schools that parents choose to investigate and from which they ultimately select—whether researchers use average failure rate, selectivity, or other measures to characterize schools in each choice set.

So parents make school choices for—and sometimes with—their children in different ways, with different resources and perhaps different logics of choice. But thus far, these choice-related perceptions and behaviors have not been studied in the context of efforts to expand housing opportunity for disadvantaged parents and their children. Likewise, the interplay of housing and school choice in the lives of low-income families and the prospects for changing *how* choices are made thanks to an exit from inner-city poor communities have not been examined in the growing body of research on how and why families choose the schools they do.

Drawing on these lessons and debates, we turn next to what we learned about MTO families' choices, exploring in depth the patterns we previewed, with several family cases, earlier in the chapter.

HOW MTO FAMILIES LOOKED FOR "GOOD" SCHOOLS

Information Poverty

Most MTO parents were information poor about school choice. Based on our interview data, only one in six of the parents in the experimental-complier group *who made school choices* cited formal sources of information, such as teachers or school staff, about school offerings. Just under half reported specific steps they took to find out which schools were academically promising—even if the choice set was limited in quality. Information poverty did not vary across treatment groups, suggesting that relocation itself did little to change access to information. In this respect, our findings echo a growing research literature, which indicates that most parents, and most notably low-income and minority parents, do not have any formal assistance or counseling when they choose schools for their children (Bulman 2004).[9]

When they had school choices to make, MTO parents relied heavily on referrals provided by their networks of relatives and friends. For the most part, these contacts were also low-income people with limited education and knowledge of school options. Neighbors in new, less poor locations were cordial strangers or casual acquaintances at best, as we showed in chapter 6, not sources of information or other aid. Movers rarely "converted" new locations into significant new social resources. Not only did MTO parents not receive formal counseling, then, but as other studies have shown, these parents' social contacts were probably less "productive," in terms of information quality and referral, than the contacts of higher income parents tend to be (Bell 2005).

Danielle's case, which we introduced above, shows how housing choices, the school-choice set, and poor information combined to undermine school opportunity for the experimental group. Danielle's daughters, Kia and Shauna, attended a well-run neighborhood school when they lived in a low-poverty inner suburb south of Boston. When the family moved back to inner-city Boston, to a high-poverty area, the choice set was poor, and Danielle relied on her cousins to help her choose, in effect, the least bad school she could find in the area. (Thanks to court-ordered desegregation, Boston parents have some choice among public schools, starting with elementary.) But that school was a disappointment, and after both daughters had been "jumped" (assaulted) and one found herself fighting constantly, her grades dropping, Danielle wanted them out of that school.

Some word-of-mouth advice was valuable, however. The small number of parents in the experimental group who moved successfully and were able to find out about higher performing schools also typically learned about these schools through word of mouth—but not from neighbors or relatives. Michelle, one such parent in the Boston experimental group, explained the choice to send her daughter to a stronger school, with enrollment by admissions exam, outside of Boston:

Q: How did she end up going there?
A: My girlfriend is a schoolteacher, and her daughter was up at the high school.... She told me the schools that she had applied to and she did plenty of research on the schools. So I didn't have to do much research because she already did it all for me.
Q: Could she just sign up for the school, or was there any kind of lottery system for which children got to go there?
A: Yeah, there are. There's a couple of categories. One, you have to be in Boston public school. And they go by your records, your grade records.
Q: Oh, you have to do well in school to get in?
Q: Yes, she's an honor roll student.

While the data are not available, it is likely that the majority of MTO parents, including many in the experimental group who relocated successfully, had themselves attended predominantly minority, poor, and under-performing schools. Almost two-thirds had not completed high school, making it hard for them to determine an academically promising school for their children. In Boston and New York, where students are often given the option of selecting a theme high school, a few MTO parents were attracted by the name or theme of a school and used these to determine whether the school was good or appropriate for their children. Jada in New York and Bianca in Boston, whose families successfully relocated to a low-poverty neighborhood and managed to remain in them for years, are cases in point.

Knowing that his daughter wanted to be a pediatrician, Jada's father supported her choice of the Academy of Health Careers high school. Our ethnographer observed as father and daughter went through a long list of schools provided by the New York City school district and selected that school based on the name indicating its focus, unaware—until our fieldworker pointed it out—that the school's graduation rate was just 40 percent. Jada's family had left the inner city for a safe, low-poverty neighborhood in Staten Island, where she attended an assigned neighborhood school. Jada was active at school, and her parents were obviously pleased at the education she was receiving. But now faced, for the first time, with a school choice not dictated by their housing location, Jada's parents were struggling with limited information on how to choose well.

In Boston, Shenice supported her daughter Bianca's choice to attend Boston Tech Academy specifically because it guaranteed students the use of a laptop computer and the choice to keep it, for $1, upon graduation. Shenice had applied to the METCO program, which would have bused Bianca to a high-performing school district in suburban Boston. But when Bianca was not admitted, Shenice did not push her to apply to a selective exam school in Boston, saying the prospect intimidated her daughter. Shenice liked Boston Tech's focus on computers and considered it a sign of a "good" school. Like Jada's father, Shenice was unaware that her daughter's school was one of Boston's under-performing, predominantly nonwhite and poor schools. Mother and daughter, who associated racial diversity and technology with school opportunity, were baffled when the school year began and they noticed that few white students attended Boston Tech.

Information poverty is also limiting the higher education choices of MTO children. Many express the desire to attend college and the expectation that they will do so. For some, the lesson at home was clear: College can help you have a better life than your struggling parent. Robin, for example, relied on her mother's advice and the MTO relocation counselor to move with her three children to a suburb east of Los Angeles, near a local college that she hopes her daughter, Terri (age 16), will attend once she finishes high school. Robin says of Terri:

> She learn from me, doing, accomplishing stuff.... She see how hard I had to work. I had to struggle raising 'em [my children] by myself. She like try to do something different, go to college.... I had learned the hard way, and she seen it, and she grew up with me, because I had her young, so she got to really see how it is, how hard it is in life. So that is probably why she is more successful now. And she see how hard it is once you get off track. She see how she had to fall back, going to summer school, so now she trying to do more, better, more productive, and she doing a lot better. [Interview]

Yet in Robin's family and others, we noted confusion about academic requirements, financial aid, course and career options, and more—the patterns common among less educated parents in America.

Take Jaclyn, age 17, and her mother Roxanne, who was also caring for two grandsons when we got to know her family, in a suburb of Los Angeles, in 2004. They were part of the MTO experimental group, and Roxanne, like other MTO parents, was thrilled to put the L.A. schools behind them. And she had been attentive to her child's needs. When she noticed Jaclyn struggling with "just adding," she went to the school and asked them to test her daughter. "It wasn't like she wasn't trying to do the work. She would try," Roxanne remembers. The testing pointed to a learning disability, so Roxanne enrolled Jaclyn in special classes.

Jaclyn told us that she liked her high school—she was about to enter her senior year—and definitely wanted to go on to college. But then it turned out she meant, perhaps, a trade school. She had made plans "far in advance," she said. She wanted to be a veterinarian. But as with many teenagers, her plan was hardly written in stone. "What about those people who take care of *wild* animals?" she wanted to know. "Do they pay you to do that? I either want to work with animals or do fashion design." In a home economics class, she had made a shirt and a purse.

On one of our visits, Jaclyn was concerned about her school's counselor, who did not seem to care much about placing students. One of her friends, for example, found out too late that she did not have the credits needed to graduate. Jaclyn's friends, she told us, did not talk much about going to college, though she believed several planned to do so, nor did the teachers at her school talk to their students about college. So we pressed for more details on her plans. "What do you think about going to a trade school versus a community college or a four-year college?" our ethnographer asked Jaclyn. "I talked to my mom and the man in the career center [at school]," she replied. "He said that Cal State is a good place to go and take up your major." So we asked how that would be different from going to a vocational school. "I'm not sure how it would be different, except that they'd ask for loans. I think you'd get more education and not have to pay."

Soon, Jaclyn told us that she had begun attending meetings about different colleges. "On Wednesday," she said, "they had a meeting, and [the University of California] Berkeley came there, and it was pretty nice. They said you could go off campus and there was like parties and stuff." Jaclyn had little to draw on in her immediate family or kin network. "My mom don't even know that much about college," she said, "because she didn't even graduate [high school]. My oldest niece, Showana, went to ITT Tech. So she go with computers." Her mother told us that Jaclyn could talk to other girls in her school about college, but Jaclyn did not seem to be learning much from them.

Jaclyn did not understand the requirements for applying to a nearby Cal State campus—or any other college. "I think they [school staff] said November third was the last day to register," said Roxanne. "Register for what?" we inquired. "For any college, I guess." And she added, "[Jaclyn] was thinking about going to Long Beach Community College, because she was saying that it would be better for her, that they could offer her what she needed or something. Her grade point average isn't high enough for her to go to Cal State, and plus, I can't afford for her to go, and I don't think she's gonna get a scholarship. So we trying to figure out what's best for her right here. I don't know anything about that. Maybe you can give her some thoughts about that, help her get where she needs to be, cuz oh, man…" she sighed.

On a later visit, after much confusion, Jaclyn had an informed plan. The counselor at her school's career center told her that she lacked the credits to enter a four-year college, that she should apply to a community college she liked and plan to transfer to a four-year institution later. He would help her apply for financial aid. As we left the field, Jaclyn was applying to two community colleges nearby. She and her mother had attended an informational meeting on the Cal Grant aid program for low-income families and, with assistance, completed the paperwork.

It is not clear whether MTO children attending high schools in lower poverty areas, or outside of central-city school districts, are getting more or better college counseling than counterparts enrolled in inner-city schools. Again, as MTO unfolded, the options to attend charter and magnet schools, some of which emphasize stronger college and career counseling, expanded. What is clear is that MTO parents are not well prepared to advise their children on how to gain admission and finance higher education, let alone how to make the most of the opportunity once they clear those hurdles.

Safety First

Consistent with the desire to live in much safer neighborhoods, about one-quarter of the MTO parents we interviewed, including about one in seven choosers—those who had a choice of public schools from a given residential address—emphasized safety and order as the key mark of a "good" school. MTO parents consistently emphasized that safety and discipline, and the absence of violence or gang activity, in particular, made a school good or bad. Safety and order—in particular, low classroom disruption—*are*, we should note, important indicators of school quality that directly affect learning. But among the choosers, one in seven appeared to make these the overwhelming priorities when assessing school quality, to the exclusion of academic opportunity indicators. Though this sample size is small, limiting our ability to make inferences about the MTO population as a whole, we did not observe differences across treatment groups in this cultural logic, even, for example, when families moved from low-poverty areas back to poorer ones in the inner city. And, we must note, it is a well-founded logic for parents whose "choices" have historically been defined by a lack of choice and by dramatic inequalities. But the logic of *avoiding* school risks does not ensure that parents will make the most of school choices to *garner* academic opportunities.

School safety concerns appeared to be more common among MTO families in Los Angeles, which was experiencing a surge of gang-related problems when we conducted our interviews and ethnographic visiting in 2004 and 2005. Denise, a mother in the Los Angeles experimental group whom we introduced above, talked about the differences between the "ghetto" school in her old neighborhood and the "great" school her children attend now. The latter has "rules" and "they don't play around," she said, and "that is what I like about it."

Kimberlyn, also a parent in the Los Angeles experimental group, lamented having to move her son Damian (age 17) from a better high school in the San Fernando Valley, where the family had relocated to find a low-poverty neighborhood, back to L.A.'s inner-city schools. Kimberlyn complained of some racial harassment in her apartment complex in the Valley, but eventually, she told us, she decided to move back to an inner-city neighborhood in South Los Angeles to be closer to family, friends, and what she perceived to be better access to institutional resources, such as job training. The best she felt she could do for Damian was move him from one inner-city high school (the assigned one) to another, modestly safer one. Kimberlyn accomplished this by giving the school district the address of a friend rather than her own new address. "Gangs is everywhere," she told us. While we visited the family, Damian was at risk of not graduating and was, said Kimberlyn, "not taking school seriously and getting an attitude."

While safety concerns were much more common among the families who continued to live in or who moved back to poorer, central-city neighborhoods than other participating families, these concerns also shaped the school choices of some MTO families living in the inner suburbs, where poverty and distress increased dramatically in the 1990s. April's school choice for her children, which we profiled at the beginning of this chapter, reflected deep concern about those changes.

Some MTO parents felt they had to choose between the lesser of two evils. For example, Robin, a black mother in the Los Angeles experimental group whom we introduced in the discussion of information poverty above, moved first to an eastern suburb, and then later to another nearby suburb. After the latest move, Robin opted not to move her daughter, Terri, out of the local high school despite the fact that Terri had been jumped by girls there and was seen ditching school (being truant). Among other challenges, Terri was struggling to fit in at a school of mostly white and Mexican students, yet her mother saw a stark contrast with inner-city schools left behind. Robin explained:

> Yeah, L.A. schools are worse than out here. These schools are just now getting bad, but L.A. schools are way worse. I'd have to walk them to school when I didn't have a car.... [But here], they sent a form home saying that if I wanted her to be switched over to [another high school], that they could transfer her over there, and then, I don't know who she heard it from, but they said that that school is worse than the one she go to. So she decided not to go. I was like, yeah, if you are going to be in more trouble there, might as well stay where you at. Eventually they'll leave you alone, you know. It's not like she's just a bad girl for somebody to pick on. [Fieldnote]

Trusting that Terri, who was new at her school, was no longer going to hang out with the "bad crowd," Robin decided to keep her daughter there and not risk exposing her to a less familiar, and perhaps worse, environment. But as we outlined above, the decision was based on very limited information. Robin also passed on the option of transferring Terri to a school in a nearby city, where Robin considered the schools to be better, because of the difficult commute. In this case, Robin's decision seemed to be a wise one, because based on follow-up visits, Terri soon adapted, made new friends, volunteered at the local library, joined two student organizations, and got a part-time job—all while doing better academically.

In other cases, the priority placed on safety helps explain why a small number of experimental-group parents who stayed in the same school district also kept their children in the same (pre-move) schools after the family moved, that is, schools serving high-poverty neighborhoods anchored by public housing projects. In these instances, both parents and children noted that even if the schools in their old neighborhood were dangerous, their risks were well understood and therefore less threatening. For example, parents pointed to their hard-won knowledge about "gang colors" and which groups of children "caused trouble." Moving their children to a new school could mean moving them into new gang territory where the "colors" were less well understood and avoided. Some youth were also hesitant to move from schools they knew were unsafe because they had a network of friends they could rely to defend them ("watch their backs"), or because they had established understandings with "troublemakers" who would, in turn, offer needed protection. Adam, a teen in the Section 8 comparison group in Los Angeles, left a new school to return to his old neighborhood school. "I want to be somewhere where I am more comfortable," he told us. "You know, I really don't know nobody [at the other school], all those other gangsters over there don't know me."

Counter-Examples: Seeking Out Academically Promising Schools

While some MTO parents emphasized safety and order as the overriding indicators of school quality, others also expressed an interest in engaged and caring teachers, as well as after-school programs or other resources for their children. About half the MTO parents we interviewed who were aware of school choices available to them spoke about taking extra steps to find schools that were not only safe but also academically promising in these other dimensions.[10] As researchers have found for other low-income parents who seek to protect and enrich their children in spite of risks in school and in the neighborhood (Elliott et al., 2006; Furstenberg et al., 1999; Jarrett 1999), a small number of achievement-oriented MTO parents also supplemented their "safety first" school choices with special arrangements.

Some of these parents were the better educated among MTO participants. There is Pamela, the retired nurse in the New York City control group, who successfully enrolled her children, Tricia and Eamon, in a selective college preparatory school in the Bronx. She keeps them engaged in after-school programs and special classes and has seen to it that they visited top colleges as early as middle school. And there is Jessica, the college-educated elementary school science teacher, who carefully researched the best school options for her son, James, after the family returned to Harlem.

But a handful of other, less well-educated MTO parents also took extra steps to find the right learning opportunities for their children. Monica, a mother in the Los Angeles experimental group, enrolled her two sons in a Catholic school. Though the school is in their old neighborhood, a relatively poor enclave of Latino immigrants, Monica works at the school and knows it to be disciplined and safe. The school is operated by the church the family attends, and the school-church community is a major focus of their family life.

Likewise, Laura and her children, in the New York control group, are actively involved in the charter school they attend in their inner-city community. Laura is a high school dropout and became a mother as a young teen. Her children participate in after-school programs at their charter school, and two of Laura's older sons work at the school. During our fieldwork, one was pursuing his GED (high school equivalency) because it was an employment requirement.

A few parents took extreme measures to find enriching schools far beyond their neighborhoods. For example, one mother in Los Angeles provided her employer's address as her own in order to get her children into the schools in that affluent community, a two-hour bus ride from their home.

Finally, some schools, though chosen for safety reasons, turned out to be academically enriching. As we noted above, Robin's daughter Terri adapted successfully to her high school in an eastern suburb of Los Angeles, though Terri was in the minority as a black student there and got jumped early on by trouble-making students. Along with extracurricular involvement, a part-time job, and stronger grades, Terri had developed what experts describe as essential to the learning process: productive relationships with her teachers. As Terri told us, "You could put me in a class right now, and I could be the only black student, with that teacher, I wouldn't care. Cuz I know that teacher, and I know so much about that teacher, and I feel comfortable with that teacher teaching me."

More resourceful choices by some MTO experimental compliers reflected either a more educated parent—with both the cultural logic of schools as settings for enrichment and the superior information on schools that improves the choice process—or the rare presence of a social contact, such as the schoolteacher friend cited earlier, who provided "extraordinary" information. Again, though, these valuable contacts were not neighbors, and in general, those who relocated to low-poverty areas did not garner significant new information resources or other aid from neighbors.

Other Concerns that Limited Enrollment in "Better" Schools

MTO parents, like parents everywhere, generally favored schools for their children that were near the home or otherwise conveniently located. Low-income parents are especially likely to report convenient location as a priority, especially if they do not own automobiles or have access to good public transportation.[11] Laura in New York also explained that she liked having her children in a school nearby because she could get to them quickly if "anything were to happen." Very few emphasized the risk of lost academic credit, access to social supports, or the importance of making school and school-based friendships a source of stability for children amidst the disruption of moving.

A few parents had arrangements with relatives or friends who lived in the former neighborhood, trusted people to pick up their children or watch them after school. Dana, a mother in the L.A. experimental group, detailed her decision to have her children sleep over at a relative's home in the old neighborhood to accommodate her work schedule:

> A: She left elementary and she graduated fifth grade from over in [the neighborhood where the family had lived in public housing], because I was still working, so that was my only childcare. And grandmamma, she would send them to school, [and then] I brought them home.
> Q: But so she went up through fifth grade at the same school over by [the development]? And even when you had moved out to [your new neighborhood]?
> A: I kept her there [old neighborhood] because, by me driving the school bus, I would have to be at work at 4:30 in the morning.... And it was kind of hard for me to get them up and drive. So what I'd do is I'd leave them there [at grandmother's] during the week, and then on the weekends I'd bring them home.

A handful of those mover parents who did not change their children's schools after a move did so because they wanted to preserve their children's friendships and not force their children to find new friends or peers in new schools. Both parents and children mentioned that friendships were important for safety, but also for academic and social development. The parents felt that moving had disrupted other aspects of their children's lives and so wanted to keep school life and friendships more stable. Finally, not having good information with which to compare schools and their standards across different neighborhoods, a handful of parents specifically reported "good grades" at the old school, even if its standards and test scores were low relative to alternatives, as a sign that the school was a good fit for their children.

SUMMARY AND IMPLICATIONS

MTO produced limited improvements in school context, certainly much more limited than those produced by the Gautreaux housing desegregation program that inspired MTO. MTO did not get children to significantly better schools for two main reasons: first, because "choice sets" were limited: the program did not enable most of them to *move* to and *stay* in high-performing school districts or attendance zones; and second, because choice effectiveness was limited, too: the MTO program did not address participants limited resources and logics for choosing the most effective schools. Our work strongly corroborates prior findings on how low-income parents choose schools and why they choose the schools they do, while examining the special context of assisted housing mobility. Among other things, this special context allowed us to examine the question of whether the logic of choice, or the social networks and other resources that support effective choosing, shifts when poor, inner-city families move to less poor areas. Sadly, we find that it may not—at least for many families—if they are served by a relocation-only strategy.

As we showed in chapter 7, families who relocated through MTO did not move to high-performing, wealthier suburban school districts but rather to neighborhoods in the outer ring of cities or the relatively disadvantaged inner suburbs. What is more, many families in the MTO experimental group—typically citing rising rents and utility costs or problems with the housing unit or landlord—moved back, over time, to poorer neighborhoods, in tight and costly rental housing markets, with weaker and typically more dangerous schools. The instability and scarcity of quality, affordable housing for low-income families—and the absence of any such housing in many high-performing suburban districts—has not thus far received attention in the evolving literature on school choice, although again, for most families at all income levels, housing choices define school choices. Moreover, so much of the research on how neighborhoods affect child and family success centers on conditions *sufficient* for producing those effects—such as better peer influences or high-performing schools and other institutional resources—without confirming the most basic necessary condition: being able to live in a given type of neighborhood long enough for it to matter.

Yet wider options do not mean much if one cannot exercise them effectively. Most MTO parents, like many low-income families nation-wide, drew on very limited information resources, such as word-of-mouth referrals from ill-informed relatives or friends—or even their children. Across all treatment groups, parents generally lacked the information required to determine which schools were of genuinely high academic quality. The families lacked institutional guidance, better placed contacts, or other supports. Also, experimental-group movers were not able to convert less poor locations into significant new social resources. That is, their social networks remained insular and limited in function, focused on relatives or small circles of close friends.

Next, many MTO families also made choices that belie expert views about how parents *should* choose schools and, more to the point, about what parents should value most. Their choices centered on avoiding ghetto-type risks rather than garnering (broader) academic opportunity. MTO families came from some of the most dangerous public housing communities in the nation, and most said they volunteered for the program to get away from drugs and gangs. Following that logic, it is perhaps not surprising that some MTO parents asked little more of the schools than somewhat better safety and order.

Finally, the need to juggle caregiving, work, and other demands encouraged some parents to enroll their children in the schools that were closest to the home or most conveniently located to their sources of social support. So did the desire to protect children's built-up friendships as a source of emotional stability amidst the disruptions of moving and growing up poor.

Future efforts might define "opportunity" communities to include local school performance and help low-income families stay in, not just get to, such communities. School-choice demonstrations likewise point toward specific ways to inform the school choices of low-income (or other) parents, such as by making information on school performance more transparent and the choice process less time consuming.

We revisit and extend these and other ideas in the book's concluding chapter. Since housing choices *are* school choices for 7 of the 10 children in America who attend public schools, the limits of this particular relocation-only experiment for the inner-city poor should not dissuade policy makers and practitioners from making bolder, more savvy efforts in the future.

But we turn our attention next to the other major hope that MTO would help participating families get ahead in their lives, not just improve the quality of their lives by making them safer and less fearful day to day. We turn next to the hope that MTO would generate moves to job opportunity.

Chapter 9

Finding Work

Consider two very different cases of the role of relocation in the economic lives of low-income African-American women. Anique and her daughter Clara left public housing in a high-poverty, high-crime neighborhood of South Los Angeles nine years ago. Since then, Anique has struggled to line up steady work and childcare while bouncing from apartment to apartment in L.A.'s sprawling housing market. At one point, her daily commute was 70 miles each way, from Long Beach where her mother and sister provided the childcare she needed, to her job in Riverside County. But Anique had considerable work experience, and the skills and confidence that often come with that experience, at the time of her move. As we completed our visits with her in 2005, she and Clara were living in a neighborhood that felt safe, across the street from Anique's steady new job as a child-support investigator with county government.

Kimberlyn and her two teenaged boys also relocated from public housing projects in South L.A., to a much safer neighborhood in the San Fernando Valley. Kimberlyn credits that relocation—her "last chance," she recalls—with getting her away from an abusive relationship. While her boyfriend was out one night, a friend helped her sneak out of the apartment she had shared with him. Although the new neighborhood provided safer, better schools, which Kimberlyn prized, for her sons, she experienced racial harassment from white neighbors in her apartment complex. Plus, Kimberlyn was on welfare when she moved and had almost no work experience or credentials. When she could not or would not secure, in the Valley, the job training and other resources she knew she needed, she moved her family back to South L.A. and put her sons back into the much more disruptive and dangerous schools there. Over the months we visited her and the boys, Kimberlyn was unable to line up steady work and was back on welfare after stints as a security officer and brief spells in training. The childcare her sister provided in South L.A. abruptly disappeared, and her mother's daily needs had become a major burden as Kimberlyn struggled to get ahead.

For roughly half a century, policy makers and researchers have debated the impacts of place, and in particular of living in inner-city ghettos, on employment and economic self-sufficiency. Images of the welfare-dependent or socially isolated ghetto poor, together with evidence of a growing "spatial mismatch" between suburban job growth and the urban neighborhoods where low-skilled people are concentrated, fueled an interest in housing policy as a tool for shifting the geography of economic opportunity (Abrams 1955; Briggs 2005a; Downs 1973). And as we showed in chapter 3, when evidence on the Gautreaux housing desegregation program in metro Chicago suggested that low-income African-American parents who moved to the suburbs had better odds of getting a job, planners envisioned Moving to Opportunity (MTO) as a chance to realize this potential on a larger, multiregion scale, with more rigorous evaluation. The challenge was significant, since most MTO adults were on welfare when they enrolled in the experiment; only about one-quarter were working (Orr et al., 2003).

MTO was not designed to directly address participants' employment status or employability, including the skills and credentials deficit, lack of childcare and transportation, illness, or other barriers to work that low-skill single mothers often face. Yet the experiment had the research-based expectation that if families moved to low-poverty neighborhoods, adults could become employed or get better jobs by moving closer to areas of job growth, gaining more useful job networks (a form of social capital) with more advantaged neighbors who could recommend job openings or even vouch for them, and/or gaining momentum from a community environment with stronger work norms and higher status "cultural capital"— different, planners believed, from the jobless, socially isolated ghettos the families were leaving behind. That is, the expectations about employment gains were rooted in three mechanisms with fairly direct effects: space, networks, and norms. MTO planners, and researchers who soon began to debate the trajectory the experiment might follow, imagined possible indirect effects on employment as well, such as the possibility that safer neighborhoods might reduce stress and anxiety, making adults more capable of pursuing jobs or training. On the other hand, observers argued, families might lose access to social ties which are often sources of childcare, transportation, and other work supports, as well as preexisting employment relationships. In other words, moving away from high-poverty public housing might or might not, in fact, mean moving to *job* opportunity. And it might include a loss of supportive "community."

At some MTO sites, there was encouraging evidence of early impacts— of employment gains and declines in welfare receipt at some sites—yet at the interim mark some four to seven years after random assignment, there were no treatment effects on employment, earnings, or self-sufficiency (Orr et al., 2003). As evaluators pointed out, many MTO adults, regardless of treatment group, had made significant gains in a strong economy, and all had felt the effects of the federal welfare reform in 1996—the nation's most sweeping reform of an entitlement program in a generation. At the interim mark, more than twice as many MTO adults were working in all three treatment groups (Orr et al., 2003)—this over a period in which labor markets were tight and time limits on welfare assistance began to show effects—and many other MTO families, as program counselors learned early on, were simply not "job ready." They showed significant barriers to work, in the form of chronic illnesses, low skills, very limited work experience, and other traits (Popkin, Harris, and Cunningham 2001). So the market and entitlement reform effects may have swamped any treatment effect of MTO, at least in the short run. Moreover, as we examined in chapter 7, by the interim point, many experimental-group families had moved on to somewhat poorer neighborhoods, for a range of reasons. Yet additional analyses of the interim impacts survey suggest that the employment picture might be more complex and mixed than initially thought, with positive effects for subgroups of adults or particular sites, including earnings gains in Los Angeles.

We set out to understand these puzzles, focusing on the social processes that might tie place of residence to economic opportunity. We found that several factors contributed to the "noneffects" of this relocation-only experiment on employment and earnings. First, some job-ready parents in MTO found it challenging to secure a three-way match among the locations of their jobs, housing, and sources of social support (childcare, in particular). As in Anique's case, this was particularly tough where the job market was turbulent, access to affordable housing unstable, and informal social support vital but unpredictable. For example, a worker's shift might change, requiring childcare at a different time. The aunt or mother or cousin providing that childcare became unavailable. The commute became untenable, so the family had to move quickly, but the options available in a tight and costly housing market were poor. The wrong choice might require another sudden move.

Second, few of the MTO adults "converted" new housing locations into new social and institutional resources, and some did struggle to retain their pre-move social resources, such as accessible childcare, usually provided by relatives at no cost. As we detailed in chapter 6, those who relocated through MTO typically made casual ties, if any, to new neighbors. As skeptics of the "social-capital-gain" thesis had predicted, the movers rarely got job leads, let alone endorsements, from their neighbors—no more than they obtained information about school options, as we showed in the last chapter.

But third, we found several ways in which neighborhoods can matter—as locations—even where neighbors do not. For example, "successful" relocation actually led to a loss of proximity to entry-level job centers, new job creation, and net job growth in at least one of the MTO labor markets. On the other hand, relocating enabled some youth to build much more diverse friendships and a broader repertoire or toolkit of "soft skills" that they perceive to be important for upward mobility—notwithstanding some pains of acculturating to new social expectations in new neighborhoods and schools. In plainer terms, fitting in was hard, but learning to fit in came with certain rewards in career entry and advancement, these young people felt. We show how MTO youth experienced this cultural compromise, which has received considerable attention in the debates over minority academic achievement and the stigmas associated with "ghetto culture" on one hand or "acting white" on the other.

Those three findings focus on the job-ready adults and youth who participated in MTO. But MTO was broadly targeted. Eligibility was not restricted according to skill levels, work experience, or—more to the point—being healthy enough to hold down a job. The fourth factor, as we have already hinted, was the large share of MTO adults who were *not* job ready. The numbers were far beyond what the Gautreaux program, which served a less disadvantaged population about a decade earlier, had led planners to expect. Relocation alone was no solution to the employability problems facing the most disadvantaged MTO adults, and in some cases, it may have been harder, say, for a chronically ill or depressed parent to find the supports they would need, for themselves and their children, to become employable.

These findings indicate both the usefulness and the limits of a broadly targeted, relocation-only policy strategy for the inner-city poor, as well as the dangers of assuming that less poor neighborhoods are advantageous for poor residents across the board. We begin with a closer look at the evidence behind the employment expectations, then profile the interim outcomes, and show how MTO families experienced the search for work and career alongside other struggles.

HOPES AND PRIOR EVIDENCE

As we previewed above, prior research, as well as the effort to plan MTO, pointed to several ways that residing in a particular neighborhood might affect employment, whether directly or indirectly. The three most-cited mechanisms were: reducing the spatial mismatch between job locations and workers' housing locations; gaining more useful social networks; and improving the "normative climate" of the worker's (or job seeker's) neighborhood of residence.

Spatial Mismatch

In a seminal 1968 article, following a series of urban riots that swept America's cities, economist John Kain proposed that the poor in economically isolated ghettos would suffer from the growing spatial mismatch between *job locations*, which were becoming more and more decentralized away from central business districts and toward less dense suburbs, and the *housing locations*, in segregated urban neighborhoods, to which many racial minorities were consigned. That same year, the Kerner Commission advised that economic opportunity in our nation had taken on a distinct spatial, color-coded form, with the fortunes of "two Americas"— white and nonwhite—drifting apart (see chapter 2).

While the evidence is complex, much research supports the contention that the decentralization pattern later labeled "job sprawl" makes low-skill and minority workers—who have limited housing choices in suburban areas—less likely to learn about job openings, more likely to face high commuting costs, more likely to quit when job locations shift significantly, and more likely to be rejected by employers based on residence in a stigmatized ghetto (Fernandez and Su 2004; Gobillon, Selod, and Zenou 2007; Ihlanfeldt and Sjoquist 1998; Tilly et al., 2001). While African-American workers live closer than whites to job concentrations in the aggregate, for example, because African Americans are more concentrated in cities and because job density is still highest in central cities, this also means that African Americans live closer to a large number of competing workers (S. Raphael 1998). Mouw (2000) found the labor force within 10 miles of African Americans' homes to be 48 percent larger in Chicago and 76 percent larger in Detroit, for example, than the labor force within that radial distance from whites' homes in those cities.

Yet other researchers have argued that ease of travel is the missing link in much spatial mismatch research. Controlling for the fact that employed people are more likely than the unemployed to own cars, Ong and Miller (2005) find that car ownership is a much better predictor of employment, for men and women in Los Angeles, than is living near to job locations.[1] Using a similar model, Ong (2002) also finds a significant independent effect of car ownership for welfare recipients seeking employment in metro L.A.—one of our three study sites.

But since skill mismatches and other barriers also shape labor market outcomes, what might a *shift* in residence accomplish? In the nonexperimental Gautreaux desegregation program, which in effect assigned families to neighborhoods rather than to treatment groups, Popkin, Rosenbaum, and Meaden (1993) found that minority women who relocated from inner-city Chicago neighborhoods to middle-class suburbs 15–30 miles away were more likely to be employed, holding their education level and other factors equal, than counterparts who stayed within the city of Chicago, though not at higher wages. More recent research on Gautreaux outcomes has incorporated long-run administrative data on employment and welfare receipt and tested a variety of neighborhood traits. Mendenhall et al. (2006) find that mothers who relocated to more racially integrated, nonpoor neighborhoods spent 7 percent less time on welfare, were employed at a rate 6 percent higher, and earned $2,200 more per year (on average) than women who relocated to poorer and more racially isolated areas. Mothers in the integrated group were more likely to report available jobs near their homes, as well as superior institutional resources, including training and educational opportunities. These results, while nonexperimental, strongly suggest that particular forms of relocation *can* positively affect the employment prospects of low-income, mostly low-skill mothers.[2] But like most research on Gautreaux, the evidence does not tell us *why* those results developed and what may have changed over time, as families' lives changed and as they moved about in the housing market.

There is strong evidence that housing opportunity shapes proximity to job growth. Nationally, spatial mismatch improved in the 1990s only for African Americans, and this was because of residential mobility, that is, African Americans moving closer to jobs rather than the other way around (Raphael and Stoll 2002). Yet some observers have argued that uneven metropolitan restructuring could lead to a *loss* of access to proximate, skill-appropriate jobs, such as in rebounding downtowns, through moves toward lower poverty neighborhoods outside the urban core (Briggs 1997). And again, it may be that transportation access, more than proximity per se, is the major driver of access to jobs.

Finally, scholars have shown that employers stigmatize some job seekers according to their place of residence, considering a "ghetto address" a marker for less reliability or job preparedness (Kirschenman and Neckerman 1991; Tilly, Moss, Kirschenman, and Kennelly 2001). So leaving behind a low-status address should be a plus, all else being equal, in the job market.

In the short to medium run, the spatial mismatch mechanism—more precisely, the idea that relocation of low-income, mostly low-skill adults and their children would lead to a reduction of mismatch—hinges on an important, two-part condition: that relocation would (a) move the disadvantaged closer to jobs for which they are or can become qualified (b) in sectors that are hiring. This may be very dependent on the character of particular local markets, and it may also depend on the business cycle. Also, spatial- mismatch research has addressed transportation as a factor mediating access to jobs, but it has not, thus far, given much attention to the three-way match between place of residence, job location, *and* the reliable sources of informal support, such as childcare at no or low cost, that remain critical for disadvantaged parents in the labor force. If our nation provided decent childcare, at a reasonable price, to every parent who wanted to work, this third leg of the stool would not be so critical.

Job Networks and Social Capital

Many jobs are found through informal networks rather than more formal means of search (Granovetter 1995; Ioannides and Loury 2004; Lin 2001; Putnam 2000). Helpful social contacts may provide job seekers information on openings (a referral function), "put in a good word" with the employer on behalf of the job seeker (an endorsement or vouching function), and provide childcare, mentoring, or other needed support to help someone stay employed. Segregated networks can provide a quick route to bad jobs, though, with lower wages, few benefits, and poor working conditions; there is evidence that racial minorities are overly reliant on co-ethnics, that is, members of their own racial/ethnic group (Fernandez and Fernandez-Mateo 2006). Networks can also play a variety of roles for employers, at various stages, including recruitment and screening (Fernandez and Fernandez-Mateo 2006; Ioannides and Loury 2004). Networks, then, can mediate both spatial "matches" and mismatches by shaping access to information, endorsements, and support that connect job seekers to particular niches of the labor market, though we have much to learn about *how*.

Beyond "what you know," then, "who you know" can serve as a key social resource or source of social capital (Putnam 2000). This is crucial if we care about how the disadvantaged in our society get ahead, not just get by, thanks to their social contacts—and the contacts of those contacts. But the networks of the poor, especially if they are racial minorities, tend to be more limited, strained, and insular—meaning less diverse and thus narrower in their range and function—than those of higher income people (review in Briggs 1998). The disadvantaged tend to be missing particular kinds of social connections that could be helpful. For example, in a study of public housing residents living near the Brooklyn waterfront, Kasinitz and Rosenberg (1996) found that physical proximity to the large concentration of high-wage jobs did little for the mostly African-American poor in public housing, who lacked social connections to the unions that brokered those jobs. K. Newman (1999) and Sullivan (1989) found similar patterns in neighborhood-based job networks and employer hiring, emphasizing how some employers use the referral networks of their current employees to favor nonlocal (outside-the-neighborhood) hires over local ones. O'Regan and Quigley (1993) likewise implicated weak or missing networks and the racial segregation of workers in minority youth unemployment. And Kleit (2001), in a study comparing clustered versus dispersed public housing residents, found that the latter were more likely to *have* diverse social networks but less likely to *ask* their neighbors for help when looking for a job.

Having a tie is one thing, but activating it or mobilizing its resources is quite another (Allen 2007; Lin 2001). And asking for help does not guarantee that one will receive it. Sociologist Sandra Smith (2005) used a phrase her interviewees reported—"don't put my name on it"—to capture the guardedness that led social contacts of the African-American poor, including relatives, to withhold aid even when they were in a position to provide it. "There's a job opening you can apply for, but don't tell them I recommended you, don't put *my* name on it" was what these contacts told their relatives or friends, in effect, because they feared tarnishing their reputations thanks to the job seeker's unreliable behavior. An endorsement, let us acknowledge, does not mean much if it comes from someone known to recommend unreliable people; the opposite confidence is at work in the immigrant job referral "machine," as many employers, who rely on their immigrant employees to recruit co-ethnics, recognize. The issue for extremely poor African Americans is not just social isolation from more advantaged useful contacts, Smith argues—a focus of the underclass debate we examined in chapters 2 and 6—but rather a culture, in the sense of learned coping behavior, that displaces cooperation and needed assistance. That culture revolves around distrust (withholding aid from those one deems unreliable) and a do-it-myself "defensive individualism"—not seeking aid, if one is likely to be denied, as a way of preserving one's dignity (Smith 2007).

Relocation might enhance job-related social capital, then, but for relocation to matter, one must (a) be willing and able to make new contacts, (b) activate them in useful ways, tapping (c) usefully positioned individuals who are (d) willing to provide aid. Yet as we showed in chapter 6, many movers focused on their preexisting networks of kin, close friends, or other strong ties, and few were "joiners" (engaging themselves in neighborhood churches or secular groups). So in terms of both having opportunity for contact and seizing on that opportunity, relocation might not encourage MTO participants—in particular, those in the experimental group who moved away from high-poverty areas—to "convert" their new locations into new social resources for getting ahead.

Neighborhood Norms and Cultural Capital

Some scholars and social critics have suggested that high-poverty, racially isolated neighborhoods, particularly where joblessness is chronic and pervasive, may lose a strong culture of work, for example in the form of adult role models who demonstrate that work is respectable and that it leads to a better life (Mead 1992; Wilson 1987). Other observers have emphasized capability rather than motivation to succeed in the mainstream world of work, stressing how living in socially isolated ghettos could undermine norms of interaction and the "soft skills"—such as understanding the social expectations of the workplace, including those of supervisors and customers—needed to succeed in the world of work (Anderson 1994; Kirschenman and Neckerman 1991; K. Newman 1999; Small and Newman 2001).

The latter perspective suggests that a socially learned "toolkit" (Swidler 1986), and not just formal educational credentials or indicators of job-related hard skills, is an important part of career success. It is particularly important for disadvantaged strivers, who must acquire new cultural capital, and cross race, class, and other social boundaries, as they work to get ahead in their lives (Bourdieu and Passeron 1990; DiMaggio and Mohr 1995; Erickson 1996; Lamont and Molnar 2002; Valentine 1971).[3] But role modeling, some scholars emphasize, does not automatically develop when low-status racial minorities move into socially different neighborhoods (Briggs 1997). In fact, influential role modeling is relatively rare across race and class boundaries (Joseph, Chaskin, and Webber 2007).[4]

Low-income African-American parents who managed to get to and stay in mostly white, middle-class suburban neighborhoods through the Gautreaux program did report very different neighborhood norms, and also new capabilities for themselves and their children, when they contrasted those neighborhoods with the inner-city Chicago neighborhoods they had left behind (Rosenbaum, DeLuca, and Tuck 2005). And neighborhood institutions, schools most important, should organize young in-movers' exposure to new expectations, not informal neighboring. Carefully conducted experiments offer powerful evidence that inner-city children educated in desegregated, middle-class, mostly white schools have more racially and socioeconomically diverse friendships, work in less segregated occupations, and feel more comfortable in majority-white environments than counterparts schooled in the inner city (Crain and Wells 1994).

But adults or youth in MTO might struggle to acculturate to new expectations, or they might resent and resist fitting in—"going along to get along," as the old saying goes. These complicated possibilities underscore the play of race, class, and other social boundaries in our society—and, in particular, in the schools, neighborhoods, and other settings where expectations clash about appropriate versus inappropriate behavior. The stakes, and the costs of our myopia about these issues as a society, have only grown with media interest in ghetto-culture "reality" shows, arguments over public and private use of the words "nigger" and "ho'" (whore), and other controversies.[5]

In *Keepin' It Real*, a study of these dynamics in high school, sociologist Prudence Carter (2005) found some minority students very comfortable straddling different expectations from teachers, parents, and peers, for example, about adopting or not adopting a middle-class Anglo-American style of dress, speech, and self-presentation (for example, body language). They associated "acting white" with a cultural style, not the effort to excel academically. But other students, who also believed that education could pay off for them, resented the way that teachers put down their "street" style. And these youth were less likely to straddle effectively—in part because they chose to resist (see also Valentine 1971). Likewise, anthropologists of education, focusing on ethnically diverse high schools, have distinguished youth who encounter incongruent expectations in family, peer, and school cultures and who manage the "border crossings" effectively from those who do not manage them well or find them insurmountable (Phelan, Davidson, and Cao 1991).

There is some evidence from qualitative interviews of African-American MTO youth in Baltimore that adolescent boys had greater difficulty than girls "fitting in" socially after relocating to low-poverty areas, including suburban neighborhoods. The boys made specific reference, like the resisters in Carter's school study, to expectations—particularly from white, better-off neighbors—that they (the youth) resented and, in some cases, felt they could not meet (Clampet-Lundquist et al., 2006).

We simply do not understand well the conditions under which newcomers to a setting are likely to choose to "go along" (assimilate), resist, or a bit of both, or how the likelihood that they will be accepted in a given social setting, regardless of their own choices, might be shaped by factors beyond their control. Also, most research on these issues tends to give us point-in-time views in one or a small number of schools. Our study of MTO has allowed us to examine, over months of visiting parents and their children—some of them grown up and moved out on their own—the experiences of *different* youth in the same families (older and younger siblings), who went through school and neighborhood transitions at different stages (in childhood, for example, versus early or middle adolescence). The experiment also allows us to examine how the *same* young people experience different school communities, for example, relocating from an inner-city context to a higher status suburban one and back again. We even watched some of these moves unfold, and adjustments to new schools and other settings develop, while we were in the field.

Potential Losses and Barriers

Research suggests other reasons for caution as well, including possibilities that MTO might lead adults and youth to lose ground economically after relocating away from high-poverty neighborhoods. As we previewed above, some observers worried that relocated adults might lose contact with valuable coping resources—informal caregiving, small emergency loans, and other aid from social ties—that are particularly crucial for low-income people (Greenbaum 2006; Venkatesh 2000, 2006). Relocation might force a trade-off, in effect, between one set of (familiar) social resources and another valuable-to-have-but-hard-to-come-by set (Briggs 1998). Also, those MTO adults who were working when they entered the program might lose valuable employment relationships and struggle to replace them, adding to the employment instability that the most disadvantaged appear to face as they enter or reenter the world of work (Herr and Wagner 2007; Newman 1999).

The risks of such losses, and the possible rewards of relocating as well, must be considered in the specific context in which low-skill, low-income single mothers look for work: safe, reliable, and inexpensive childcare is hard to secure; flexible, low-cost transportation is critical and too often missing; and for many who live in public housing in high-poverty areas—in developments that have become a housing of last resort for the ill and disabled poor—chronic physical and mental health problems pose particularly high barriers to everyday functioning, not to mention finding and keeping a job (Popkin, Cunningham, and Burt 2005).

MTO EMPLOYMENT EFFECTS SO FAR

Early evidence on the experiment's employment effects was encouraging, if mixed. Within two to four years of the random assignment that followed enrollment in MTO, experimental-group compliers (those who successfully relocated to low-poverty neighborhoods) in Baltimore were

15 percent less likely than control-group families to be receiving welfare; and the experimental group as a whole was 5 to 7 percent less likely than controls to be on welfare (Ludwig, Duncan, and Ladd 2003). However, comparable analysis for MTO families in Boston found no differences in either welfare recipiency or employment.

Four to seven years after random assignment, the interim evaluation of MTO found no significant impacts on employment, earnings, or receipt of public assistance across the five MTO sites (table 9.1; Orr et al., 2003). Notably, about twice as many MTO adults were working, in all three treatment groups, as compared with baseline measures at the start of the experiment. Researchers, as we noted above, cautioned that market cycles and policy shifts—specifically, the strong job economy of the late 1990s and the shift from an entitlement-based welfare program to Temporary Assistance for Needy Families—may have swamped any treatment effects of MTO at the interim mark.

Later analyses have examined subgroup outcomes (by site, age, and other traits) and nonexperimental effects, for example, the association between months residing in low-poverty areas (as a proxy for "treatment intensity") and employment. When interim results are disaggregated by site, there are significant, if modest, effects on employment for experimental-group families in Los Angeles and earnings increases in New York (Kling 2006). Moreover, there are modest employment gains among younger adults (women under 33 years of age) in the experimental group, as well as earnings gains of about $33 per week, four to five years after random assignment (Kling, Liebman, and Katz 2007). In addition, using the interim survey data, we find, net of conventional employment predictors, that MTO adults who moved to low-poverty *suburban* neighborhoods earned $75 more per week than those in control neighborhoods. And Clampet-Lundquist and Massey (2006) examined the association between MTO employment outcomes and residence in neighborhoods that are both low in poverty and racially integrated. Emphasizing prior evidence that "non-poor African-American areas are not comparable socially or economically to the non-poor neighborhoods inhabited by other groups" (8), the researchers underscore that while Gautreaux achieved both economic and racial desegregation, MTO achieved only the former—and only for a time. They find that 85 percent of the program population spent no time in an integrated (less than 30 percent minority), low-poverty census tract. They also find a significant association between duration-weighted exposure to low-poverty areas and employment and welfare receipt over time. We cannot know whether it is the case that *something about living in these areas* gave MTO adults a boost or whether living in such areas reflects *unmeasured traits* of those adults that made them more successful in the job market.[6] Given the ongoing mobility in the MTO population, though, which we explored in chapter 7, we strongly agree with these and other researchers that the lack of measurable *treatment* effects on employment in MTO cannot be reasonably interpreted as ruling out *neighborhood* effects on employment.

Table 9.1. MTO Interim Impacts on Employment and Earnings

	Control mean	Experimental vs. Control		Section 8 vs. Control	
		ITT	TOT	ITT	TOT
Adult employment and earnings (self-report)					
Currently employed (n=3517)	52.2%	1.4% higher (0.021)	3.0% higher (0.044)	2.6% higher (0.023)	4.4% higher (0.039)
Currently employed full-time, i.e., 35 or more hours per week at all jobs (n=3488)	39.4%	0.1% lower (0.021)	0.2% lower (0.044)	0.1% higher (0.023)	0.1% higher (0.038)
Currently employed with weekly earnings above poverty (n=3311)	32.9%	0.8% lower (0.020)	1.7% lower (0.043)	1.6% higher (0.022)	2.6% higher (0.037)
Annual individual earnings in 2001 (n=3311)	$8,899	$137 (449)	$292 (957)	$47 higher (495)	$79 higher (829)
Adult employment and earnings (administrative data, n=4070)					
Annualized fraction of quarters employed, first through fourth years after random assignment	43.0%	1.7% lower (0.012)	3.6% lower (0.025)	0.1% lower (0.013)	0.2% lower (0.021)
Annualized earnings, same period	$5,847	$215 lower (254)	$456 lower (539)	$55 lower (288)	$89 lower (470)
Youth employment and earnings, ages 14–19 (administrative data, n=2619)					
Fraction of quarters employed in 2001	22.2%	0.6% higher (0.014)	1.4% higher (0.031)	1.8% higher (0.015)	2.9% higher (0.025)
Earnings during 2001	$1,366	$77 higher (140)	$173 higher (315)	$170 higher (133)	$277 higher (216)

Source: Orr et al. (2003: 129, 130), adult survey and state Unemployment Insurance records (CA, IL, MA, MD, NY). Only includes adults randomly assigned through December 1, 1997.

Note: ITT = intent-to-treat (includes compliers who successfully relocated to low-poverty neighborhoods at enrollment and noncompliers who did not), TOT=treatment-on-treated (compliers only, divided by the site lease-up rate). Control means and impact estimates are regression-adjusted with robust standard errors (not shown).

* p<.05 (Statistically significant at the 95 percent confidence level)

Furthermore, the nonexperimental analyses highlight key predictors of higher employment rates and earnings for MTO adults, including age (younger is better), education, employment status at program entry, disability status, and household composition (for example, having teenagers in the household, who do not require adult supervision and who can supervise younger siblings).

Finally, Turney et al. (2006) use qualitative interviews with 67 Baltimore MTO families, plus mapping of job locations and transit routes, to examine the mechanisms that underlie MTO's employment effects. While members of the experimental and control groups faced the same barriers to work, the researchers find that unemployed experimental-group adults are "cycling in and out of jobs" whereas "more of the unemployed controls are permanently detached from the labor force" (36). Employed MTO participants in both groups were heavily concentrated in the health care and retail sectors, for which control-group adults' better access to public transit offered some advantage. In addition, while experimental-group adults were more likely to have employed neighbors, few neighbors were employed in the health and retail sectors, and experimental-group adults were less likely (than their control-group counterparts) to consult their neighbors about jobs; this underlines the importance of distinguishing *potential* access to job aid from the *mobilization* of those social resources. Leaving aside tangible effects on job getting, experimental-group adults spoke about their employed neighbors as a source of pride and motivation.

These recent findings suggest that the relationships between place of residence, job networks, and institutional resources, such as public transit, are more complex and location specific than the "strong" causal version of MTO expected, that is, with all advantages accruing to the group that relocated away from high-poverty neighborhoods. Going beyond the brief discussion above, the findings further suggest that some place-based mechanisms of influence, such as neighborhood norms, might shape particular measures of employment (persistence in the labor force *over* time, for example) and not others (job holding at a given *point* in time, say).

Drawing on these insights and the varied approaches outlined above, we present our findings next, distinguishing job-ready adults and youth, whose experiences we focus on first, from the extremely disadvantaged MTO adults who were not job ready but nevertheless managed to relocate successfully through the program.

LESSONS ABOUT JOB-READY MTO ADULTS AND YOUTH

We began by examining the geography of entry-level jobs in the MTO metro areas—not employment rates by neighborhood but actual job locations—against the housing locations of all MTO families in the interim survey. For most MTO adults, entry-level jobs were the only realistic prospect. Then we mined our interview data for a representative look at the job search and job holding experiences of MTO adults and youth (including the commuting experience), as well as their perceptions of the neighborhood and the world of work, in their own words. Then we drew on the ethnographic fieldnotes, from our months of visiting a subgroup of 39 families, for a deeper understanding of how the families' social connections and daily routines—such as juggling childrearing, work, and other tasks in one or a series of neighborhoods—fit in the picture.

Spatial Mismatch

Consistent with Turney et al.'s (2006) findings for MTO families in Baltimore and Chicago, our interviews indicated that MTO families in all treatment groups and complier categories were heavily concentrated in health care, retail, and social services. They worked as home health aides, nurse's assistants, childcare providers, janitors, security guards, office assistants, bill coders, and entry-level staff in social service programs. In Los Angeles and Boston, these jobs were highly dispersed, but in New York, many commuted to the dense retail and health care job center that is Manhattan.

Like other local indicators, employment data are often challenging to acquire and organize at the micro level of neighborhoods or other small areas. We were able to compile fine-grained, recent local data on entry-level jobs and job turnover in distinct industry sectors for just two of the five MTO metro areas: Chicago and Los Angeles.[7] Though Chicago was not one of the sites we had investigated in depth (with qualitative interviews and ethnographic fieldwork), we wanted as much variety as possible in the spatial analysis, and we suspected that different trajectories of economic change in different parts of the country could lead to very different mismatch patterns. This turned out to be the case, as we discuss below.

Because long-run patterns of decentralization might mask the more short-run changes that coincided with the MTO relocation, we focused on a medium-term observation window, based on the data reporting periods, that includes both up and down turns in the job market. We conducted the analysis separately for four industries known to be major sources of entry-level jobs for low-skill workers (K. Newman 1999): retail trade, transportation and warehousing, health care and social assistance, and accommodation and food services, and then for the four industries combined. We estimated the number of entry-level jobs, using $20,000 per year as a proxy for that level, located within 1, 5, 10, and 20 miles of MTO families in all three treatment groups.[8] The range is important: In a transit-rich area, 1 or 2 miles away counts as close by, but in a sprawling, car-reliant region such as Los Angeles, 5 to 10 miles is still quite proximate, still well below the average commute.[9] We computed two measures to get a more robust view of the dynamics of job "opportunity": net job growth and new jobs created.

Table 9.2. MTO Interim Impacts on Spatial Access to Low-wage Jobs and Job Openings, 1998–2002, as of Most Recent Residential Location

	Control mean	Experimental vs. Control		Section 8 vs. Control	
		ITT	TOT	ITT	TOT
Los Angeles					
Net job growth within 1 mile of residence	109 (74)	180 (144)	281 (225)	1 (99)	1.3 (137)
New job creation within 1 mile of residence	294 (198)	481 (385)	752 (602)	1 (264)	1.3 (347)
Jobs within 1 mile of residence+	4,492 (3,025)	7,351 (5,886)	11,486 (9,197)	22 (4,036)	29 (5,311)
Net job growth within 5 miles of residence	7,900 (485)	-3,306* (588)	-5,166* (919)	-998 (671)	-1,313 (883)
New job creation within 5 miles of residence+	21,208 (1,301)	-8,890* (1,578)	-13,891* (2,466)	-2,699 (1,800)	-3,551 (2,368)
Jobs within 5 miles of residence+	32,4240 (19,874)	-135,855* (24,108)	-212,273* (37,669)	-41,178 (27,494)	-54,181 (36,176)
Net job growth within 10 miles of residence	13,196 (482)	-1,387 (653)	-2,138* (1,020)	-300 (671)	-395 (883)
New job creation within 10 miles of residence	35,398 (1,296)	-3,731* (1,757)	-5,762* (2,745)	-829 (1,806)	-1,089 (2,376)
Jobs within 10 miles of residence+	541,833 (19,834)	-57,232* (26,892)	-89,425* (42,019)	-12,631 (27,643)	-16,620 (36,372)
Chicago					
Net job growth within 1 mile of residence	7 (0.3)	0 (0.4)	0 (1.1)	1 (1)	1.5 (1.5)
New job creation within 1 mile of residence	57 (3)	-1 (3)	-3 (9)	8 (5)	12 (8)
Jobs within 1 mile of residence+	1,250 (63)	-29 (71)	-83 (203)	174 (102)	260 (152)
Net job growth within 5 miles of residence	107 (4)	-4 (5)	-11 (14)	-6 (6)	-9 (9)
New job creation within 5 miles of residence+	882 (33)	-43 (43)	-123 (123)	-44 (45)	-66 (67)
Jobs within 5 miles of residence+	18,804 (679)	-936 (894)	-2,674 (2,554)	-801 (935)	-1,196 (1,396)
Net job growth within 10 miles of residence	392 (10)	-8 (15)	-23 (43)	-16 (14)	-24 (21)
New job creation within 10 miles of residence	3,176 (82)	-85 (116)	-243 (331)	-128 (113)	-191 (169)
Jobs within 10 miles of residence+	66,656 (1,731)	-1,741 (2,453)	-4,974 (7,008)	-2,674 (2,376)	-3,991 (3,546)

Sources: Census Zip Business patterns (1998, 2002), Census Transportation Planning Package (2000), Local Employment Dynamics (2001, 2003), Abt Associates geocoded tracking data for MTO households. See endnotes for specifications of "growth" and "creation."
+ Figures for jobs within 1, 5, and 10 miles are observed measures, not estimates.

Note: ITT = intent-to-treat (includes compliers and noncompliers), TOT=treatment-on-treated (compliers only, divided by site lease-up rate for each treatment group).
* p<.05 on t-test.

As of the interim mark, we found that the experimental group in metro Los Angeles (i.e., both the compliers who made the program relocation and the noncompliers who did not) lived in neighborhoods with fewer low-wage jobs, less net job growth, and less job creation within 5 and 10 miles, in aggregate, than their control group counterparts (table 9.2). And the difference is *greater* if we consider the compliers only. The lower job density of experimental-group areas helps explain the differences in job growth and creation; job-denser areas appear to have seen more growth in the late 1990s and early 2000s. There was no significant difference in job concentrations within 1 mile in L.A., however, and no apparent impact at all in Chicago, where the volume of low-wage jobs and job growth are dramatically lower than L.A.'s overall. Section 8 compliers moved to locations with essentially the same number of low-wage job opportunities as control-group counterparts. The treatment-group differences in L.A., which was the far more dynamic job market between 1998 and 2002, are even more striking if we focus on the compliers. The average growth in low-wage jobs over that period was 65 percent *lower* for experimental compliers than for control compliers (the group that hypothetically would have successfully leased up if offered the location-restricted voucher) within 5 miles of the most current address, and 16 percent lower within 10 miles.

These results confirm that relocating, through the MTO program, to a low-poverty census tract outside the inner city did not *necessarily* mean relocating to a job-rich zone, at least not on average. The data available also indicate that starting points and changes in the geography of entry-level job openings are quite localized, quite specific to particular metro job and housing markets, contrary to the simple version of the spatial mismatch argument.[10] As prior researchers have emphasized, however, the geographic proximity of jobs is just a piece of the puzzle. To understand what shapes access to jobs, we must examine job seekers experiences and choices.

Our interviews taught us that MTO mothers in the experimental group balanced competing concerns about safety, access to employment, and access to childcare in a variety of ways, depending on their outlook and circumstances, and that each factor had important implications for the quality of their housing locations as "platforms" for employment success. In effect, the challenge for these low-income, low-skill parents, most of them single mothers, was lining up spatial matches that included jobs, housing and vital job *support*—especially reliable childcare that was usually obtained within networks of reciprocal, but often unstable, support (cf. Henly 2002).

About one in seven mothers in the experimental group specifically identified the loss of convenient access to public transit as a "price" they paid to get out of the projects to safer neighborhoods. For example, when we asked Nicole, a mother in the Boston experimental-complier group, how her current, low-poverty neighborhood compared to the one left behind in terms of worries and stress, she replied:

> The stress here is more just transportation issues. How am I going to get from here to the doctor's today? ... I don't have money for a bus, which is an hour-and-a-half walk. And if it's pouring rain and cold, with two babies, you can't walk an hour to a bus stop anyway. In South Boston and Dorchester, I didn't have worries like that. Um, but it was just more concern for my kid's safety.

As we showed in chapter 5, most experimental compliers cited safety and security, not better job or school opportunities, as their top reasons for moving, But a handful of MTO adults (about 1 in 10), when asked why they had chosen their current neighborhood, specifically mentioned relocating to be closer to jobs they *already* had. In New York, where participants in the experimental group did realize a significant gain in earnings over their control group counterparts, working participants had somewhat higher skill levels and more work experience. They held jobs that appear to offer more upward mobility as well. They are certified childcare providers, para-professionals, retail managers, teachers, and even graduate students; some have left housing assistance altogether. Rhadiya, for example, a mother in the New York experimental group who used her voucher to reduce her commute time, found she could earn more:

> RHADIYA: I started while I was in Manhattan and then I moved here where I was closer to work, which was a plus for me. Yeah, it's like now 10 minutes [away].
> INTERVIEWER: How far was it when you were in Manhattan? How long did it take you?
> R: It took me like an hour and 15 minutes.
> I: So it must be a big relief.
> R: Yes, definitely. Yeah, and I also do a lot of overtime. Like my annual salary was like 24, 26, but that year, I made close to 40,000.

Likewise, in Los Angeles, where experimental compliers were more likely to be employed as of the interim evaluation, the successful combined new housing locations with access to job training and placement, sometimes through temp agencies. Denise, a mother in this group, temped for four years for her current employer before they offered her a permanent position. But the neighborhood she found with her MTO housing voucher helped her keep commuting time well below the average for MTO adults in L.A. The evidence suggests that the MTO intervention, limited to relocation though it was, contributed to the economic prospects of low-income parents such as Rhadiya and Denise. Although these women were indeed more likely than others in the program to succeed "on their own," the assisted relocation accelerated their mobility prospects, helped them achieve work-related strategies in which place of residence was one key element.

However, the balancing acts these women sustain are extraordinary, and progress is generally in stutter steps, as the most intensive job interventions for the hard-to-employ have found (Herr and Wagner 2007). For example, Sabrina, a mother of two in the Boston experimental complier group, left public housing in the inner-city neighborhood of Roxbury, moved to Quincy, an inner suburb to the south of Boston, moved back to the inner city near her old "project" neighborhood, and finally returned to Quincy, where she has lived, using a housing voucher, ever since. She described the effect of the lower poverty Quincy environment on her life as a single mother:

> It gives you a sense of confidence. It's a better area and it's up to you to decide what you want to change. I don't feel like my life is in any danger. I never had that feeling here. Safety was a big worry there [in the projects].

Sabrina emphasized the importance of her living environment for setting out to work. Her case emphasizes place as an enabler, though not a guarantor, of job prospects. Though Sabrina did spend a while on welfare when living in public housing, she began her career as an office assistant in a Boston hospital at age 16, so she had considerable work experience by the time she enrolled in MTO.

Anique, a mother in the L.A. experimental-complier group whom we introduced in the opening pages of this chapter, had more trouble aligning steady work, affordable housing, and childcare, though her rental voucher and relocations helped. Her pre-move employment as a telemarketer and bill collector helped her find better work as she moved, but in a turbulent labor market, she suffered repeated spells of unemployment and financial hardship, including the loss of her housing voucher (when her attempt to purchase a small home failed) and bankruptcy. She initially relocated from public housing in South Los Angeles to the nearby suburb of Compton. After eventually landing a job in Riverside County, some 40 miles east of Compton, Anique moved to a town where she had an aunt and uncle to help look after her children. But when her relatives left the state, Anique and her daughter Clara had to move to Long Beach to live with Anique's mother. Then Anique was laid off from her job, thanks to company relocation, and so they stayed put for almost two years. "It was hard to even get a place," she says. "Everything just went downhill, downhill…" Other jobs ended because of downsizing.

She changed jobs again during our fieldwork. Based on her work experience, she was hired as a child-support investigator in Riverside County, but her daily commute from Long Beach was about 70 miles each way, which often meant leaving the house before 5 A.M. and having very little time with her daughter each day. Anique gradually saved enough to rent an apartment in Riverside, right across the street from her job. However, because they were now far from the social support Anique's mother and sister provided, Clara, now 11, was home alone after school each day. Anique has found some support services nearby and feels her apartment complex is quiet and safe, but she also reports experiencing racial harassment in the neighborhood.

Anique is a revelatory case: a mother whose job, housing, and support locations remained unstable for a long period of time, challenging her to bring them into alignment, although she was an "instant success" at the narrow task of completing the MTO-assisted relocation away from a high-poverty neighborhood.

Other MTO participants emphasized the risks associated with job changes, that is, starting over "at the bottom"—an outlook at odds with the notion that wider housing choices will lead low-income people to pursue better jobs. Interviews with these participants highlight the real trade-offs individuals face when switching jobs, such as losing their seniority within an organization, interrupting their job history, or losing benefits temporarily while they work through a trial period with a new employer.

Low-wage work is often particularly unstable as well as inflexible (Edin and Lein 1997; Henly 2002; K. Newman 1999). Some employed MTO participants, such as Anique, were clearly not mobile *enough* in the housing market to keep up with employer restructuring, as prior research on spatial mismatch has underscored. This suggests the need for a more dynamic view of housing-to-work connections, especially for the very low-income households that receive housing assistance. Assisting the *first* move, even if it is well targeted to the adults with the best odds of benefiting, represents a kind of bet that job locations will be in a stable relationship to the new housing location—or that harried, low-skill single parents will be able to quickly change jobs or change housing to reestablish a fit.

For example, a handful of MTO mothers in the experimental group who moved back to poorer areas (though not necessarily to the public housing neighborhood) cited access to job training and placement as a key factor in that choice—consistent with recent research findings that challenge the notion that higher neighborhood poverty is invariably associated with fewer organizational resources (Small and McDermott 2006)—along with access to informal childcare provided by relatives or close friends in those "move-back" areas. But these strategies, which also connect housing to work, did not always pan out. Kimberlyn, the second L.A. experimental complier we introduced early on, struggled in one way in her low-poverty neighborhood in the San Fernando Valley: lacking credentials, work experience, and confidence in herself, and feeling isolated and unwelcome. Moving back to the inner city led to a different set of struggles, as the childcare her sister provided abruptly disappeared, and Kimberlyn could not manage to complete training and find steady work. She inquired widely about jobs and training opportunities, and during our fieldwork, she began, but never completed, training in cosmetology and other fields, as well as an associate's degree program. Constantly needy family members, now near at hand, and her son's dangerous school added to Kimberlyn's stress and anxiety.

In general, this range of patterns underscores the diversity of background and circumstance in the MTO population. But it also confirms the role a neighborhood can play as a *location*, important for what they allow one to access *from* the neighborhood (including childcare and after-school programs, a reasonable commute to work or training, etc.), as opposed to a *social world* (significant as a context for human development through social interaction or influence through observation). In one sense, of course, this is merely a restatement of the commonplace, enshrined in the real estate industry, that location is a central feature of housing quality. But in the context of MTO, the distinction between location and social world is important, given the range of mechanisms that planners and researchers thought might operate once low-income, mostly low-skill families with children relocated. In the range of balancing acts outlined above, while neighborhood locations were sometimes important, *neighbors* were generally not—at least for MTO adults—whether as working role models, sources of job referral, or providers of childcare or other supports for work. We turn to these and other functions of networks next.

Job Networks

At the interim evaluation point, only 16 percent of MTO experimental compliers reported that they got their current or most recent job through a referral provided by a friend, relative, or acquaintance in the current neighborhood. Networks are just one method of job search, of course. Like others in the market, MTO job seekers also used newspaper ads, the internet, and walk-in applications to find their jobs. But where networks did play a role, MTO adults in our study were more likely to get useful referrals from job training program staff or fellow job seekers they met in those programs, and from friends or co-workers, than from neighbors. Here again, those who entered MTO with some work history, and the confidence and contacts that come with a history of job holding, were at an advantage. Some adults also got useful referrals from kin or from another trusted source, such as a pastor.

The lack of job referrals from neighbors in low-poverty areas, meanwhile, reflected limited *opportunity* for meaningful social contact (the chance to form more useful ties) with neighbors, a *wariness* about forming such ties to neighbors, and a lack of willingness to *activate* ties to neighbors in order to get referrals or other aid. As for the hoped-for but unrealized gains in social capital, then, those who relocated rarely "converted" their lower poverty address, even if they managed to keep it for years, into significant new social resources.

As we showed in chapter 6, most experimental compliers who were living in low- or relatively low-poverty neighborhoods at the time of our interviews had only casual contact with neighbors, greeting them or chatting briefly outside their homes but often not knowing their names, visiting them in their homes, or exchanging anything more. Like suburbanites across the country, MTO parents reported that their low-poverty neighborhoods were quieter and safer than the inner city. But without formal institutional ties to connect them to neighbors, and given the ongoing housing mobility that undercut the formation of relationships in new places, interactions were fleeting. A handful of MTO parents did participate in secular groups of one kind or another, and a larger minority were churched, but these organizations tended to be outside the neighborhood. For some MTO women and their children, racial strains acted as barriers, too: A small number of cases reported active harassment, others a perception of strained interaction. In general, there was little to encourage neighboring. Mothers described neighbors left behind (in public housing) as social but often untrustworthy, whereas neighbors in low-poverty areas were usually perceived to be trustworthy but not social. Some MTO adults specifically attributed this to their new neighbors' busier, work-oriented lifestyles or their preferences for "keeping to themselves."

Furthermore, as we emphasized in chapter 6, preestablished networks—to relatives, in particular—dominated the social lives of most MTO adults and their children. These networks defined the most important socializing, social support exchanges, and sources of influence from social contacts. And these were overwhelmingly disadvantaged networks, with adults that were often poorly educated, unstably employed, and, in the case of many male contacts, struggling to overcome the employment effects of a criminal record and incarceration. In a small number of cases, moves back to poorer neighborhoods specifically reflected the need for more social support, primarily from relatives, or the need to provide caregiving when kin became ill or disabled. But in other instances, as we have shown, parents moved to get *away* from relatives they saw as risky or burdensome.

Clearly, some movers did lose *convenient* access to useful social resources they had at baseline. But in general, they did not lose contact. To the contrary, the old ties traveled with MTO movers, and useful new job contacts, where they developed, were rarely in the neighborhood.

Neighborhood Norms and Cultural Capital

Beyond gains in neighborhood safety and feelings of security and calm, a number of MTO experimental compliers who made it to low-poverty areas—like counterparts in the suburban Gautreaux group—took great pride in their neighbors' working. Parents in the ethnographic sample who stressed this specifically emphasized the importance of this climate of working people for their children's healthy development. A few explicitly complained about the lack of commitment to getting ahead among those able to work in the projects and about the discouragement. For example, when we asked Jackie, an experimental complier in L.A., whether she believed that most of her neighbors worked, she replied as follows, emphasizing the contrast with the environment in which she had grown up in public housing:

> Yeah. I see people leaving out, because I used to go to work, construction for security, at like five in the morning. And I see people leaving out 4:00, 4:30. And then you can hear the gates opening and close, the cars just going in and out, or walking through the hallways, the aisle-ways. I think mostly everybody get up and go to work. Except the older people.... [Whereas in the projects] I think that's what really made me get a job. Because I grew up seeing everybody that *don't* work. And all I used to say is, "I want a check with my name on it." And everybody used to say, "You want a check?" I say, "Watch. When I grow up, I'm going to get me a check with my name on it." Nobody believed me.

Jackie considered her prior neighbors' disbelief a motivator. That is, she wanted to prove them wrong. Like about one-quarter of movers we interviewed, Jackie differentiated herself from those whom she perceived to lack the right values or get-ahead attitude and motivation. This is a moral logic that ethnographic studies of low-wage work and community life in poor neighborhoods have uncovered consistently since the 1960s (see, e.g., Hannerz 1969; K. Newman 1999).

Not all MTO movers described their public housing neighborhoods as hostile to work, though. A handful of MTO parents specifically argued that, in the post-welfare reform era, everybody "has to work" regardless of neighborhood environment.

As we noted in the previous section, frequent moving is hardly a recipe for forming useful social ties in new neighborhoods. "Demonstration effects" alone may be a boon to the next generation, however. The interim survey found that adolescent girls in the experimental group were 22 percent more likely to be in school and 16 percent less likely to be idle than counterparts in the control group (Orr et al., 2003). In addition to the freedom from fear we explored in chapter 5, we believe that positive role models, even distal ones, may be contributing to these positive treatment effects on girls. When asked about the positive influences of their low-poverty neighborhood on girls, some mothers in the ethnographic sample, which we visited repeatedly to understand attitudes toward childrearing and perceptions of neighborhood, specifically emphasized the climate of work. Jackie, for example, told us:

> It gives the kids a different atmosphere, because it's a lot of working people out here. And everybody's always busy. If they're not in school [or] working, they're doing something. So you never really just see anybody just hanging around.

Brianna, also a mother in the L.A. experimental complier group, put it this way, emphasizing what she and her daughter notice about neighbors:

> Well because she sees like our neighbors to go to work, come home. Just seeing, I think a lot of people [work].... That's why you see the people leave

and go to work, you know. I see a lot of that, and I think she look up to that. You know, she watch that. She's very observant.

But what about the cultural "toolkits" young people acquire growing up in one type of neighborhood, or family, versus another? Some young adults in the experimental- complier group show how relocation *can* dramatically expand the range of cultural expectations young people experience as they mature. With those experiences comes the opportunity to develop a broader cultural repertoire or toolkit, including higher status class manners and other soft skills to enhance employment prospects and upward mobility. These cases also reflect the strains of acculturating to new expectations. Here, we draw on our ethnographic sample—the group we were able to get to know best. And we were able to gather these in-depth data only for girls.[11] We cannot know how prevalent these patterns are in the MTO population as a whole, or how exactly the boys compare to the girls. But again, fine-grained data help shed light on social mechanisms that are still poorly understood, particularly in the context of housing policy that aims to expand opportunity.

Kaliyan is an 18-year-old freshman in the California State University system. Born to Cambodian refugee parents living in public housing, she has moved often since childhood, from the projects in South L.A., when she was 10, to Reseda (a middle-income, mostly white community in the San Fernando Valley), thanks to MTO, then to Van Nuys (a more ethnically and economically diverse Valley community), and on to Pasadena and Duarte (also diverse, with more active gangs, as she remembers) in the San Gabriel Valley. In Pasadena, she lived with an African-American foster family for a while, because her parents had divorced, and relationships within her family had disintegrated. (Extremely strained family relationships were common among the refugee parents and youth we interviewed in MTO.)[12] Her father encouraged his children to assimilate, even discouraging them from having Cambodian friends in the projects. "My dad always used to say that your business will be everywhere if you have Cambodian friends."

Her peer relationships, formed mostly in school, ranged from middle- and upper-income teens driven (in her view) by brand-name consumption to gangs of low-income Asian youth she turned to, in the poorer Valley communities, to help her find a sense of belonging and self-worth. She often felt terribly out of place, becoming bulimic and suicidal at one point, experimenting with drugs—which were easy to get from white kids in the Valley, who were using them all the time—and joining a girl gang. The gang, she remembers, was all about ethnic pride and standing your ground. But that was "stupid," she concluded, and eventually, she found a way to operate in different cultural worlds without feeling incapable or "lesser than."

Kaliyan, who refers to her "white side" and "minority side" when explaining these experiences to us, has had to recognize and respond to a wide variety of social boundaries and expectations, including different class cultures, in different school-community settings:

> "Like at my high school, there were really rich people, so I didn't fit in.... Actually, I realized it in elementary school. I remember thinking, I just can't afford to do that.... I [the fieldworker] asked her, "What do you think was hardest for you growing up?" Kaliyan replied, "Trying to fit in. Doing the popular thing. I remember when I first moved out here [to the San Fernando Valley], all the girls were doing ballet or cheerleading or something. Then in middle school, everyone was a mall rat. In high school, it was racing. It was really hard for me because I wasn't allowed to go out. That's my 'minority' side," explained Kaliyan. She continued, "Then my white side was being forced to like things like Britney Spears, NSync. Everyone was into [brand names like] Hollister and Abercrombie [& Fitch]. People were driving Jettas and going to Tiffany's [jewelry store]. I was going to school with a bunch of MTV girls, all these white girls." "Why didn't you like the people you were hanging around with?" the fieldworker asked. "Because I didn't always like what they did," replied Kaliyan. "It's hard to go from being poor to being Barbie Doll-ish.... I always thought I wasn't good enough. All those people had money. White people have money. They'd talk about me and stuff
>   ... I mean, these were the girls I was trying to impress all the time."

Even though Kaliyan still struggles with "being different," she has developed racially diverse friendships, skills at fitting in, and valuable knowledge about the usefulness of social networks for getting ahead. She has held several jobs in retail, a sector she describes as "color coded" in terms of who can work where to serve what racial group of customers. And she appears to confidently use her budding networks to get better jobs. Kaliyan has even pledged a sorority in college because she heard that "they're good for networks and lifelong connections. Like if you want to get a job here or there, your sorority might be able to help you out...You know, you hear these stories of people getting jobs because they belong to the same sorority or fraternity. I've heard stories of people getting jobs in Congress and...big corporations." Kaliyan, who now lives in the San Fernando Valley with her boyfriend and his parents, has come quite a social distance from the South L.A. projects.

Isabela is a 23-year-old Latina whose family left the South L.A. projects for Canoga Park, a middle-income area in the San Fernando Valley, when she was entering high school. Her younger brother, Rudy, is 11 years younger; he made the move before entering elementary school. Though Isabela often got into fights while in high school in the Valley, and although she had learned a very relevant skill (how to defend herself) back in the projects, she remembers learning a different "way to be" in the Valley. She described it to us as how to be "proper" rather than "ghetto." There was "less drama" and less picking fights in the Valley, she recalls; teachers took more of an interest in her, and she learned how to behave around "people who are more upper class," including "sitting up straight."

She believes that this helped her when she decided to enter the Marines and had to deal with its strict demands. We asked her to explain her reference to a "ghetto style":

> She explained, "leaning back, always being casual. Always have attitude when out, even in other neighborhoods."... She said that she doesn't want to act like that anymore and that her L.A friends make fun of her. They say to her, "You're so serious. The military has you brain washed." But she said that they are not allowed to "act ghetto" in the military. If they are caught slouching or talking in a casual and off-handed way they will get yelled at, "You're not in the ghetto."... She attributes so much of her "change" with both spending time in the Valley and the military, and I [the fieldworker] wanted to figure out what affected what. She speculates that moving to the Valley made her military experience easier: "If I hadn't moved to the Valley, I would have been naïve to other races. The Valley taught me how to fit in."... She explained that the Valley was a safer neighborhood, so she had more friends and could leave the house more. So she had more opportunities to socialize. She had a diverse group of friends and was comfortable with diversity.

Isabela was very self-conscious about the family's class status in the more affluent Valley context. She remembers changing the way she dressed and got her hair done, and her mother remembers these things as well. "She always had to have everything special," says Esperanza. Isabela also remembers asking her mother to drop her off at the back of a mall so that her Valley friends would not see their beat-up car.

Isabela worries that her younger siblings, who live with her parents now back in South L.A., are "becoming more ghetto." She points to Rudy, who spent his elementary school years in the Valley but has returned to inner-city L.A. for high school. He had to acculturate in the other direction. He stopped wearing khaki pants and shirts with collars, although they were purchased at a thrift store, because his peers said, "Here comes the Valley Kid," and they teased him, "Are you a high roller?" Rudy was ahead of his class when his family returned to inner-city L.A. and its schools, but based on what her son reports about the classrooms in his South L.A. school, his mother Esperanza fears that he downplays what he knows in order to fit in. As our fieldwork progressed, Rudy was getting into trouble at school more and more, disrupting his classes. His mother explained his strategy, "Say, ok, I'm not going to listen to him [the teacher]. I'm as bad as you."

Meanwhile, Isabela avoids spending time with her family except when she has to help out. When she completed her service in the Marines, she moved to Downey, a southern suburb about a half hour drive from her mother, stepfather, and younger siblings. The housing is more expensive in Downey, but she marks her move there, initially to live with a boyfriend while she holds down several part-time jobs, as a step up from her family's life in South L.A. "I'm not going backwards," she says. Her younger brother Rudy, meanwhile, says, "She thinks we live ghetto."

Some adolescents in MTO also experienced these boundary cross-ings—particularly where African-American families found themselves a shrinking minority in mostly Mexican or Mexican and white schools in greater L.A.—and we met them at an earlier stage of making sense of it all. When Terri, age 16, found herself struggling in school and harassed by fellow students, her mother Robin pushed her to change her habits and change her friends. At first, she resisted, but later, she told us, "I cut myself off from the…And they thought I was trying to be better than them. It's like, I am!" As we visited this family, in a county east of Los Angeles, over the course of the school year, Terri's grades picked up; she got involved in several clubs at school; and she got a part-time job. Terri, who is African American, also described changes in her circle of friends: "I don't really like hanging around African-American people now," she told us. We asked Terri what being African American means to her, and she said:

> Cuz most of the African Americans are sort of ghetto and all of that, so…that's why I used to do, I don't want to do the same thing…. I want to try different stuff. And like…all the people I used to hang around with were African American. I don't want it to be like that, because when I do get out there and go to college, I'm not going to know how to experiment with other races and stuff—and what they like, and what they dislike, and all of that. So it's better to know now, to get ready for college.

The female friends Terri identified were mostly Mexican, but her male friends remained mostly African American. And Terri is part of an extended family network that attends a large African-American church every weekend, with relatives driving in from miles away. She admires her cousin, who has graduated college and is planning to go to grad school. In other words, she does not lack for positive African-American role models or ongoing participation in traditional African-American community institutions. But Terri has decided she wants to get ahead; she changed her peer group of girlfriends to reflect that, and, at least for now, she associates African Americans in her school with "ghetto" behavior and outlook, with not striving or succeeding. More than that, she believes that an insular, same-race circle of friends would deprive her of the exposure she needs to other racial and ethnic groups and their expectations.

These cases shed light on the processes of "navigating" varied cultural expectations and acquiring new cultural capital as well as new ways to position oneself. First, as a general matter, the experiences of MTO youth who relocated away from high-poverty neighborhoods fell into several, relatively distinct categories. Many continued to lead quite insu-lar lives, socializing in the "bubble" of their kin network, as we showed in chapter 6, and attending schools where informal social expectations, as distinct from formal academic ones, were not so different from those they had seen before (see chapter 8). Others, such as Kaliyan, Isabela, and Isabela's younger brother Rudy—who was pressured to acculturate in reverse, from higher status "Valley Kid" to ghetto-style, when his parents moved back to the inner city—experienced more radical shifts in the expectations of teachers and/or peers. In a third category are the minority of MTO youth whose *at-home* experiences, regardless of neighborhood context, were equipping them to function in a world of mainstream middle-class expectations. These were young people being raised by the more educated parents in MTO.

Second, for lower status youth, as the typical life course would predict, the first experience of challenging new expectations was in peer groups based at school, only later in the workplace or military or other settings. Segregation between schools, which tracks housing segregation, indeed helps to delineate boundaries between different cultural worlds—in particular, we have emphasized, between different *class cultures*—and the toolkits needed to succeed in them. But schools, as Prudence Carter and other scholars have shown, are also divided internally, and this means MTO youth had some room to engage or avoid particular cultural expectations regardless of where they lived and went to school. What is more, young people respond in a variety of ways. Some learn to operate in multiple worlds, while others will not or cannot accommodate wide-ranging expectations. Kaliyan and Isabela help illustrate what particular trajectories of relocation *make possible* through broader exposure, not what MTO-type interventions can assure in the way of transferring valuable cultural capital to highly disadvantaged youth.

Third and finally, as Carter emphasizes, some who acquire the valued cultural capital—the proverbial right stuff in terms of the cultural pecking order in America—eagerly assimilate, after some period of strain, and leave familiar ways behind, rather than "straddling." Parents help shape these choices, both through direct encouragement or discouragement and through whatever they do, or do not do, to give their children a sense of worth in spite of the disadvantages they face. As anthropologists Phelan, Davidson, and Cao (1991) put it, some young people, in crossing cultural borders constantly, must actively deny aspects of who they are, and their emotional struggles are easily overlooked by parents, teachers, and other adults in their lives. Both Kaliyan and Isabela, for example, recall these struggles, and both have distanced themselves, as they transition to the independence of adulthood, from their families and the neighborhoods where they grew up. Some children and parents perceive this distancing, like the distancing from risky and burdensome kin that we examined in chapter 6, as—like it or not—a feature of getting ahead through wider housing opportunity. New cultural capabilities come at a price. Change includes loss and, for some, the mixed feelings that come with loss.

Beyond the issue of having or not having an adequate cultural toolkit, the normative dimension of employment includes the "rightful" place of work in our lives, which William Julius Wilson and other scholars have treated as "attachment" to working. A small minority of the experimental compliers—about 1 in 10—were not working at the time of our in-depth qualitative interviews and emphasized this normative belief about work:

their desire to focus on their children and the security of public assistance income compared to an insecure paycheck with no benefits. In this view, which other researchers have documented among low-skill, low-income mothers (Edin and Lein 1997), work is associated with insecurity and shortchanging one's children, not with advancement or self-respect.[13] And while discussions of pro-work norms generally assume *readiness* to work, as we show next, about a fifth of MTO families highlighted major barriers that made them, in effect, not ready at all.

EXTREME DISADVANTAGE: THE NON-WORK-READY

Many MTO adults face major barriers to work that were not directly addressed by the intervention. Beyond skill and credentials, transportation, and childcare, there were basic health and mental-health barriers. It is not clear that changes in spatial access to jobs, job networks, or normative support for work *could* have significantly benefited those who were not job ready. Nor is it clear that changes experienced through a relocation-only intervention could make them more job ready.

Almost 40 percent of MTO participants were not in the labor force (neither working nor looking for work) at the time of the interim evaluation survey (Orr et al., 2003). These patterns reflect, in part, the severe disadvantage that characterized families living in high-poverty public housing—in some of the toughest neighborhoods of the target cities—by the early 1990s (Popkin, Cunningham, and Burt 2005). About 23 percent of MTO participants received Supplemental Security Income (SSI) at the interim mark, a benefit primarily granted to individuals who are unable to work because of chronic health problems, which are concentrated in poor, high-risk neighborhoods to an extraordinary degree, as we showed in chapter 4.

Although experimental movers did experience a major reduction in depression, and a modest one in obesity, by the interim mark, just under a fifth of these adults reported that problems such as depression, asthma, diabetes, heart problems, and obesity continued to interfere with their ability to look for work or keep a job after their initial move. For example, Yolanda, a mother in Boston describes how a severe trauma that occurred more than five years ago continues to limit her ability to work:

> My problem started in '97. I got depression and anxiety. I get panic attacks.... All of this is a result of a trauma I had at the projects...there was a fire and the smoke came in from the bottom of the door. The building did not burn because it was made of bricks, but it traumatized me so much...when I saw the two-year-old baby burn in the crib.... My children were small.... The fireman tore down the door and grabbed the children. It was during wintertime, and they had to give them oxygen because they were asphyxiating. *Fieldworker: Did it affect you? Could you work during those years?* I worked until this happened.

In some cases, the chronic health problems were physical—and equally overwhelming. Erika, the experimental complier we introduced in chapter 1, in the suburbs south of Boston, has not worked for many years due to poor health. She must go to the hospital several times per week, sometimes every day, and takes medication for stomach pain and chronic headaches. The year before we started to visit, she had an asthma attack and was diagnosed with walking pneumonia, then congestive heart failure and the related problem of edema (fluid buildup) in her legs. When walking around became difficult, she became obese, making it harder still to stay active on her weakened legs. Erika uses an electric scooter to get around.

In other cases, enormous caregiving demands, including the burden created by family members' problems, compounded the strains imposed by chronic health problems. Roxanne, the experimental-group mother in Los Angeles whom we described in the previous chapter, cares for her daughter Jaclyn (age 17) as well as two teenage foster children, whose mother is a drug addict. But during the period we visited her, she was also caring for two infant grandsons until her daughter could regain custody. Plus, one of Roxanne's foster children was skipping school frequently and not coming home at night. Roxanne's daily routines were all consuming, especially caring for the infants, as well as exhausting: She has diabetes and arthritis and was frequently short of breath.

As we noted earlier, vital supports for work were also a consideration for many movers. Problems lining up childcare and transportation continued to undermine employment for many participants after moving. One mover in a low-poverty neighborhood outside L.A. said:

> But since I've got here, the problems I had. Like I leave to go to work like 4 in the morning. Well, there's no childcare open. It's only like maybe four day cares in the whole city.… And they all have limits on how many kids they could [take]. So that's the problem. I don't have, they don't have like the YMCA. They don't have things like that here [in this neighborhood]. *Fieldworker: So do you have childcare?* I don't have nothing. I can't afford it on my own. So I been dealing with, like, certain family members. But now, next week, they're all moving to Arizona.

As we explore in the next chapter, the struggles of the extremely disadvantaged raise serious questions about targeting: who gets served, and who should be, by MTO or other programs to tackle ghetto poverty in effective and humane ways.

SUMMARY AND IMPLICATIONS

It is simple enough to think of reasons that escaping high-poverty, high-crime inner-city neighborhoods through MTO would not be enough to affect the employment or earnings of the participants *on average*, at least by the interim mark when evaluators took careful measurement.

First, there were the big factors outside the experiment's control. Welfare reform, though not factored into MTO's design, came into effect as the experiment unfolded, helping to push millions off public assistance and into the low-wage workforce. At the same time, the strongest job economy since the Second World War—a much bigger driver of local employment rates than any social program—made labor markets tight in the early years of MTO (before the downturns that followed the collapse of the stock market bubble in 2000–2001 or the later economic crisis, which began in 2007). True, the experimental groups in Los Angeles and New York show some treatments effects, but MTO families were, as of the interim, roughly twice as likely to be in the labor force *regardless* of treatment group. Only time will tell whether market cycles somehow interact with the MTO "treatment" in ways we do not yet understand.

Second, on the flip side, many who relocated through MTO—and many counterparts, in the other treatment groups, who did not—were not work ready, and the modest, up-front adjustment supports at some sites (see chapter 3) could not begin to make them work ready. About one-fifth of MTO families are disabled by chronic physical or mental-health problems or both. And others were all but barred from effective job search, let alone regular job-holding, by their lack of vital job supports. Childcare and transportation were major ones, as they typically are for very low-income single parents. But caring for elderly or infirm relatives factored in, too, along with caring for other people's children. Many MTO families entered the experiment extremely disadvantaged as well as extremely underserved by our frayed and incomplete safety net and support systems.

What the focus on average effects—the staple measure in experimental science—misses, however, is the important ways in which a change of address *did* matter for many MTO families, along with the reasons why. We have focused, in this chapter and throughout the book, on variation in experiences and choices, on the fact that—with a few notable exceptions—there was no average experience. One reason we do this is to go well beyond the relatively uninformed hopes about the geography of jobs, social networks, or other factors that fueled expectations about how MTO would affect economic opportunity. But another reason is to shed light on how better informed efforts might function in the future, as part of a rebuilt opportunity agenda in a stunningly unequal society.

We found that *neighborhoods* can matter even when *neighbors* do not, especially for adults, who do not enter new school communities when they move—do not join the institutional life of new neighborhoods much at all, in fact. At least in terms of the proxy measures of new job creation and net job growth, moving to low-poverty neighborhoods, as we showed for metro Los Angeles, did not necessarily reduce the spatial mismatch between residences and job locations. And single parents without reliable, high-quality, low-cost, institutionally provided childcare had to line up support, housing, and work locations—and commutes among them—in complicated ways that the one-dimensional version of spatial mismatch, with jobs sprawling toward the promising suburbs, simply does not capture. For some families, such as Anique's, the alignment remained unstable for long periods of time, requiring enormous determination and more than a little luck. For other families, the arrangements were stable, if limiting. As we will explore in the concluding chapter, this is one on a list of challenges that housing policy cannot resolve on its own. This most ambitious of American housing experiments cannot help but reflect the major gaps, as we noted above, in how we support work *and* make it pay.

On the other hand, neighborhoods are more than job locations where institutions create specific expectations, with the potential to educate newcomers. At least some youth in MTO have acquired valuable new forms of cultural capital, which should help them navigate mainstream, middle-class expectations in a variety of settings, including higher education and the workplace. Acculturating was a strain, at least for children who moved after acquiring one identity in ghetto neighborhoods only to find that new peers had very different expectations of them. Schools organized this exposure to new expectations, as they did in the best documented school desegregation efforts. There should be less strain for those who moved very young, at least if the families are able to stay out of ghetto neighborhoods. But they are also different for children who live in ghetto-poor, segregated areas but whose parents isolate them from the streets. Some parents, like Patricia, the tireless 73-year-old in our study, manage to connect their children to higher status schools and other institutions, where "ghetto style" is, at most, a discussion topic or an occasional mode in the repertoire, and not the norm—not the only known way to present oneself.

When different neighbors matter most for disadvantaged young people, then, it is—as a number of researchers conjectured—because the character of neighborhood institutions matter (Jencks and Mayer 1990; Leventhal and Brooks-Gunn 2000; Sampson, Morenoff, and Gannon-Rowley 2002). Some of the consequential resources they provide are social, though, not material. This, too, is an important lesson for future policy and practice.

Chapter 10

Lessons

> *Interviewer:* In what ways do you think you have been successful in your life?
>
> *Anique* (Parent, MTO Los Angeles): Maintaining employment through all the layoffs and downsizing, where I didn't have to end up goin' back on welfare. Getting my daughter out of the [public housing projects]. And I'm still working on everything else.

GREAT EXPECTATIONS REVISITED

The curious thing about big ideas is the variety of ways they can be undone. Some—such as tackling global climate change—confront deeply seated beliefs and political interests. Other ideas, such as the idea that helping poor people move out of ghettos could dramatically improve their lives, face other kinds of challenges.

One is what we have called the strong-idea-weakly-implemented problem. Launched in 1994, the Moving to Opportunity (MTO) experiment has, in certain important respects, offered a modest test of a powerful idea. It was, like all social programs, imperfectly planned and implemented. To be fair, the terrain was largely uncharted and the information available to Congress and the implementing agencies quite limited. They made reasonable choices, perhaps the best possible at the time, about how to define "opportunity neighborhoods," for example, and also about who, among the inner-city poor, were in a position to benefit from an intervention limited to a change of address. Like the participating families, moreover, the planners and implementers faced a range of barriers beyond their control.

MTO is rich in lessons, to be sure, but the intervention, while ambitious in its hopes, was modest in the supports it offered to those who participated, at least when viewed against the potential we outlined in chapter 3 or the severity of disadvantage so many of the participants faced. MTO's effects so far, and any that are documented over the longer run, should be judged in that context. And *some* of those effects, most of all on safety and feelings of security, are simply extraordinary.

Of course, this verdict—"big and important idea receives partial test"— is not the stuff of news headlines. But acknowledging this is one of the ways we make progress, as a society, on important and long-ignored problems. We can learn a great deal when our efforts fall short, and we should not let the shortcomings obscure the significant, but easily undersold, successes. "Quality-of-life" impacts sound like consolation prizes, for example, not major successes, until you think about what it would be like to have *your* child grow up in an urban war zone and then get a ticket out. We agree with Nobel economist Amartya Sen (2001) that "freedom from fear" is an essential element of social progress. It is no substitute for a high-wage job, but nor can its value be overestimated. It is priceless.

MTO participants cited neighborhood safety as their top reason for entering the program, and it was clearly their biggest and most immediate gain. Yet our results show that safety has meaning for adolescent girls beyond the lower exposure to gang violence and drug trafficking documented in earlier MTO research. As their own comments and those of their mothers indicate, girls who moved from high to lower poverty neighborhoods have also benefited from a dramatic change in the level of their "female fear" (Gordon and Riger 1989)—the fear of sexual harassment, coercion and rape—and the ways in which it impedes women's lives. Both adolescent girls and their mothers who moved to and managed to stay in low-poverty areas are very aware of the dangers they have left behind and are cognizant of feeling much less anxious and afraid. It is striking that even though these families left high-risk, high-poverty public housing six to nine years before we interviewed them, the threats are still very vivid. In contrast, those who are still living in—or who have moved back to—high-poverty neighborhoods speak of their fears, the often extreme strategies they use to protect themselves (or their daughters), and the consequences the girls have faced—pregnancy, sexually transmitted disease, domestic violence, and sexual assault.

Relocation is a powerful, low-cost tool for dramatically reducing this fear and risk, which, we argue, is a key reason girls responded to MTO much better than boys. And the risk to receiving neighborhoods is trivial, as we have shown, particularly where relocatees are widely dispersed in the housing market. More than a move to opportunity, then, this experiment provided a *move to security*. For their part, however, many MTO boys have experienced the change very differently, struggling to make new friends in low-poverty areas, confronting isolation and boredom, sustaining connections to risky neighborhoods through their parents and relatives, and perceiving a more hostile welcome in low-poverty neighborhoods than did the girls. A relocation-only intervention was simply not enough to help these very low-income young minority males make healthier transitions.

As for opportunity in the wider sense, relocation alone will never compensate for the major barriers low-skilled people face in our economy, in particular the absence of good schools, expanded access to college and relevant training, and critical supports for work, such as health care and childcare—or for the downward pressure on wages created by economic restructuring and the decline of organized labor. What is more, initiatives to expand housing opportunity for the inner-city poor should not substitute for investing in the revitalization of distressed neighborhoods. Both place-based and people-based policies should be pursued in smart ways; both are central to creating a more equitable geography of opportunity (Blackwell and Bell 2005; Briggs 2005b). But MTO and similar efforts show *some* of the promise of assisted housing mobility, and we know more than ever about how to deliver on and expand that promise. Hard-won lessons point the way toward a next generation of strategies that should be smarter in multiple dimensions.

In this chapter, we discuss three major lessons of our work and a number of secondary ones. Framed in terms of risk and choice, the first lesson concerns the challenges of *staying* out of risky neighborhoods once one has managed to leave one through the program's support; the second concerns the role of social ties in perpetuating *exposure* to risk—in the form of dangerous behavior—regardless of one's neighborhood of residence; and the third concerns the power and limits of choice, narrowly defined, as a mechanism for improving lives.

The first lesson is about the quiet crisis of affordable rental housing: There is far too little of it in the urban areas where economic growth is concentrated in our country. The stock has been eroding for decades now. And what little exists is much too concentrated in a handful of neighborhoods, within those regions, that are either highly distressed or vulnerable to decline. The aims of MTO have been significantly undermined by this dual reality—the shortfall and the geographic concentration. But our larger worry goes well beyond the experiment. The scale of this crisis, and the backbreaking cost of rental housing to families on the bottom, is all too invisible, generally an afterthought, in America's debates about poverty and economic opportunity. As we noted in chapter 4, even the most ambitious proposals to increase wages for the lowest paid workers and to expand the Earned Income Tax Credit (a popular wage supplement) fall far short of the asking rents in economically vibrant cities and suburbs, where job opportunity will likely be concentrated in the years ahead. So our first priority is to closely examine the lessons of MTO for this important issue, which has too long been absent from the nation's "opportunity agenda."

The second major lesson concerns the "community question" raised about encouraging poor people to relocate. Critics worried about a loss of community, particularly in the form of social support from loved ones and familiar institutions, such as churches that have long served poor and minority neighborhoods. To the contrary, most often, MTO families kept their social worlds centered on kin, and that was part of the problem. The most vulnerable among the poor are embedded in personal "communities" of kin that often expose those vulnerable families to extraordinary risk and burden no matter where they live. There are more weaknesses to such "strong" ties than low-income housing policy, or allied support systems, are currently designed to handle.

The third major lesson has to do with great expectations about choice, the notion that choice-driven programs tap the efficiency of the market and empower the poor at the same time. This idea has always been in the "DNA" of the federal government's housing voucher program, enacted in 1974, which is the nation's largest expenditure to meet the housing needs of very low-income people. It is a central idea in education and health care reform, too. And thanks to a burgeoning field at the intersection of economics and psychology, "choice architecture" should be a core concern for planners and social reformers in a wide array of fields, as Cass Sunstein and Richard Thaler argue in *Nudge* (2008). The attention to how we organize choices, and not just to people's preferences in the abstract, is encouraging and overdue.

Yet for poor people who have lived segregated lives in dangerous, high-poverty neighborhoods, conventional choice programs offer little room to maneuver, thanks to a limited choice set, what we have called information poverty, the limited comparisons the "choosers" are in a position to make on their own, and, sometimes, a logic of choice focused on avoiding violence and other risks—not necessarily on garnering "opportunity." Put simply, that logic of choice reflects the fact that many poor people do not know what they are missing, just around the bend, because they have never had it, and no one they know and trust has ever had it.

We take up these lessons in turn and conclude with a bottom-line message about the idea that inspired this uniquely American experiment. Along the way, we highlight recommendations for policy, practice, and future research.

"OPPORTUNITY" WITHOUT AFFORDABLE HOUSING

Many discussions of MTO and related efforts to tackle ghetto poverty in low-income housing, including the sensationalized "American Murder Mystery" magazine article we discussed in chapter 2, have put the cart before the horse. For children and families to benefit significantly from the chance to live in better neighborhoods, they must be able to live in them securely over a period of time. This is not a sufficient condition, but it is a necessary one, and it was largely overlooked in the design and implementation of the experiment, just as the corresponding shortcoming—the fact that so many MTO families have struggled to stay in low-poverty neighborhoods—has often been missed in media accounts of the experiment's effects on education, employment, and other social outcomes.

It is also overlooked by some of the nation's most respected policy analysts when they apply textbook assumptions to our housing crunch and the spillover effects it creates. Commenting, during the 2008 primary season, on the Democratic presidential candidates' policy proposals, economist Rebecca

Blank explained why she favored John Edwards's proposal to dramatically expand the number of housing vouchers rather than work on the supply side to ensure affordability. "Compared to vouchers," she wrote, "building new low-income housing is a less efficient and usually more expensive way to help low-income families find affordable housing. *Because vouchers can be used in any neighborhood and give families choice about where they live, they should be favored in our national housing policy*" (emphasis added).[1]

That is an increasingly heroic assumption in tight, expensive housing markets. And the underlying forces that drive that expense have not changed, in spite of the economic crisis that engulfed America, beginning with the spate of foreclosures in 2006 and 2007 and then the capital market crunch and hemorrhaging of jobs by late 2008. As we showed in chapter 4, the shortage of rental housing in safe neighborhoods that *stays* affordable, even as markets grow tight and prices soar, is a major problem for our country. It is also a glaring gap in many debates about promoting economic opportunity and security—cutting poverty, to be sure, but extending economic security *up* the income ladder as well. Observers are right to focus on the forces that depress wages for those on the bottom of the job market, but no wage remedy in sight—not planned increases in the federal minimum wage, not local movements to supersede federal requirements with a "living wage," not more generous wage supplements from the Earned Income Tax Credit—can hope to close the gap between asking rents and wages without a concerted housing strategy, too. One of the worst-case scenarios is a future defined by still more luxury rental production as the low-rent housing stock continues a long-run disappearing act.

Addressing this crunch calls for working aggressively on the supply side of the market—with much larger-scale affordable housing preservation efforts as well as new production, with an inclusionary approach across cities and suburbs—and not just expanding the voucher program (Comey, Briggs, and Weismann 2008; Joint Center for Housing Studies 2006a; Katz and Turner 2007). Local efforts to tie vouchers to subsidized housing developments show particular promise,[2] as do efforts—which are few and far between for now—to reduce the cost of developing new housing, even market-rate housing, to ease the supply crunch for low- and moderate-income tenants. Without vouchers or similar subsidies, most "affordable" housing production simply does not produce units affordable to extremely low-income families. These are the families at greatest risk of homelessness, with all the social costs and family impacts that implies, and of instability—constant moving in search of a decent, safe, affordable home. That instability, as we have underlined, directly undermines hopes for connecting disadvantaged families to the resources in better neighborhoods. It also undermines children's academic achievement, healthy relationships to teachers and peers, and emotional well-being.

But we badly need more research on landlord behavior and the types of rules and incentives that developers, whether private or nonprofit, would respond to now. We also need to learn more about options for making housing search by low-income renters more efficient and effective, especially in tight markets.

THE "COMMUNITY" RISK—REAL AND IMAGINED

Critics of MTO and similar efforts to deconcentrate urban poverty worried that helping poor people to leave very poor neighborhoods would lead to a loss of social support (Goetz 2003; Venkatesh 2000), also that higher income neighbors probably would not incorporate poor newcomers into community life anyhow. The first worry was largely unfounded, at least for MTO families, and the second misstates the problem. In general, families in most urban and suburban neighborhoods keep to themselves, especially in big cities and suburbs, as MTO movers found everywhere. It is mainly local institutions that connect neighbors to one another, not informal neighboring—except where most people in the neighborhood stay put over long periods of time, and this is rarely the case for renters.

Too much research and policy aimed at neighborhoods still treat the neighborhood of residence as the primary neighborhood of influence for healthy child and family development. The MTO case shows how misleading this assumption can be. The neighborhood of residence functioned mainly as a decent *location*, with less exposure to violence, not a *social world*. Second neighborhoods, where important kin were based, were the most important social sites for many MTO families. If anything, the most disadvantaged were, as predicted by earlier research, particularly reliant on relatives and so most likely to maintain strong ties to some other neighborhood. This almost always meant a high-poverty, segregated neighborhood, and not necessarily the one the MTO family (nuclear family) left behind when it left public housing. Some MTO parents actively distanced themselves from problematic relatives, but this was the exception, and it often took place only when the parent had been overtly victimized in some way. The more subtle costs of long-run exposure to risk did not raise flags, for most MTO parents, and produce such distancing.

Yes, much vital social support for MTO families came from loved ones, most of them relatives. But the dominant view of kin networks as supportive communities misses what we have called the weakness of strong ties, in three dimensions. First, there is the problem, identified a generation ago but rarely addressed in social programs, of excessive obligations, which held MTO families back: chronic financial demands, house guests who disrupted family routines and parental attention, and other kinds of burdens.

Second, there is the much less acknowledged problem of exposure to risk, such as early drug and alcohol use, drug dealing, gang violence, and domestic violence. Strong attachment to kin structured much of this exposure after families relocated to low-poverty areas. MTO adolescents' "friends," they told us, were often cousins, uncles, or nephews, and some were engaged in delinquent or criminal behavior. Most of the absent fathers for youth in our study were in jail or ex-offenders or irregularly employed because of addiction or criminal careers. Compounding the "relative risk," as Gretchen Weismann (2008) found using our data, MTO parents were less likely to think of relatives as sources of risk and so less likely to monitor their children when they visited relatives or to buffer their children from the risks that abounded in the lives of their relatives and the neighborhoods those relatives occupied.

The third weakness is less obvious: An overwhelming focus on one's kin ties displaces the formation of other kinds of ties. This happens for two main reasons. One is opportunity for contact: With demanding daily routines and little time to socialize, and without much exposure to institutions where they might form new and useful ties, many parents in MTO—but especially the most disadvantaged—focus on the social networks into which they were born. Compounding this availability factor is distrust: wary of friends or other close ties to nonkin, the extended family remains the main pool for active ties. When parents did form broader relationships, it was through the workplace or social programs, or they maintained a few cherished friendships made in public housing or school during childhood.

Social relations represent a much trickier target for policy intervention than, say, the scarcity of well-located and affordable rental housing. This is especially true when the ties in question are a family's closest ties—ties of blood and deeply felt obligation. But we believe that three broad strategies have shown promise. The first is offering healthy, developmental alternatives to socializing with risky relatives. After-school programs, weekend and summer programs, and other youth-serving institutions are the most tested examples here. But proposals to, in effect, extend schooling down to the pre-K years—in the form of universal, high-quality early childhood education—are also relevant, as are the longer school days now operating in some charters and other schools. The keywords, of course, are *healthy* and *developmental*—something more than custodial day care.

The second strategy is less obvious and also less tested, at least in the arena of social programs. We will call it relationship management and support: helping people to better manage the risks, and make the most of the resources, in their important relationships. This may strike as even more meddlesome social engineering—the overreaching "nanny state" telling poor people how to treat their own relatives. But directing people, or managing their choices, is not what we have in mind. And there are important precedents for this. One is in innovative family-strengthening programs, already at work, that take a holistic approach and include skill-building for clients in the important arena of personal relationships. Practitioners and researchers are calling this a "full frame" approach to working with the most disadvantaged parents and their children (Smyth, Goodman, and Glenn 2006). These families pay a severe price for the underfunding and fragmentation in our social service systems, as well as the failure of those systems to adequately account for the role of kin networks and neighborhood context.

Other precedents are decidedly middle-class, of course: Family therapy is all about managing healthier relationships. And a booming industry of "personal effectiveness" coaches helps professionals better manage work relationships, better manage themselves as emotional beings, and otherwise attain their goals. Given these respected approaches available to middle and upper-income people, why should we ignore this important lever for change—relationship management—when serving poor people with smarter programs?

The third strategy is more indirect: to make disadvantaged families less *reliant* on risky kin relationships for the aid they need to get by or get ahead. Holistic strategies for family economic success are an important part of this, but so are institutional substitutes for some of the specific functions poor people consistently tap their strong ties to handle, such as job referrals. There is ample evidence, for instance, on what it takes to provide effective "job matching" for low-skilled people, with weak job networks, who face multiple barriers to work (Harrison and Weiss 1998; Herr and Wagner 2007).

As for research, we need to move beyond documenting risk and counting up social ties and exchanges. We need to understand, in much more nuanced ways, how adults and their children come to *recognize* and *manage* various types of risk in their strongest social ties. Avoidance is clearly one common strategy, but are there others? Again, the key reasons we need more insight into these things are that people raised with a sense of strong obligation to kin seem less mindful, on average, of the risks and less able to sever the ties, than they are in the case of other types of relationships, such as friendships or acquaintanceships.

CHOICE AS AN OPPORTUNITY ENGINE

In America, we are deeply enamored of choice as a mechanism for improving lives, both in consumer markets and public policy. Proponents claim that vouchers, choice counseling, consumer "report cards," and other mechanisms promise greater competition, efficiency, transparency, and quality in "public service markets," such as public education, and also in housing—a complex private market shaped by government policy in a host of important ways. Our work illuminates the serious problems on both the demand and supply side of this promise.

On the supply side, echoing our arguments about housing scarcity above, the choice set in low-income housing is often abysmal in high-cost markets: Live in a lousy apartment in a decent neighborhood or a better unit in a risky neighborhood. Deal with substandard housing—heaters that do not work, leaks that do not get fixed, pests that run rampant no matter how good a housekeeper one may be—or the well-documented hazards of unsafe neighborhoods. Families in MTO differed in their willingness to make particular trade-offs, and blind luck helped determined their outcomes, too. In general, we find that very low-income families on housing assistance take what they can get, making the most of proximity to loved ones, managing in substandard or crowded units for the sake of their children, and otherwise settling. The fact that many in our country do not, as a practical matter, have very good options to choose *from*, even if they are given housing or school vouchers or other forms of assistance, suggests a wide gulf between optimistic, middle-class conceptions of choice as empowering and the realities of choice for the most disadvantaged.

On the demand side, some choices—among retirement savings plans, "exotic" subprime mortgages or other credit instruments, and, for many families, the right schools and neighborhoods—are particularly complex to make. Choosing well demands not-easily acquired types of information and subtle judgments about that information (Thaler and Sunstein 2008). Beyond information and skill, comparison shopping also requires time, transportation, and other precious resources, which the very poor frequently do not have.

In lieu of better evidence on how low-income people actually make choices, the debate in housing policy, especially over rental vouchers, often revolves around stylized versions of the supply- versus demand-side explanations of segregation. In the strong (unqualified) form of the supply-side story, at least for tight housing markets, poor families who win the "lottery" of housing assistance are desperate to live in more racially and economically integrated areas, but market discrimination and scarcity thwart their dream of a better life in a better place. In this telling, even voucher holders who receive information, transportation, or other supports have little *meaningful* choice. In the strong demand-side narrative, families only integrate when they are obliged to do so by government planners. Assisted housing mobility, in this telling, reflects the integrator's ideal and not the preferences of families served. Yes, all parents may want the safest possible places for their children, say the demand-side purists. But the inner-city poor, most of whom are racial minorities, also want the comfort of familiarity and social acceptance, as well as support from loved ones—even if that means enduring more dangerous and resource-poor areas.

Based on the decade-plus experience of families in the MTO experiment and the wide range of data we integrated to write this book, we find that the supply-siders are right about constraints (though our fieldwork was not set up to detect discrimination as a contributor), while the demand-siders largely misconstrue the role of preferences, at least in the tight housing markets where much economic growth and inequality are concentrated in America.

Yes, intense market pressure in greater Boston, Los Angeles, and New York over MTO's first decade, and the huge number of highly poor neighborhoods in the latter two in particular, as well as the limits and flaws in the housing voucher program, were major barriers for many families. Most tried to stay in low-poverty areas, but only some succeeded. The less stably housed the family, the more this was true—because each new move forced the family to navigate anew, with little room to maneuver in the choice of best-possible neighborhoods—and this shaped many trajectories (of moves over time) that led experimental compliers (the focus of hopes in the program) to live in poorer neighborhoods. Housing voucher holders clearly avoid searching in neighborhoods where they expect that landlords will refuse to accept the government subsidy, for example, whether or not this is actually the case. Sometimes, they hire rental agents, poll friends and relatives, and otherwise compensate for their limited information and time and for the stigmas the voucher carries.

For some families, getting a housing voucher *is* like winning the lottery; decent units in desired neighborhoods are available and can be located in time; inspectors and landlords cooperate in textbook fashion; and the unit remains affordably priced for years. For others, the dearth of minimally acceptable units, the insecure opportunity to live in a safer neighborhood when one does gain a foothold, and each arduous new search are all reminders of what it means to rent housing on the bottom of the income ladder in extremely costly and tight markets—and with a government housing subsidy that is often rejected in "better" neighborhoods, even when the advertised rent is within reach.

Expanding the choice set for the voucher program calls for expanding and accelerating the focus on supply-side strategies with an inclusionary approach in many markets. It could include post-move (second or *n*th move) counseling, which shows promise in local studies. Short of that, it means searching on behalf of families in order to generate wider options, as Gautreaux placement agents did in the program's first wave, and then working with private landlords to ensure that decent, leased units will remain affordable and in program compliance as long as possible. This need not deny families the opportunity to lease up elsewhere, but it would put the onus of the arduous search task in the most competitive markets on the agencies offering housing assistance. Another way to expand choices is by strengthening protection from source-of-income discrimination by landlords (refusing to accept a tenant because they hold a governmental rental voucher). And finally, proposals to create a housing allowance in the Earned Income Tax Credit, which would transfer subsidies directly to tenants without triggering the stigma of a voucher, also show promise for meeting some housing needs (Dreier 2008). But many proposals to help the working poor will not address the many extremely low-income nonworking households that rely on vouchers.[3]

The finding that different voucher holders are willing to make different trade-offs also underscores the importance of transportation as a determinant of accessibility. "Car vouchers" and other tools could mitigate the trade-off between living in a safer neighborhood and having the desired level of access to one's social supports and cherished institutions, such as "church homes," as well as jobs or education and training programs.

Finally, a host of reforms to the federal voucher program hold the promise of "changing the defaults," in the lingo of choice architecture (Thaler and Sunstein 2008). As housing expert Barbara Sard explains it, the aim would be to shift the defaults that channel very low-income people, especially racial minorities, toward poor neighborhoods again and again—because poor renters have limited capacity to search and because landlords in those weak submarkets are most likely to accept vouchers and therefore represent the easiest placements. The new default, in our view, could be to get matched by a capable intermediary, whether public or private agency, to an available unit (or set of options) in a safe, accessible, more resource-rich community. The family could refuse such an option and move to a more familiar neighborhood, which often means a poorer and more segregated one. But the default would offer an alternative first.

Creating such a default calls for changes in staffing, information systems, and other elements of operating capacity in housing programs, as well as changes in how resources are allocated. Such reforms could shift the rules and incentives for the landlords and housing agencies that do so much to *create* the choice set families face. This, and not a myopic focus on influencing the choosers—the families searching for decent housing, in better neighborhoods, against the odds—is the key to changing outcomes. It is also an urgent issue, since the epidemic of foreclosures, as we showed in chapter 2, has reignited stereotypes about poor renters with vouchers. Avoiding concentrations of vouchers in weak rental submarkets, such as neighborhoods in decline or on the verge, is vitally important.

As for choice in the education arena, MTO produced limited improvements in school context, certainly much more limited than those produced by the Gautreaux housing desegregation program that inspired MTO. MTO did not get children to significantly better schools for two main reasons: first, because "choice sets" were limited (the program did not enable most of them to *move* to and *stay* in high-performing school districts or attendance zones); and second, because choice was limited, too (the MTO program did not address participants' limited resources and logics for choosing the most effective schools).

Where MTO families had school choices to make beyond the choice of neighborhood, that is, where children were not assigned according to school attendance zones, they did not always make the best choices. Here again, information poverty was a big barrier, and the fact that relocating did not produce broader, less insular social networks contributed to that intangible but very limiting form of poverty. Beyond this, the rationale of choice some parents applied also shaped the outcomes. By rationale, we mean the cultural logic that low-skilled parents, raised in dangerous neighborhoods and schools and embedded in networks of relatives and friends with similar experiences brought to bear in making school choices for their children. For these parents, choices centered on avoiding ghetto-type risks rather than garnering (broader) academic opportunity. Most MTO families said they volunteered for the program to get away from drugs and gangs. Following that logic, it is perhaps not surprising that some MTO parents asked little more of their children's schools than somewhat greater safety and more orderly classrooms.

Future efforts might define "opportunity" communities to account for local school performance and, again, help low-income families stay in, not just get to, such communities. School choice demonstrations likewise point toward specific ways to inform the school choices of low-income (or other) parents, such as by making information on school performance more transparent and comprehensible and the choice process less time consuming and daunting.

A SUCCESS MODEL

Figure 10.1 presents a simple logic model for understanding the strengths and weaknesses of assisted housing mobility as a tool for (a) improving the quality of life of the poor or (b) helping them escape poverty (Briggs and Turner 2006). Logic models, also known as *theories of change*, consist of a set of causes and effects, outlined in a sequence or chain, to clarify the premises and contingencies on which success depends (Hatry and Wholey 1999). (Note: A more detailed model of social mechanisms is in the appendix, figure A.1.)

In this book, we have elaborated on these causes and effects, as well as the threshold conditions and contingencies. We are particularly concerned that policy makers, implementers, and researchers alike understand the latter. That is, what must obtain for the potential of these initiatives to be realized, and where are the initiatives most vulnerable? Here are some of the most important factors and a summary of our recommendations:

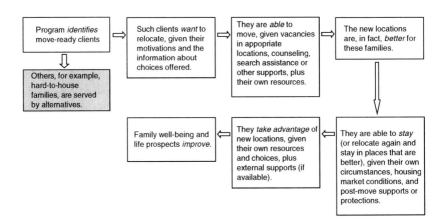

Figure 10.1 Basic Logic Model: Assisted Housing Mobility

Targeting people: Target the move-ready, and help those who are not ready with alternative supports. We use "readiness to move" to refer to families' level of functioning vis-à-vis the demands of relocation and of adapting successfully to take advantage of the resources in new neighborhoods (Briggs and Turner 2006). Better targeting of people is crucial if social programs are to produce the results we need and secure sustained political support (Schuck and Zeckhauser 2006). Edward Goetz (2003) and other critics of poverty concentration have argued that mobility programs "cream" only the most able to succeed, the upwardly mobile. Yet about one-quarter of MTO families were severely disadvantaged. Some of these families were not suited, at least not initially, to a relocation program. Researchers and practitioners have called some of them the "hard to house" (Popkin, Cunningham, and Burt 2005). They need intensive case management and supports, which are more effectively delivered at well-staffed sites, such as "supportive housing" developments.

In chapter 5, we explained that many public housing developments had, by the late 1980s, become so distressed that they resembled war zones. In an ongoing demonstration program focused on the most disadvantaged Chicago public housing residents, counselors have encountered severe depression and uncontrolled schizophrenia well beyond expectations, as well as symptoms of posttraumatic stress disorder. Relocation counseling has gone nowhere, and the program is adapting to focus on intensive services, transitional jobs, and other supports (Popkin et al. 2008). Providing such alternative supports to the hard-to-house while targeting the move-ready is not creaming—which implies that *only* the most able get any help.

The larger problem is that the low-income housing field has been much slower than the field of workforce development, which coined the label "readiness to work" decades ago, to understand and respond to the wide range of client strengths and needs. MTO's approach to screening and support services is one illustration of that lag (Turner and Briggs 2008). For those who *are* suited to benefit, "mobility plus" efforts—relocation tied to other key supports, such as work supports and workforce development, plus transportation help—could help them escape poverty, not just make the experience of persistent poverty less life threatening, nerve-wracking, and depressing.

Targeting places: We know a great deal about the kinds of neighborhoods that pose serious risks to children and families but much less about how to define the "opportunity-rich" neighborhoods to which MTO-type efforts could help families move. We suggest that, instead of simple proxies, such as a neighborhood's racial composition or poverty rate, destination neighborhoods should be targeted on the basis of concrete opportunities, such as community safety, quality schools, or access to skill-appropriate jobs. New efforts to do just that are emerging in civil rights cases—as part of devising smarter remedies for public housing segregation—and also among federal reformers.[4]

Helping participants stay in better neighborhoods, not just get to them: Our housing policy recommendations above outline the need as well as promising policy options.

Helping families leverage the value, and mitigate the risks, of new neighborhoods: Moving improves outcomes for many families, but moving is no panacea for the problems associated with persistent family poverty. And some families need additional assistance in order to take full advantage of new opportunities or to cope, say, with the different adjustments that low-income minority girls and boys seem to face after they relocate. Innovative local approaches to "responsible relocation," such as in a Baltimore regional housing campaign, point the way.

FINAL THOUGHTS

The strategy underlying MTO—"assisted housing mobility" for the inner-city poor—is a powerful, and indeed essential tool for fighting ghetto poverty. Minimally, it provides a direct and cost-effective way to dramatically improve the *quality* of poor people's lives by buffering them from the violence in ghetto neighborhoods. This can happen even when a neighborhood is just a location, not a community of social exchange. The dramatic improvements in safety and security, indexed by striking reductions in depression and anxiety for women and girls, are enough to make MTO worthwhile. And the costs and risks are low, particularly when viewed as preventive investments and when compared to the costs of crisis intervention. But future efforts could do more still, as we have outlined, to make relocation part of a larger recipe for getting ahead—for *escaping* poverty.

In 1968, the Kerner Commission recognized expanded housing opportunity as a vital part of the national agenda to create equal opportunity in a persistently segregated nation. Nothing we have learned since suggests that its overall vision was flawed—or that segregation is somehow taking care of itself. But assisted housing mobility is extraordinarily vulnerable, as we have underscored, to the strong-idea-weakly-implemented problem. Its success depends on a—for now—extraordinary chain of cooperation, running from tenants through landlords, housing agencies, and in some cases, support services and community institutions. In many ways, moreover, we have structured our housing markets to make it hard for this strategy to succeed. We should, by all means, call on the poor to make the best possible choices about their own lives. But rewriting the rules of housing markets, with housing assistance as a part, is simply beyond their reach. It is up the rest of us—the public, policy makers, planners, and businesspeople—to level the playing field. It is also in our collective interest to do so since the nation has become much more ethnically diverse, in recent decades, and more economically unequal at the same time.

Different "choice architecture" will not help much where the supply of affordable housing choices is very deficient. As we explain in chapter 4, that is not the case across America, in spite of arguments about "national" crises of affordable rental housing. But it is the case in the expensive housing markets where much of the country's economic growth has concentrated. In those places, we can supply better choices, and we can improve the architecture everywhere, i.e., the presentation of choices and the defaults and other incentives for helping people make the healthiest choices they can.

Beyond these considerations, the anti-poverty strategy for which MTO is one ambitious form is vulnerable, like every other important idea about improving lives through social programs, to unfounded assumptions about how persistently poor people can actually escape risks, wherever they are able to live. In the same way that neighborhoods can matter (as good or bad locations for leading one's life) even when one's neighbors do not (as social resources), so high-risk ghetto neighborhoods exert a pull—most of all, through the strong ties of kinship—long after families have moved out. In a general sense, researchers have noted this for nearly a century, going back to the early studies of immigrant ghettos in Chicago, for example. Our work documents that pull in the context of a program that specifically sought to ensure moves to opportunity *without* engineering the social lives its participants then chose to lead. Again, for many MTO families, we found, the destination neighborhoods were simply not "communities" in ways that planners and observers had hoped. Yet the mental model of the neighborhood of residence as a causal sandbox, *determining* social influences and social contact, endures. Our main concern is not how researchers model causes and effects, though that is certainly at issue here as researchers and funders pay increased attention to how contexts—key social settings, such as schools, youth programs, and neighborhoods—function or dysfunction on behalf of young people. Rather, our main concern is that future efforts not downplay the degree to which many of the chronically disadvantaged cling to and lean on the most important people in their lives and, at the same time, are held back by them.

As we completed this book, researchers were launching the "final" impact evaluation of MTO, a test of how the parents and children are doing 10 to 13 years after they enrolled. But no evaluation of this experiment will ever be final, in the sense of providing the last word. Evaluations are conducted on the administrative schedules of researchers and their sponsors. Often, as in the case of MTO, they are imprinted in legislation to convey policy makers' best guesses about when there might be something worth learning. But MTO families write their own stories as they lead their lives, and those stories unfold on their own schedules. Our job has been to give voice to some of the persistent threads in those stories, in hopes that the wider world might learn something and choose to act.

Appendix

Studying Moving to Opportunity

OPTIONS AND CHOICES

We had a number of options for examining and then explaining the Moving to Opportunity experiment—its accomplishments, shortcomings, and surprises. Perhaps the most obvious was to emphasize the story of families managing an often daunting array of changes in their lives. We might center the study on parenting, daily routines, and sources of risk and resilience in the lives of adults and children in the experiment (Furstenberg et al., 1999). Another option was to focus on the question of upward mobility—the "to opportunity" emphasis of the experiment—by drawing on what scholars and practitioners have learned about how people complete school, get ahead (or not) in the American labor market, build wealth, and so on in the face of major structural forces that tend to reproduce inequality (Massey 2007; Neckerman and Torche 2007; Newman and Massengill 2006). Though MTO planners were not focused on helping families "succeed" at *staying* out of high-poverty areas, just helping them to *get* out, getting ahead in the housing market was another natural element of this mobility or "attainment" perspective on MTO. Both traditions (human development and status attainment) have shown interest in the question of how neighborhood context affects the well-being and life fortunes of children and families—in particular, of disadvantaged families.[1] But having written and advocated for years on behalf of disadvantaged communities, we also had the sense that broader changes in neighborhoods, cities, and metropolitan regions should be tracked, as part of the study, and linked to family fortunes at the micro-level. This is in the rich demographic tradition, specifically area-based analysis, which sometimes includes studies of the "ecology" of human development—the contexts working *around* parents and children to affect their well-being (Bronfenbrenner 1979).

Finally, there was the important, but until now largely overlooked, story of designing and launching the intervention itself. Our collective experience with this extraordinary social experiment goes back two decades: John helped to conceive, design, and implement it when he worked at U.S. HUD, and he coedited the book of early-impact studies (Goering and Feins 2003); Sue was on the original Gautreaux study team—whose work inspired the federal government to create MTO—and she later led the qualitative component of the interim MTO evaluation (Orr et al., 2003); and Xav did research on a similar quasi-experiment in housing desegregation in Yonkers, New York, and later ran the HUD policy development and research office, where the MTO evaluation was sponsored and managed. We knew that, unlike many poverty researchers, who merely observe the poor, we could draw on studies of the policymaking process, as well as implementation research, to understand what the program, as *planned change* in the lives of very poor people, did or did not anticipate and why, how the delivery of the program shaped family experiences, how larger structural forces—such as changes in other domains of social policy, market trends, and other forces—undermined planners' hopes, and so on.

We chose, of course, to include elements from each of these important traditions, and the body of the book is structured accordingly: how MTO was designed and launched, the character of the city and regional contexts and the changes in same as MTO unfolded, and then the family-level experiences (tied back to the first two domains). All are part of MTO's "story" as an American experiment. And the first two turn the mirror on us as a country, whereas a narrow focus on the families might encourage the reader to hold this story at arms length, not to mention make unwarranted assumptions about why families make the choices they do—or why they have those choices to make in the first place.

In this brief appendix, we provide details on our data and methodology, to help the reader make judgments about our findings and the ways we have discussed their implications. But we have another aim as well. Large-scale, mixed-method efforts of this kind remain rare, in part because they are challenging to design, get funded, and carry out and in part because most research training tends to narrow researchers' view, as well as their professional comfort zone, leading to much more one-dimensional approaches. We believe that studies of this kind are vitally important for understanding complex problems as well as systematic efforts to tackle them through social reform. We believe that scholars, sponsors, and consumers of research cannot afford to turn away from the challenges or to stop seeking out better ways to generate useful new knowledge. For all these reasons, we close by discussing, in a more personal way, what we learned from the challenges of doing this work, and we provide advice for future efforts with similar goals.

GENESIS AND OVERVIEW

It was the mammoth but puzzling Interim Impacts Evaluation study, conducted four to seven years after families enrolled in MTO, that triggered our work. It first surfaced what appeared to be anomalous, incongruous, and unexpected effects of MTO. Why would girl movers do so well and boys so poorly, at least in comparative terms? Why would adult's mental and physical health improve but not their employment or wages? How could the studies of Gautreaux have found such significant impacts on children's education while MTO studies have found virtually none? Given that the Chicago region was the locus for Gautreaux and also one of the five MTO sites, the divergence appeared even more puzzling. Either the earlier research was flawed or reflected vastly different causal forces, or else we all needed a more nuanced appreciation of what it will take to change the lives of very poor families moving from public housing ghettos in America's inner cities.

The Three-City Study of MTO was conceived, then, as a large-scale, mixed-method study focused on unraveling, as best we could, these puzzles in three MTO sites: New York, Boston, and Los Angeles (HUD authorized a second team, with whom we shared analyses, to do follow-up research in Baltimore and Chicago).[2] We obtained geocoded MTO survey data, collected in the Interim Evaluation, under special agreement with HUD and Abt Associates, to examine housing trajectories and locations over time, school choices, and other outcomes. We set to work, with help from the National Neighborhood Indicators Project, mining the data on census tracts ("neighborhoods"), zip codes and other small-area geographies, as well as entire cities and metro areas. But our major thrust was new qualitative data on the families in MTO, collected through in-depth qualitative interviews and ethnographic fieldwork—repeat visiting, with a range of interview styles, in addition to participant observation of life as MTO families lived it.

Before we present the essentials on our data and methodology, we need to clarify the key features of MTO itself and the important ways in which the experiment has evolved. It is not, by any stretch, a pure test of "neighborhood effects," and because this is easily missed in both public and scholarly debates, we outline what we believe MTO is and is not testing.

BACKGROUND: WHY LAUNCH A SOCIAL EXPERIMENT? WHAT IS MTO TESTING?

Those who study the effects of different neighborhood contexts on child and family success struggle with the fact that families are not randomly sorted into neighborhoods. Because different families have and make different housing choices, life outcomes—and the processes that shape them—may reflect key traits of families and not necessarily the influences of their neighborhood environment. To further complicate the puzzle, important neighborhood influences appear to be *managed* differently by different types of families, meaning that traits of families and of neighborhoods interact and may shift over time (Ellen and Turner 2003; Furstenberg 1993; Furstenberg et al., 1999). In general, a randomized social experiment is the best-available way to determine the impact of

neighborhoods over and above family-level influence. Because participants in the MTO demonstration were randomly assigned to treatment
groups, the effects of the treatment (intervention) should be *attributable
to the experiment* rather than to the characteristics of the families. But it
is very important to recognize, as we will explain, that this may not be
attributable to living in particular kinds of neighborhoods.

In 1994, MTO's local program managers invited very low-income residents of public housing and project-based assisted housing to participate
(see chapter 3). All were in high-poverty neighborhoods of Baltimore, Boston, Chicago, Los Angeles, and New York. The mean baseline location was
a striking 56 percent poor in 1990—much higher than the 40 percent
threshold that analysts have used to define extreme or "ghetto" poverty
concentration (Jargowsky 1997). Over 5,300 families applied, and just
over 4,600, 93 percent of whom were black or Hispanic, met payment
record and other basic eligibility requirements. Those families were randomly assigned to one of three treatment groups: a control group (families
retained their public housing unit but received no new assistance), a Section 8 comparison group (families received the standard counseling and
voucher subsidy, for use in the private market), or an experimental group.
The experimental-group families received *relocation counseling* (focused on
opportunities to live in low-poverty areas) and *search assistance* (often in
the form of accompanied visits and transportation to vacant units); the
supplemental services provided and the specific roles played by public versus nonprofit housing agencies varied considerably across the sites (Feins,
McInnis, and Popkin 1997). The experimental group also received a voucher
useable only in a low-poverty neighborhood (less than 10 percent poor as
of the 1990 census), with the requirement that the family live there for
at least a year. After the initial placement, no families received additional
relocation counseling or special assistance from the program, nor did any
face program-imposed locational restrictions after the first year. So there
was no feature of the demonstration to specifically encourage families to
choose another low-poverty neighborhood if and when they moved on.

Of the 1,820 families assigned to the experimental group, just under half
(47 percent or 860) found a suitable apartment and moved successfully
(leased up) in the time allotted, becoming the program's "compliers"—a
20 percent improvement over the Gautreaux program. The experimental-group families most likely to lease up had fewer children, access to a
car, more confidence about finding an apartment, greater dissatisfaction
with their origin neighborhood, and no church ties to the origin neighborhood; a looser rental market and more intensive counseling services were
also significant predictors of success (Shroder 2003). The program's early
impacts included dramatic improvements in neighborhood poverty rates
and participants' reports of safety and security—but not rates of racial
integration (Feins 2003).

Housing tenure, housing assistance receipt, and the frequency of
moves, which are both cause and effect of broader housing choices and

opportunities, did not change significantly for any of the treatment groups. By the interim mark, that is, the evaluation point four to seven years after random assignment, about 70 percent of MTO households continued to receive some form of housing assistance; about 90 percent (in all three groups) were still renters; and the low-income renters who dominate the MTO patterns showed the comparatively high rates of residential mobility that characterize poor renters nationwide; there were no substantial differences among treatment groups in length of time residing in their current housing unit (Orr et al., 2003:61–66, C-16, D-1). Members of the experimental group were still much more likely to report feeling safe, to report less social disorder in their neighborhoods, and to report feeling satisfied with their neighborhoods (Orr et al., 2003:42).

But what, in fact, *is* the treatment, and what is MTO testing? Like other social experiments, MTO has evolved in the real world and not under controlled laboratory conditions. The experiment's value as a window on neighborhood effects, the experience of relocation by very low-income families, and other important topics have recently drawn considerable debate from leading social researchers (Clampet-Lundquist and Massey 2008; Ludwig et al. 2008; Sampson 2008; Sobel 2006).

Several features of the experiment's evolution hold particularly important implications for our research design and for the interpretation of our results. First, 67 percent of the experimental-complier group had moved at least once more by the interim mark, and according to Orr et al. (2003), that group was only half as likely (18 vs. 38 percent) as compliers who stayed put to be living in a neighborhood less than 10 percent poor. MTO's program content helped families *get* to particular kinds of neighborhoods, not *stay* in them or move to *similar* neighborhoods over time. But additional moves introduce additional family-level selection effects on locational outcomes over time, making it difficult to attribute particular outcomes to the intervention as one moves beyond treatment-group differences to analyze outcomes for distinct subgroups within the treatment groups (as we do). For this reason in particular, most of our results are descriptive in nature, not presented as unbiased estimates of treatment effects or "program causality" (Kling, Liebman, and Katz 2007) but rather as robust accounts of what families experience and why they make the choices they do.

Second, many of the low-poverty areas that served as initial destinations for the experimental group have changed over time, through no choice of the participants. Census data show that while most were relatively stable in terms of income levels, almost half (45 percent) were becoming poorer in the 1990s (Orr et al., 2003), even as many inner-city neighborhoods were becoming less poor.

Third, about 70 percent of the control group had also moved by the interim mark—most to other poor neighborhoods but with a mean reduction in neighborhood poverty rate from 51 percent to 34 percent (when compared to control-group members who did not move). One reason for these moves was public housing demolition and revitalization programs, HOPE VI most important, which received a major boost from federal policy and local mayors and advocates just as MTO was starting up. But the key point is that many members of the MTO control group are movers, too, some with vouchers, about one quarter living in neighborhoods below 20 percent poverty by the interim point, rather than members of a fixed-in-place comparison category.

Still, at the interim point that preceded our fieldwork by about two years, families in the MTO experimental group were about 13 percent more likely than the control group, and experimental compliers 27 percent more likely, to be living in very low- poverty areas; the experimental group had also lived in such areas for longer periods of time (Orr et al., 2003:42). The experimental group has had an exceptional experience vis-à-vis the dominant pattern for low-income housing assistance nationwide.

MTO is thus a test of at least two important things for families who used to live in high-poverty public housing and project-based assisted housing: (a) the experience and effects of *living* in much lower poverty neighborhoods over some period of time; and (b) the experience and effects of *relocating*, after initial counseling and search assistance, to low-poverty neighborhoods, and, in some cases, relocating again to a range of neighborhood types, while raising children and handling other life challenges.

In the next section, we outline how we designed and conducted our study to address these important features of the experiment.

TACKLING THE PUZZLES: DESIGN, DATA, AND METHOD

We focused on "how" and "why" questions: To better understand what statistical analyses of close-ended surveys have been unable to explain, we employed mostly qualitative methods, and we integrated our analyses of multiple types of data, both quantitative and qualitative. We focused on the mechanisms that might help explain the puzzling effects and noneffects highlighted in the interim evaluation, and we began with a simple model of the intervention, which emphasizes hoped-for (positive) effects (figure A.1). In general, these mechanisms have been much less well understood than broad statistical relationships between, say, living in a particular kind of neighborhood and the likelihood that one will drop out of high school or become a teen parent. Qualitative approaches are particularly important for understanding why participants in social programs make the choices they do, as well as for understanding significant variation *within* treatment groups, unlike the dominant tradition in experimental science, which is to focus on average treatment effects.[3]

Our family-level data were collected in 2004 and 2005—about 6 to 10 years after families' initial placement through the MTO program and about 2 years after the interim survey data were collected. First, we

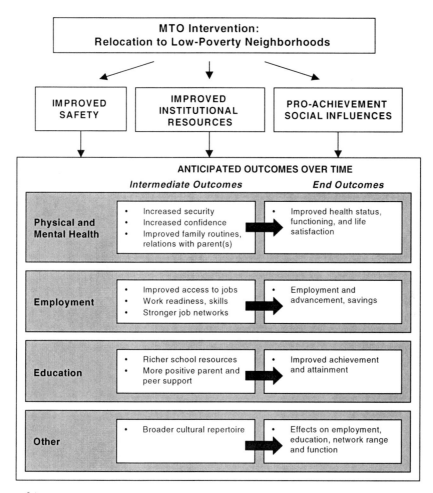

Figure A.1 Mechanisms and Effects in MTO (Path Diagram)

randomly selected 122 families, conducting a total of 278 semistructured, in-depth qualitative interviews with parents, adolescents, and young adults in all three treatment groups, including compliers and noncompliers in the experimental and Section 8 comparison groups (sampling randomly from all three groups within the stratum of families who had an adolescent child resident in the home at the time of the interview, see table A.1). We oversampled families in Los Angeles because it was the site with the highest lease-up rate for MTO experimental group families and because a large number of L.A. families were excluded from the interim survey because they had moved after 1997. Overall, we conducted 81 interviews in Boston, 120 in Los Angeles, and 77 in New York. We offered financial incentives to participate. The response rate was 70 percent, and the combined cooperation rate for the interviews—consents as a share of eligible families contacted, excluding those we could not find due to deaths or our inability to locate the family—was 79 percent.[4]

Next, we launched "family-focused" ethnographic fieldwork (Burton 1997; Weisner 1996), visiting a subset of 39 interviewed families repeatedly over a period of six to eight months. In recruiting this subset, which included only control-group and experimental-group complier families and thus allows for treatment-on-treated (TOT) analysis, we oversampled families who were still living in suburban school districts—considering these to be "locationally successful," at least in relative terms.[5] The cooperation rate for the ethnographic subsample was 70 percent.

Chi-square tests confirm that both samples are quite representative of the much larger population of MTO families surveyed at the interim mark (n=2,720), both in terms of background traits and employment status—though our final sample modestly underrepresents Hispanics and overrepresents families on welfare—and a range of other social outcomes (table A.2). It may be that nonworking parents were more available for ethnographic visiting and/or more enticed by the financial incentives we offered. Analysis of refusals indicated that either parents felt too busy to "deal with" repeat visiting or, for their own reasons, did not want to share more about their lives. We accounted in our qualitative analyses— for example of social relations, routines, and other topics—for the modest underrepresentation of working families in the ethnography. Ethnic representation was less an issue, since we did not conduct direct comparisons of Hispanic and African-American families.

The *qualitative interviews*, which were conducted in English, Spanish, and Cambodian, let us explore a variety of issues, including neighborhood environment, housing, health, education, and employment. The sample covers the full range of outcomes (from very successful to highly distressed) for all three MTO treatment groups and both complier statuses, a key to generating representative results. Interviews with parents averaged

Table A.1. Three-City Interview Sample (Overview)
Number of Families, by Site, Treatment Group, and Complier Status

	Experimental Group		Section 8 Comparison Group		Control Group	*Row Total*
Site	Complier	Noncomplier	Complier	Noncomplier		
Boston	17	4	7	1	10	*39*
Los Angeles	22	4	10	3	14	*53*
New York	16	5	4	1	4	*30*
Total	55	13	21	5	28	*122*

Note: The sites indicate metro areas, though all public housing developments targeted by MTO were in the central city. The response rate for the interview sample was 70 percent and the adjusted cooperation rate 79 percent. The ethnographic sample (N=39 families) was drawn from the interview sample, as described in text.

Table A.2. Descriptive Statistics: Three-City Interview and Ethnographic Samples Compared to Interim Impacts Evaluation Sample

	Interim Evaluation Sample (n=2,720 households)	Qualitative Interview Sample (n=122 households)	Ethnographic Sample (n=39 households)
Demographic traits			
Adult female	98%	98%	95%
Children female	53%	53%	49%
Household head is black non-Hispanic	43%	54%	46%
Household head is Hispanic	46%	35%	39%
Family size: 2-4 children under 18	64%	68%	62%
Locational and social outcomes			
2000 Neighborhood poverty rate (2002 locations)			
Living in a neighborhood less than 10% poor	8%	10%	14%
Living in a neighborhood more than 30% poor	58%	50%	35%
Residential mobility: Moved 1 to 3 times	58%	61%	69%
Adult ever completed high school	37%	41%	36%
Adult employed	52%	55%	44%
Total household income (mean)	$16,703	$18,514	$16,278
Respondent or child receiving TANF	31%	40%	53%
Adult Body Mass Index (BMI, mean)	30	30	30
Adult psychological distress index (mean)	0.33	0.32	0.35
Child psychological distress index (mean)	0.27	0.21	0.22
Child ever arrested	12%	16%	28%
Youth risky behavior index (mean)	0.40	0.36	0.38

Note: The Interim Impacts Evaluation Sample column includes three of the five MTO sites: Boston, Los Angeles, and New York. Column headers indicate total sizes for each sample; cell sizes vary minimally due to missing data. Locations are as of the 2002 Interim Impacts Survey (Orr et al. 2003). "TANF" is Temporary Assistance to Needy Families. BMI of 30 or higher indicates obesity.

one to two hours; interviews with adolescents and young adults averaged 45 minutes to an hour. The young-adult children are the first cohort of MTO's "next generation" to age into adulthood, and prior research on MTO has ignored the experiences of this age group entirely. Including them allowed us to examine the transition to adulthood and, in many cases, to make sibling comparisons within families.

To enhance validity and extend our data on priority themes, the *ethnographic fieldwork* added direct observation to what participants reported about their attitudes, choices, and outcomes. The fieldwork focused on the core constructs of families' lives, such as daily routines to "get life accomplished" (Burton 1997), important social relations, and the details of engagement (or lack of same) in their neighborhood of residence and other neighborhoods, such as those where relatives or close friends lived. The fieldwork was a blend of "naturalistic" or unstructured interviewing, semistructured interviewing, and direct observation of family life inside and outside the home. This core-constructs approach, combining informal interviewing and participant observation, provides a robust source of inferences about social processes and other causal mechanisms to complement formal interviews that are focused heavily on the outcomes themselves (Weisner 1996). Unlike more established traditions in ethnography, such as community, in-school, or peer-group studies, family-focused ethnography centers on developing rich, valid accounts of family-level decisions and outcomes, including efforts to support children, elders, or other family members.

We analyzed both the interview and fieldnote data using MTO's treatment-group structure and also analyzed the fieldnotes (beyond that structure) on the basis of exposure (years in low-poverty environments or suburban school districts or both), patterned social relations, and other dimensions. The latter centered on within-treatment-group variation.

A team of trained coders coded the approximately 300 hours of transcripts for key themes and issues; the coding included checks for interrater reliability. The coded transcripts were loaded into QSR6 qualitative database software, which allows for crosscutting analysis by codes and respondent characteristics (e.g., sorting by adolescent girls talking about safety and school). The ethnographic fieldnotes (for a total of 430 visits) were linked to the interview transcripts and selected interim evaluation data, coded by trained fieldworkers (with reliability checks), and then analyzed using EthnoNotes, which facilitates multisite team ethnography (Lieber, Weisner, and Presley 2003). This included both family and group-level analyses in the form of memo-ing (Miles and Huberman 1994).

The third element of the study, which we term *scans*, focused on the changing contexts in which MTO families are leading their lives, for example the economic and social changes at the neighborhood, city, and metropolitan levels that are reshaping the geography of risks and resources over time. The scans analyzed census and administrative data at the neighborhood, city, metropolitan region, and other levels, including data from the National Center for Education Statistics, the National Neighborhood Crime Study, and other sources.

Consistent with a mixed-method, and not just multi-method, research strategy, we have triangulated our data analyses both within and between key components of the study, for example: among the ethnographic field-note analysis, housing market trend analysis, and statistical survey analysis to understand housing trajectories (types) over time; and within the ethnographic analysis to understand important social relations, as *reported* by MTO participants and also *observed* directly by our fieldworkers.

As discussed in chapter 1, the integration of distinct types of data is crucial for generating richer, more valid results and actionable specifics to guide decision-makers. Mixed-method approaches are also crucial for building better theory, over time, from a base of complex and mixed results. But it is important to appropriately interpret the different types of data and appreciate their limitations.

LESSONS LEARNED

As the reader will have guessed by now, we learned our biggest lessons the hard way. First, many of the systems established to support and regulate modern research in the last century—that is, human subjects protection, data storage, even personnel management—are simply not adequate for "networked" twenty-first century projects, in which activities are distributed across geography and institutional boundaries. At one point, for example, each member of our team of 15 ethnographers was supervised by a principal investigator living in Boston, submitted weekly invoices to the Urban Institute in Washington, and shared their data via encrypted e-mail or stored them on a secure, Web-based server at UCLA's Fieldwork Lab. Each of us had to patch together and master a host of information systems—one for fieldnote coding and secure storage, another for reporting hours and getting paid, a third for exchanging nonsensitive data, others for group scheduling—in order for the project to function effectively. And each participating institution presented its own rules. At one point, that included the City University of New York, Harvard, MIT, the Urban Institute, and UCLA. The study had to clear three human subjects reviews at three institutional review boards (Harvard, MIT, UI), each with its own priorities and special requests. We had not anticipated the bureaucratic complexity we would face, and dealing with it consumed valuable time. Our happiest discovery was BaseCamp—an award-winning software application that made the analysis and reporting stage of our work infinitely easier, with a host of intuitive functions tailor-made for distributed team projects. Collaborators need these kinds of management tools, and perhaps a few waivers or up-front interorganizational agreements, to smooth the path.

Second, it is vitally important for the study leaders (principal investigators) to understand and value the integration of methods—what it means to do integrated, *mixed*-method work, as distinct from running *multiple* methods in parallel. But it is also vital, and much harder, for every research assistant to understand and value that integration as well. On one hand, the implications of this for research design and management are straightforward: cross-training of staff, developing data collection instruments and coding schemes in an integrated way, and constant reinforcement of the need to triangulate across data sources during the analysis and reporting. But doing those things is not easy even for veteran researchers with advanced training. It is harder still for newcomers to research, who are eager to do discrete (read: neatly contained) analysis, to acquire and feel mastery of one method at a time, and even to draw inferences as they go rather than go through the laborious task of mining not one but two or more mountains of qualitative data, alongside quantitative analyses. Next time, we would invest even more in integrating early and often—all the way to the finish.

But third, our overall division of labor for the qualitative components of our study—focus the in-depth interviews on a broad array of issues and focus the ethnographic fieldwork on core constructs first and foremost—paid off well. It can be challenging to convince eager graduate students or other research assistants that the details of daily routines and social relations are worth learning and relearning (updating) on each visit. Other topics cry out for attention, especially "opportunity" topics, such as experiences at school or in the job market. But investigating the core routines and social relations of family life provides much more robust views of exposure (to particular kinds of settings) and interaction than the obvious alternative: using ethnographic fieldwork to "scoop up" little bits of data along a broad waterfront. Such scooping up would turn ethnography, in the end, into mere serial qualitative interviewing, robbing the method of its principal value: naturalistic, rather than formal, interaction with subjects and, by combining interviewing with sharp observation, the power to reveal meanings and motivations and place them in context. In hindsight, focusing first and foremost on the core constructs was also vital since we underestimated the time it would take to connect consistently, for in-depth conversation and observation, with our subjects. The adults were willing, in principle, to participate, but hard to rely on, given their preferences, the ups and downs of family life, and circumstances beyond their controls. The young boys in particular, signed on but remained more wary, on average, and more skeptical about the usefulness of spending time with field researchers than their female counterparts. Travel distances ate up the clock as well, especially in sprawling greater Los Angeles, where the MTO sample is scattered across hundreds of square miles. In the end, it was simply not possible, on time and on budget, to complete most of the additional topical work we had planned.

Our final and most important message about mixed-method research is the simplest one: Dare to try. Researchers, like their subjects, have comfort zones, and so do their funders and other partners. But the questions we pursue demand that we make a career-long habit of stretching ourselves. This is especially true where complex, ambitious, and easily misunderstood social interventions are concerned. The stakes are too high to do any less.

Notes

CHAPTER ONE

1. See the Housing Act of 1949; and Millennial Housing Commission (2001); Newman and Schnare (1997).

CHAPTER TWO

1. "Hurricane Katrina," *The Economist* (September 1, 2005).

2. "Katrina's Silver Lining," *New York Times*, September 8, 2005.

3. See, for example, Leslie Kaufman, "An Uprooted Underclass, under the Microscope," *New York Times* (September 25, 2005); "A Voucher for Your Thoughts: Katrina and Public Housing," the *Economist* (September 24, 2005); Xavier de Souza Briggs and Margery Austin Turner, "Fairness in New New Orleans," *The Boston Globe* (October 5, 2005); and Briggs (2006).

4. Emily Brady, "In the Projects, Hope and Hard Knocks," *New York Times* (April 13, 2008).

5. Ghettos are distinguishable from ethnic "quarters," or what are now termed *enclaves*, where members of a given ethnic group largely choose to settle (Marcuse 2005). Such quarters were recorded at least as far back as ancient Rome (Briggs 2004). They helped define the immigrant city at the turn of the twentieth century in America, and they once again dot the urban and suburban landscape in a new era of immigration (Alba and Nee 2003).

6. We refer here to "family" housing units occupied primarily by working-age adults and their children, not the units set aside for elderly households, which remained predominantly white in many cities. The latter, as courts found, were often "protected" by discriminatory local agencies.

7. Originally planned as two developments—Pruitt for blacks and Igoe, across the street, for whites—the Pruitt-Igoe complex became a black-only development when the Supreme Court ruled planned segregation unconstitutional (Rainwater 1970).

8. Whites migrated, too, and a significant pattern of white outmigration to newer and more affluent suburbs, as well as continued white avoidance of neighborhoods with a noticeable black presence, made many of the "destination neighborhoods" of middle-class minorities progressively more segregated and poor over time (Ellen 2000; Orfield 1997; Quillian 1999). This unwelcome pattern does not diminish the impact of minority middle-class outmigration on inner-city ghetto poverty—the point on which we focus in text. On the challenges facing the black middle class, as well as its political interests and attitudes toward race integration and class status, see Pattillo (2000, 2007) and Lacy (2007).

9. Paul Krugman, "Republicans and Race," *New York Times* (November 19, 2007).

10. Small and Newman (2001) examine the impact of Wilson's work on later scholarship about the family, culture, and neighborhood in relation to persistent poverty.

11. Specifically, a census tract had to be one standard deviation or more about the national mean on all four of these traits to be considered an underclass tract. For details, see Ricketts and Sawhill (1988), and Mincy and Wiener (1993). Jargoswky and Yang (2006) finds the same divergence between high-poverty concentration and underclass social traits for in the latest (Census 2000) analysis, as well as a greater decline in the number of underclass as opposed to high-poverty neighborhoods. See also Jargowsky (2003), Kingsley and Pettit (2003). On the relevance of the underclass concept for poor Hispanics and their neighborhoods, see J. Moore (1993).

12. Bane and Ellwood found that most "entries" and "exits" to and from poverty status owed to a *change in income* (thanks to losing or getting a job, for example) or a *change of family status* (thanks to marriage or separation), or both.

13. Pattillo (2003) has argued for a "wide-lens" definition of urban ghettos, one more consistent with early twentieth-century conceptions of spatial exclusion and disadvantage, as opposed to the "tight" metric of extreme poverty concentration employed since Wilson (1987). A larger number of neighborhoods, she points out, and many nonpoor people, especially middle-class and lower middle-class African Americans and Hispanics, suffer the costs of ghettoization.

14. For a critical history of urban renewal at work, see, in particular, M. Anderson (1964), Gans (1962), Jacobs (1961), and Keyes (1969). For a contemporary look at the long-run costs of urban renewal for black communities, as well as newer threats from urban redevelopment, see Fullilove (2004).

15. See, for example, reviews and evidence in Briggs (2008), Fullilove (2004), Goering and Feins (2003), Greenbaum (2006), Imbroscio (2008), Joseph et al. (2007), Pattillo (2007), Popkin et al. (2004), Popkin and Cove (2007), Schwartz and Tajbahksh (1997),), and Venkatesh (2000, 2006).

16. The Center on Budget and Policy Priorities estimates that a total of 200,000 units were demolished between 1995, when Congress and the Clinton Administration agreed to rescind a "one-for-one" replacement requirement, and 2008—75 percent of these as part of HOPE VI. The remaining 25 percent were demolished under a federal "viability" rule, enacted by Congress in 1996, under which housing agencies identified and demolished severely distressed developments with low vacancy rates that could not be redeveloped cost effectively.

17. HUD defines "very low income" as at or below 50 percent of the median income of the county or metropolitan area in which the voucher-using family chooses to live. HUD conducts rent surveys and sets ceiling rents, as well as housing quality standards that the local agency administering the voucher program must ensure via property inspections. See U.S. Department of Housing and Urban Development, "Housing Choice Vouchers Fact Sheet" (no date) online at www.hud. gov. The typical voucher holder lives in a poor and somewhat racially segregated neighborhood, though not as poor or segregated as the typical resident of public housing (Newman and Schnare 1997), as we discuss in chapters 3 and 6. Were this not the case—that is, if vouchers delivered broad neighborhood "choice," as countless policy statements have hoped—planners might simply have provided housing vouchers without the special assistance or requirements that MTO included.

18. See, for example, Steve Sailer's blog at isteve.blogspot.com/2008/06/hanna-rosin-in-atlantic-american-murder.html (June 8, 2008) [accessed June 26, 2008].

19. *From Poverty to Prosperity: A National Strategy to Cut Poverty in Half* (Washington, DC: Center for American Progress, 2007).

20. Acknowledging the challenges of defining ghetto-poor neighborhoods, we use the figure calculated by Jargowsky and Yang (2006). This is poor persons living in census tracts that met Ricketts and Sawhill's (1988) definition of "underclass," with exceptionally high levels on four measures: males out of the labor force, school dropout, unwed parenting, and dependence on public assistance. Jargowsky and Yang found the total population of such tracts to be just under 2.2 million and note that the main reason for decline in the number of tracts that meet the underclass definition was a drop in high levels of high school dropout and public assistance receipt. Fifty-seven percent of underclass tracts are also high-poverty tracts, with a poverty rate of 40 percent or more.

CHAPTER THREE

1. These and other data in the chapter are drawn from agency documents and published research, as well as John Goering's notes and recollections of his more than two decades on the HUD policy and research staff.

2. No author, "Refugee from Racial Hostility is Killed in Apartment Robbery," *New York Times* (September 3, 1993).

3. The subsidies were called "certificates" at the time, but we have used the more universal label. Federal involvement in such "demand-side" programs, that is, programs that subsidize the consumer in the private market rather than providing a unit at below-market rent (a supply-side strategy), dates back to the Section 23 Leased Housing Program created in 1961. HUD launched a major test of household behavior in response to demand-side subsidies with the Experimental Housing Allowance Program in 1970. A regular program was authorized by Section 8 of the Housing and Community Development Act in 1974, which included a rental "certificate" program. Vouchers, with similar requirements, were added in 1983. In 1998, the Quality Housing and Work Responsibility Act consolidated the demand-side programs into a single Housing Choice Voucher program, though the label "Section 8" is still commonly used. For details on how the program works, see information online at www.hud.gov or the Center on Budget and Policy Priorities' housing policy and research program.

4. The key concern is selection bias. The first generation of Gautreaux studies compared families who had successfully moved to suburban areas, and were still living in those areas year later, with those who moved within the central city. They did not include families who tried to relocate outside the city but failed or those who had moved to the suburbs but later moved back to the city—meaning the early research probably exaggerated the average effects of the program by focusing on a select group. Managers kept limited information on participants, making it hard to track down a more representative program population years later. Gautreaux did not employ random assignment, but rather screened and selected participants, in the early years, whom counselors thought could succeed in suburban locations. As such, there was no way to disaggregate the effects of housing mobility counseling from the effects of selective relocation to largely white, middle-class suburbs and their schools. See further discussion in Orr et al. (2003:3–4). Subsequent research has used administrative data and interviews covering a more

representative sample of Gautreaux program participants to enhance the validity of the original findings and generate new evidence on long-run effects (see, e.g., De Luca and Rosenbaum 2003; Keels et al. 2005).

5. Like other agencies with multifaceted missions and years of shifting oversight by Congress and the White House, HUD faced competing pressures. On one hand, it had an obligation, under the Fair Housing Act of 1968, to "affirmatively further fair housing," and this included neighborhood standards for targeting low-income housing assistance (cf. Tegeler 2005). While HUD may have had wide discretion in addressing this mandate, as the Reagan-Bush years illustrated, this mandate could be extremely difficult, if not impossible, to pursue in the face of political opposition. It did not help that neither Congress nor the courts had ever bolstered or clarified the broad mandate in the 1968 law.

6. HUD staff memo.

7. Housing and Community Development Act of 1992, "Conference Report" to accompany H.R. 5334 (October 5, 1992). Report 102–1017, Washington, DC: U.S. Government Printing Office. See Section 152 on MTO's authorization.

8. Kenneth J. Cooper, "Gingrich Pledges a Major Package of Spending Cuts Early Next Year," *Washington Post* (December 13, 1994).

9. About 9 in 10 MTO volunteers came from public housing, while 1 in 10 were living in multifamily "assisted" housing developments, run by private, for-profit or nonprofit landlords rather than public housing agencies. Both groups came, by the program's design, from high-poverty neighborhoods. For simplicity, we use "public housing" hereafter to describe both groups.

10. Research conducted under the MTO small-grants competition was circulated and critiqued in 1997 and compiled and published in Goering and Feins (2003).

11. Extensive research on all of these programs is publicly available online, from Abt Associates (HOPE VI, MTO), MDRC (Jobs-Plus), Public/Private Ventures (Bridges to Work), and the Urban Institute (HOPE VI, MTO). Some of the programs—HOPE VI, in particular—have also been discussed extensively in the popular media, trade publications in housing and community development, and scholarly journals. For an integrative review of this set of programs and discussion of their policy implications, see Turner and Rawlings (2005).

12. The housing counseling model used for MTO was derived directly from the Gautreaux program, and Gautreaux counselors trained the new MTO nonprofit groups. MTO was largely designed to replicate the core features of Gautreaux and not to find innovative new means of offering counseling advice. There was, as we emphasized in text, no rigorous evidence on the forms and effects of mobility counseling when MTO began.

13. *Notice of Funding Availability, Moving to Opportunity Demonstration*, U.S. Department of Housing and Urban Development (August 1993).

14. In 1988, Congress included a "one-strike" provision, as part of the Public Housing Drug Elimination Act, to authorize such screening and enable evictions from public and assisted housing. But HUD retained discretion over enforcement, and in 1994, only two of the five MTO sites included this screen. In 1996, one-strike became mandatory for all public housing agencies.

15. In the first phase of MTO enrollment and placement in Los Angeles, a nonprofit human service provider, Beyond Shelter, partnered with a fair-housing advocacy organization. While the former was very effective at providing early

support services, the latter organization did poorly, and the relationship between the two organizations was strained. Beyond Shelter declined to bid for second-round funding.

16. Lacking funding and other supports, the organization—an icon for fair-housing advocates for decades—closed its doors in 2006.

17. See, in particular, research on the psychological sense of threat and "invasion" that accompanies intergroup competition for material resources as relative group sizes shift (Blalock 1967; Goldsmith 2004; Pettigrew 1998).

18. Larry Carson and Pat Gilbert, "Plan to Resettle Families from Inner City Fuels Fears," *The Baltimore Sun* (July 1, 1994).

19. Larry Carson, "Housing Controversy Replay," *The Baltimore Sun* (August 7, 1994).

20. Lori Montgomery, "U.S. Plan to Spread out the Poor Creates a Storm," *Detroit Free Press* (July 14, 1994).

21. Carson and Gilbert (1994).

22. Ann Mariano, "Hill Panel Halts Plan to Move Poor families," *Washington Post* (September 3, 1994).

23. Ed Brandt, "Relocation Program Won't Grow: New Money Halted in Housing Plan for Inner City Families," *Baltimore Sun* (September 10, 1994).

24. Michael Olesker, "Playing on Fears: DePazzo Exploits Stereotype of Poor," *Baltimore Sun* (September 6, 1994).

25. Karen De Witt (March 28, 1995).

26. Senior HUD staff waited until late 1995 and then used the unspent MTO funds for a new, less intrusive demonstration program, Regional Opportunity Counseling (ROC), which operated for a few years in 16 public housing authorities.

27. For evidence on the property value impacts of subsidized housing, both developments and vouchers, see Ellen (2007), Freeman and Botein (2002), and Galster, Tatian, and Smith (1999).

28. For much of George W. Bush's presidency (2001–2006), it was the Republican-led Congress that resisted the administration's deepest proposed cuts and most sweeping reforms in voucher allocation. Still, funding dropped, and the lack of stability in funding thwarted program planning and management at the local level. See, for example, Douglas Rice and Barbara Sard, "The Effects of the Federal Budget Squeeze on Low-Income Housing Assistance," Washington, DC: Center on Budget and Policy Priorities, February 2007; and Poverty and Race Research Action Council, "The Section 8 Program and Access to Opportunity: An Agenda for Policy Reform," Washington, DC: Author, 2007. Under Democratic leadership after the elections of November 2006, Congress proposed improvements to the HOPE VI public housing redevelopment program and reforms to the housing voucher program to stabilize funding levels, streamline features that discourage landlord participation, tie vouchers to subsidized developments where units will remain affordable, and enhance clients' access to better units and neighborhoods. See Barbara Sard and Leah Staub, "House Bill Makes Significant Improvements in 'HOPE VI' Public Housing Revitalization Program," Washington, DC: Center on Budget and Policy Priorities, January 2008; and Will Fischer and Barbara Sard, "Senate Bill Would Update and Streamline Housing Voucher Program," Washington, DC: Center on Budget and Policy Priorities, March 2008. We discuss these developments, as well as future prospects, in the book's concluding chapter.

29. Rachel L. Swarns, "Top U.S. Housing Official Resigns," *New York Times* (March 31, 2008).

CHAPTER FOUR

1. Here, we allude to the distinction between measures to *reduce* segregation levels by changing patterns of residential settlement (who lives where) and measures to mitigate the social *costs* of segregation, such as spatial disparities in exposure to violence and other problems, without affecting the levels of segregation, that is, without changing who lives where. See Briggs (2005b).

2. See, in particular, Berube, Katz, and Lang, editors (2003, 2005, 2006) and Pack (2002).

3. Leaving aside the MTO metros, a second subgroup of the "winning" regions—metro Charlotte, North Carolina; Las Vegas, Nevada; and Phoenix, Arizona; for example—had no large industrial base in the past, and therefore no major deindustrialization to recover from, but instead boomed with the expansion of service jobs and the migration trend toward the Sun Belt in recent decades. While these areas have been hard hit by the foreclosure crisis, their structural foundations, including attractive locations and relatively low cost of living, are likely to keep them competitive for years to come.

4. Authors' calculations, using Census Bureau data.

5. The Boston Indicators Project (Boston: The Boston Foundation, 2008).

6. Sam Roberts, "In Manhattan, Poor Make 2 Cents for Every Dollar to the Rich," *New York Times* (September 4, 2005).

7. For a review of the content and tone of reports by major national commissions on housing needs, as well as scholarly research, from the late 1960s forward, see Briggs (2005).

8. HUD defines worst-case housing needs for unassisted renters as: falling below 50 percent of area median income and either (a) paying more than half of household income for housing ("severe rent burden") or (b) living in "severely substandard" housing or both.

9. Worst-case needs grew among all major racial groups, and of the 5.99 million total reported by HUD, 3.1 million were non-Hispanic white, 1.3 million were non-Hispanic black, and 1.2 million were Hispanic in 2005.

10. Like the trends in the poor population that we discussed in chapter 2, the worst-case needs population is dynamic, with a large number of households reporting short spells of worst-case needs and a smaller share facing long spells. Based on the Census Bureau's Survey of Income and Program Participation, HUD reported, for example, that 33 percent of the households with worst-case needs in 2002 had "exited" that status a year later, though most of those still reported "moderate rent burden" (paying between 30 and 50 percent of their income for rent). Some households exited by receiving housing assistance, some by income gains, and some by becoming homeowners.

11. HUD determines the fair market rent (FMR) at the 40 percent ("modest") level of the median gross rent, based on local market surveys. The average national FMR for a two-bedroom apartment was $900 for 2007. As of spring 2008, federal policy would leave that FMR far out of reach in lower-income households in much of the country even under the scheduled increases in the minimum wage, up to $7.25 per hour by July 2009 (NLIHC 2008).

12. One reason New York City has seen growth primarily in the luxury condo market over the past decade is that by the late 1990s, developing unsubsidized rental housing for any income group had become financially unfeasible (Salama, Schill, and Stark 1999).

13. For an in-depth historical analysis of suburban exclusion, see also Fogelson (2005).

14. Clearly, some types of moves have long been associated with social mobility as well as escape from undesirable places. But as every parent knows, moving can be harmful as well. Recent research on child and adolescent development has underscored the deleterious effects of frequent moving on children and adolescents, net of other factors, including poorer emotional health, weaker academic outcomes, strained family relationships, smaller and less stable peer networks, and even a greater risk of gravitating toward deviant or delinquent peers after arriving in new schools and communities (Barlett 1997; Haynie and South 2005; Haynie, South, and Bose 2006; Pribesh and Downey 1999).

15. For example, HUD can enable local housing agencies to apply for "exemption rents," especially where such flexibility would enable voucher users to lease up in better neighborhoods and agencies can make vouchers portable across jurisdictions.

16. The opposite trend occurred across states and multistate census regions: Income became more evenly distributed in the latter half of the twentieth century. The pattern, argue Massey and Fischer (2003), reflects a growth in affluence in the South as well as increases in poverty in the Northeast and Midwest over a long period of economic restructuring and migration across regions.

17. The sharp decline in extremely poor tracts in a single decade was driven largely by the "exit" of such tracts to the next category down (moderately poor), while the expansion in moderately poor (20–40 percent poor) tracts was driven by those exits (one-quarter of the total change) and by many nonpoor (<20 percent poor) tracts becoming moderately poor (about one-half of the total change; Briggs and Keys 2009).

18. Using Earned Income Tax Credit data for 1990 and 2005, researchers found that the working poor were more heavily concentrated in very poor neighborhoods by 2005 (Kneebone and Berube 2008).

19. The migration of much larger numbers of poor immigrants to metro Los Angeles, primarily from Mexico, is clearly part of the story. But different spatial patterns in economic restructuring across U.S. regions, as well as other factors, may also be playing a role.

20. Peter Dreier, "Poverty in the Suburbs," the *Nation* (September 20, 2004). World Wide Web page www.thenation.com [accessed April 30, 2008].

21. The researchers defined *middle-income neighborhoods* as census tracts with an average income in the range of 80 to 120 percent of median income for the metro area. Unlike studies using the federal poverty line, this area median income (AMI) approach controls for differences in median income and cost of living, and thus allows standardized comparisons, across metro areas.

22. Blacks, in particular, are unlikely to exit racially mixed or predominantly black neighborhoods for predominantly white ones, and if they do enter the latter type, they are likely to exit them for the first two types—a trajectory pattern that helps reproduce major differences in the kinds of neighborhoods that blacks and whites experience over time (South and Crowder 1997). Hispanic fortunes appear to vary by major national groupings, with Mexican Americans showing

patterns similar to those of blacks, and Cuban Americans approximating whites. Most Asian Americans show patterns similar to whites, with the notable exception of low-income Southeast Asian refugees, who are ghettoized in the housing market much like low-income blacks.

23. High rates of immigration through the 1990s and 2000s have combined with concentrated settlement patterns to decrease rates of Asian and Hispanic exposure to whites over the past two decades. In part, this reflects a clustering that is typical for newly arrived immigrants, especially those whose first language is not English. Immigrants arrive faster than they can "diffuse" (spread out) across the housing market; plus ethnic enclaves offer a range of supports that new arrivals can use, from finding housing to securing a job and childcare, obtaining familiar food, celebrating religious and cultural traditions, and more (Alba and Nee 2003).

24. Katz and Turner (2007) summarize the locational data for rental housing produced, for example, by HUD's HOME block grant program and the Treasury Department's Low Income Housing Tax Credit (LIHTC) program, which is now the principal source of capital subsidy for affordable rental housing production in the United States. See also Goering, Kamely, and Richardson (1994), Massey and Denton (1993), and Schill and Wachter (1995).

25. Many "affordable" housing programs primarily serve low- and moderate-income families—families between 50 and 80 percent of area median income or 80 and 100 percent, respectively, rather than the very low-income families (with incomes below 50 percent of area median) that are the exclusive focus of the public housing and rental voucher programs. One reason for this is that most housing developments are not financially feasible if they try to serve very low-income tenants who do not bring additional, ongoing subsidies (e.g., vouchers). Reaching the very low-income group is known as deep targeting, and some of the most important developments in the housing field—including the effort to develop more mixed-income housing in suburban areas—do such deep targeting only rarely. When they do so, it is often because vouchers are "tied" to the "hard" units that also receive capital subsidies (see Citizens Housing and Planning Association 2008; Katz and Turner 2007). In Montgomery County, Maryland's much-admired inclusionary zoning program, the local public housing agency is able to acquire a small share of units mixed into new, market-rate, multifamily housing developments—creating a portfolio of "scattered-site" public housing to serve very low-income tenants (Hogan 1996).

26. Economists Sandra Newman and Joseph Harkness (2000) found, using a geocoded version of the Panel Study of Income Dynamics matched to housing assistance data, that between 1968 and 1990, nearly two-thirds (62 percent) of assisted households moved from one extremely poor neighborhood to another, another 18 percent moved to a neighborhood between 30 and 40 percent poor, 10 percent moved to a neighborhood between 20 and 30 percent poor, and just 6 percent moved to a neighborhood less than 20 percent poor.

27. See Will Fischer and Barbara Sard, "Senate Bill Would Update and Streamline Housing Voucher Program" (Washington, DC: Center on Budget and Policy Priorities, March 2008).

CHAPTER FIVE

1. See, for example, Ellen and Turner (2003); Leventhal and Brooks-Gunn (2000); Leventhal and Brooks-Gunn (2003); Sampson, Morenoff, and Gannon-Rowley (2002).

2. See for example Goetz 2003, Imbroscio 2007, or Rosin 2008.

3. For a discussion of the long-term implications of these threats for the life chances of low-income adolescent girls, and how this affects risky sexual behavior, see Furstenberg, Brooks-Gunn, and Morgan (1987) and Kendall-Tackett, Williams, and Finkelhor (1993).

4. Not surprisingly, fear of sexual victimization accounts for gender differences in adolescents' fear of other forms of victimization (May 2001). Further, girls' sense of the danger posed by sexual victimization may be compounded by the risk of contracting AIDS and other sexually transmitted diseases; girls in urban contexts are more likely than their suburban counterparts to voice fear of the physical dangers associated with sexual intercourse, such as vulnerability to AIDS and pregnancy (Tolman 1996).

5. Several studies of urban adolescents found that a measure of perceived neighborhood "ambient hazards"—including experience of personal threats as well as disorder—was positively associated with early sex and mental health problems, once family and neighborhood socioeconomic status were held constant (Aneshensel and Sucoff 1996; Upchurch, Sucoff, and Levy-Storms 1999). Links between urban adolescents' reports of exposure to neighborhood disorder and their increased likelihood of engaging in risky sexual behavior have also been observed (Chen et al. 1997; Harding 2006).

6. See work on low-income female caregivers (e.g., for review and discussion, see Quane et al. 2008).

7. Of the 71 youth who discussed peer influences, 23 boys mentioned peers as good influences, as compared to 26 girls; in contrast 15 boys said their peers were bad influences, while only 7 girls cited negative influences.

CHAPTER SIX

1. Strictly speaking, collective efficacy centers on the *micro*-neighborhood. It includes elements of "proximate" trust and cohesion, as well as expectations about what others will do, that have meaning in a very localized conception of who one's neighbors are. In our MTO research, as in other studies, parents and their children sometimes defined "neighborhood" much more expansively, for example as a catchment area for daily routines, which might be carried out largely by car and span miles in each direction.

2. On the concept of excessive obligations and its implications for upward mobility, see also Portes and Sensenbrenner (1993).

3. On "the strength of weak ties," as well as ties across boundaries of race and socioeconomic status, see Granovetter (1973, 1995) and Briggs (2007).

4. In Herbert Gans's (1962) early formulation, neighbors are found, but friends are chosen, and race, class, and life stage, not physical proximity (or propinquity) alone, appear to be the consistent drivers of friendship in neighborhoods (see review in Briggs 1997).

5. This is a form of *free riding*, that is, individuals benefiting from stocks of social capital even if they do not contribute to those stocks through interaction (Putnam 2000).

6. That is, this mode of analysis does not determine "treatment effects," in the scientific shorthand.

7. Recall that this sample includes both the experimental compliers and control-group members, unlike the complier-only discussion (of "movers' experiences") earlier in the chapter, where we discussed the typology.

8. See, in particular, Menjívar (1995) and Dominguez and Watkins (2003). As Menjívar shows in the case of Salvadorean immigrants, for example, "The new-comers could not earn money to start supporting themselves quickly after they arrived, while relatives already in the U.S. not only had to support the newcomers but could not even get back the money they had lent the person to make the jour-ney north. These circumstances were often the basis for hostile and potentially explosive situations within families. By cutting off the flow of material assistance, and hindering the sharing of in-kind services, this situation effectively debased the viability of a network because it undermined the reciprocity upon which kinship support networks are sustained" (229).

9. Note that this is not a summary of difference findings, for example from sta-tistical analysis. It is clear from the in-depth, qualitative evidence on the movers' experiences. And what about MTO children? Our data do not allow us to care-fully address the question of whether the experiment had the effect of encourag-ing school-age children to form more diverse friendships, for example, at school. The evidence in chapter 9 is that relocation gave at least some MTO youth access to dramatically different social worlds than they knew in high-poverty neighbor-hoods left behind. And this was largely through school-based friendships and acquaintanceships. New friendships in new worlds came with dramatically dif-ferent expectations about appropriate behavior and cultural knowledge—what scholars term *cultural capital*—as well.

CHAPTER SEVEN

1. Jason DeParle, "The Slamming Door," *New York Times Magazine* (October 20, 1996).

2. Barry Schwartz, Hazel Rose Markus, and Alana Conner Snibbe, "Is Freedom Just Another Word for Many Things to Buy? That Depends on Your Class Status," *New York Times Magazine* (February 26, 2006). See also B. Schwartz (2004).

3. The TOT column is not a simple comparison of compliers to control-group members. It is that comparison adjusted (divided) by the lease-up rate, by site. This is to allow for the fact that not all members of the control group, had they been assigned instead to the experimental group, would have leased up (relo-cated) successfully in low-poverty neighborhoods. The TOT figures thus estimate the benefit of being in the experimental- group subset who leased up as compared to a hypothetical subset of the control group that would have done so. See Orr et al. (2003:B7-B10).

4. From the standpoint of causal inference, additional moves introduce addi-tional family-level selection effects on locational outcomes over time, making it difficult to attribute particular outcomes to the intervention as one moves beyond treatment-group differences to analyze outcomes for distinct subgroups within the treatment groups (as we do). For this reason in particular, most of our results are descriptive in nature, not presented as unbiased estimates of treatment effects, that is, of *program causality* (cf. Kling, Liebman, and Katz 2007).

5. When all subsidies are considered, of course, middle- and upper-income households receive much more support from government—largely in the form of federal tax deductions that subsidize homeowners.

6. There is a large research literature. See, in particular, Clark and Dieleman (1996), Newman and Duncan (1979), Rossi (1955), Speare (1974), and Speare, Goldstein, and Frey (1975).

7. Most demographic research on housing patterns describes aggregate patterns for groups over time, not the *trajectories* of individual households, obscuring important features of housing choice and also of supply. A recent body of research finds that blacks are far more likely than whites to move from one poor neighborhood to another and also to reenter a poor neighborhood fairly quickly after residing outside of one. The latter factor—"recurrence"—helps explain blacks' much longer exposure than whites to neighborhood poverty over time (Quillian 2003; South and Crowder 1997; Sharkey 2008; Timberlake 2007), a gap that is not explained by racial differences in income or household structure. That gap persisted into the 1990s, even as extreme poverty concentration declined, and appears to be dominated by black renters (Briggs and Keys 2009). Since the 1960s, geographers, sociologists, and other analysts of "vacancy chains" have modeled churning, filtering, and other *system*-level dynamics, whether with simulations or empirical data (Clark 1965; Chase 1991; Emmi and Magnusson 1994; Persky and Felsenstein 2008; White 1971). These models are of some value for studies, such as ours, that aim to understand variation in *household*-level experiences and outcomes.

8. Researchers have documented the high prevalence of these problems where public housing has been demolished and "vouchered out" in favor of mixed-income redevelopment (Popkin, Cunningham, and Burt 2005; Popkin and Cove 2007; Snell and Duncan 2006; Varady and Walker 2007) and in recent public housing desegregation programs (Pashup et al. 2005).

9. Some local housing programs appear better able than others to help assisted households navigate tight markets. For example, research on less studied markets—such as Alameda County, California, where local housing agencies are well managed—shows relatively high lease-up rates over the long run even among families who used vouchers in unfamiliar suburbs, where the rental market was often tight (Varady and Walker 2007).

10. See, in particular, Varady and Walker's (2007) study of Alameda County, California's effort to help housing-voucher holders relocate to suburban areas where few vouchers were in use.

11. This is revealing for descriptive purposes, but clearly does not allow us to attribute treatment effects, given the selectivity. Most initial relocation happened in the latter half of the decade, though the program employed the available 1990 tract poverty data. We employed Census 2000 rates for tract poverty and thus isolate transitions across neighborhood poverty levels that reflect residential mobility from any that owe to substantial change in neighborhood poverty levels. We further limit this reporting to cases for which valid address data were available at multiple observation points: at initial relocation, in the year 2000, and again at the interim evaluation point in 2002. Households not included in this analysis were somewhat more likely to be Hispanic, in the labor force, with a high school/GED, and living in a lower poverty neighborhood at the time of the interim survey, though differences were generally modest (*p*<.05, data available from the authors).

12. Families in our study reported reasons for moving for each of their address spells, from original lease-up to the qualitative interview in 2004.

13. The HOPE VI program replaces public housing developments with mixed-income developments, offering a share of the new units to prior residents. But public housing agencies, at the MTO sites and elsewhere, also carry out large-scale "modernization" programs from time to time, and these require tenants to resettle.

Some tenant households do not return to their public housing unit following the modernization work.

14. We avoid any estimates of prevalence here and employ a case-study approach because we were able to collect valid data on multiple housing searches only for a subset of families (n=19).

CHAPTER EIGHT

1. Alliance for School Choice, *www.allianceforschoolchoice.org/New/SchoolChoice. html* [accessed May 28, 2008].

2. METCO is extremely popular among low-income parents in inner-city Boston and remains heavily oversubscribed due to funding limitations. In-depth research indicates that many of its participants struggle to straddle the different social expectations at home and school but believe the benefits outweigh the strains over the long run (Eaton 2001). In the next chapter, we return to this theme of youth adapting to new expectations in new settings (after relocation).

3. This section draws primarily on the ethnographic cases, that is, the subset of 39 families for whom we have both in-depth qualitative interviews and in-depth fieldnote data.

4. The interim impacts evaluation administered its own nationally standardized protocol—the Woolcock-Johnson achievement tests for math and reading—rather than relying on school grades, because of the variability in grading and curricular emphasis across schools and school districts (Orr et al., 2003).

5. Sanbonmatsu et al. (2006:31) acknowledge that self reports may reflect different frames of reference, for example higher expectations on the part of young experimental compliers who never attended inner-city schools. Also, other mediators of educational outcomes, such as adults' employment or parenting practices, are less amenable to relocation-only interventions, and MTO interim survey data suggested minimal impacts of the program on those.

6. Our calculations, using interim impacts evaluation survey data provided by Abt Associates with HUD approval.

7. Across all five MTO sites, experimental compliers who were attending school in the same district at baseline and the interim survey mark four to seven years later were somewhat less likely (23.7 percent vs. 37 percent) to have been school choosers (our calculations, using interim survey data).

8. Our analysis does not focus on the question of whether school preferences differ by race and class, for which research evidence is mixed (cf. Weiher and Tedin 2002; Wells 1993). Our concern, rather, is with the character and range of those preferences among MTO families, how they interact with so-called choice sets, and whether they shift with a significant relocation.

9. We do not compare information poverty across treatment groups since the experiment was even less able to offer parents in the control group and Section 8 comparison groups significant new choices to make.

10. This refers to the experimental-complier subgroup.

11. For example, in the carefully evaluated Alum Rock school-voucher demonstration, 70 percent of low-income parents cited "location" as the primary reason for choosing their children's schools. This choice factor has been widely documented (Maddaus 1990; Hastings and Weinstein 2007).

CHAPTER NINE

1. To account for that correlation, Ong and Miller (2005) employ an instrumental variable approach.

2. The latest generation of Gautreaux research uses administrative data not only to track outcomes over longer periods of time but to ensure a broader, more representative program population.

3. The interest in bicultural or multicultural consciousness and social skill goes back at least as far as DuBois's *The Souls of Black Folk* (1903), though DuBois's emphasis was on the oppressive burden, for blacks, of trying to operate in a world run by white people's rules while knowing one would always be inferior and excluded—a pattern he called "double consciousness." This interest was revived in the late 1960s and early 1970s, especially among education researchers (see, e.g., Valentine 1971). It has also appeared frequently in literature and autobiography by persons of color, for example Maya Angelou's *I Know Why The Caged Bird Sings* (1969).

4. If there are gains to be made through relocation, it is not clear what it would take for *role modeling* or *peer effects* (which hinge on social interaction with neighbors) or what scholars call *demonstration effects* (which do not hinge on interacting, just observing) to operate effectively across race, class, or other social boundaries in neighborhoods. On the latter, see Rubinowitz and Rosenbaum (2000) and Tienda (1991). Joseph, Chaskin and Webber (2007) underline the distinction between *proximal* role modeling (up close and personal) and *distal* role modeling (resting on observation).

5. See, illustratively, Vanessa Jones, "The Ghetto Culture Machine," *Boston Globe* (April 25, 2007).

6. Liebman et al (2004:24) compare experimental and nonexperimental results from different survey populations, concluding that "estimates using non-experimental approaches are not at all consistent with those from the experimental approach, casting doubt on the validity of non-experimental estimates. Furthermore, the selection patterns necessary to reconcile the experimental and non-experimental results are complex and differ across subgroups, suggesting that it will not generally be possible to identify the direction of bias in non-experimental estimates."

7. Data on business establishments come from Census Zip Business Patterns (BP), on earnings from the Census Transportation Planning Package (CTPP), Part 2, by place of work and industry, on overall turnover in the job type from Local Employment Dynamics (LED) data, and on MTO residential locations from Abt Associates tracking data for the program population (thanks to HUD). The LED data were not available for other MTO metros.

8. For example, we calculated a low-wage net aggregate job growth indicator, by industry, for each MTO participant's zip code at the time of the interim survey as follows:

$$\begin{array}{l} N \\ J_{mk} = \Sigma \; T_p e_c l_p g_c, \; if \; d_{mp} < k, \\ z = 1 \end{array}$$

where J_{mk} is the number of new, low-wage jobs within k distance of the MTO participant's interim survey zip code m, T_p is the number of establishments in zip code p, N is the number of zip codes, e_c is the ratio of employees to establishments in county c, l_p is the ratio of workers earning more than zero but less than $20,000 per year (about twice the minimum-wage rate) to all workers with earnings in zip code p, g_c is the ratio of the net number of jobs gained (or new jobs created) to the number of workers who were employed by the same employer in both the current and previous year in county c, zip code p is in county c, and d is distance from the centroid of zip code m to the centroid of job location zip code p. To convert the tract-level CTPP data (used to calculate l_p) to the zip code level, we applied a transformation to estimate the portion of a tract that is within a zip code, then weighted the tract-level data accordingly. Therefore, the zip code level number of workers is equal to the sum of the number of workers in all overlapping tracts, weighted by the portions of the tracts that fall within the zip code. Next, we applied a distance equation to calculate the distance between the MTO residential zip code centroids and that of each job-location zip code, and then we summed the new, low-wage jobs in all zip codes within the specified distance.

9. On the other hand, beyond 20 miles, the differences among treatment groups are nominal, since most MTO families did not move that far.

10. Additional analyses should examine changes in the competition for jobs by relocation group, yielding, in effect, a competition-adjusted view on spatial access to entry-level job opportunity in MTO metro areas. We are grateful to economist Steve Raphael for suggesting this.

11. The boys were more elusive (more difficult to schedule and keep visits with), on average, than the girls, as well as less forthcoming when we could visit with them. This is sadly consistent with the interim survey finding that "girls fared better than boys" in the process of relocation. We were therefore able to collect substantial data from boys on a more limited range of core themes—daily routines, social relations, and neighborhood engagement—and we mine those data to examine boy-girl differences in chapter 5, in particular.

12. The experience of the violent Pol Pot dictatorship, made infamous for its forced-labor "killing fields," and the arduous transition to America help explain these tragic strains (see Chan 2003, 2004). But the fact that some refugee youth in our study, who spoke only English, could not communicate with their own parents, who spoke only Cambodian, exacerbated the strains. Refugees make up a significant share of public housing residents in some cities (mostly government-designated *refugee resettlement areas*). Yet there is very little research on the refugee experience in low-income housing programs. We over-sampled Cambodians at the Los Angeles site, and hired an interpreter to enable us to interview all of the parents in these families, to address this gap.

13. Child and family development researchers have explored this theme as part of the normative conception of good parenting and also as a struggle to establish viable routines that balance childrearing (household work) and paid employment (see, e.g., Lowe and Weisner 2003; Lowe et al., 2005).

CHAPTER 10

1. Rebecca Blank, "How to Wage the Next War on Poverty: Advising and Grading the Candidates," *Pathways* (Winter 2008), pp.17–20.

2. See, for example, "Building the Stock: Targeted Project-Based Rental Assistance to Create More Deeply Affordable Permanent Housing," Citizens Housing and Planning Association and The Boston Foundation, March 2008.

3. Yet it is vital that assisted relocation not be thought of as simply a matter of counseling, more generous payment levels, or locational restrictions on vouchers. Wider landlord participation demands responsive housing agencies. Given the highly uneven performance, support, and regulation of local public housing agencies to date, policy makers should assess the role of real estate agents in this picture. In the shorthand of optimization, we have a low-income housing assistance policy—the rental voucher program, which serves about 2 million of the nation's poorest households at a given time—that is engineered to minimize cost to the taxpayer subject to an inconsistently enforced minimum standard of housing unit quality. The program lacks a robust rule or incentive to ensure the best-possible *neighborhood* quality or family *stability* in good locations, especially in the tight markets (with demand pressure and volatile prices) where those mechanisms are needed most.

4. See various reports by the Inclusionary Communities Project, Kirwan Institute, and Poverty and Race Research Action Council, plus in the case of *Thompson v. HUD*, 404 F.3d 821 (4th Cir. 2005).

APPENDIX

1. There is a large literature. See critical reviews and discussion in Briggs (1997, 2004), Brooks-Gunn, Duncan, and Aber (1997), Ellen and Turner (2003), Jencks and Mayer (1990), Leventhal and Brooks-Gunn (2000), and Sampson, Morenoff, and Gannon-Rowley (2002).

2. Our work was funded by the Annie E. Casey, Fannie Mae, Rockefeller, Smith Richardson, and William T. Grant Foundations, as well as the U.S. Department of Housing and Urban Development (which provided authorization, in addition to funding).

3. For an overview of experimental research design and analysis, see Campbell and Stanley (1963) and Shadish, Cook, and Campbell (2002). On evolving analytic approaches for social experiments specifically, see Bloom (2005), and for MTO, see Orr et al. (2003). On choice making in social programs, see Duncan, Huston, and Weisner (2007) and Schuck and Zeckhauser (2006).

4. We made multiple attempts to locate all eligible respondents, including calling (when valid phone numbers were available), sending mailings, and using the team's ethnographers to knock on respondents' doors. Abt Associates, which maintains the tracking database, requested updated information from its tracking service and searched the National Change of Address database. In addition, we sent some addresses to the National Opinion Research Center's tracking service. Finally, where possible, the team's ethnographers went to the last known address and attempted to obtain a new address and/or telephone information for the respondent. This final cooperation rate was computed excluding those we were unable to contact due to deaths or invalid addresses.

5. We also drew a special sample of Southeast Asian refugee families at the Los Angeles site, because of the large number of refugee families receiving housing assistance in Los Angeles and other refugee gateway cities and the very limited research base on their special needs.

Works Cited

Abrams, Charles. 1955. *Forbidden Neighbors: A Study of Prejudice in Housing*. New York: Harper.

Acevedo-Garcia, Dolores. 2003. "Future Directions in Residential Segregation and Health Research." *American Journal of Public Health* 93:215–221.

Alan Guttmacher Institute. 1994. "Sex and America's Teenagers." Author, New York.

Alba, Richard D. and Victor Nee. 2003. *Remaking the American Mainstream: Assimilation and Contemporary Immigration*. Cambridge, MA: Harvard University Press.

Albert, B., S. Brown, and C. Flanigan. 2003. "14 and Younger: The Sexual Behavior of Young Adolescents." National Campaign to Prevent Teen Pregnancy, Washington, DC.

Allen, Ryan P. 2007. "'I Don't Expect to Go and Beg from Them': The Logic of Refugee Social Tie Activation." Minneapolis, MN: University of Minnesota.

Alvi, Shahid, Martin D. Schwartz, Walter S. DeKeseredy, and Michael O. Maume. 2001. "Women's Fear of Crime in Canadian Public Housing." *Violence Against Women* 6:638–661.

Anderson, Elijah. 1991. *Streetwise: Race, Class, and Change in an Urban Community*. Chicago: University of Chicago Press.

———. 1994. "The Code of the Streets: How the Inner-City Environment Fosters a Need for Self-Respect and a Self-Image Based on Violence." *Atlantic*, pp. 80–94.

———. 1999. *Code of the Street: Decency, Violence, and the Moral Life of the Inner City*. New York: W.W. Norton.

Anderson, Martin. 1964. *The Federal Bulldozer: A Critical Analysis of Urban Renewal*. New York: McGraw-Hill.

Aneshensel, Carol S. and Clea A. Sucoff. 1996. "The Neighborhood Context of Adolescent Mental Health." *Journal of Health and Social Behavior* 37:293–310.

Apgar, William C. and Allegra Calder. 2005. The Dual Mortgage Market: The Persistent of Discrimination in Mortgage Lending. Pp. 101–149 in *The Geography of Opportunity: Race and Housing Choice in Metropolitan America*, edited by X. d. S. Briggs. Washington, DC: Brookings Institution Press.

Auletta, Ken. 1982. *The Underclass*. New York: Random House.

Bane, Mary Jo and David Ellwood. 1986. "Slipping Into and Out of Poverty: The Dynamics of Spells." *Journal of Human Resources* 1–23.

Barlett, Sheridan. 1997. "The Significance of Relocation for Chronically Poor Families in the U.S.A." *Environment and Urbanization* 9:121–131.

Basolo, Victoria and Mai Thi Nguyen. 2006. "Does Neighborhood Matter? The Neighborhood Conditions of Housing Voucher Holders by Race and Ethnicity." *Housing Policy Debate* 16:297–324.

Bell, Courtney. 2005. "All Choices Created Equal? How Good Parents Select 'Failing' Schools." National Center for the Study of Privatization in Education, Teachers College, Columbia University, New York.

Bellah, Robert N. 1985. *Habits of the Heart : Individualism and Commitment in American Life*. Berkeley, CA: University of California Press.

Belsky, Eric S. and Rachel Bogardus Drew. 2007. "Overview: Rental Housing Challenges and Policy Responses." Pp. 14–56 in *Revisiting Rental Housing*, edited by N. P. Retsinas and E. S. Belsky. Washington, DC: Brookings Institution Press.

Berube, Alan, Bruce Katz, and Robert Lang, editors. 2003. "Redefining Urban and Suburban America: Evidence from Census 2000, Volume 1." Washington, DC: Brookings Institution Press.

———. 2005. "Redefining Urban and Suburban America: Evidence from Census 2000, Volume 2." Washington, DC: Brookings Institution Press.

———. 2006. "Redefining Urban and Suburban America: Evidence from Census 2000, Volume 3." Washington, DC: Brookings Institution Press.

Berube, Alan and Elizabeth Kneebone. 2006. "Two Steps Back: City and Suburban Poverty Trends, 1999–2005." Washington, DC: Brookings Institution.

Blackwell, Angela Glover and Judith Bell. 2005. "Equitable Development for a Stronger Nation: Lessons from the Field." Pp. 289–309 in *The Geography of Opportunity: Race and Housing Choice in Metropolitan America*, edited by X. d. S. Briggs. Washington, DC: Brookings Institution Press.

Blalock, H. M. 1967. *Toward a Theory of Minority Group Relations*. New York: Wiley and Sons.

Bloom, Howard S. 2005. "Learning More from Social Experiments." New York: Russell Sage Foundation.

Bluestone, Barry and Bennett Harrison. 1982. *The Deindustrialization of America: Plant Closings, Community Abandonment, and the Dismantling of Basic Industry*. New York: Basic Books.

Bobo, Lawrence D., Melvin L. Oliver, James H. Johnson, and Abel Valenzuela. 2000. "Analyzing Inequality in Los Angeles." Pp. 3–50 in *Prismatic Metropolis: Inequality in Los Angeles*, edited by L. D. Bobo, M. L. Oliver, J. H. Johnson, and A. Valenzuela. New York: Russell Sage Foundation.

Bonastia, Christopher. 2006. *Knocking on The Door: The Federal Government's Attempt to Desegregate the Suburbs*. Princeton, NJ: Princeton University Press.

Bourdieu, Pierre and Jean Claude Passeron. 1990. *Reproduction in Education, Society, and Culture*. Newbury Park, CA: Sage Publications.

Bourgois, Philippe. 1995. *In Search of Respect: Selling Crack in El Barrio*. New York: Cambridge University Press.

Briggs, Xavier de Souza. 1997. "Moving Up Versus Moving Out: Neighborhood Effects in Housing Mobility Programs." *Housing Policy Debate* 8:195–234.

———. 1998. "Brown Kids in White Suburbs: Housing Mobility and the Multiple Faces of Social Capital." *Housing Policy Debate* 9:177–221.

———. 2003. "Housing Opportunity, Desegregation Strategy, and Policy Research." *Journal of Policy Analysis and Management* 22:201–206.

———. 2004. "Traps and Stepping Stones: Neighborhood Dynamics and Family Well-being." Faculty Working Paper RWP04–015, John F. Kennedy School of Government, Harvard University, Cambridge, MA.

———. 2005a. "More *Pluribus*, Less *Unum*? The Changing Geography of Race and Opportunity." Pp. 17–41 in *The Geography of Opportunity: Race and Housing Choice in Metropolitan America*, edited by X. d. S. Briggs. Washington, DC: Brookings Institution Press.

———. 2005b. "Policy and Politics: Changing the Geography of Opportunity." Pp. 310–341 in *The Geography of Opportunity: Race and Housing Choice in Metropolitan America*, edited by X. d. S. Briggs. Washington, DC: Brookings Institution Press.

———. 2007. "'Some of My Best Friends Are…': Interracial Friendships, Class, and Segregation in America." *City & Community* 6:263–290.

———. 2008. "Maximum Feasible Misdirection: Reply to Imbroscio." *Journal of Urban Affairs* 30:131–137.

Briggs, Xavier de Souza and Benjamin Keys. 2009. "Has Exposure to Poor Neighborhoods Changed in America? Race, Risk, and Housing Locations in Two Decades." *Urban Studies* 46:429–458.

Briggs, Xavier de Souza and Margery Austin Turner. 2006. "Assisted Housing Mobility and the Success of Low-Income Minority Families: Lessons for Policy, Practice, and Future Research." *Journal of Law and Social Policy* 1:25–61.

Brody, Gene H., Xiaojia Ge, Rand Conger, Frederick X. Gibbons, Velma McBride Murry, Meg Gerrad, and Ronald L. Simons. 2001. "The Influence of Neighborhood Disadvantage, Collective Socialization, and Parenting on African-American Children's Affiliation with Deviant Peers." *Child Development* 72:1231–1246.

Bronfenbrenner, Urie. 1979. *The Ecology of Human Development : Experiments by Nature and Design*. Cambridge, MA: Harvard University Press.

Brooks-Gunn, Jeanne, Greg J. Duncan, and Lawrence Aber, editors. 1997. *Neighborhood Poverty*. New York: Russell Sage Foundation.

Browning, Christopher R., Tama Leventhal, and Jeanne Brooks-Gunn. 2005. "Sexual Initiation in Early Adolescence: The Nexus of Parental and Community Control." *American Sociological Review* 70:758–778.

Bruch, Elizabeth E. and Robert D. Mare. 2006. "Neighborhood Choice and Neighborhood Change." *American Journal of Sociology* 112:667–709.

Bulman, Robert. 2004. "School-Choice Stories: The Role of Culture." *Sociological Inquiry* 74:492–519.

Burton, Linda and Robin Jarrett. 1991. "Studying African-American Family Structure and Process in Underclass Neighborhoods: Conceptual Considerations." Paper presented at *annual meeting of the American Sociological Association*. Cincinnati, OH.

Burton, Linda M. 1997. "Ethnography and the Meaning of Adolescence in High-Risk Neighborhoods." *Ethos* 25:208–217.

Burton, Linda M., Donna-Marie Winn, Howard Stevenson, and Sherri Lawson Clark. 2004. "Working with Black Clients: Considering the "Homeplace" in Marriage and Family Therapy Practices." *Journal of Marital and Family Therapy* 30:397–411.

Campbell, Donald T. and Julian C. Stanley. 1963. *Experimental and Quasi-Experimental Designs For Research*. Dallas: Houghton Mifflin.

Cannon, Lou. 2003. *Governor Reagan: His Rise to Power*. New York: Public Affairs.

Carter, Prudence L. 2005. *Keepin' It Real: School Success Beyond Black and White*. New York: Oxford University Press.

Case, Ivan D. 1991. "Vacancy Chains." *Annual Review of Sociology* 17:133–154.

Chan, Sucheng. 2003. *Not Just Victims: Conversations with Cambodian Community Leaders in the United States*. Chicago: University of Illinois Press.

———. 2004. *Survivors: Cambodian Refugees in the United States*. Chicago: University of Illinois Press.

Charles, Camille Zubrinsky. 2005. "Can We Live Together? Racial Preferences and Neighborhood Outcomes." Pp. 45–80 in *The Geography of Opportunity: Race and Housing Choice in Metropolitan America*, edited by X. d. S. Briggs. Washington, DC: Brookings Institution.

Chen, Yu-Wen, Arlene R. Stiffman, Li-Chen Cheng, and Peter Dore. 1997. "Mental Health, Social Environment, and Sexual Risk Behaviors of Adolescent Service Users: A Gender Comparison." *Journal of Child and Family Studies* 6:9–25.

Citizens Housing and Planning Association. 2008. *Strategies for Creating More Deeply Affordable Housing*. Boston: Author.

Clampet-Lundquist, Susan, Kathryn Edin, Jeffrey R. Kling, and Greg J. Duncan. 2006. "Moving At-Risk Teenagers Out of High-Risk Neighborhoods: Why Girls Fare Better than Boys." Working Paper #509, Industrial Relations Section, Princeton University, Princeton, NJ.

Clampet-Lundquist, Susan and Douglas Massey. 2006. "Neighborhood Effects on Economic Self-Sufficiency." In *Annual Meeting of the Eastern Sociological Society*. Boston, MA.

Clampet-Lundquist, Susan and Douglas S. Massey. 2008. "Neighborhood Effects on Economic Self-Sufficiency: A Reconsideration of the Moving to Opportunity Experiment." *American Journal of Sociology* 114:107–143.

Clark, William. 2005. "Intervening in the Residential Mobility Process: Neighborhood Outcomes for Low-Income Populations." *Proceedings of the National Academy of Sciences* 102:15307–12.

Clark, William A.V. 1965. "Markov Chain Analysis in Geography: An Application to the Movement of Rental Housing Areas." *Annals of the Association of American Geographers* 55:351–359.

Clark, William A.V. and Frans M. Dieleman. 1996. *Households and Housing: Choice and Outcomes in the Housing Market*. New Brunswick, NJ: Rutgers University Press.

Clotfelter, Charles T. 2004. *After Brown: The Rise and Retreat of School Desegregation*. Princeton, New Jersey: Princeton University.

Comey, Jennifer, Xavier de Souza Briggs, and Gretchen Weismann. 2008. "Struggling to Stay Out of High-Poverty Neighborhoods: Lessons from the Moving to Opportunity Experiment." The Urban Institute, Washington, DC.

Cooksey, Elizabeth, Ronald R. Rindfuss, and David K. Guilkey. 1996. "The Initiation of Adolescent Sexual and Contraceptive Behavior during Changing Times." *Journal of Health and Social Behavior* 37:59–74.

Crain, Robert L. and Amy S. Wells. 1994. "Perpetuation Theory and the Long-Term Effects of School Desegregation." *Review of Educational Research* 64:531–553.

Crane, Jonathan. 1998. *Social Programs That Work*. New York: Russell Sage Foundation.

Danielson, Michael N. 1976. *The Politics of Exclusion*. New York: Columbia University Press.

DeLuca, Stefanie and James E. Rosenbaum. 2003. "If Low-Income Blacks Are Given a Chance to Live in White Neighborhoods, Will They Stay? Examining Mobility Patterns in a Quasi-Experimental Program with Administrative Data." *Housing Policy Debate* 14:305–45.

Devine, Deborah J. et al. 2003. "Housing Choice Voucher Location Patterns: Implications for Participant and Neighborhood Welfare." Washington, DC: U.S. Department of Housing and Urban Development.

DiMaggio, Paul and John Mohr. 1995. "The Intergenerational Transmission of Cultural Capital." *Research in Social Stratification and Mobility* 14:167–199.

Dominguez, Silvia and Celeste Watkins. 2003. "Creating Networks for Survival and Mobility: Social Capital Among African-American and Latin-American Low-Income Mothers." *Social Problems* 50:111–135.

Downs, Anthony. 1973. *Opening Up the Suburbs: An Urban Strategy for America.* New Haven: Yale University Press.

———. 2007. "Introduction: Why Rental Housing is the Neglected Child of U.S. Shelter." Pp. 1–13 in *Revisiting Rental Housing*, edited by N. P. Retsinas and E. S. Belsky. Washington, DC: Brookings Institution Press.

Dreier, Peter. 1995. "Putting Cities on the National Agenda." *Urban Affairs Review* 30:645–656.

———. 2008. "Housing the Working Poor." *Shelterforce*, 2007, pp. 9–13.

Du Bois, W. E. B. 1899. *The Philadelphia Negro: A Social Study.* New York: B. Blom.

Duncan, Greg J., Aletha Huston, and Thomas Weisner. 2007. *Higher Ground: New Hope for the Working Poor and Their Children.* New York: Russell Sage Foundation.

Eaton, Susan E. 2001. *The Other Boston Busing Story: What's Won and Lost Across the Boundary Line.* New Haven, CT: Yale University Press.

Edin, Kathryn and Maria Kefalas. 2005. *Promises I Can Keep: Why Poor Women Put Motherhood Before Marriage.* Berkeley: University of California Press.

Edin, Kathryn and Laura Lein. 1997. *Making Ends Meet: How Single Mothers Survive Welfare and Low-Wage Work.* New York: Russell Sage Foundation.

Ehrenreich, Barbara. 2001. *Nickel and Dimed: On (Not) Getting By in America.* New York: Metropolitan Books.

Ellen, Ingrid Gould. 2000. *Sharing America's Neighborhoods: Prospects for Stable Racial Integration.* Cambridge, MA: Harvard University Press.

———. 2007. "Spillovers and Subsidized Housing: The Impact of Subsidized Rental Housing on Neighborhoods." Pp. 144–159 in *Revisiting Rental Housing*, edited by N. P. Retsinas and E. S. Belsky. Washington, DC: Brookings Institution Press.

Ellen, Ingrid Gould, Tod Mijanovich, and Kerri-Nicole Dillman. 2001. "Neighborhood Effects on Health." *Journal of Urban Affairs* 23:391–408.

Ellen, Ingrid Gould and Margery Austin Turner. 2003. "Do Neighborhoods Matter and Why?" Pp. 313–338 in *Choosing a Better Life? Evaluating the Moving to Opportunity Social Experiment*, edited by J. Goering and J. Feins. Washington, DC: Urban Institute Press.

Elliott, Delbert S., Scott Menard, Bruce Rankin, Amanda Elliott, William Julius Wilson, and David Huizinga. 2006. *Good Kids from Bad Neighborhoods: Successful Development in Social Context.* New York: Cambridge University Press.

Ellwood, David T. 1988. *Poor Support: Poverty in the American Family.* New York: Basic Books.

Emmi, Philip C. and Lena Magnusson. 1994. "The Predictive Accuracy of Residential Vacancy Chains Models." *Urban Studies* 31:1117–1131.

Erickson, Bonnie H. 1996. "Culture, Class, and Connections." *American Journal of Sociology* 102:217–251.

Feins, Judith 2003. "A Cross-Site Analysis of MTO's Locational Impacts." Pp. 81–114 in *Choosing a Better Life? Evaluating the Moving to Opportunity Experiment*, edited by J. Goering and J. Feins. Washington, DC: Urban Institute Press.

Feins, Judith D., Debra McInnis, and Susan J. Popkin. 1997. *Counseling in the Moving to Opportunity Program*. Washington, DC: U.S. Department of Housing and Urban Development.

Feins, Judith D. and Rhiannon Patterson. 2005. "Geographic Mobility in the Housing Choice Voucher Program." *Cityscape* 8:21–47.

Fernandez, Roberto M. and Harris David. 1992. "Social Isolation and the Underclass." Pp. 257–279 in *Drugs, Crime and Social Isolation: Barriers to Urban Opportunity*, edited by A. Harrell, V and G. E. Peterson. Washington, DC: Urban Institute Press.

Fernandez, Roberto M. and Isabel Fernandez-Mateo. 2006. "Networks, Race, and Hiring." *American Sociological Review* 71:42–71.

Fernandez, Roberto M. and Celina Su. 2004. "Space in the Study of Labor Markets." *Annual Review of Sociology* 30:546–569.

Finkel, Meryl and Larry Buron. 2001. *Study on Section 8 Voucher Success Rates, Volume 1: Quantitative Study of Success Rates in Metropolitan Areas*. Washington, DC: U.S. Department of Housing and Urban Development.

Fischel, William A. 2001. *The Homevoter Hypothesis: How Home Values Influence Local Government Taxation, School Finance, and Land-Use Policies*. Cambridge, MA: Harvard University Press.

Fischer, Claude. 1982. *To Dwell Among Friends: Personal Networks in Town and City*. Chicago: University of Chicago Press.

Fischer, Claude S. 2002. "Ever-More Rooted Americans." *City & Community* 1:175–193.

Fogelson, Robert M. 2005. *Bourgeois Nightmares: Suburbia, 1870–1930*. New Haven: Yale University Press.

Freeman, Lance and Hilary Botein. 2002. "Subsidized Housing and Neighborhood Impacts: A Theoretical Discussion and Review of the Evidence." *Journal of Planning Literature* 16:359–378.

Frey, William. 2006. "Diversity Spreads Out: Metropolitan Shifts in Asian, Black, and Hispanic Populations Since 2000." Metropolitan Policy Program, The Brookings Institution, Washington, DC.

Fullilove, Mindy Thompson. 2004. *Root Shock: How Tearing Up City Neighborhoods Hurts America, and What We Can Do About It*. New York: One World/ Ballantine Books.

Furman Center for Real Estate and Urban Policy. 2005. *State of New York City's Neighborhoods 2005*. New York University, New York, NY.

Furstenberg, Frank. 1993. "How Families Manage Risk and Opportunity in Dangerous Neighborhoods." Pp. 231–258 in *Sociology and the Public Agenda*, edited by W. J. Wilson. Newbury Park, CA: Sage Publications.

Furstenberg, Frank F., Thomas D. Cook, Jacquelynne Eccles, Glen H. Elder, and Arnold Sameroff. 1999. *Managing to Make It: Urban Families and Adolescent Success*. Chicago: University of Chicago Press.

Furstenberg, Frank F. Jr. , Jeanne Brooks-Gunn, and S. Phillip Morgan. 1987. *Adolescent Mothers in Later Life*. New York: Cambridge University Press.

Gabriel, Stuart and Frank Nothaft. 1988. "Rental Housing Markets and the Natural Vacancy Rate." *AREUEA Journal* 16:419–429.

Gabriel, Stuart A. and Frank Nothaft. 2001. "Rental Housing Markets, the Incidence and Duration of Vacancy, and the Natural Vacancy Rate." *Journal of Urban Economics* 49:121–149.

Gallagher, Megan, and Beata Bajaj. 2007. "Moving On: Assessing the Benefits and Challenges of HOPE VI for Children." HOPE VI: Where Do We Go from Here? Brief 4. Washington, DC: The Urban Institute.

Galster, George C. 2003. "Neighborhood Dynamics and Housing Markets." Pp. 153–171 in *Housing Economics and Public Policy*, edited by K. Gibb and T. O. Sullivan. Oxford, England: Blackwell.

Galster, George C., Jackie Cutsinger, and Jason C. Booza. 2006. "Where Did They Go? The Decline of Middle-Income Neighborhoods in Metropolitan America." Metropolitan Policy Program, The Brookings Institution, Washington, DC.

Galster, George C. and Sean P. Killen. 1995. "The Geography of Metropolitan Opportunity: A Reconnaissance and Conceptual Framework." *Housing Policy Debate* 6:10–47.

Galster, George C., Peter Tatian, and Robin Smith. 1999. "The Impact of Neighbors Who Use Section 8 Certificates on Property Values." *Housing Policy Debate* 10:879–918.

Gans, Herbert J. 1962. *The Urban Villagers: Group and Class in the Life of Italian Americans*. New York: Free Press.

———. 1990. "Deconstructing the Underclass: The Term's Dangers as a Planning Concept." *Journal of the American Planning Association* 56:271–289.

———. 1995. *The War Against the Poor: The Underclass and Antipoverty Policy*. New York: Basic Books.

Garbarino, James, Kathleen Kostelny, and Nancy Dubrow. 1991. *No Place to Be a Child: Growing Up in a War Zone*. San Francisco: Jossey-Bass.

Glaeser, Edward, Jospeh Gyourko, and Raven Saks. 2006. "Urban Growth and Housing Supply." *Journal of Economic Geography* 6:71–89.

Glaeser, Edward and Jacob L. Vigdor. 2001. "Racial Segregation in the 2000 Census: Promising News." Metropolitan Policy Program, The Brookings Institution, Washington, DC.

Gobillon, Laurent, Harris Selod, and Yves Zenou. 2007. "The Mechanisms of Spatial Mismatch." *Urban Studies* 44:2401–2427.

Goering, John. 1986. "Introduction." Pp. 1–18 in *Housing Desegregation and Federal Policy*, edited by J. Goering. Chapel Hill, NC: University of North Carolina Press.

———. 2005. "Expanding Housing Choice and Integrating Neighborhoods: The MTO Experiment." Pp. 127–149 in *The Geography of Opportunity: Race and Housing Choice in Metropolitan America*, edited by X. d. S. Briggs. Washington, DC: Brookings Institution Press.

Goering, John and Judith Feins. 2003. "Choosing a Better Life? Evaluating the Moving to Opportunity Social Experiment." Washington, DC: Urban Institute Press.

Goering, John, Ali Kamely, and Todd Richardson. 1995. "Location and Racial Composition of Public Housing in the U.S." Office of Policy Development and Research, U.S. Department of Housing and Urban Development, Washington, DC.

Goetz, Edward. 2003. *Clearing the Way: Deconcentrating the Poor in Urban America*. Washington, DC: Urban Institute Press.

Goldsmith, Pat Antonio. 2004. "Schools' Role in Shaping Race Relations." *Social Problems* 51:587–612.

Gordon, Margo and Stephanie Riger. 1989. *The Female Fear*. New York: Free Press.

Gormley, William T. and David Leo Weimer. 1999. *Organizational Report Cards.* Cambridge, MA: Harvard University Press.

Granovetter, Mark. 1973. "The Strength of Weak Ties Hypothesis." *American Journal of Sociology* 78:1360–1380.

———. 1995. *Getting a Job: A Study of Contacts and Careers, Second Edition.* Cambridge, MA: Harvard University Press.

Greenbaum, Susan. 2006. "Comments on Katrina." *City and Community* 5:109–113.

Greener, Ian. 2008. "Markets in the Public Sector: When Do They Work, and What Do We Do When They Don't?" *Policy & Politics* 36:93–108.

Hainer, Peter. 1991. "Sharing Kith and Kin: A Study of Kinship Behavior, An Approach to Explanation." Unpublished Ph.D. dissertation, Department of Anthropology, Brandeis University, Waltham, MA.

Hannerz, Ulf. 1969. *Soulside: Inquiries into Ghetto Culture and Community.* New York: Columbia University Press.

Harding, David J. 2006. "Violence as a Neighborhood Effects Mechanism." in *Annual Meeting of the American Sociological Association.* Montreal, Quebec, Canada, August 10.

Harper, Gary W., Christine Gannon, Susan E. Watson, Joesph A. Catania, and M. Margaret Dolcini. 2004. "The Role of Close Friends in African-American Adolescents' Dating and Sexual Behavior." *The Journal of Sex Research* 41:351–362.

Harrington, Michael. 1962. *The Other America: Poverty in the United States.* Baltimore: Penguin Books.

Harrison, Bennett and Marcus S. Weiss. 1998. *Workforce Development Networks: Community-Based Organizations and Regional Alliances.* Thousand Oaks, CA: Sage Publications.

Hartung, John and Jeffrey R. Henig. 1997. "Housing Vouchers and Certificates as a Vehicle for Deconcentrating the Poor." *Urban Affairs Review* 32:403–419.

Hastings, Justine S. and Jeffrey M. Weinstein. 2007. "Information, School Choice, and Academic Achievement: Evidence from Two Experiments." Working Paper 13623, National Bureau of Economic Research, Cambridge, MA.

Hatry, Harry P. and Joseph S. Wholey. 1999. *Performance Measurement: Getting Results.* Washington, DC: Urban Institute Press.

Haynie, Dana L. and Scott J. South. 2005. "Residential Mobility and Adolescent Violence." *Social Forces* 84:361–374.

Haynie, Dana L., Scott J. South, and Sunita Bose. 2006. "The Company You Keep: Adolescent Mobility and Peer Behavior." *Sociological Inquiry* 76:397–426.

Henly, Julia 2002. "Informal Support Networks and the Maintenance of Low-Wage Jobs." Pp. 179–203 in *Laboring Below the Line,* edited by F. Munger. New York: Russell Sage Foundation.

Herr, Toby and Suzanne L. Wagner. 2007. *Beyond Barriers to Work.* Chicago: Project Match.

Hipp, Lena and Mildred E. Warner. 2008. "Market Forces for the Unemployed? Training Vouchers in Germany and the U.S.A." *Social Policy and Administration* 42:77–101.

Hirsch, Arnold R. 1983. *Making the Second Ghetto: Race and Housing in Chicago, 1940–1960.* New York: Cambridge University Press.

Hogan, James. 1996. *Scattered-Site Housing: Characteristics and Consequences.* Washington, DC: U.S. Department of Housing and Urban Development.

Holzer, Harry. 2006. *Reconnecting Disadvantaged Young Men: Improving Schooling and Employment Outcomes*. Washington, DC: Urban Institute Press.

Ihlanfeldt, Keith R. and David Sjoquist. 1998. "The Spatial Mismatch Hypothesis: A Review of Recent Studies and Their Implications for Welfare Reform." *Housing Policy Debate* 9:849–892.

Imbroscio, David. 2008. "[U]nited and Actuated by Some Common Impulse of Passion: Challenging the Dispersal Consensus in American Housing Policy Research." *Journal of Urban Affairs* 30:111–130.

Ioannides, Yannis M. and Linda Datcher Loury. 2004. "Job Information Networks, Neighborhood Effects, and Inequality." *Journal of Economic Literature* 42:1056–1093.

Jacobs, Jane. 1961. *The Death and Life of Great American Cities*. New York: Random House.

Janowitz, Morris. 1952. *The Community Press in an Urban Setting*. Glencoe, IL: Free Press.

Jargowsky, Paul. 1997. *Poverty and Place: Ghettos, Barrios, and the American City*. New York: Russell Sage Foundation.

———. 2003. "Stunning Progress, Hidden Problems: The Dramatic Decline of Concentrated Poverty in the 1990s." Washington, DC: The Brookings Institution.

Jargowsky, Paul A. and Mary Jo Bane. 1991. "Ghetto Poverty in the United States, 1970–1980." Pp. 235–273 in *The Urban Underclass*, edited by C. Jencks and P. E. Petersen. Washington, DC: Brookings Institution Press.

Jargowsky, Paul A. and Rebecca Yang. 2006. "The "Underclass" Revisited: A Social Problem in Decline." *Journal of Urban Affairs* 28:55–70.

Jarrett, Robin L. 1999. "Successful Parenting in High-Risk Neighborhoods." *The Future of Children* 9:45–50.

Jarrett, Robin L. and Linda M. Burton. 1999. "Dynamic Dimensions of Family Structure in Low-Income African-American Families: Emergent Themes in Qualitative Research." *Journal of Comparative Family Studies* 30:177–187.

Jencks, Christopher. 1970. "Education Vouchers: A Report on Financing Education by Payments to Parents." Center for the Study of Social Policy, Cambridge, MA.

———. 1992. *Rethinking Social Policy*. Cambridge, MA: Harvard University Press.

Jencks, Christopher and Susan E. Mayer. 1990. "The Social Consequences of Growing Up in a Poor Neighborhood." Pp. 111–185 in *Inner-City Poverty in the United States*, edited by L. E. Lynn and M. G. H. McGeary. Washington, DC: National Academy Press.

Jencks, Christopher and Paul Petersen. 1991. "The Urban Underclass." Washington, DC: Brookings Institution Press.

Johnson, Heidi. 2009. *Vulnerable Youth and the Transition to Adulthood: Youth in Distressed Neighborhoods, ASPE Research Brief* Washington, DC: The Urban Institute.

Johnson, Michael P. 2005. "Spatial Decision Support for Assisted Housing Mobility Counseling." *Decision Support Systems* 41:296–312.

Joint Center for Housing Studies. 2006a. "America's Rental Housing: Homes for a Diverse Nation." Harvard University, Cambridge, MA.

———. 2006b. "State of the Nation's Housing: 2006." Harvard University, Cambridge, MA.

Joseph, Mark L., Robert J. Chaskin, and Henry S. Webber. 2007. "The Theoretical Basis for Addressing Poverty Through Mixed-Income Housing." *Urban Affairs Review* 42:369–409.

Kadushin, Charles and Delmos Jones. 1992. "Social Networks and Urban Neighborhoods in New York City." *City and Society* 6:58–75.

Kain, John. 1968. "Housing Desegregation, Negro Employment, and Metropolitan Decentralization." *Quarterly Journal of Economics* 32:175–197.

Kasarda, John D. and Morris Janowitz. 1974. "Community Attachment in Mass Society." *American Sociological Review* 39:328–339.

Kasinitz, Phillip and Jan Rosenberg. 1996. "Missing the Connection: Social Isolation and Employment on the Brooklyn Waterfront." *Social Forces* 43:180–195.

Katz, Bruce and Margery Austin Turner. 2007. "Rethinking U.S. Rental Housing Policy: A New Blueprint for Federal, State, and Local Action." Pp. 319–358 in *Revisiting Rental Housing*, edited by N. P. Retsinas and E. S. Belsky. Washington, DC: Brookings Institution Press.

Katz, Lawrence F., Jeffrey R. Kling, and Jeffrey B. Liebman. 2001. "Moving to Opportunity in Boston: Early Results of a Randomized Mobility Experiment." *Quarterly Journal of Economics* 116:607–654.

Katz, Lawrence, Jeffrey R. Kling, and Jeffrey Liebman. 2003. "Boston Site Findings: The Early Impacts of Moving to Opportunity." Pp. 177–211 in *Choosing a Better Life? The Moving to Opportunity Social Experiment*, edited by J. Goering and J. Feins. Washington, DC: Urban Institute Press.

Kaufman, Julie E. and James E. Rosenbaum. 1992. "The Education and Employment of Low-Income Black Youth in White Suburbs." *Educational Evaluation and Policy Analysis* 14:229–240.

Keels, Micere, Greg J. Duncan, Stefanie DeLuca, James Rosenbaum, and Ruby Mendenhall. 2005. "Fifteen Years Later: Can Residential Mobility Programs Provide a Permanent Escape from Neighborhood Crime and Poverty?" *Demography* 41:51–73.

Kendall-Tackett, Kathleen A., Linda Meyer Williams, and David Finkelhor. 1993. "Impact of Sexual Abuse on Children: A Review and Synthesis of Recent Empirical Studies." *Psychological Bulletin* 113:164–180.

Kerner Commission. 1968. "Report of the National Advisory Commission on Civil Disorders (Kerner Commission)." U.S. Government Printing Office, Washington, DC.

Keyes, Langley C. 1969. *The Rehabilitation Planning Game*. Cambridge, MA: MIT Press.

Kilpatrick, Dean G., Ron Acierno, Benjamin Saunders, Heidi S. Resnick, Connie L. Best, and Paula P. Schnurr. 2000. "Risk Factors for Adolescent Substance Abuse and Dependence: Data From A National Sample." *Journal of Consulting and Clinical Psychology* 68:19–30.

Kingdon, John W. 1984. *Agendas, Alternatives, and Public Policies*. Boston: Little Brown.

Kingsley, G. Thomas and Kathryn Pettit. 2003. "Concentrated Poverty: A Change in Course." Research Brief, National Neighborhood Indicators Project, The Urban Institute, Washington, DC.

Kingsley, G. Thomas and Katherine L.S. Pettit. 2008. "Have MTO Families Lost Access to Opportunity Neighborhoods Over Time?" Three-City Study of Moving to Opportunity Brief No. 2. The Urban Institute, Washington, DC.

Kirschenman, Joleen and Kathryn Neckerman. 1991. "'We'd Love to Hire Them, But…': The Meaning of Race for Employers." Pp. 203–232 in *The Urban Underclass*, edited by C. Jencks and P. E. Peterson. Washington, DC: Brookings Institution Press.

Kleit, Rachel Garshick. 2001. "The Role of Neighborhood Social Networks in Scattered-Site Public Housing Residents' Search for Jobs." *Housing Policy Debate* 12:514–573.

Kling, Jeffrey R. 2006. "Moving to Opportunity." in *Conference on Causal Inference in Neighborhood-Based Research*. University of Chicago, Chicago, IL.

Kling, Jeffrey R., Jeffrey B. Liebman, and Lawrence F. Katz. 2007. "Experimental Analysis of Neighborhood Effects." *Econometrica* 75:83–119.

Kling, Jeffrey R., Jens Ludwig, and Lawrence F. Katz. 2005. "Neighborhood Effects on Crime for Female and Male Youth: Evidence From a Randomized Housing Voucher Experiment." *Quarterly Journal of Economics* 120:87–130.

Kotlowitz, Alex. 1991. *There Are No Children Here: The Story of Two Boys Growing Up in the Other America*. New York: Doubleday.

Krieger, Nancy. 1994. "Epidemiology and the Web of Causation: Has Anyone Seen the Spider?" *Social Science Medicine* 39:887–903.

Lacy, Karyn R. 2007. *Blue-Chip Black: Race, Class, and Status in the New Black Middle Class*. Berkeley: University of California Press.

Ladd, Helen. 2002. "School Vouchers: A Critical View." *Journal of Economic Perspectives* 16:3–24.

Ladd, Helen F. and Jens Ludwig. 2003. "The Effects of MTO on Educational Opportunities in Baltimore." Pp. 117–151 in *Choosing a Better Life? The Moving to Opportunity Social Experiment*, edited by J. Goering and J. Feins. Washington, DC: Urban Institute Press.

Lamont, Michèle and Virag Molnar. 2002. "The Study of Boundaries in the Social Sciences." *Annual Review of Sociology* 28:167–195.

Leif, Beth and Susan Goering. 1987. "The Implementation of the Federal Mandate for Fair Housing." Pp. 227–267 in *Divided Neighborhoods*, edited by G. Tobin. Newbury Park, CA: Sage Publications.

Lemann, Nicholas. 1991. *The Promised Land: The Great Black Migration and How It Changed America*. New York: Vintage Books.

Leventhal, Tama and Jeanne Brooks-Gunn. 2000. "The Neighborhoods They Live In: The Effects of Neighborhood Residence on Child and Adolescent Outcomes." *Psychological Bulletin* 126:309–337.

———. 2003. "Moving to Opportunity: An Experimental Study of Neighborhood Effects on Mental Health." *American Journal of Public Health* 93:1576–1582.

Levy, Frank. 1987. *Dollars and Dreams: The Changing American Income Distribution*. New York: Russell Sage Foundation.

Lewis, Oscar. 1966. *La Vida: A Puerto Rican Family in the Culture of Poverty*. New York: Random House.

Lieber, Eli, Thomas S. Weisner, and Matthew Presley. 2003. "EthnoNotes: An Internet-Based Field Note Management Tool." *Field Methods* 15:405–425.

Liebman, Jeffrey B., Lawrence Katz, and Jeffrey Kling. 2004. "Beyond Treatment Effects: Estimating the Relationship Between Neighborhood Poverty and Individual Outcomes in the MTO Experiment." IRS Working Paper 493, Princeton University, Princeton, NJ.

Liebow, Eliott. 1967. *Tally's Corner*. Boston: Little, Brown.

Lin, Nan. 2001. "Toward a Network Theory of Social Capital." Pp. 3–29 in *Social Capital: Theory and Research*, edited by N. Lin, K. Cook, and R. Burt. New York: Aldine de Gruyter.

Lindblom, Charles E. 1959. "The Science of "Muddling Through." *Public Administration Review* 19:79–88.

Lipsky, Michael. 1980. *Street-Level Bureaucracy: Dilemmas of the Individual in Public Services*. New York: Russell Sage Foundation.

Logan, John. 2001. "Ethnic Diversity Grows, Neighborhood Integration Lags Behind." Lewis Mumford Center, University at Albany, Albany, NY.

Long, Larry. 1992. "International Perspectives on the Residential Mobility of America's Children." *Journal of Marriage and the Family* 54:861–869.

Lowe, Edward D. and Thomas S. Weisner. 2003. "'You Have to Push It—Who's Gonna Raise Your Kids?': Situating Childcare and Childcare Subsidy in the Daily Routines of Lower Income Families." *Children and Youth Services Review* 25:225–262.

Lowe, Edward D., Thomas S. Weisner, and Aletha C. Huston. 2005. "Childcare Instability and the Effort to Sustain a Working Daily Routine." Pp. 121–144 in *Developmental Pathways Through Middle Childhood*, edited by C. R. Cooper, C. T. Garcia-Coll, W. T. Bartko, and H. M. Davis. New York: Routledge.

Lucas, Wendy. 1997. "Perry Hall, Baltimore, Maryland Housing, and Neighborhood Study: Putting FHA Housing on the Map." Washington, DC: U.S. Department of Housing and Urban Development.

Ludwig, Jens, Greg J. Duncan, and Paul Hirschfield. 2001. "Urban Poverty and Juvenile Crime: Evidence from a Randomized Housing-Mobility Experiment." *Quarterly Journal of Economics* 116:665–679.

Ludwig, Jens, Greg J. Duncan, and Helen Ladd. 2003. "The Effects of MTO on Children and Parents in Baltimore." Pp. 153–175 in *Choosing a Better Life? Evaluating the Moving to Opportunity Experiment*, edited by J. Goering and J. D. Feins. Washington, DC: Urban Institute Press.

Ludwig, Jens, Jeffrey B. Liebman, Jeffrey R. Kling, Greg J. Duncan, Lawrence F. Katz, Ronald C. Kessler, and Lisa Sanbonmatsu. 2008. "What Can We Learn about Neighborhood Effects from the Moving to Opportunity Experiment?" *American Journal of Sociology* 114:144–188.

Maddaus, John. 1990. "Parental Choice of Schools: What Parents Think and Do." *Review of Research in Education* 16:267–295.

Marcuse, Peter. 1995. "Interpreting 'Public Housing' History." *Journal of Architectural and Planning Research* 12:240–258.

———. 2005. "Enclaves Yes, Ghettos No." Pp. 15–30 in *Desegregating the City: Ghettos, Enclaves, and Inequality*, edited by D. P. Varady. Albany, NY: State University of New York Press.

Martin, Elmer P. and Joanne Mitchell Martin. 1978. *The Black Extended Family*. Chicago: University of Chicago Press.

Massey, Douglas S. 2007. *Categorically Unequal: The American Stratification System*. New York: Russell Sage Foundation.

Massey, Douglas S. and Nancy A. Denton. 1993. *American Apartheid: Segregation and the Making of the Underclass*. Cambridge, MA: Harvard University Press.

Massey, Douglas S. and Mary Fischer. 2003. "The Geography of Inequality in the United States, 1950–2000." *Brookings-Wharton Papers on Urban Affairs*:1–30.

Massey, Douglas S. and Garvey Lund. 2001. "Use of Black English and Discrimination in Urban Housing Markets." *Urban Affairs Review* 36:452–469.

May, David C. 2001. "The Effect of Fear of Sexual Victimization on Adolescent Fear of Crime." *Sociological Spectrum* 21:141–174.

McArdle, Nancy. 2003. "Beyond Poverty: Race and Concentrated Poverty Neighborhoods in Metro Boston." The Civil Rights Project at Harvard University, Cambridge, MA.

McClure, Kirk. 2001. "Housing Subsidy Programs and the Concentration of Poor and Minority Households." in *Annual Meeting of the Association of Collegiate Schools of Planning*. Cleveland, OH.

———. 2006. "Do Tight Housing Markets Inhibit Racial, Ethnic, and Poverty Deconcentration?" in *Annual Meeting of the Association of Collegiate Schools of Planning*. Fort Worth, TX.

McDougall, Harold. 1993. *Black Baltimore*. Philadelphia: Temple University Press.

McLoyd, V. C. 1998. "Socioeconomic Disadvantage and Child Development." *American Psychologist* 53:185–204.

Mead, Lawrence M. 1986. *Beyond Entitlement: The Social Obligations of Citizenship*. New York: Free Press.

———. 1992. *The New Politics of Poverty: The Nonworking Poor in America*. New York: Basic Books.

Menard, Scott and David Huizinga. 2001. "Repeat Victimization in a High-Risk Neighborhood Sample of Adolescents." *Youth & Society* 32:447–472.

Mendenhall, Ruby, Stefanie DeLuca, and Greg Duncan. 2006. "Neighborhood Resources, Racial Segregation, and Economic Mobility: Results from the Gautreaux Program." *Social Science Research* 35:892–923.

Menjívar, Cecilia. 1995. "Kinship Networks Among Immigrants: Lessons from a Qualitative Comparative Approach." *International Journal of Comparative Sociology* 36:219–232.

Merry, Sally Engle. 1981. *Urban Danger: Life in a Neighborhood of Strangers*. Philadelphia: Temple University Press.

Miles, Matthew B. and A. Michael Huberman. 1994. *Qualitative Data Analysis*. Thousand Oaks, CA: Sage Publications.

Milkman, Ruth. 2006. *L.A. Story: Immigrant Workers and the Future of the U.S. Labor Movement*. New York: Russell Sage Foundation.

Mincy, Ronald J. and Susan J. Wiener. 1993. "The Underclass in the 1980s: Changing Concepts, Constant Reality." The Urban Institute, Washington, DC.

Moore, Joan and Raquel Pinderhughes. 1993. "In the Barrios: Latinos and the Underclass Debate." New York: Russell Sage Foundation.

Moore, Mark H. 1990. "What Sort of Ideas Become Public Ideas?" Pp. 55–83 in *The Power of Public Ideas*, edited by R. B. Reich. Cambridge, MA: Harvard University Press.

———. 1995. *Creating Public Value*. Cambridge, MA: Harvard University Press.

Mouw, Ted. 2000. "Job Relocation and the Racial Gap in Unemployment in Detroit and Chicago, 1980 to 1990." *American Sociological Review* 65:730–753.

Moynihan, Daniel Patrick. 1965. "The Negro Family: The Case for National Action." U.S. Department of Labor, Washington, DC.

Murray, Charles A. 1984. Losing Ground: American Social Policy, 1950–1980. New York: Basic Books.

National Commission on Severely Distressed Public Housing. 1993. *The Final Report of the National Commission on Severely Distressed Public Housing: A Report to the Congress and the Secretary of Housing and Urban Development*. Washington, DC: U.S. Government Printing Office.

Neckerman, Kathryn M. and Florencia Torche. 2007. "Inequality: Causes and Consequences." *Annual Review of Sociology* 33:335–357.

Newman, Katherine S. 1988. *Falling from Grace: The Experience of Downward Mobility in the American Middle Class*. New York: Free Press.

Newman, Katherine S. 1999. *No Shame in My Game: The Working Poor in the Inner City*. New York: Knopf and Russell Sage Foundation.

Newman, Katherine S. and Rebekah Peeples Massengill. 2006. "The Texture of Hardship: Qualitative Sociology of Poverty, 1995–2005." *Annual Review of Sociology* 3:423–466.

Newman, Sandra. 1995. "Poverty Deconcentration as a Policy Strategy." Occasional Paper No. 17, Institute for Policy Studies, Johns Hopkins University, Baltimore.

Newman, Sandra and Joseph Harkness. 2000. "Assisted Housing and the Educational Attainment of Children." *Journal of Housing Economics* 9:40–63.

Newman, Sandra J. and Greg Duncan. 1979. "Residential Problems, Dissatisfaction, and Mobility." *Journal of the American Planning Association* 45:154–166.

Newman, Sandra J. and Ann B. Schnare. 1997. "'… And a Suitable Living Environment': The Failure of Housing Programs to Deliver on Neighborhood Quality." *Housing Policy Debate* 8:703–741.

O'Connor, Alice. 2007. *Poverty Knowledge*. New York: Russell Sage Foundation.

Oliver, Melvin. 1988. "The Urban Black Community as Social Network: Toward a Network Perspective." *Sociological Quarterly* 29:623–645.

Ong, Paul M. 2002. "Car Ownership and Welfare-to-Work." *Journal of Policy Analysis and Management* 21:239–253.

Ong, Paul M. and Douglas Miller. 2005. "Spatial and Transportation Mismatch in Los Angeles." *Journal of Planning Education and Research* 25:43–56.

O'Regan, Katherine and John Quigley. 1993. "The Effect of Social Networks and Concentrated Poverty on Black and Hispanic Youth Employment." *Annals of Regional Science* 27:327–342.

Orfield, Myron. 1997. *Metropolitics: A Regional Agenda for Community and Stability*. Washington, DC and Cambridge, MA: Brookings Institution Press and Lincoln Institute of Land Policy.

———. 2002. *American Metropolitics: The New Suburban Reality*. Washington, DC: Brookings Institution Press.

Orlebeke, Charles J. 1999. "The Evolution of Low-Income Housing Policy, 1949–1999." *Housing Policy Debate* 11:489–520.

Orr, Larry, Judith D. Feins, Robin Jacob, Erik Beecroft, Lisa Sanbonmatsu, Lawrence F. Katz, Jeffrey B. Liebman, and Jeffrey R. Kling. 2003. "Moving to Opportunity for Fair-Housing Demonstration: Interim Impacts Evaluation." U.S. Department of Housing and Urban Development, Washington, DC.

Pack, Janet Rothenberg. 2002. *Growth and Convergence in Metropolitan America*. Washington, DC: Brookings Institution Press.

Pancs, Romans and Nicolaas J. Vriend. 2004. "Schelling's Spatial Proximity Model of Segregation Revisited." *Journal of Public Economics* 91:1–24.

Park, Robert Ezra. 1952. *Human Communities: The City and Human Ecology*. Glencoe, IL: Free Press.

Park, Robert Ezra, Ernest Watson Burgess, Roderick Duncan McKenzie, and Louis Wirth. 1925. *The City*. Chicago: University of Chicago Press.

Pashup, Jennifer, Kathryn Edin, Greg J. Duncan, and Karen Burke. 2005. "Participation in a Residential Mobility Program from the Client's Perspective: Findings from Gautreaux Two." *Housing Policy Debate* 16:361–392.

Pattillo, Mary. 2003. "Extending the Boundaries and Definition of the Ghetto." *Ethnic and Racial Studies* 26:1046–1057.

Pattillo, Mary E. 2007. *Black on the Block: The Politics of Race and Class in the City.* Chicago: University of Chicago Press.

Pattillo-McCoy, Mary. 2000. *Black Picket Fences: Privilege and Peril Among the Black Middle Class.* Chicago: University of Chicago Press.

Pelletiere, Danilo, Keith E. Wardrip, and Sheila Crowley. 2008. "Out of Reach, 2007–2008." National Low Income Housing Coalition, Washington, DC.

Pendall, Rolf. 2000. "Why Voucher and Certificate Holders Live in Distressed Neighborhoods." *Housing Policy Debate* 11:881–910.

———. 2007. "Opposition to Housing: NIMBY and Beyond." *Urban Affairs Review* 35:112–136.

Pendall, Rolf, Arthur C. Nelson, Casey J. Dawkins, and Gerrit J. Knaap. 2005. "Connecting Smart Growth, Housing Affordability and Racial Equity." Pp. 219–246 in *The Geography of Opportunity: Race and Housing Choice in Metropolitan America*, edited by X. d. S. Briggs. Washington, DC: Brookings Institution Press.

Perkins, Douglas D. and Ralph B. Taylor. 1996. "Ecological Assessments of Community Disorder: Their Relationship to Fear of Crime and Theoretical Implications." *American Journal of Community Psychology* 24:63–107.

Persky, Joseph and Daniel Felsenstein. 2008. "Multipliers, Mark-Ups, and Mobility Rents: In Defense of "Chain Models" in Urban and Regional Analysis." *Environment and Planning A*:2933–2947.

Peterson, Paul E. and David E. Campbell. 2001. *Charters, Vouchers, and Public Education.* Washington, DC: Brookings Institution Press.

Pettigrew, Thomas F. 1998. "Inter-group Contact Theory." *Annual Review of Psychology* 49:65–85.

Phelan, Patricia, Ann Locke Davidson, and Hanh Thanh Cao. 1991. "Students' Multiple Worlds: Negotiating the Boundaries of Family, Peer, and School Cultures." *Anthropology & Education Quarterly* 22:224–250.

Polikoff, Alexander. 2006. *Waiting for Gautreaux: A Story of Segregation, Housing, and the Black Ghetto.* Evanston, IL: Northwestern University Press.

Popkin, Susan J. and Elizabeth Cove. 2007. "Safety is the Most Important Thing: How HOPE VI Helped Families." The Urban Institute, Washington, DC.

Popkin, Susan J., Mary K. Cunningham, and Martha R. Burt. 2005. "Public Housing Transformation and the 'Hard to House.'" *Housing Policy Debate* 16:1–24.

Popkin, Susan J., George C. Galster, Kenneth Temkin, Carla Herbig, Diane K. Levy, and Elise K. Richer. 2003. "Obstacles to Implementing Public Housing Desegregation: Lessons Learned from Eight Consent Decrees." *Journal of Policy Analysis and Management* 22:179–199.

Popkin, Susan J., Victoria Gwiasda, Lynn Olson, Dennis Rosenbaum, and Larry Buron. 2000. *The Hidden War: Crime and the Tragedy of Public Housing in Chicago.* New Brunswick, NJ: Rutgers University Press.

Popkin, Susan J., Laura E. Harris, and Mary K. Cunningham. 2001. *Families in Transition: A Qualitative Analysis of the MTO Experience.* Washington, DC: The Urban Institute.

Popkin, Susan J., Bruce Katz, Mary K. Cunningham, Karen D. Brown, Jeremy Gustafson, and Margery A. Turner. 2004. *A Decade of Hope VI: Research Findings and Policy Challenges.* The Urban Institute, Washington, DC.

Popkin, Susan J., Diane K. Levy, Larry Buron. 2009. "Has HOPE VI Transformed Residents' Lives? New Evidence From the HOPE VI Panel Study." *Housing Studies* 24:477–502.

Popkin, Susan J., James E. Rosenbaum, and Patricia Meaden. 1993. "Labor Market Experiences of Low-Income Black Women in Middle-Class Suburbs." *Journal of Policy Analysis and Management* 12:556–573.

Popkin, Susan J., Brett Theodos, Caterina Roman, Elizabeth Guernsey, and Liz Getsinger. 2008. "The Chicago Family Case Management Demonstration: Developing a New Model for Serving 'Hard to House' Public Housing Families." The Urban Institute, Washington, DC, June.

Portes, Alejandro and Robert Sensenbrenner. 1993. "Embeddedness and Immigration: Notes on the Social Determinants of Economic Action." *American Journal of Sociology* 98:1320–1350.

Pressman, Jeffrey L. and Aaron B. Wildavsky. 1973. *Implementation: How Great Expectations in Washington are Dashed in Oakland.* Berkeley, CA: University of California Press.

Pribesh, Shana and Douglas B. Downey. 1999. "Why are Residential and School Moves Associated with Poor School Performance?" *Demography* 36:521–534.

Putnam, Robert D. 2000. *Bowling Alone: The Collapse and Revival of American Community.* New York: Simon & Schuster.

Quane, James M. 2008. "Low-Income Female Caregivers' Expectations for their Adolescent Sons or Daughters in Disadvantaged Urban Neighborhoods." Unpublished paper, John F. Kennedy School of Government, Harvard University, Cambridge, MA.

Quane, James M., Bruce Rankin, Pamela Joshi, and William Julius Wilson. 2008. "Complex Lives and Compounded Problems: Understanding the Effects of Work and Welfare." Unpublished paper, John F. Kennedy School of Government, Harvard University, Cambridge, MA.

Quercia, Roberto G. and George C. Galster. 1997. "The Challenges Facing Public Housing Authorities in a Brave New World." *Housing Policy Debate* 8:535–569.

Quigley, John M. and Steven Raphael. 2004. "Is Housing Unaffordable? Why Isn't It More Affordable?" *Journal of Economic Perspectives* 18:191–214.

Quillian, Lincoln. 1999. "Migration Patterns and the Growth of High-Poverty Neighborhoods, 1970–1990." *American Journal of Sociology* 105:1–37.

———. 2003. "How Long Are Exposures to Poor Neighborhoods? The Long-Term Dynamics of Entry and Exit from Poor Neighborhoods." *Population Research and Policy Review* 22:221–249.

Ragin, Charles. 1987. *The Comparative Method: Moving Beyond Qualitative and Quantitative Strategies.* Berkeley: University of California Press.

Rainwater, Lee. 1970. *Behind Ghetto Walls: Black Families in a Federal Slum.* Chicago: Aldine.

Raj, Anita, Elizabeth Reed, Elizabeth Miller, Emily Rothman, and Jay G. Silverman. 2007. "Contexts of Condom Use and Non-condom Use among Young Adolescent Male Perpetrators of Dating Violence." *AIDS Care* 19:970–973.

Raphael, Jody. 2001. "Public Housing and Domestic Violence." *Violence Against Women* 7:699–706.

Raphael, Steven. 1998. "The Spatial Mismatch Hypothesis and Black Youth Joblessness: Evidence from the San Francisco Bay Area." *Journal of Urban Economics* 43:79–111.

Raphael, Steven and Michael A. Stoll. 2002. "Modest Progress: The Narrowing Spatial Mismatch Between Blacks and Jobs in the 1990s." Metropolitan Policy Program, Brookings Institution.

Rawlings, Lynette A., Laura E. Harris, and Margery Austin Turner. 2004. "Race and Residence: Prospects for Stable Neighborhood Integration." The Urban Institute, Washington, DC.

Renzetti, Claire M. 2001. "One Strike and You're Out: Implications of a Federal Crime Control Policy for Battered Women." *Violence Against Women* 7:685–698.

Ricketts, Erol R. and Isabel V. Sawhill. 1988. "Defining and Measuring the Underclass." *Journal of Policy Analysis and Management* 7:316–325.

Rieder, Jonathan. 1985. *Canarsie: The Jews and Italians of Brooklyn Against Liberalism*. Cambridge, MA: Harvard University Press.

Riis, Jacob A. 1890. *How the Other Half Lives: Studies Among the Tenements of New York*. New York: Penguin Books.

Roisman, Florence. 2007. "Affirmatively Furthering Fair Housing in Regional Housing Markets." *Wake Forest Law Review* 42:333–391.

Roman, Caterina G., Carly R. Knight, Aaron Chalfin, and Susan J. Popkin. 2009. "The Relationship of the Perceived Environment to Fear, Physical Activity and Health in Public Housing Developments: Evidence from Chicago." *Journal of Public Health Policy* 30:S286-S308.

Rosenbaum, Emily, Laura Harris, and Nancy A. Denton. 2003. "New Places, New Faces: An Analysis of Neighborhoods and Social Ties Among MTO Movers in Chicago." Pp. 275–310 in *Choosing a Better Life? Evaluating the Moving to Opportunity Social Experiment*, edited by J. Goering and J. D. Feins. Washington, DC: The Urban Institute Press.

Rosenbaum, James. 1995. "Changing the Geography of Opportunity by Expanding Residential Choice: Lessons from the Gautreaux Program." *Housing Policy Debate* 6:231–270.

Rosenbaum, James, Stefanie DeLuca, and Tammy Tuck. 2005. "New Capabilities in New Places: Low-Income Black Families in Suburbia." Pp. 150–175 in *The Geography of Opportunity: Race and Housing Choice in Metropolitan America*, edited by X. d. S. Briggs. Washington, DC: Brookings Institution Press.

Rosenbaum, James E. and Susan J. Popkin. 1991. "Employment and Earnings of Low-Income Blacks Who Move to Middle-Income Suburbs." Pp. 342–356 in *The Urban Underclass*, edited by C. Jencks and P. E. Peterson. Washington, DC: Brookings Institution Press.

Rosin, Hanna. 2008. "American Murder Mystery." *Atlantic Monthly* July/August:40–54.

Rossi, Peter. 1955. *Why Families Move*. Glencoe, IL: Free Press.

Rubinowitz, Leonard and James Rosenbaum. 2000. *Crossing the Class and Color Lines: From Public Housing to White Suburbia*. Chicago: University of Chicago Press.

Salama, Jerry J., Michael H. Schill, and Martha E. Stark. 1999. *Reducing the Cost of New Housing Construction in New York City*. A Report to The New York City Partnership and Chamber of Commerce, The New York City Housing Partnership and The New York City Department of Housing Preservation and Development. New York: New York University School of Law, Center for Real Estate and Urban Policy.

Sampson, Robert J. 1999. "What Community Supplies." Pp. 241–292 in *Urban Problems and Community Development*, edited by R. Ferguson and W. Dickens. Washington, DC: Brookings Institution Press.

———. 2008. "Moving to Inequality: Neighborhood Effects and Experiments Meet Social Structure." *American Journal of Sociology* 114:189–231.

Sampson, Robert J., Jeffrey Morenoff, and Thomas Gannon-Rowley. 2002. "Assessing 'Neighborhood Effects': Social Processes and New Directions in Research." *Annual Review of Sociology* 28:443–478.

Sampson, Robert J., Jefferey D. Morenoff, and Stephen W Raudenbush. 2005. "Social Anatomy of Racial and Ethnic Disparities in Violence." *American Journal of Public Health* 95:224–232.

Sampson, Robert J., Stephen W. Raudenbush, and Felton Earls. 1997. "Neighborhoods and Violent Crime: A Multilevel Study of Collective Efficacy." *Science* 277:918–924.

Sanbonmatsu, Lisa, Jeffrey R. Kling, Greg J. Duncan, and Jeanne Brooks-Gunn. 2006. "Neighborhoods and Academic Achievement: Results from the Moving to Opportunity Experiment." *Journal of Human Resources* 41:649–691.

Schacter, Jason P. 2001. "Geographical Mobility: 2002 to 2003." Washington, DC: Current Population Reports, U.S. Census Bureau.

Schelling, Thomas. 1971. "Dynamic Models of Segregation." *Journal of Mathematical Sociology* 1:143–186.

Schill, Michael H. 2005. "Regulations and Development: What We Know." *Cityscape* 8:5–19.

Schill, Michael H. and Susan M. Wachter. 1995. "Housing Market Constraints and Spatial Stratification by Income and Race." *Housing Policy Debate* 6:141–168.

Schön, Donald and Martin Rein. 1994. *Frame Reflection: Toward the Resolution of Intractable Policy Controversies*. New York: Basic Books.

Schuck, Peter H. and Richard J. Zeckhauser. 2006. *Targeting in Social Programs: Avoiding Bad Bets, Removing Bad Apples*. Washington, DC: Brookings Institution Press.

Schwartz, Alex and Tajbakhsh. 1997. "Mixed-Income Housing: Unanswered Questions." *Cityscape* 3:71–92.

Schwartz, Barry. 2004. *The Paradox of Choice: Why More is Less*. New York: ECCO.

Sen, Amartya Kumar. 2001. *Development as Freedom*. New York: Oxford University Press.

Shadish, William R., Thomas D. Cook, and Donald Thomas Campbell. 2002. *Experimental and Quasi-Experimental Designs for Generalized Causal Inference*. Boston, MA: Houghton Mifflin Company.

Sharkey, Patrick. 2008. "The Intergenerational Transmission of Context." *American Journal of Sociology* 113:931–969.

Shroder, Mark D. 2003. "Locational Constraint, Housing Counseling, and Successful Lease-Up." Pp. 59–80 in *Choosing a Better Life? Evaluating the Moving to Opportunity Social Experiment*, edited by J. Goering and J. Feins. Washington, DC: Urban Institute Press.

Silverman, Jay G., Michelle R. Decker, Elizabeth Reed, Emily Rothman, Jeanne Hathaway, Anita Raj, and Elizabeth Miller. 2006. "Social Norms and Beliefs Regarding Sexual Risk and Pregnancy Involvement Among Adolescent Males Treated for Dating Violence Perpetration." *Journal of Urban Health: Bulletin of the New York Academy of Medicine* 83:723–735.

Simons, R. L., Christine Johnson, Jay J. Beaman, Rand D. Conger, and Les B. Whitbeck. 1996. "Parents and Peer Group as Mediators of the Effect of Community

Structure on Adolescent Behavior." *American Journal of Community Psychology* 24:145–171.

Skiba, Russell J., Robert S. Michael, Abra Carroll Nardo, and Reece Patterson. 2001. "The Color of Discipline: Sources of Racial and Gender Disproportionality in School Punishment." Policy Research Report #SRS1, Indiana Education Policy Center, University of Nebraska, Lincoln, NE.

Small, Mario Luis. 2008. "Lost in Translation." Pp. 165–171 in *Workshop on Interdisciplinary Standards for Systematic Qualitative Research*, edited by M. Lamont and P. White. Washington, DC: National Science Foundation.

———. 2004. *Villa Victoria: The Transformation of Social Capital in a Boston Barrio*. Chicago: University of Chicago Press.

Small, Mario Luis and Monica McDermott. 2006. "The Presence of Organizational Resources in Poor Urban Neighborhoods." *Social Forces* 84:1697–1724.

Small, Mario Luis and Katherine Newman. 2001. "Urban Poverty after the Truly Disadvantaged: The Rediscovery of the Family, the Neighborhood, and Culture." *Annual Review of Sociology* 27:23–45.

Smith, Sandra. 2007. *Lone Pursuit: Distrust and Defensive Individualism among the Black Poor*. New York: Russell Sage Foundation.

Smith, Sandra Susan. 2005. "'Don't Put My Name on It': Social Capital Activation and Job-Finding Assistance among the Black Urban Poor." *American Journal of Sociology* 111:1–57.

Smyth, Katya Fels, Lisa Goodman, and Catherine Glenn. 2006. "The Full-Frame Approach: A New Response to Marginalized Women Left Behind by Specialized Services." *American Journal of Orthopsychiatry* 76:489–502.

Snell, Emily K. and Greg J. Duncan. 2006. "Child Characteristics and Successful Use of Housing Vouchers." *Housing Policy Debate* 17:727–754.

Sobel, Michael S. 2006. "What Do Randomized Studies of Housing Mobility Demonstrate? Causal Inference in the Face of Interference." *Journal of the American Statistical Association* 101:1398–1407.

South, Scott J. and Kyle Crowder. 1997. "Escaping Distressed Neighborhoods: Individual, Community, and Metropolitan Influences." *American Journal of Sociology* 102:1040–1084.

Speare, Alden, Jr. 1974. "Residential Satisfaction as an Intervening Variable in Residential Mobility." *Demography* 11:173–188.

Speare, Alden, Jr., Sidney Goldstein, and William H. Frey. 1975. *Residential Mobility, Migration, and Metropolitan Change*. Cambridge, MA: Ballinger.

Stack, Carol. 1974. *All Our Kin: Strategies for Survival in a Black Community*. New York: Harper and Row.

Stack, Carol and Linda Burton. 1993. "Kinscripts." *Journal of Comparative Family Studies* 24:157–175.

Stuart, Guy. 2000. "Segregation in the Boston Metropolitan Area at the End of the Twentieth Century." The Civil Rights Project at Harvard University, Cambridge, MA.

Sullivan, Mercer. 1989. *Getting Paid: Youth Crime and Work in the Inner City*. Ithaca, NY: Cornell University Press.

Swidler, Ann. 1986. "Culture in Action: Symbols and Strategies." *American Sociological Review* 51:273–286.

Tegeler, Philip D. 2005. "The Persistence of Segregation in Government Housing Programs." Pp. 197–216 in *The Geography of Opportunity: Race and Housing*

Choice in Metropolitan America, edited by X. d. S. Briggs. Washington, DC: Brookings Institution Press.

Thaler, Richard H. and Cass R. Sunstein. 2008. *Nudge: Improving Decisions About Health, Wealth, and Happiness.* New Haven: Yale University Press.

Tienda, Marta. 1991. "Poor People and Poor Places: Deciphering Neighborhood Effects on Poverty Outcomes." Pp. 244–262 in *Macro-micro Linkages in Sociology*, edited by J. Huber and B.E. Schneider. Newbury Park, CA: Sage Publications.

Tilly, Chris, Phillip Moss, Joleen Kirschenman, and Ivy Kennelly. 2001. "Space as a Signal: How Employers Perceive Neighborhoods in Four Metropolitan Labor Markets." Pp. 304–339 in *Urban Inequality: Evidence from Four Cities*, edited by A. O'Connor, C. Tilly, and L. Bobo. New York: Russell Sage Foundation.

Timberlake, Jeffrey. 2007. "Racial and Ethnic Inequality in the Duration of Children's Exposure to Neighborhood Poverty and Affluence." *Social Problems* 54:319–342.

Tolman, Deborah L. 1996. "Adolescent Girls' Sexuality: Debunking the Myth of the Urban Girl." Pp. 255–271 in *Urban Girls: Resisting Stereotypes, Creating Identities*, edited by B. J. Leadbeater and N. Way. New York: New York University Press.

Tönnies, Ferdinand. [1887] 1955. *Community and Society (Gemeinschaft und Gesellschaft)*. Translated by C. P. Loomis. London: Routledge and Kegan Paul.

Tubman, J. G., M. Windle, and R. C. Windle. 1996. "Cumulative Sexual Intercourse Patterns among Middle Adolescents: Problem Behavior Precursors and Concurrent Health Risk Behaviors." *Journal of Adolescent Health* 18:182–191.

Turner, Margery Austin and Xavier de Souza Briggs. 2008. "Assisted Housing Mobility and the Success of Low-Income Minority Families: Lessons for Policy, Practice, and Future Research." The Urban Institute, Washington, DC.

Turner, Margery Austin and Lynette A. Rawlings. 2005. "Overcoming Concentrated Poverty: Ten Lessons for Policy and Practice." The Urban Institute, Washington, DC.

Turner, Margery Austin and Stephen L. Ross. 2005. "How Racial Discrimination Affects the Search for Housing." Pp. 81–100 in *The Geography of Opportunity: Race and Housing Choice in Metropolitan America*, edited by X. d. S. Briggs. Washington, DC: Brookings Institution Press.

Turney, Kristin, Susan Clampet-Lundquist, Kathryn Edin, Jeffrey R. Kling, and Greg J. Duncan. 2006. "Neighborhood Effects on Barriers to Employment: Results from a Randomized Housing Mobility Experiment in Baltimore." Pp. 137–187 in *Brookings-Wharton Papers on Urban Affairs 2006*, edited by G. Burtless and J. R. Pack. Washington, DC: Brookings Institution Press.

U.S. Department of Housing and Urban Development. 1999. "Moving to Opportunity for Fair Housing: Current Status and Initial Findings." Office of Policy Development and Research, Washington, DC.

————. 2007. "Affordable Housing Needs 2005: Report to Congress." Office of Policy Development and Research, Washington, DC.

Upchurch, D. M., C. A. Sucoff, and L. Levy-Storms. 1999. "Neighborhood and Family Contexts of Adolescent Sexual Activity." *Journal of Marriage and the Family* 61:920–933.

Vale, Lawrence J. 1993. "Beyond the Problem Projects Paradigm: Defining and Revitalizing Severely Distressed Public Housing." *Housing Policy Debate* 4:147–174.

———. 2000. *From the Puritans to the Projects: Public Housing and Public Neighbors*. Cambridge, MA: Harvard University Press.

———. 2006. "The Ideological Origins of Affordable Homeownership Efforts." Pp. 15–40 in *Chasing the Dream: New Perspectives on Affordable Homeownership*, edited by W. M. Rohe and H. L. Watson. Ithaca, NY: Cornell University Press.

Valentine, Charles A. 1971. "Deficit, Difference, and Bicultural Models of Afro-American Behavior." *Harvard Educational Review* 41:137–157.

Varady, David P. and Carol Walker. 2007. *Neighborhood Choices: Section 8 Housing Vouchers and Residential Mobility*. New Brunswick, NJ: CUPR Press.

Varady, David P. and Carol C. Walker. 2000. "Vouchering Out Distressed Subsidized Developments: Does Moving Lead to Improvements in Housing and Neighborhood Conditions?" *Housing Policy Debate* 11:115–62.

———. 2003. "Housing Vouchers and Residential Mobility." *Journal of Planning Literature* 18:17–30.

Venkatesh, Sudhir Alladi. 2000. *American Project*. Cambridge, MA: Harvard University Press.

———. 2006. "Sociology and Katrina." *City & Community* 5:115–118.

Vera, Elizabeth M., Le'Roy E. Reese, Roberta L. Paikoff, and Robin L. Jarrett. 1996. "Contextual Factors of Sexual Risk-Taking in Urban African-American Preadolescent Children." Pp. 291–307 in *Urban Girls: Resisting Stereotypes, Creating Identities*, edited by B. J. Leadbeater and N. Way. New York: New York University Press.

Von Hoffman, Alexander. 1995. "Vision Limited?: The Political Movement for a U.S. Public Housing Program, 1919–1950." Working Paper W96–3. Joint Center for Housing Studies, Harvard University, Cambridge, MA.

Wang, Xinhao and David P. Varady. 2005. "Using Hot-Spot Analysis to Study the Clustering of Section 8 Housing Voucher Families." *Housing Studies* 20:29–48.

Weiher, Gregory R. and Kent L. Tedin. 2002. "Does Choice Lead to Racially Distinctive Schools? Charter Schools and Household Preferences." *Journal of Policy Analysis and Management* 21:79–92.

Weismann, Gretchen. 2008. "The Relative Risk: Parenting, Peers, and Poverty in the Three-City Study of Moving to Opportunity." Unpublished Ph.D. dissertation, Department of Urban Studies and Planning, Massachusetts Institute of Technology, Cambridge, MA, June.

Weisner, Thomas. 1996. "Why Ethnography Should Be the Most Important Method in the Study of Human Development." Pp. 305–324 in *Ethnography and Human Development: Context and Meaning in Social Inquiry*, edited by R. Jessor, A. Colby, and R. Shweder. Chicago: University of Chicago Press.

Wellman, Barry. 1979. "The Community Question: The Intimate Networks of East Yorkers." *American Journal of Sociology* 84:1201–1231.

———. 1988. "Networks as Personal Communities." in *Social Structures: A Network Approach*, edited by B. Wellman and S. D. Berkowitz. New York: Cambridge University Press.

———. 2001. "Physical Place and Cyberplace: The Rise of Personalized Networking." *International Journal of Urban and Regional Research* 25:227–252.

Wellman, Barry and Scott Wortley. 1990. "Different Strokes from Different Folks: Community Ties and Social Support." *American Journal of Sociology* 96:558–588.

Wells, Amy Stuart. 1993. *Time to Choose: America at the Crossroads of School Choice Policy*. New York: Hill and Wang.

White, Harrison. 1971. "Multipliers, Vacancy Chains, and Filtering in Housing." *Journal of the American Institute of Planners* 37:88–94.

Wilson, William Julius. 1987. *The Truly Disadvantaged: The Inner City, the Underclass, and Public Policy.* Chicago: University of Chicago Press.

———. 1996. *When Work Disappears: The World of the New Urban Poor.* New York: Knopf.

Wirth, Louis. 1928. *The Ghetto.* Chicago: University of Chicago Press.

———. 1938. "Urbanism as a Way of Life." *American Journal of Sociology* 44:1–24.

Yinger, John. 1995. *Closed Doors, Opportunities Lost: The Continuing Costs of Housing Discrimination.* New York: Russell Sage Foundation.

Zhou, Yu and Dowell Myers. 2006. "Convergence or Divergence in Los Angeles: Three Distinctive Ethnic Patterns of Immigrant Residential Assimilation." *Social Science Research* 36:254–85.

Index

CPSIA information can be obtained at www.ICGtesting.com
Printed in the USA
BVOW052237171011

273883BV00003B/4/P

7285